Francis Beckett is a freelance journalist, writing regularly for the New Statesman, the Guardian and the Times Educational Supplement about education as well as politics and contemporary history.

His other books are: Enemy Within, about Britain's Communists was published in 1995 to critical acclaim; and The Rebel Who Lost His Cause, about the extraordinary personal and political odyssey of his own father, published in 1999.

He is a former Labour Party press officer and a former president of the National Union of journalists. His first play, The Sons of Catholic Gentlemen, was broadcast by LBC in September 1997.

CLEM ATTLEE

Francis Beckett

Politico's
PUBLISHING

Published in Great Britain 2000
by Politico's Publishing
8 Artillery Row
Westminster
London
SW1P 1RZ

Tel 020 7931 0090
Fax 020 7828 8111
Email publishing@politicos.co.uk
Website http://www.politicos.co.uk/publishing

First Published by Richard Cohen Books 1997

First published in paperback 2000

A catalogue record of this book is available from the British Library.

ISBN 1 902301 70 6

Typeset in Baskerville by Palimpsest Book Production Limited, Polmont, Stirlingshire and Politico's Publishing

Printed and bound in Great Britain by Creative Print and Design

Contents

Introduction

With almost any other subject, the biographer can rely on the odd anguished soul-bearing letter, or the testimony of a sympathetic friend or lover, but not with Clement Attlee. You can see why George VI thought he ought to have been called Clam, not Clem.

So I'm pleased that many people who knew him – his surviving friends and relatives, reviewers like Roy Jenkins, Roy Hattersley, Jack Jones and Lord Longford, his former aide Sir David Hunt – seem to think I got pretty near to the essence of the man. The only people who thought I had him wrong seemed to be those who loathed him, like Gerald Kaufman, or who loathed his works, like the former right wing Tory MP Robert Rhodes James.

And I'm even nearer now – since the hardback edition was published three years ago, I've spoken to four people who came as close as anyone to being his confidantes, and I'll tell you about them in a moment.

He was a man whom we need to understand, especially now. Few politicians, even Prime Ministers, leave Britain radically different from the way they found it. Among Labour Prime Ministers, only one made real, tangible, lasting changes to the way people live in Britain. Attlee, Prime Minister from 1945 until 1951, led the government which created the National Health Service, made Britain's first and only serious assault on poverty, and built most of the features of the welfare state.

Perhaps only us post-war baby-boomers understand the magnitude. Some of us think the changes turned Britain, for the first time, into a civilised society (and three decades later, Margaret Thatcher turned it back again). Others think they are the cause of Britain's decline (and three decades later Margaret Thatcher rescued the national backbone). But we all know they matter terribly. They were the context and texture of our youth.

I was born in 1945, four days after VE day and a month before

Clement Attlee became Prime Minister. I had my childhood illnesses in NHS hospitals. My parents did not have to worry about enormous hospital bills, as their parents would have done. Between the ages of 11 and 13 I attended Rickmansworth Grammar School in Hertfordshire, and later Keele University, both of them monuments to the Attlee government: purpose-built and newly opened at the start of the 1950s to cope with the new customers created by the swift implementation of the 1944 Education Act and the raising of the school leaving age; light, airy and modern, with young and idealistic teachers who enjoyed what they did.

Even so, I did not entirely appreciate the social revolution which had happened during my first six years on this earth. With my friends I thought New Jerusalem was round the corner, its arrival hindered only by what we believed was the conservatism of the Labour government under Harold Wilson. We did not realise that we were living in New Jerusalem. Before the Attlee government, working class parents could not afford the doctor, and relied on folk remedies – old wives tales – to treat their children's ailments. Before the first world war 163 of every 1,000 children died before their first birthday – it is 15 per 1,000 today. The figure was twice as high for working class children. Of those who survived, one in four did not live beyond the age of four.

Working class children in the 1930s seldom had enough to eat and received just enough education to enable them to do routine work. A father out of work meant a family near starvation. But in the 1950s, better pay and shorter hours of work gave people leisure for the first time. Older children, especially those at work, had disposable income. Children became serious consumers, able to make choices and support those choices with cash.

What kind of a man was it whose government could have done all this? Rumour had it that he was a grey, humourless little man who, fortunately, had some great men around him. Churchill is supposed to have called him 'a modest little man with plenty to be modest about.' Almost certainly Churchill never said that. (I have my own candidate for the authorship, and you will find his name in Chapter Seven.) Churchill, who recognised a formidable politician when he saw one, knew that Clem had little to be modest about, and was, in his own understated way, as immodest as Churchill himself.

Everyone knows the aphorism. Few people know Clem's affectionate, typically pronounless, devastatingly accurate aphorism about Churchill. 'Trouble with Winston. Nails his trousers to the mast. Can't get down.'

The myth of insignificance suited everyone. It suited Clem, who could get away with radical policies more easily because he did not seem alarming or exciting. It suited Conservative newspapers, which presented him as a weak, ineffectual leader who could easily be pushed around by dangerous lefties like Nye Bevan. It suited ambitious rivals like Herbert Morrison.

Even Clem's official biographer, Kenneth Harris, appears to accept that Clem was, as Hugh Dalton put it at the time, an 'accidental' leader, and that had it not been for the special circum stances of 1931, we would probably never have heard of him. In a sense every Prime Minister owes his rise partly to luck, but this is much less true of Clem than of, say, Harold Wilson and Tony Blair, who owed their position as Labour leader to the sudden, early and unexpected death of their respective predecessors.

The dull, grey Clem is also a myth. He wrote poetry all his life, and dreamed of being a poet. And far from being a passenger in the government he ran, he was its guiding intellect and its engine room too, more firmly in charge that most Prime Ministers. If the Conservatives had won the 1945 election, the revolution would not have happened. If Labour under a different leader had won, less would have been done.

It is often said that Clem Attlee could never survive in 1990s politics, because he lacked an 'image', and wanted the Labour Party to say exactly what it believed, rather than what it thought the electorate wanted to hear.

But images are not a recent invention. Stanley Baldwin, Ramsay MacDonald, Winston Churchill – they all had an image, and so did Clem. A wise man, he ensured that his 'image' was always close to the reality, avoiding Neil Kinnock's ambitious attempt to create an entirely new persona. And he saw Labour's convoluted constitution, with its complicated checks and balances and its trade union block vote, as a strength and not a weakness. He brought the left into his cabinet, most obviously in the shape of Aneurin Bevan, even though Bevan had almost been expelled from the Party only a year previously.

So how close did I get to the man? I was the first writer to have access to the extraordinary series of letters he wrote after his wife's death to a young American journalist, Patricia Beck, whom he had met on the campaign trail during the 1950 election. The letters were among the most revealing that Attlee ever wrote. It was clear that, after his wife's early death, Patricia Beck became, for the rest of his life, closer to him than any other living person. They met several times a week, and as he grew more frail, he came to need her friendship more and more.

But until recently, I had not talked to Ms Beck. After the book was published, I found her, and went to her small house in one of those wonderful granite terraces in St Andrews.

The front door opens straight onto the street, and the moment she opened it I knew why she had mattered to Attlee. She was tall and slim, with a dignity and a sense of seriousness about her. She spoke and behaved quietly and – there's no other word for it – decorously. I was not at all surprised when she explained why she had settled in Britain. 'I find American society extremely violent in its attitude of mind. They rant and rave about individualism but they are the most conforming people. Coming to Britain was like slipping into an old and favourite overcoat. In Britain I found a genuine appreciation of the need for change.' She has the slightest hint of an American accent still, but you hardly notice it in a woman with such perfect British manners.

She confirmed some things for me. We know that when he resigned as Labour leader in 1955, Clem supported Hugh Gaitskell as his successor, but I was sure he had really wanted Aneurin Bevan, and felt that Bevan had made this impossible. I had never hoped to get it confirmed from so authoritative a source. 'He terribly wanted Bevan to succeed him as leader' Patricia Beck told me. 'He was very disappointed about that.'

Patricia was born in Seattle in 1923, joined Life magazine as a young journalist in 1945, and was sent to London to cover the Prime Minister's campaign for re-election in 1950, during which she followed the Prime Minister's car, which was driven by the Prime Minister's wife. Vi Attlee was widely thought to be a terrible driver and a difficult and neurotic woman, but Patricia said: 'Our driver said she was a marvellous driver, especially on winding roads in Derbyshire. And she was very competent, and always pleasant and relaxed.'

At the end of the campaign 'we felt we had to do something for the Attlees who had been so kind to us.' So they bought a volume of Blake's poems 'because they were relevant to his attitude to society' and Patricia handed it in at Downing Street. As she was leaving, he came to the door and waved the book at her.

She liked both the old-fashioned courtesy of the Attlees, and their politics. She had admired Franklin and Eleanor Roosevelt, and 'I felt, hurrah, someone's carrying on their work.' She was 'entranced by his vision and sense of fair play. People speak of him as dull, but that's because they don't give a damn themselves.'

In September 1951 she went to Ceylon, and had a mild dose of polio. He heard about it somehow, and wrote to her. Later that year, back in the USA, she read that he was in hospital, and sent him a batch of books and a piece of beef. 'You had rationing in Britain then. There were companies in New York which specialised in sending food parcels to British friends.' Years later Clem told her the beef had turned out to be maggoty.

She returned to London in 1953 to work at Reuters, and he invited her to tea at the House of Commons. Three years later, she left to help found a small news and public relations agency.

She saw the Attlees regularly, and they corresponded, but it was after Vi died in 1964 that she and Clem became really close, and he came to depend on her. He introduced her to the new Prime Minister, Harold Wilson. By then he had become very weak and frail, and she said to Wilson: 'Can't anything be done for Clem?' Wilson said he had offered him a place in the Chelsea Hospital, but Clem turned it down. She thought he should have taken it. He would have liked the company of old soldiers like himself. 'He used the word 'fellowship' over and over again. It was an idea that mattered to him.'

Although she thought a great deal of him, he started to become a burden. She was working very hard, and he seemed to need her around more and more. He was looked after by an old soldier, Alf Laker, who was also a trained nurse. 'Laker was very experienced and tremendously kind. If he had any ambitions for himself, I was never aware of it. He would ring and say, Lord Attlee wants to know if you will come to dinner. We would have a tray in front of the fire. One day I went out to lunch with him, and when I got back he was on the telephone to say, will you have dinner with me in the Athenaeum. I couldn't face it.'

'We laughed a lot together' says Patricia. 'Also he liked someone who could listen, and I loved listening to him. He would sing bits of songs from musicals he and Vi had seen together, the kind of things that rhyme moon and June.'

The second of my new contacts was Clem's oldest daughter,

Janet. I'd concentrated on her younger sister Felicity, believing that Janet's insights had all been gobbled up by Kenneth Harris. I was wrong. Janet was the child who inherited some of his political beliefs and skills, who has had an active and effective political life of her own in the USA (somewhat hampered by becoming a US citizen rather late in life), and she offered one special insight which no one else had thought of.

Everyone who studies Clem asks the question: how did he manage to be so self-contained, to have so little need to unburden himself on anyone? How can anyone bear the crushing burdens of the premiership in the immediate post war years, go home to his wife every evening, and never talk politics with her? She suggested that, as with so many men of his generation, it probably went back to his time as a soldier in the First World War.

'I think he simply shut the door on it. That's why he was so reserved, so inaccessible to everyone,' she said. 'His brother Tom was the only person who knew him – even Vi didn't. With me he'd open the big chest where he kept his war medals, he'd show me the hole in his leg where he'd been shot. But what really hurt him were the boys he's worked with in Limehouse – none of them came back. He'd drilled them, trained them to be soldiers – did he wonder if he'd done it rather too well?'

The First World War legacy was a crucial element in the way he handled his first government job, as Postmaster General in 1931, she says. He knew that when your son was killed at the front in the First World War, you heard about it by telegram. So he brought in gold-braided greetings telegrams. You could see before you opened it that it wasn't announcing a death.

She offered other stories which I wish I'd got into the book. How over Sunday lunch he would organise general knowledge quizzes with the children, how he first kissed Vi in Windsor Park, how Janet's relationship with him (unlike that of her sisters) revolved round games of strategy like bezique, probably because he could see that she was the only one of his four children with a real political brain. 'Until I was 30 I thought I was like my mother,' says Janet, who physically resembles her mother 'but then I realised I was like my father.'

My third new interview was with Peter Morris, who became a Transport House press officer in 1952. Peter had a new and appealing story about Clem's lifelong devotion to Vi.

'At the Labour Party conference, he'd be on the platform and every 20 minutes or so he'd stop doodling, look at Vi who was knitting, smile, wave, then he went back to his doodling, she to her knitting. They went on all day like that.'

I was right, Peter said, to say he deeply disliked Herbert Morrison, but mistaken to say he only read The Times. 'He read the Daily Herald, which told him how far too the left he could go without alienating the right wing trade union leaders.' And great public meetings were not what he was best at. The 11 year old Morris heard him speak at an election meeting in 1938, where Morris's uncle was the Labour candidate. 'He made his usual unemotional speech and in the middle he said: 'Neville Chamberlain keeps asking for more time. If I were the judge, he would get it.' It took the audience a few seconds to realise he had made a joke.'

My fourth interviewee contacted me. I'd quoted from some letters I'd seen from the elderly Clem's letters to a teenager called Geoffrey, who had written to him for an interview. And afterwards I received a letter from a middle aged writer called Geoffrey Elborn, who had enjoyed the book, and wondered whether I might like to know the story behind the letters.

Geoffrey had conceived a distant admiration for the great man. After they had corresponded a little (see page 317) Clem invited him to visit the flat in Kings Bench Walk where Laker was looking after him. It was the year Clem died, and Geoffrey was able to paint a more vivid picture of the great man in old age and infirmity than I have done:

'Laker brought in tea for me, and coffee for A. He did not touch the coffee, but drank a glass of either port or claret. A asked a little about my school, and we spoke about poetry, the romantic mainly. He then said he was tired and wanted to sleep, but suggested I look at his books.

'He had gone to the trouble of looking out Dunbar's poem In Praise of the City of London because of my being Scottish. He showed me some books Churchill had inscribed to him, one reading: 'Best wishes to Clem for a speedy recovery – don't read this though.'

'When A was fast asleep, I crept out quietly and spoke to Laker, who . . . said that Lord A is ageing very quickly and is growing very blind, which he hates, as he loves reading . . . He does not care for any room in the flat, except the sitting room, and Laker dresses him there. He uncharacteristically refuses to smoke his pipe now (I used to send him Cut Golden Bar). He had two cigarettes while I was there . . .

'The Queen is very fond of A . . . If she sees A at some function, she makes a beeline for him. He cannot go to the Lords any more, and this depresses him – he lives for politics. I asked if my letters were a nuisance and L said: 'Oh, no. He loves getting mail, as he likes doing something.'

These four people added to my understanding of the man. They also corrected some mistakes. Here Peter Morris was especially valuable, for he found out the truth about the poem reprinted on page 137, which I had thought was written by Clem Attlee himself.

I have used their information to correct errors. But shortage of time prevented me from doing the fairly considerable rewrites of some passages which their information justified. I hope that putting it here will enable the reader to benefit from it.

One last point. Throughout the book I have referred to him as Clem. This may seem presumptuous. He was 62 when I was born and had we met, he would certainly have expected me to call him Lord Attlee. He was an Edwardian who never got used to the post war habit of calling casual acquaintances by their first name, preferring the public school habit of calling people he had known for years by their unadorned surname.

But after two years getting as close to him as I could, referring to him throughout as Attlee did not look right to me.

FRANCIS BECKETT
September 2000

1

The Making of a Young Conservative

On 5 January 1883, Mr Henry Attlee, a respected London solicitor, rose at 7 am and held family prayers in his large Putney home, with the servants present, at 7.30. He led his children into the breakfast-room just before 8 and picked up his copy of *The Times*. Mr Attlee followed the same routine every morning, but perhaps that morning he glanced first at the top left-hand corner of the front page before delving into his paper. If he did so, he was reassured. There it was, in the births column, following *The Times* house-style:

> On the third Inst, at Westcott, Putney, to the wife of
> HENRY ATTLEE, a son.

That was how England learned of the arrival of the man who, six decades later, was to lead the government which changed fundamentally the way his countrymen lived. The announcement was exactly what its subject would have wanted, if he had been consulted in the matter. It was discreet, it was conventional, and it committed him to absolutely nothing.

Having checked that the birth of his seventh child, his fourth son, had been announced in the proper manner, Mr Attlee put on his frock-coat and top hat and left the house in good time to walk to Putney station and take his accustomed 9 am train to the city and the Billiter Square offices of Druces and Attlee, a firm so solidly established that it can be found in the City of London to this day, modestly listed as one of the tenants at the imposing entrance of Salisbury House, a luxurious 1960s office block at 163/4 London Wall. There is still an Attlee among the senior partners.

The Attlees were upper middle-class. It was a rigid class society divided into masters and servants, a division which, in the next century, Henry Attlee's son was to do more than any other single human being to undermine. Henry Attlee, whose morning routine did not alter at all because he acquired a son on that day in January, may also have read on the front page of *The Times* some personal advertisements placed by people of his own class.

'Can any LADY RECOMMEND a thoroughly trustworthy middle aged servant as WORKING HOUSEKEEPER for a country house, where three are kept in the kitchen', Mrs Milligan from Caldwell Hall in Burton-on-Trent wished to know. Mrs Lushington of Hampshire required 'a strong, active woman, as COOK' and offered 'good wages, but no beer'. Mr Stubbs of South Kensington wrote: 'TO ARMY RIDING MASTERS, retired officers, or Educated NCOs, WANTED, a good horseman, under 12 stone. Gentlemanly berth, likely to be permanent.'

The closing years of the nineteenth century in Britain saw a society growing each year more certain that its values and its class divisions were forever, and were the best way for human beings to live. Henry Attlee and his colleagues and friends were as sure of the morality and the permanence of unbridled capitalism, and of the moral value of material success, as many people have again become in the closing years of the twentieth century, and as insensitive to the human misery it creates.

The gulf between wealth and poverty was widening at the end of the nineteenth century, just as it is widening again now, as the twentieth century dies. In the year of Clement Attlee's birth, 1883, the Rev Andrew Mearns of the Evangelical Church wrote a pamphlet called *The Bitter Cry of Outcast London* which described the teeming, fetid mess of buildings and misery in the East End where thousands of men, women and children were herded together like ill-treated animals in their own filth. 'While we have been building our churches and solacing ourselves with our religion, and dreaming that the millennium was coming, the poor have been growing poorer, the wretched more miserable, and the immoral more corrupt,' he wrote.

> Tens of thousands are crowded together ... To get into [the slums] you have to penetrate courts reeking with poisonous and malodorous gases arising from accumulations of sewage and refuse scattered in all directions and often flowing beneath your feet ... Up rotten staircases ... Down dark and filthy passages swarming with vermin ... [to] the dens in which [live] these thousands of beings who belong, as much as you, to the race for which Christ died.

One or two families lived in each filthy room, eight feet square, whose windows were stuffed with rags to keep out the rain. He piled example on example.

> In one cellar [live] a man ill with smallpox, his wife just recovering from her eighth confinement, and the children running about half-naked and covered with dirt. Here are seven people living in one underground kitchen, and a little dead child lying in the same room. Elsewhere is a poor widow, her three children, and a child who had been dead thirteen days. Her husband, who was a cabman, had shortly before committed suicide.

Others cannot afford even this shelter, and 'huddle together upon the stairs and landings, where it is no uncommon thing to find six or eight in the early morning'. Children suffer most in the slums, especially if they and their parents are among the majority who earn their living honestly, which is far harder than earning it dishonestly: 'How long must the little hands toil before they can earn the price of the scantiest meal!' The answer, often, is seventeen hours a day. 'Here in a cellar are nine little ones. You can scarcely see across the room for smoke and dirt. They are without food and have scarcely any clothing . . .'

Children 'often pass the whole day without a morsel of food' and die like flies.

> An inquest was held into the death of a little baby. A man, his wife and three children were living in that room . . . This dead baby was cut open in the one room where its parents and brothers and sisters lived, ate and slept, because the parish had no mortuary . . .

Slum-dwellers are the prey of greedy landlords who squeeze them for rent and give nothing in return.

> Two old people have lived in one room for 14 years, during which time it has only once been partially cleansed. The landlord has undertaken that it shall be done shortly, and for the past three months has been taking sixpence a week extra for rent for what he is thus *going to do*. This is what the helpless have to submit to; they are charged for these pestilential dens a rent which consumes half the earnings of a family . . .
>
> And so Dives makes a richer harvest out of their misery, buying up property condemned as unfit for habitation, and turning it into a gold-mine because the poor must have shelter somewhere, even though it be the shelter of a living tomb.

Landlords, says Mr Mearns, in what must then have been an original and evocative expression, are 'grinding the faces of the poor'. He concluded, as Clement Attlee concluded two decades later after working in the same parts of the East End as Mr Mearns, that 'without state interference nothing effectual can be accomplished upon any large scale.' The adult Clement Attlee would have shared his view that the Church was spending far too much of its time ministering to the rich. But he would have quarrelled with the idea that some good had been accomplished when belief in Jesus was instilled into poor people. 'And on his miserable bed, amidst squalor and want and pain, a poor blind man dies with the prayer upon his lips "Jesus lover of my soul, let me to thy bosom fly."' Clem would have thought the old man was being subjected to one final cruel deception.

All this was happening less than ten miles, but on another planet, from the comfortable Putney house where Clement Attlee was born and grew up. We may be absolutely certain that he had no idea what was going on on the other side of the same city, and that when he found out, more than two decades later, the discovery changed his life. 'We were, I think,' wrote Clem in his autobiography, 'a typical family of the professional class brought up in the atmosphere of Victorian England.' He enjoyed a happy, secure, comfortable childhood in a house in Portinscale Road, Putney, built in the 1870s. Portinscale Road runs off West Hill, the long and tree-lined hill which leads up from Wandsworth towards Wimbledon. Henry named the house 'Westcott' after the hamlet where his own father's Surrey corn-mills stood. Soon after Clem was born, he built a new wing which made the house truly spacious even by the standards of the Victorian upper middle classes. Its ground floor had a dining-room, a drawing-room, a study and a full-size billiards room. Upstairs was a day nursery which was also used as a schoolroom, a night nursery for the three small children, three large bedrooms, two small bedrooms and a box-room. Outside was a big garden and a tennis court, and the drive was big enough to admit carriages, though Henry Attlee did not keep one. The family employed a cook, housemaid and parlourmaid, who lived in, and a gardener and governess who came in daily.

The children loved the garden. Decades later Clem's brother, Tom, could describe every inch of it. It ran the full width of the Victorian house, which was as wide as four or five substantial suburban houses today. Three-quarters of the back wall of the house was covered with ivy and fronted by a great tall tree. Steps led down from an imposing panelled Victorian back door onto a terrace running the width of the house, then a steep grassy bank leading down to a huge, neat lawn. Beyond the lawn, narrow gravel paths led among the shrubs, and beyond them was the best place of all: the kitchen garden, full of fruit bushes and trees, with a marrow-pit which smelled strongly of growing things and of manure. And there, any day, you would find the gardener, Mr Gee, whom Tom described as 'a good-natured fellow with that inexhaustible patience which the unwearying chatter of childhood demands'. There the younger children, Tom (three years older than Clem, and all his life the brother to whom he was closest), Margaret (five years older than Clem), Clem himself and Laurence (a year younger) would build palaces, forts and railways out of any pieces of stone and wood they could find lying around.

Putney in those days, though only six miles from the centre of London, was almost a village, surrounded by fields, farms, country pubs and market-gardens. You could dimly hear from the Attlees' home the sound of the horses' hooves which was the London traffic. Years later Clem's brother Tom recalled Putney High Street:

> Old, dark, bricked houses and decorous shops . . . [led] up from the river to the steep slopes of Putney Hill with its square, opulent houses in large, shady gardens. Beyond them the Heath was still wild, and at its edge watched by great blocks of houses, comfortable, solid, smelling of plum-cake and beeswax; quiet, dignified, set in grounds that were almost small estates, with gardeners' cottages in their far-off corners among cucumber frames and potting-sheds.

Clem himself remembered.

> Horse drawn traffic involved the dropping of a large amount of ordure . . . In the wet weather the streets were seas of mud churned up by the hoofs of the horses and splashed freely over pedestrians by the wheels of the vehicles . . . Standing in our garden one could hear the roar of London traffic as the horse-hoofs beat on the paved streets. I recall the dust in summer and the mud in winter . . .

For more than 200 years the Attlee family had been solid and comfortably-off citizens of Surrey. Clem's grandfather, Richard Attlee, made a considerable sum of money from his corn-mill. He took two of his seven sons into the business and set two more up in business on their own. Henry, the ninth of his ten children, was educated privately, largely by the vicar, in Brockham, Surrey. In the family papers there survives a splendid letter, written by Henry Attlee in 1856, when he was fourteen. The copperplate handwriting is utterly perfect:

> My dear father, It is with great satisfaction I announce the pleasing

intelligence of the holidays which will commence on the fourteenth instant on which day I look forward to joining the family circle at Dorking. I hope you will find me improved in my studies and that I have made good use of the time and opportunities afforded me. I have heard several very impressive sermons by Mr Pugh at St Johns Church. Your dutiful son, Henry Attlee.

Two years later he was articled to the solicitors Druces, where he rose to become senior partner in 1897, when Clem was fourteen, and to rename the firm Druces and Attlee. He became one of His Majesty's Lieutenants of the City of London and eventually, in 1906, President of the Law Society. He enjoyed the gentlemanly pursuits of cricket and shooting, was interested in early English literature, and was a Liberal and an admirer of Mr Gladstone.

Henry married Ellen Watson, the oldest of the seven children of Thomas Watson, Clem's only living grandparent, who had inherited plenty of money and did not to have to work, devoting his life to his enthusiasm for art and literature. He was secretary of the Art Union of London, which published reproductions of good pictures at moderate prices. He had a white beard and the unmistakable air of a late-Victorian aesthete.

Thomas Watson lived with his four unmarried daughters and his son in Wandsworth, then the village next door to Putney, now a teeming inner-London suburb. Henry and Ellen settled in Putney so as to be near Ellen's family. The children went to their grandfather's house a lot, often sleeping overnight in a big four-poster bed. It was another place which Clem and Tom remembered all their lives with happiness. It was, said Tom, 'built of dark brown-red bricks in the reign of Queen Anne, with heavy gables, small sash windows, a big wisteria clutching its front. It sat low behind heavy iron railings, peering across the flat expanse of Wandsworth Common. When you shoved back the catch of the tall gate with a sixpence, a narrow flagged path led you to the low front door, past a shrubbed lawn on your right and a disused coach-house on your left.' Inside, the house was full of engravings, books, statuettes, silver tea-caddies, all dimly lit by candles, oil-lamps and some gaslight. The whole place smelled of old leather, plum cake and pipe tobacco, 'a restful, welcoming, comfortable smell' according to Tom. Clem remembered particularly the big bedroom belonging to two of the aunts because he spent four weeks in it recovering from some childhood illness; it had 'a very wavy floor and fascinating cupboards which we always thought ran a very long way down into the house'. This house too had a fine garden, with a great cedar tree, a lawn, a greenhouse and winding paths, contrasting sharply with the world outside, where trams rattled past and the pavements were dusty and hard.

Henry and Ellen Attlee's first child, Robert, was born in 1871, twelve years before Clem. The eighth and youngest, Laurence, was born the year after Clem, in 1884. The Attlees were relaxed and affectionate parents by the standards of the time. Henry was of medium height, and most of his face was hidden by one of those great, bushy Victorian beards, but he was not at all the distant Victorian father-figure which his photograph would suggest. His older sons remembered him coming home excited after winning a case he had fought all the way to the House of Lords and racing them round the garden, breaking one of the strictest rules of the house by jumping through the rows of runner-beans. By the time the three youngest children arrived – Tom, Clem and Laurence – he was more likely to challenge his sons to a game of billiards than a race round the garden. Perhaps this was why billiards became Clem's favourite game, and the only one he ever excelled at.

Ellen Attlee was no stereotype Victorian mother either. She was educated to a level which many Victorians would have considered inappropriate for a woman. She had her father's knowledgeable love of the arts and literature, spoke excellent French and passable Italian, played the piano, sang and painted in water-colours. But the centre of her being was her family. She had a husband whom she admired and adored, and eight healthy and affectionate children, for whom she lived, and who returned her love. Her own mother had died young, and Ellen had brought up her five sisters and her brother, so by the time it came to bringing up her own eight children, she already had plenty of practice. It was perhaps fortunate that bringing up children was something she enjoyed doing.

On summer mornings young Clement was sometimes allowed to walk part of the way to the station with his father, trotting alongside the dignified top-hatted and frock-coated figure. In the evenings Henry drank precisely one glass of claret over dinner with his family, then retired to his study to prepare his paperwork for the next day, or to rehearse a court appearance. On Sundays the children were dressed in their best clothes and taken to church – in the morning for the main service, in the afternoon for a children's service, in the evening for yet a third service. It was boring, but it was also a routine that added to their abundant sense of the security and permanence of things. Religion was at the core of the family, and

Clem was introduced to the Bible at an early age. An early reader, he was found at about the age of four making diving gestures from a chair and repeating the Bible quotation which had inspired him, 'Divers of them came from far.'

It was a united, religious, happy, affectionate late-Victorian family. But just because it was so self-contained, there was a tendency for the Attlee children to go out into the world unwillingly and unprepared. Why face an uncomprehending and possibly hostile world when everything you need for your happiness is here, in your parents' house? Especially when Ellen Attlee felt a little jealous of her children seeking friends outside the family circle. Partly as a result, Clem was an acutely shy child outside the family, though he was lively and argumentative inside it. From an unpublished fragment of autobiography it is clear that shyness was the bane of his childhood, and he stayed shy, even when he was Prime Minister.

Ellen grew up with conservative views of the sort people meant when they said, 'I'm not political at all, I'm conservative.' Clem remembered his mother, whenever politics was mentioned, trying tactfully to change the subject. She was one of those well-brought-up middle-class people who think there is something indecent and dangerous about discussing politics. The children, including Clem, took their lead from her. One of Clem's earliest memories was of walking with some of his brothers and sisters on the rocks in the Isle of Wight. Someone shouted out in a cockney accent: 'Look at those little kids walking on the rocks.' Clem's elder brother Bernard replied, 'Essence of vulgarity,' which, Clem later said, 'we thought a very fine retort.'

So in Ellen Attlee's eyes, her husband's main, perhaps his only defect, was not so much that he was a Liberal, but that he was tasteless enough to talk about it. He had once even thought of standing for Parliament, but his senior partner persuaded him to stay with the firm. He had Liberal values that were considered very advanced. He thought poverty and hardship to be evils, while many of his contemporaries believed that they were positive virtues, proving the competitiveness and virility of our national life.

When Clem was born, Henry Attlee's political hero, William Gladstone, was in the third year of his second term of office as Prime Minister. Gladstone was the prophet of the great Liberal causes which were close to Henry Attlee's heart: Irish home rule, friendship with the Boers in South Africa, universal education. All three causes were passionately opposed by the Conservatives and by most of the professional middle class. When Clem was two, in 1885, the Conservatives returned to power and ruled continuously for the next twenty years, except for breaks of a few months in 1886 and less than three years between 1892 and 1895. By the time Clem was sixteen Britain was fighting the Boers, and when Clem himself entered politics Irish home rule seemed further away than it had to his father.

Coupled with his radicalism Henry Attlee believed in the Victorian values of hard work and material success. He worked hard and prospered. When Clem was thirteen Henry bought a splendid seventeenth-century holiday home in Thorpe-le-Soken near the Essex coast, with 200 acres of land, a farmhouse and several cottages. There the family spent their Easter and summer holidays, playing tennis, cricket and bicycle-polo and shooting rabbits.

Attlee girls were educated at home, but the boys were sent to a small private school when they were five – all except Clem, who was kept at home until he was nine, learning from his mother and his sisters' governesses, and roaming at will among his father's large collection of books. This may have been because his size worried his parents. He was much the smallest of a family which in general grew to medium height, and by the time he went to school his brother Laurence, eighteen months younger, was taller than Clem. Big Victorian families, even well-to-do ones, thought themselves very lucky if they did not lose at least one child, often the smallest and sickliest one. A family rumour has it that Clem was kept at home because they believed he would never live to be a man, and his short life should be made as happy, fulfilling and secure as possible. Whatever the reason, it certainly meant that he got a better education than a private school would have offered: languages and music from governesses and his well-educated mother, poetry from his father's books. It stuck. At the age of seventy, he created a precedent for a British socialist by addressing the Socialist International conference in Milan in fluent Italian, and he was still translating Italian Renaissance literature for fun.

One of the governesses, Miss Hutchinson, came to the Attlees from a much more famous family – the Churchills, where she had been employed to teach young Winston. She might perhaps have seen Winston as a future Prime Minister, but it would surely never have occurred to her that he would be succeeded in Downing Street by little Clement Attlee. In the 1880s she brought a story to the Attlee household that one day while she was teaching Winston a maid came in and asked Miss Hutchinson if she had rung the bell. Winston replied: 'I rang. Take away Miss Hutchinson, she is very cross.'

Like many clever, bookish children, Clem seems to have been blessed with a mind like a sponge. 'It wasn't so much the amount he read but the amount he could remember,' said his brother Laurence years later. He would bury himself in books – poetry, history, literature and the bound volumes of *Punch* with their wonderful cartoons followed by several lines of dialogue. He developed his lifelong love of poetry; though only nine years old, he mourned the death of Lord Tennyson in 1892. 'From the time that I could read, and even before, I have had an intense pleasure in poetry,' he once wrote. He loved arguing – not in order to propound strongly held views, for he had none at that time, but as an intellectual exercise. When Clem finally went to school the standard of his teaching abruptly dropped. He followed Tom to Northaw Place, a boarding preparatory school at Potters Bar in Hertfordshire. The two clergymen who ran it were interested in cricket and in the Bible, in that order, and in very little else. No-one bothered Clem with academic demands, so he picked up endless cricket statistics and an encyclopaedic biblical knowledge, played cricket adequately but without any distinction and, when they left him alone, read poetry.

In 1896 he was sent to one of those dreadful institutions used by the English upper classes to beat their sons into men fit to govern an Empire. Henry Attlee chose Haileybury in Hertfordshire, partly on the rather poor grounds that the cricket-loving clergymen at Northaw Place recommended it. But he was also a member of the school council – a governor, as we would put it – and had helped create, as an offshoot from Haileybury and a tribute to its military traditions, the United Services College in Westward Ho!, a public school for future army officers. This was the school which Rudyard Kipling, one of Clem's favourite poets, had attended and used as the model for *Stalky & Co*, and it was run on similar lines to Haileybury. Kipling wrote of it:

> There we met with famous men
> Set in office o'er us
> And they beat on us with rods
> Faithfully with many rods
> Daily beat on us with rods
> For the love they bore us.

It may also have weighed with Henry Attlee that Haileybury's headmaster, unlike most public school headmasters, shared his pro-Boer sympathies. Canon Edward Lyttleton's aunt was married to Gladstone, and the year before Clem arrived, the former Prime Minister himself was a guest at Speech Day. Haileybury's imposing buildings surround a huge square quadrangle. It was designed in 1806 by a Cambridge graduate still only in his twenties who had taken the world of architecture by storm. William Wilkins had already designed Downing College, Cambridge, and later designed London's National Gallery. The exterior of one of the four sides of Haileybury is like a rehearsal for the National Gallery, with its great Greek colonnades.

Clem, at thirteen, was taken up the long tree-lined drive, through a large arch and into the biggest academic quadrangle in Europe. The buildings enclosing the quadrangle are divided into houses, and all boys go into one of the houses. Attlee joined Lawrence House, where he was to sleep in a long dormitory housing perhaps fifty boys, with bare steel beds about 3 feet apart. If he was lonely and frightened, he has left no record of the fact. It was never his style to dwell on his emotions. Tom was already at Haileybury, hating it. Going back each term, away from his comfortable and loving home, was a torment to him, including as it did the ordeal of 'bagging places' where you tried to get a place for the term in Hall near your friends and away from your enemies. 'How wretched the new boy felt,' wrote Tom, 'who, coming in late, found every place apparently occupied and was pitchforked in somewhere, to the freely expressed disgust of his reluctant neighbours; and realised that this was to be his place for the term.' He hated 'the windswept quad, the formroom with its inky desks and draughts' where enemies lurked. Tom hated the cruelty of boys who tormented others for their amusement. But neither brother seems to have known, or remembered, the prefect who threw himself in the path of a train and died instantly in 1897, during Clem's second year at the school. In a letter to Lyttleton, the prefect gave as good a definition of bullying as any sociologist, accusing three other boys of 'a regular, organised attempt, and a successful one, to undermine my influence and make miserable my life, by cowardly and insidious means, and to make me an object of scorn to all.'

Unlike Tom, Clem made himself at home easily and without apparent trauma, as he did everywhere he went throughout his life, whether it was the East End of London or the House of Lords. It was a gift he had, and as a result he felt a lifelong happiness about, and loyalty to, any place in which he spent an appreciable part of his life.

His letters home, mostly to his much older sister Mary, reveal no hint of unhappiness. They are mostly about inter-house competitions, cricket matches and the weather. 'Yesterday we played Bedford Grammar School and beat them by 3 points to nothing. Crowds of little Bedford boys came down to watch the match. Apparently they are allowed to wear light clothes and knickerbockers there at least the smallest ones did. Did not Mother and Mig Clem's older sister Margaret) give you a weird account of our footer match with Dulwich. Mother *would* think all the men were being killed.'

Perhaps having an elder brother at the school made things easier. The two spent a lot of time together, for Tom had been desperately lonely before Clem arrived. Sixty years later Clem was still willing to drag an unwilling Tom – who had nothing but dislike for his old school – to an Old Haileyburian dinner. The school's recently published history records that Clem visited often, liked meeting other Old Haileyburians, and left instructions that his Garter Banner should go to the school after his death.

But he disliked the dirt: 'Our sanitary needs were supplied by three rows of earth closet.' In the long, narrow, dark dining-room with its brown wall, ceiling and gallery, 'forks and spoons were washed by being thrown in a large tub of hot water and stirred with a brush, hence the well justified warning "Never smell a college spoon" ... Lower boys had to pig it in the form rooms or class rooms where there was no privacy and a good deal of opportunity for bullying. The food was extremely bad at first but improved later. It was disgustingly served. I can clearly remember thinking often that one of the blessings of leaving would be decent food properly served.' Lyttleton believed the boys should have minimum comforts and a daily cold bath, and urged parents not to send their sons food-hampers.

Clem was small and played games, as he put it, 'keenly but without distinction' in a place where you were either a 'blood' (good at games) or you were a nobody. So you might have expected him to be unhappy, or at least bullied a little as, probably, his brother Tom had been. But the only hint of it is in the first draft of his autobiography which, like most things that were at all revealing, he removed from the published version: 'The chief bugbear of the small boys in the House was an uncouth and brutal youth called Archer Clive whose activities were however restricted by the prefects . . . I was small and very shy. Self-conscious to a degree, blushing very readily, a phenomenon frequently taken advantage of by other boys. This was called "making him smoke!" I was also at this time very much of a prig.' When Clem was Prime Minister, a Haileybury contemporary, Brian Harley, wrote a letter to a newspaper which had attacked him and suggested he was a Haileybury failure: 'When he dropped the mask which the non-athletic wore as protection against the "bloods" he was interesting and amusing.'

As with most public schools, you could be beaten readily, by any of the masters or even by a prefect. Clem enjoyed the Officers' Training Corps, and managed to be beaten only once, during the Boer War, after Lyttleton refused to give the boys their expected half-day's holiday the day Ladysmith was relieved. Many of the boys thought this was because of his pro-Boer sympathies. Whatever the reason, much of the school rebelled and marched down to the neighbouring town of Hertford, then on to Ware, about three miles further on, roaring patriotic songs all the way. Lyttleton beat at least seventy boys that day. Lyttleton had less respect for the classics than most public school heads, but loved cricket. Clem's own lifelong obsession with cricket may – since he had little gift for playing it – have come from the fact that the headmasters at both his prep and public school thought playing cricket was what young men were created to do.

He was a perfectly able though undistinguished pupil, becoming a prefect but not head of house, and must have been the last boy anyone expected to become Haileybury's only Prime Minister. He was so shy that he could hardly bring himself to speak in the school's Literary and Debating Society. He was given the job of running the house library because he had read all the books, but no-one advised him what to read. 'Had I been guided in reading I might have ended up as a blameless history don.' But he displayed, probably unconsciously, a talent which was to serve him well all his life. For a small, shy bookworm without any talent for games, he contrived to stay out of trouble most of the time. If anyone knew what to look for, they might have seen a natural politician in the making.

In 1901, Queen Victoria died and Clement Attlee entered University College, Oxford, joining Tom who was in his third year at Corpus Christi College. He studied modern history and specialised in the Italian Renaissance. He loved the place. 'I played all games but without distinction, amused myself on the river . . . in sailing boats, and savoured to the full all the joys of Oxford. On Sundays Tom and I would go for long walks, lunching in country inns and often ending up at Wolvercote, where my brother Bernard was vicar.' He played billiards with enthusiasm, building on those games in Putney with his father to win his only sporting prize ever, when he was a member of the University College billiards team which beat Brasenose College. It was a happy, undemanding three years, and Clem enjoyed every minute of it.

In his first year Clem shared lodgings with two other Old Haileyburians over a confectioner's shop in the high street, and spent most of his time with other Old Haileyburians, including the ever-present friend and mentor, Tom. But in his second year he moved into rooms in the college itself and started to expand his social circle, getting to know most of the 140 undergraduates there. They may not have been at Haileybury, but they were former public schoolboys, and therefore shared a common background and way of thinking with him, and he started, little by little, to break down some of his shyness. Looking back, he always thought that second year was the happiest and most carefree time in his life, when he was well established at Oxford but did not have to worry about impending final examinations.

Autobiographies of most senior politicians are full of how they took the Union by storm on entering Oxford with a bravura performance on a great issue of the day. Clem's autobiography says simply and candidly that he was much too shy ever to speak there. So far as he thought about politics at all, he still held his mother's undemanding conservative views, adding to them a certain cavalier cynicism, though he was not interested enough to join the University Conservative Club. He gave no thought to social questions and believed that only Tories were fit to govern, because they understood men. He had rejected his father's radicalism: Liberals were 'waffling, unrealistic have-nots who did not understand the basic facts of life'. This was partly comfortable habit, and partly the natural instinct of a profoundly conventional man who, if he can, prefers to swim with the tide. The spirit of the times, especially at Oxford, was Conservative and imperialist. Also, 'I had fallen under the spell of the renaissance. I admired strong, ruthless rulers.' He thought only gentlemen were fit to govern, and believed, as he wrote in an unpublished fragment of autobiography, 'in the legend of the White Man's Burden and all the rest of the commonplaces of imperialist idealism. The well-to-do were for the most part where they were because of their virtues.'

England, and especially Oxford, displayed, as the century turned, a rather repellent patriotic conservative triumphalism, not so different from the spirit of the 1980s. The Edwardian age was brassier and crasser than the Victorian age, and more crudely addicted to wealth. The Conservatives under Lord Salisbury – the last Prime Minister to sit in the Lords – had been firmly in control of government since 1895, and were to remain so until 1905. Liberalism was in decline and the Liberal Party split into warring factions. The Boer War had cranked up patriotic fervour. Class distinctions were sharper than ever. At the top was the aristocracy. Next came the higher professional classes, into which Henry Attlee's family fitted – lawyers, doctors, clergymen. Then came such people as managers, foremen and clerks. Below white-collar workers came small shopkeepers, who clung to a sort of fragile gentility which could be blown apart at any moment if the business started to fail. They worked dreadfully long hours and sweated their labour, which came from the one class below them, the manual workers.

Social historian Paul Thompson says that one look at a person's clothes was enough to place them in their class, because Edwardian society divided into three classes: those who wore tailor-made clothes, those who wore new ready-mades, and those who wore other people's cast-offs. Clem, of course, wore tailor-made clothes. He would, like any early-Edwardian young gentleman, have needed a full wardrobe: a tweed suit for the country, frock-coat for day-wear, tail-coat for formal evenings out, dinner-jacket for less formal evenings, and boots, shirts, cuffs and waistcoats of different styles to match; special clothes for bicycling, walking and all his other pastimes. Brown boots and spotted ties could be worn in the country but not in the town. Different clothes were appropriate for the morning and the afternoon. He would have had to be sure he was wearing the correct clothes at all times. The gap between rich and poor was increasing. The rich felt a collective need to flaunt their wealth.

In the first summer that Clem went to Oxford, a young man two years older than he found a job in Bristol after eight weeks out of work, delivering for a firm of mineral-water manufacturers. He had had a desperately hard childhood, with no father and a mother who died in poverty when he was eight. He had started work at the age of eleven, and in his new job his hours were 6 am to 6 pm after which he had to groom his horse. A year later his employers made him one of their permanent drivers, and a contract was signed between

'Ernest Bevin . . . hereinafter called the Servant' and the company. His pay was just under £50 a year: slightly less than a secondary school teacher in a state school, who could expect to earn between £50 and £80 a year, and a fifth as much as Clem's allowance from his father as an undergraduate, which was £250. The two men lived in different worlds, but forty-five years later Ernie Bevin was to be Clem's Foreign Secretary and his most important political ally, and together they would shape Britain's post-war foreign policy.

Oxford was not the place to learn how the other half lived. In 1900 it was simply a university town – unspoiled, ancient, untouched by commerce and even less by tourism, existing only to serve the needs of the university population. To Clem, being poor meant the sad predicament of an Old Haileyburian friend, Charles 'Char' Bailey, who wrote later: 'I wasn't very well off. If I had people coming to lunch I used to send my scout up to pinch Clement's silver. He never minded. He breathed loving kindness.' Neither was it the sort of place where you learned to question orthodoxy. Intellectual dissent had once flowered in Oxford: fifty years previously it was known as 'the home of lost causes'. But by the time Clem arrived, the pressure to turn out the sort of young man required in business and the civil service had blunted the dissenting edge, just as in the 1990s, as another new century dawns, the pressure to turn out the management types required by business is blunting the questioning edge of Britain's universities.

In his last two terms at Oxford Clem worked hard, putting in a solid eight hours a day at his books. His tutors thought he could have achieved a first-class degree if he had restricted his reading to what was strictly relevant to his work. But he had to make do with a good Second, which disappointed him. A First would have enabled him to become a Fellow of University College, and no other prospect could have given him half so much pleasure as to stay in his beloved Oxford, reading, talking, listening, getting to know more and more about art, poetry and the Italian Renaissance, writing poetry, and getting better and better at billiards. 'I left Oxford with an abiding love of the City and the University and especially of my own College,' he wrote in his autobiography.

Still, a man has to do something, so he decided in a rather desultory way to study for the bar. He knew that Henry Attlee would be happy to have another lawyer among his sons, and to have a successful solicitor for a father was, and still is, the best possible start for a young barrister. He told his first biographer, Roy

Jenkins, that he was not very keen on any career: 'I rather thought of some profession in which a living could be made while in my leisure time I could continue my reading in literature and history and learn more of art and antiquities.' This was misleading. It was not until he retired that he felt able to confess that he did have a real ambition. It was not to be a lawyer, still less a politician. It was to be a poet. He had nurtured that dream even at Haileybury, and still clung to it. He returned to live in the family home in Putney, and 1904 found him working as a pupil to Philip Gregory, a leading barrister, and studying for his bar examinations, which he passed the following year. Gregory was a hard taskmaster, especially to someone who was used to the pleasant, languid ways of Oxford. But Clem was to be grateful, years later in government, for the skill of exact drafting which he learned there.

In summer 1905, he passed his bar examinations and went to work in the family firm. He was frightfully bored there. Henry Attlee's working methods were starting to look a little old-fashioned. There were no typewriters: Mr Attlee thought they corrupted good handwriting. There was no filing system: when a file was needed, there was an invaluable clerk with a memory like an elephant. The telephone was only used to make appointments. Henry Attlee worked very hard. Clem hated it. Long hours in a dark, dirty and old-fashioned office, taking notes while the partners interviewed their clients, was not the way a young man just down from Oxford, inclined to literary romanticism, fascinated by the Italian Renaissance, and dreaming of being a poet, wanted to spend his days. With the utmost tact, because he had already developed his remarkable talent for getting his way without burning his boats, Clem left Druces and Attlee. He became the pupil of a barrister friend of his father's, Theobold Mathew, a clever, witty man whose company and work he enjoyed greatly, and then was given a place in the chambers of H. F. (later Sir Henry) Dickens, a son of Charles Dickens.

The bar traditionally is a place for rich men. In their first few years barristers do not get much work, and need a parental allowance. So Clem was a young man of leisure again, just as he had been at Oxford and, thanks to his father's money, entirely free of pressure to start earning. He did a little 'devilling' – research – for more senior barristers, and appeared very occasionally in county courts and at police courts. He was considered efficient and competent but had no particular ambition to succeed at the bar, and his progress would in any case have been hampered by his shyness.

Family breakfast in Westcott was still at 8 am sharp, after prayers. A son who did not have to get to his chambers until mid-morning was nonetheless expected to keep regular habits at home, and Clem found himself with time to kill between breakfast and work. Sometimes he killed it by walking the six miles or so to the City, or taking one of the new London County Council steamers which had just started to run from Putney Bridge to the Temple. That left a long lunch-hour, which on Wednesdays was taken care of by a luncheon club consisting of his brother Tom's literary friends from Oxford, and which met at a restaurant in the Strand. The long evenings – chambers did not normally require him to stay late – could be filled just as pleasantly. He was a member of the Hazlitt Essay Club, founded by Tom, which invited poets and writers to read and talk about their work. There was the Crosskeys, a literary club in Putney. And if there was nothing else, there was the billiards room at home, where he spent several evenings potting on his own and steadily improving. Long holidays and weekends were not a problem, either. He often spent them at his father's Essex country house, at first taking the expensive gun his father bought him until he found that shooting bored him. He learned to ride, discovered that bored him too, and travelled with friends of his parents to Belgium, France, Holland and Germany. It was a nice life. There was just one disadvantage. Attlee puts it with typical understatement: 'I became tired of doing nothing and my interest in the law was, to put it mildly, very tepid.' He was bored rigid. He ambled amiably into 1906 with little clear idea of what to do with his life. But 1906 was to change him forever.

It was an interesting year for the Attlees. In July, Henry Attlee's eminent legal career was crowned at the age of sixty-five with the Presidency of the Law Society. In his presidential address he called for reforms to the system of administering estates, and defended the distinction between barristers and solicitors.

The start of the year also saw an end to the Conservative government. It had collapsed at the end of 1905, and the January 1906 election saw the Liberals gain an overwhelming overall majority of eighty-four. The new Prime Minister, Sir Henry Campbell-Bannerman, like Henry Attlee, had been a pro-Boer and had rejected the jingoism that had sustained the Boer War. The Liberal government offered hope for the political causes dearest to Henry Attlee's heart: Irish home rule and reconciliation with the Boers in South Africa.

For Clem, 1906 was the year the East End worked its magic on his soul. He and his younger brother Laurence, who was still an under-graduate, decided to pay a visit to a youth club in Durham Road, Stepney. In 1890 some Old Haileyburyians had decided to do something to help clergy active in the working-class areas of the big cities. They had chosen Stepney because both the rector and the curate were Old Haileyburyians. They built a club, with a gymnasium, drill-hall and club rooms on the first floor, for working-class boys between fourteen and eighteen, which was open five nights a week, from 8 to 10 pm. All members joined the Territorial Army and wore a uniform on club nights, which gave them a pride in their appearance which their everyday rags could not offer. The Attlees had the vague benevolence of the conscientious upper middle-class Edwardian, a feeling that they ought to give some part of their leisure time to helping the poor. The elder brothers had helped out at boys' clubs, and Tom was putting a lot of his spare time into a club in Hoxton; an aunt managed a club for factory girls in Wandsworth, and had gone to live in a poor Wandsworth street in a flat above the club.

On that night in 1906, Laurence collected Clem from the offices of Druces and Attlee and they walked together to Fenchurch Street station and took a train. Ten minutes later, alighting at Stepney, they found themselves in a world which neither of them knew or understood – Limehouse, the heart of the slums. Clem, still in his silk hat and tail-coat, walked gingerly through the disgusting, uncleaned streets for five minutes, and looked up at Haileybury House. The sight of the Haileybury school crest on the outside wall seemed incongruous in those streets, on a dingy hall from which echoed rough cockney voices.

Inside they were greeted by Cecil Nussey, an Old Haileyburyian aged thirty-three, with a heavy, dark moustache and a magnetic personality. Nussey worked as a solicitor during the day, and ran the club every evening, living in a small house attached to it.

Clem's shyness was acute that night. He found it agonising to talk to the boys, who to him were like creatures from another planet, and even to Nussey, whose forceful dynamism he found overwhelming. It was an excruciating evening, made worse by the fact that the boys assumed that the young Attlees were persons of 'substance' and expected to be inspected. They were taken on a tour of the rooms. In one there was a squad receiving drill instruction; in another, boxing; in an upstairs room there were draughts and bagatelle. They had a long talk with Nussey, about what he was trying to do and how he was trying to do it. Despite his misery,

Clem learned enough that evening to want to come again, and he discovered more on subsequent visits. Those of the boys who were in work earned very little money, many of them as van-boys, and the little they did earn was needed to keep their families going. Some of them were working eighty or ninety hours a week, and earning barely enough to feed themselves. Their future prospects were worse than their present misery. The practice of East End employers was to employ boys between the ages of fourteen and eighteen, when they were young, fit, agile, and willing to work for next door to nothing; then throw them back onto the street before they needed sufficient wages to keep a family, and start again with fourteen-year-olds who could be sweated and exploited in their turn.

Working-class children went to the local elementary school, where they stayed until they were fourteen, then started work. At the age of twelve they could get exemption from school to work half time, and one in four London children under the age of thirteen had paid work outside school hours. Those without work could raise pennies doing odd jobs for slightly better-off people – running errands, washing steps and window-sills, catching vermin, delivering milk or meat, selling papers or matches in the street.

Clem learned something of their lives on the street, where boys generally had to fight their way to some sort of respect among their peers. He learned about their home lives. Paul Thompson in *The Edwardians* recounts an interview with a man who had been brought up in the East End at that time. His father was forced to stop working after an accident and his mother faced the humiliation of a visit from the Relieving Officer:

> This chap come down and she took the clothes off us and washed them and put them on the line see, to air . . . And this fellow come down, he'd a stick and he said, 'Oh,' he said, 'you're not destitute' he said, 'you've got clothes on the line,' he said 'and you've got a plate of fish and meat.' She said, 'Yes,' she said, 'you know how much that cost' she said, 'that cost me fourpence' . . . 'Oh' he said, 'you're not destitute' . . . You daren't have a mat on the floor. Cos we only had orange boxes for tables and chairs you see, with covers on them.

Another of Paul Thompson's interviewees in London, Will Thorn, came from a family living in two rooms, a single floor of an old house divided up. The eight children slept in one bed, their parents in another bed in the kitchen:

> We had so many addresses, we couldn't pay the rent, we had to keep

moving. And we come home from school and find your bits and pieces slung out on the road, or passed over the wall to the next bloke to look after while the landlord come in, and he found nothing there. And you was in the next garden see. He looked after 'em until we found a place. Local barrow firms even advertised: 'Keep moving, Humphreys will move you by moonlight.'

Most people of the Attlees' class were content to exploit the poor. Will Thorn recalled being sent to church to meet wealthy ladies:

You meet these old girls that stand in the porch at the church. 'Good morning Mr so-and-so, good morning Charlie so-and-so. Glad to see you at church this morning. How's your mother? Is your father at work?' 'No.' 'Well tell your mother to come round to me Wednesday or Thursday and I'll find her a day's work.' Clean the bloody house out for two bob . . .

Clem learned that for boys like Will Thorn there were none of the pleasures of childhood, except what might be provided by a place like the Haileybury Club. So there was always a waiting list for membership. And he learned the real meaning of poverty. Many of the boys did not get enough food. If they were out of work, they were seriously undernourished because in a poor family, as one of the boys told him in a phrase which was to stay with him all his life, 'You can't take the food when you haven't brought anything in.'

Life expectancy in middle-class Hampstead was fifty, in working-class Southwark thirty-six. In a healthy middle-class suburb 96 of every 100 infants would survive their first year of life. In a bad slum district one in three would die. When conscription was introduced during the Second World War it was found that four out of every five recruits had such bad teeth that they could not eat properly. All the evils of slum-dwelling identified more than two decades earlier by the Revd Andrew Mearns were still there, only more so. The rich were richer than they had been in 1883, the poor were poorer and there were more of them. Seebohm Rowntree studied poverty in York, finding twenty-eight per cent of the population, and forty per cent of schoolchildren, living below the minimum nutritional standard necessary to maintain physical health. Of 1,000 children 163 died before their first birthday. The number was twice as high for working-class children. Of those who survived, one in four did not live beyond the age of four.

Clem learned that in the East End, 300,000 people were crowded into 1,700 acres, and no doubt remembered that there were 200 acres round the holiday home in Essex which Henry Attlee had purchased when Clem was a child. He learned that two or three families were often crammed into one tiny back-to-back house; and that there was no open space because almost every available square yard had been developed to extract the last penny of profit. He learned that the ethnic mix of indigenous cockneys, Irish Catholics, and Jews fleeing Eastern European persecution, was powerful and potentially explosive. He learned what each generation has to experience over again: that the latest group of immigrants is always liable to persecution, especially where space, food and work are in short supply. In the East End in 1906 it was the Jews, and one of the last acts of the Conservative government was to bow to agitation against Jewish immigration by passing the Aliens Act, which allowed for the exclusion of immigrants who had no financial support.

Clem started coming in one evening a week, then two evenings, to help Nussey. He was amazed and delighted to find that with the unforced friendliness of the boys he was overcoming his shyness. What began as a duty started to become a pleasure. Five months after that first visit he took a commission as an officer in the Territorial Army, because otherwise he would not have been able to take a share of the responsibility for running the club. He enjoyed drilling the boys on spring evenings in the rector of Stepney's garden, marching over Wimbledon Common singing, sleeping over Saturday night in big bell-tents which the club had borrowed. The boys liked and respected him, and he felt for the first time in his life that he was doing something with a purpose. Later, after the First World War, in a book called *The Social Worker*, he described part of what was happening to him:

> Take the case of a boy from public school knowing little or nothing of social and industrial matters who decides, perhaps at the invitation of a friend or from loyalty to his old school that runs a mission, or to the instinct for service that exists in everyone, to assist in running a boys club. At first he will be shy, then on getting to know the club boys he will find himself with a new outlook and shedding old prejudices. The rather noisy crowd of boys on bicycles with long quiffs of hair turned over the peaks of their caps, whom he always regarded as bounders, become human beings to him, and he appreciates their high spirits,

and overlooks what he would formerly have called vulgarity. He goes out to referee them at football and finds that the only available ground is four miles away and he remembers that somewhere he has heard of an agitation for open spaces, while the question of getting there makes him consider transport problems, trains, rail and buses, and he may begin to enquire who is responsible for these services. He finds the boys get there so late that the moon is already getting up, and perhaps his centre-forward, on whom he had been relying, cannot get there at all; he finds it is a case of overtime, and the demand for shorter hours of labour becomes a reality . . . he realises now the value of the forty-eight hour week.

A little later he will perhaps visit one of his boys who is sick and begin to see the housing problem from the inside – perhaps the family cannot afford proper treatment for the boy, and he is forced to consider the provision now made for the sick; and further, the wages question begins to interest him after he has had a talk with the boy's father, who is in the building trade and gets only occasional work . . .

Privately he wrote years later: 'Few had boots and their clothes were just rags. Many a time I've washed their cold sore feet in winter . . .' He had come a long way from the laconic remark he made to Laurence as they travelled back to Putney after their first visit: 'Good show, that. Might look in from time to time.'

In the summer of 1906 he attended his first summer camp with the boys, at Rottingdean near Brighton, sleeping in tents. In 1907 Nussey resigned as club manager, and asked Clem to take the job in his place. Clem hesitated – not, I suspect, because he did not want the job, but because his self-confidence was still so low that he doubted whether he could do it properly. But Nussey pressed him, and at last he agreed. It paid £50 a year – about a quarter of the allowance his father paid him when he was an undergraduate – and it entailed leaving his parents' home and going to live in the small residence beside the club. It was not a full-time job. He was expected to be there in the evenings. Each morning he put on his lawyer's top hat and tail-coat, and walked through the streets of the East End to Stepney Green station. There he took a train to the Temple, to spend a boring and dispiriting day waiting for work that did not come, and looking forward to the evening, when he was going to enjoy himself and feel useful. His father continued to pay him an allowance. A young gentleman could hardly be expected to live on £50 a year.

That year the new Liberal government set up Care Committees

for schools. Its volunteer members had the task of visiting the homes of children who were obviously in need, and arranging help for them. Clem and Tom both added Care Committee work to their other duties, and learned even more about the harsh conditions of the poor.

Clem might have remained the Edwardian do-gooder, doing his bit for the less fortunate as a sort of upper-middle-class civic duty. Even now that he was a full-time social worker, Haileybury House might have been simply a temporary phase of his life which he gave to good works before returning to the real business of life, which was making money at the bar. But as months turned into years, he and his family slowly began to realise that this was not just a phase in his life. He had at last taken control of his destiny, and made a positive decision about what to do with it.

And there was another choice to be made. He spent 1906 slowly and methodically making it. 'When I give food to the poor they call me a saint. When I ask why the poor have no food they call me a Communist,' wrote the South American priest Dom Helder Camara eighty years later. That was the choice Clem Attlee had to make. Was he a saint or a communist – or socialist, at any rate? The saintly path was in the family tradition, of which his father would have heartily approved. All his brothers did some sort of social work; one of his sisters became a missionary, and the whole family, except for Clem, was partly inspired to good works by religion. At the start he, like his father, had sympathy with the methods of the Charity Organisation Society, a ghastly organisation which offered loans to tradesmen in difficulties, emigration grants or pensions to the 'respectable poor' and, for the rest, resident relief at the workhouse or nothing. The idea was to use charitable gifts as moral bribes, making it as unpleasant as possible to receive charity. Poverty was considered a sign of moral depravity. He heard one typical COS member, an Anglican parson, advocating giving poor children only burnt porridge.

This sympathy with the COS lasted only a few weeks. The trouble with charity, he wrote in *The Social Worker*, 'is that it tends to make the charitable think that he has done his duty by giving away some trifling sum, his conscience is put to sleep and he takes no trouble to consider the social problem any further.' The irrelevance and offensiveness of the COS philosophy of moral bribes became clear to him when he realised 'the fine characters of many of the boys, the heroism of the struggle with poverty, the unselfishness and neighbourly kindness which existed in a poor district'. In the next street there was a gang of small barefoot boys who had nowhere to go. He arranged for the club to be open from 7 to 8 pm – an hour before its normal opening time – for them. His senior boys volunteered to come in and teach and supervise the younger ones, even though it meant snatching a very hasty meal after a long day at work. What right had rich self-righteous clergymen to treat such people as though they were training puppies not to mess the carpet? Perhaps this was the most important revelation of all – that the boys' minds did not reflect the poverty of their homes. To the end of his life he remembered with wonder the conversations he had with them. He remembered the boy who told him that women ought to have the vote because 'only a working woman knows what a working woman has to go through'. He remembers them struggling with definitions of a gentleman, from 'a bloke what does no work' through 'a rich bloke' to 'a bloke what's the same to everybody'. Clem was impressed by the last, probably because it reflected his own view.

He met their parents, visited their homes, and saw how the poor lived. As manager he started to meet not just the boys who came to the club, but those for whom there was no room. He saw that places like Haileybury House hardly even scratched the surface of the problem. He realised, as Andrew Mearns had written the year Clem was born, that only large-scale action by the state could have any serious effect. It was not a conclusion he sought, nor one he was glad to arrive at. Clem Attlee was, and remained all his life, a profoundly conventional man, happiest swimming with the current. There was not a trace about him of the instinctive rebel which made so many charismatic socialists of his generation. If he could stay within the bounds of conventional thinking, he would be more than happy to do so. He tried hard to avoid leaving what he called his 'snug niche' in society. But he also had a logical, methodical mind and could see that unless society was organised so as to eliminate it, the wretchedness he saw all around him would continue forever. He came to socialism slowly and reluctantly, by painstakingly eliminating all possible alternatives, through his heart first and his head afterwards, mentioning (but only privately, never publicly) the 'burning anger which I felt at the wrongs which I could see around me'. There was nothing for it but to make a total break from his upbringing: 'I had been ready to do anything for the poor except get off their backs.'

Between 1905 and 1907 Clem did his work during the week and his thinking at weekends, which he spent at his parents' home in Putney, and where he and Tom thought their way to socialism together over long walks by the Thames. They talked theory and books, but also about the practical matters of running a club. Tom was now an architect, and when Clem decided that Haileybury House needed more fresh air, Tom designed a new ventilation system and superintended its installation. For Tom, too, working in a boys' club in a poor area of London – in his case Hoxton – had been a revelation. The two brothers, alike in many ways yet utterly different, used each other as sounding boards. Clem had a terribly practical mind; Tom had a tendency to wander off onto metaphysical clouds. For Tom, the easiest part of his parents' beliefs to accept was their Christianity; in fact he added to it a fervour all his own, and it was at the centre of everything he did all his life. The club where Tom was working had been founded by Christian Socialists, who had influenced him at Oxford.

Clem, on the other hand, had already quietly dropped Christianity. He did so carefully and tactfully, and gave no offence in the family home, but he did so decisively. You cannot prove that God exists by logical argument. It is a matter of faith, and Clem never had it. And that, to Clem, was that. So Tom's Christian Socialist tracts fell on stony ground. But Tom, as an architect, was also influenced by aesthetes and art critics like Thomas Carlyle, John Ruskin and William Morris, to whom he introduced his brother and whom Clem found much more helpful. Clem responded at once to Carlyle's anger and disgust, and to his appeal to the middle classes to see, and put right, the misery and ugliness in their midst. Ruskin advocated not socialism but what we now call a welfare state. The unemployed should be retrained, and if they proved unemployable, should be looked after at the state's expense. He wanted pensions for everyone. From Ruskin, Attlee learned that only the state could provide these things. From William Morris he learned that the industrial revolution had released forces of greed, cruelty and selfishness; and the task was so to organise post-industrial society that it ceased to be ugly and materialistic. Human beings should not be asked to live and work in the soulless ugliness which was the East End.

Clem turned to the poets he had loved as a boy, and found to his surprise that many of them, Shelley and Blake in particular, re-read in a new light, were on the side of revolt against capitalism and greed. He and Tom looked at co-operatives as a solution. This faith lasted just long enough for both of them to get a few suits very badly made at a tailor's shop run on co-operative lines. All this agonising might seem excessive, but the step the two brothers were about to take was one which would horrify their friends, their family's friends and the men they had been to school with. To some middle-class young men, the idea of shocking their families and friends would have been attractive. To Clem and Tom it had not the slightest appeal.

By October 1907 Clem was a socialist. The transition from being a cynical young Tory had taken just two years from that first visit to Haileybury House. The next step was to join a socialist organisation. That was not as easy as it sounds. Left-wing organisations, then as now, were suspicious, dogmatic and faction-ridden. Tom, who had been a step or two ahead of his brother all the way down the road, took Clem to the Fabian Society at Clements Inn, perhaps because it was the most middle-class of all societies, the one where they might meet men from their own background. There they met the sort of forbidding, unwelcoming socialists who, Clem was to learn, were the curse of the movement. Clem writes in his autobiography: 'Edward Pease, the Secretary, regarded us as if we were two beetles who had crept in under the door, and when we said we wanted to join the Society he asked coldly: "Why?" We said, humbly, that we were socialists and persuaded him that we were genuine.'

A few days later they went to a Fabian Society meeting and heard Bernard Shaw, Sidney Webb and H. G. Wells, and a sterile dispute about the future of the Society between several hirsute men. 'Have we got to grow a beard to join this show?' Clem asked his brother. The comfortable middle-class meeting seemed to have nothing to do with what they had seen in the East End, and the idea – still accepted by the Fabians – that the best way forward was to work through the Liberal Party seemed to them to make a nonsense of the long road they had travelled. The Fabians wanted to *give* the working-man a decent life, not encourage him to *demand* it for himself. Stepney had convinced Attlee that the working class was fit to govern.

Nor did he take to the Social Democratic Federation, a strictly Marxist organisation, doctrinally exact in the hallowed tradition of Marxist sects. That left one alternative. Clem patiently waited until an East End wharf-keeper called Tommy Williams – 'a fiery little Welshman' according to Clem's later recollection – came to

Clem Attlee

Haileybury House burning with indignation about how the Charity Organisation Society had refused to help one of the Haileybury boys. In the course of his story, he said he was a socialist, and Clem said quietly: 'I am a socialist too.' It must have taken everyone a little by surprise – the general view would have been that socialism wasn't for toffs – but though he presents the incident in his autobiography as something that just happened, Clem almost certainly acted with great deliberation and with some idea of the likely result. He never did anything by accident. The next Wednesday Tommy Williams took him to join the local branch of the Independent Labour Party. Everyone in the ILP was a member of a trade union, so he joined the only union for which he was eligible, the National Union of Clerks.

The ILP was just what he wanted. It had a general socialist objective, enshrined for years in its constitution, and not removed from Labour's constitution until the mid-1990s – 'the collective ownership of the means of production, distribution and exchange'. But it also had a clear tactical objective, to get independent representation in Parliament for working men. It was to achieve this that the Scottish miner Keir Hardie and his colleagues had founded the ILP in the year of Clem's birth. It rejected the idea that socialists should work through the Liberal Party. It had been the driving-force behind the formation of the Labour Representation Committee, which eventually became the Labour Party, and when Clem joined, it had 887 branches, 22,000 members and thirty MPs. It was not Marxist, unlike the Social Democratic Federation: the ILP did not consider socialism inevitable, and it did not talk of class war.

Almost as celebration, the years 1906 to 1908 seem to be when Clem wrote most poetry, all of it marking, in one way or another, the faith he had found. One poem was just called 'Socialism'. It's not his best, but it was a milestone on the road.

> Surely some day we'll make an ending
> Of all this wretched state of want and greed.
> Children shall reap, glad cries forth sending,
> In fields where we have sown the seed.
> All through the years mankind ascending
> Leaves the outworn and seeks a higher creed.
> In true fraternity, on love depending,
> Society fulfils its highest need.
> Man cannot rest until mankind is freed.

The Making of a Young Conservative

The countryside could move him to rapture and misery because the people he lived among could never see the open spaces. But it was the condition of the working class that moved him most:

Oh who are these that come, with no sound of trump or drum,
With the steadfast silent tramping of an army in the night,
And what the standard red, that is floating overhead?
And what is the cause of their gathering to the fight?

O, these are they that work in the pit's foul heavy mirk,
The men from shop and factory, the men from mill and field,
Dwellers in many lands, the men of horny hands,
That dig and build and fashion that the earth her fruit may yield.

These are they that sow the seed that other folk may feed,
That build the stately palaces wherein they may not dwell,
The makers of all wealth, stolen from them by stealth,
Who make a heaven for others and live themselves in hell . . .

Clem was now politically committed. His progress so far would have seemed impossible to him just two years previously.

2

The Coming of War

The twenty or so members of the ILP's Stepney branch spent most of their waking hours, like most East Enders, scratching a living for themselves and their families from the harsh and unyielding city. They had very little time to give to their politics. Only their new recruit, Clement Attlee, was sufficiently his own master at work that he could guarantee to get to evening meetings on time. And they liked him. Though from a completely different class and background, he was accepted and welcomed.

Small political organisations are good at spotting the willing workhorse with time and enthusiasm, and within a few weeks they made him branch secretary. Theoretically, he was still a lawyer, working part time at Haileybury House and attending chambers during the day, but his heart was not in it. He was neither getting briefs nor seriously looking for them, and on the few occasions he applied for jobs he was turned down, probably because, as he put it, 'socialist activities in those days were not looked on with favour'.

In the evenings he came alive. Four evenings a week were spent at Haileybury House and the fifth at the ILP branch, where eight or ten working men and their new middle-class recruit sat round a stove in a small, grimy East London church hall and discussed how best to conduct local propaganda, and how best to meet a challenge from members of the Social Democratic Federation who joined the ILP with the intention of breaking it up. This early battle was the precursor of many furious disputes with communists over the next four decades. At the weekend he refereed the boys' football matches, organised open-air meetings, and visited trade union branch meetings to help persuade trade unionists to embrace socialism. What was left of the weekend he spent in the family home in Putney.

It was an exciting time for socialists. Sir Henry Campbell-Bannerman showed some traits as Prime Minister that distinguished Clem Attlee four decades later. He was a poor public speaker with conservative habits, a strong social conscience, and unexpectedly radical policies. He was also, like Clem, underrated. A wealthy seventy-two-year-old Glaswegian of quiet respectability and fixed domestic habits, considered decent but dull, he quickly showed he could dominate a Cabinet of men who were considered far more talented than himself.

Like Clem, he thought the poverty to be found in Britain's cities disgraced the nation. All the glories of Britain are valueless, he told a Glasgow audience in 1907, 'if the men and women on whose labour the whole social fabric is maintained are doomed to live and die in darkness and misery.'

One of his government's first acts was to enable local authorities to provide free school meals for undernourished children, and the London County Council set up unpaid School Care Committees to run the scheme. Clem joined the committee for Trafalgar House School, a very large school in a poor area near Stepney Green. Each child had to be visited to ensure that the family really was destitute. Clem had regular battles with his colleagues on the committee, who wanted to keep to a minimum the number of meals provided. He recalled that his colleagues once recorded with satisfaction 'the prevalence of a wholesome feeling among parents that a stigma attaches to the receipt of meals by their children'.

The meals provided had to be supervised by volunteers, and Clem often supervised more than 400 children. He did it by organising prefects to help him – a system he had learned when a public schoolboy at Haileybury, and used at Haileybury House. The children got to know him, and he remembered all his life the barefoot little girl who came up to him in the street and said:

'Where are you going, Mr Attlee?'
'I'm going home for tea.'
'I'm going home to see if there is any tea,' said the girl.

The new Prime Minister's temperament was well illustrated by his behaviour over a Bill aimed at extending compensation for industrial injury to six million more workers. His Ministers fiercely resisted a Labour amendment to include domestic servants within the scope of the Bill. But on the last day of the Report stage, Campbell-Bannerman strolled into the chamber and listened to the Labour leader Keir Hardie arguing for their inclusion. Without consulting his Ministers, he accepted Hardie's amendment on the spot.

Campbell-Bannerman also sanctioned a secret electoral deal with

Clem Attlee

Keir Hardie's colleague Ramsay MacDonald, the Secretary of the Labour Representation Committee. The LRC, the forerunner of the modern Labour Party, was an alliance of trade unions and socialist societies, including the ILP, formed in 1900 to return Labour MPs who would form an independent party in the House of Commons. The pact was designed to avoid clashes between a Labour and a Liberal candidate which might let a Tory in. It helped ensure the huge Liberal landslide which gave Campbell-Bannerman 491 MPs (including perhaps thirty Lib-Labs), gave the LRC its first substantial parliamentary base of twenty-nine MPs (seven of them ILP-sponsored), and helped reduce the once proud Conservatives to just 132 seats.

But for Clem, it was not enough that poor people should benefit from the decency of benign Liberal politicians like Campbell-Bannerman. A Labour government would treat proper food, shelter and medicines as rights, rather than gifts which could be given and taken away. And if he was to play his part in bringing about a Labour government, there was something he had to learn to do. The Stepney ILP branch secretary was not there just to keep the minutes and organise the meetings. There was a much more forbidding duty involved: something so appalling that a couple of years earlier he could not have contemplated it.

Socialism was spread from street corners, by men standing on soap-boxes or chairs and haranguing passers-by. The branch secretary was expected to take his share of speaking at outdoor meetings. Clem was terrified. But he said he would do it – a remarkable measure of how much he had changed since the days when he was too shy an undergraduate to contemplate speaking at the Oxford Union, and of how much confidence the affection and respect of his new comrades had given him.

So on a windy night in March 1908, under a gaslamp on Barnes Street, a cold and cheerless East End street, with his coat flapping round him and his heart in his boots, he climbed on a chair and began to speak in front of five other branch members. He was glad that the light was dim, and no-one could see him blushing furiously. His voice, never his most impressive attribute, was only just audible above the wind and the hissing gaslamp, and the few passers-by quickened their pace a little. But then a dozen or so stopped and listened, and when he finished they asked questions and he answered, and when he climbed down he felt like a man who has slain a dragon. He never lost his shyness – it was with him

32

until the day he died – but it never again crippled him. He never became a great orator, and never enjoyed it much, but as the years passed he became at any rate competent.

The comradeship of those who had given him this confidence was now, and remained, the bedrock upon which his confidence rested. He treasured his occasional weekends in the countryside, but always wanted to return to Stepney, as he explained in a poem called 'Dissatisfied'.

> When in the hustle, the roar and the bustle
> Of London town
> Strange thoughts come thronging, old dreams and longing
> For sea and down
>
> I hear the thunder of waves far under
> That burst in spray
> Long combers sweeping and ripples creeping
> Across the bay.
>
> The sheepbells ringing, the wild birds singing
> By field and fold
> A note of quiet mid nature's riot
> Of blue and gold . . .
>
> But my heart keeps sighing, my soul is crying
> For town again
> For London City, its hate and pity
> Its joy and pain . . .
>
> But most beguiling the faces smiling
> Of folk I know
> The boys will greet me and comrades meet me
> So I must go.

Eight months after Clem's street corner debut, in November, Henry Attlee had a heart attack at his desk. Clem's younger brother Laurence, who was working nearby, took him home, where he died almost immediately. He was sixty-seven. His obituary in the *Solicitors' Journal* described him in similar terms to those used of his son more than half a century later: 'Acute, able and a man who knew his own mind.'

He left his eight children a total of £70,000, a magnificent sum in those days. Clem's share gave him £400 a year, which was enough to ensure freedom from money worries as long as he remained single. His father's death also meant that he no longer needed to pretend even to himself that the bar might be his future, or to consider his father's concern about his political views. Henry Attlee was too sensible a man to make an issue of it, but it had distressed him to see two sons turn to socialism.

Clem quietly stopped attending chambers and indicated that he was not interested in a temporary legal job which a friend had put his way. His life now was politics and social work. For employment he hoped for something which would bring in a little extra income, would be relevant to these two main interests, and would allow him time to pursue them. After a little searching, he found just such a job, helping the remarkable Fabian socialist Beatrice Webb organise a campaign against the Poor Law. One of the last acts of the Conservative government was to appoint a Royal Commission on the Poor Law, and to make Beatrice Webb one of its members. She, like Clem, came from the upper middle classes and never forgot the poverty and misery she saw in the East End of London. The majority of the other Commission members came from the Charity Organisation Society school of thought and tended to blame the poor for their condition.

Beatrice Webb refused to support the majority report. Her minority report offered a fully worked out blueprint for a welfare state, including a national health service. Beatrice and her husband Sidney Webb had friends in high places, and not just in socialist circles. A Conservative Prime Minister had appointed her to the Commission, and senior Liberal Ministers regarded the Webbs as excellent sources of good ideas and interesting conversation. So Beatrice hoped that her minority report might yet be implemented. She tirelessly lobbied friends in government, and set up and found finance for the National Committee for the Break-Up of the Poor Law, later called the National Committee for the Prevention of Destitution. This committee required someone to work part time finding organisations throughout the country which wished to hear one of its speakers, and making the necessary arrangements. Someone suggested to the Webbs that the young ILP activist Clement Attlee was a thoroughly efficient and reliable person.

One of his duties was to fill in when a speaker let him down at the last moment, which was how he once found himself addressing a large gathering of Liberal women in Bolton, who were expecting a Bishop, on 'Problems of Birth and Infancy'. We do not know how he managed, but Clem, awkward and uncomfortable with women, probably had even less idea about birth and infancy than the average unmarried public schoolboy of twenty-six in 1909.

Meanwhile Stepney ILP fielded Clem as a candidate for Stepney Borough Council. He polled just sixty-nine votes. It was not as awful a result as it sounds. Labour was slower to take hold in London than in other cities, and Stepney was harder going than the rest of the East End because its politics were dominated by the Union of Stepney Ratepayers, whose policy was to keep rates low. And many of Labour's natural supporters could not vote. Applicants for poor relief and many lodgers had no vote, and complicated registration procedures on moving home counted against the poor. Nonetheless, when an ILP comrade hailed him cheerfully with 'Are we downhearted?' Clem replied briskly and characteristically, 'Of course we are.'

The Webbs' campaign was equally unsuccessful. Even the more moderate suggestions of the majority report of the Royal Commission failed to find favour with the government. The Webbs were pleased with Clem's work, however, though neither of them lived to see an Attlee government at last consigning the Poor Law to history.

Clem left the job in 1909 to become Secretary of Toynbee Hall in Whitechapel, which aimed to develop relationships between universities and the working classes. This job was residential, so it meant moving out of Haileybury House. But Toynbee Hall, he found, had too many of the complacent middle-class attitudes to the poor which he had rejected when he heard them from the Charity Organisation Society. His colleagues found him too left-wing for their taste. In any case, he saw Stepney and Limehouse as his area, not Whitechapel. That year, in one of his earliest and best poems and one of the few that was published (in the *Socialist Review*), he wrote of what he felt for Limehouse.

> In Limehouse, in Limehouse before the break of day
> I hear the feet of many men who go upon their way.
> Who wander through the city.
> The grey and cruel city
> Through streets that have no pity
> The streets where men decay.
>
> In Limehouse, in Limehouse by night as well as day
> I hear the feet of children that go to work or play.
> Of children born to sorrow,
> The workers of tomorrow,
> How shall they work tomorrow
> Who get no bread today?

In Limehouse, in Limehouse today and every day
I see the weary mothers who sweat their souls away.
Poor, tired mothers trying
To hush the feeble crying
Of little babies dying
For want of bread today.

In Limehouse, in Limehouse I'm dreaming of the day
When evil times shall perish and be driven clean away.
When father, child and mother
Shall live and love each other,
And brother help his brother
In happy work and play.

It has the sentimentality of much socialist writing, but the appalling suddenness of the line 'Of little babies dying' is designed to take the reader by the throat; it would be a cold fish on whom it could fail to have effect.

So he left Toynbee Hall in 1910 to return to Limehouse. Typically, he left in good order, leaving behind a warm feeling towards him. He and Tom took an LCC flat together by the river in Limehouse. Tom was practising as an architect in the Strand and working at a hostel in Hoxton, and was active in the Wandsworth ILP. After a few months Tom married, and Haileybury House offered his brother a refuge once again. Clem was pleased that Tom's new wife Kathleen was a fellow social worker, socialist and ILP member.

That year, politics dominated Clem's life as never before, partly because it dominated the nation's life. The radical energy of the Liberal government seemed undiminished. It had introduced the first ever state pensions: tiny, available only at seventy, and with many exceptions, but a start from which future governments might build. The new President of the Board of Trade, Winston Churchill, had set up Wages Boards for some industries, consisting of representatives of employers and workers, and independent members. They had the power to set minimum rates of pay. Churchill had been lobbied by the Webbs, who had also inspired a campaign by a liberal newspaper, the *Daily News*, which revealed a few of the facts which had brought Clem Attlee to socialism. Middle- and upper-class women, some of them anyway, were distressed to find that their fine clothes were stitched by starving women working sixteen hours a day in East End cellars for less than a penny an hour. Churchill's Wages Boards were not abolished until 1993.

This measure provided Attlee's first chance to help Churchill, though Churchill did not know of it; he probably did not even hear the name Clement Attlee until many years later. But Attlee was one of the team of researchers whose information provided the ammunition on sweated labour for the Webbs to pass to the *Daily News* and to Churchill. To do this he visited several outworkers in the East End's notoriously sweated tailoring industry, and he found himself shocked all over again at the misery and exploitation he found.

Electing workers' representatives onto the Wages Boards in the East End, with its fissile mix of political and ethnic groups, was never going to be easy, and it gave Clem a chance to use one of his most valuable and rare talents – that of being trusted by all sides. He found himself chairing a meeting of four rival unions in the tailoring trade near Commercial Street, called to choose the workers' representatives. After Clem's opening speech, the whole debate was conducted in Yiddish, and the only words he could make out were 'der meister', 'der arbeiter' and 'gesweaten'. He asked the convenor whether the interruptions were questions, but was told: 'No, only abuse.' He managed to keep some sort of order even when half the audience was on its feet shouting and a man in a top hat, a long black coat and a beard leapt onto the platform, shouting and waving an umbrella. Eventually he closed the meeting and, rather to his surprise, was told that representatives had been successfully elected.

The government also tried, unsuccessfully, to cut the number of pubs in existence. Edwardians were heavy drinkers: people drank twice as much in 1910 as they did in 1930. Pubs were open all day. The rich enjoyed an excess of fine wines and spirits, and the poor found consolation from the squalor of their homes and their lives in the warmth and comradeship of pubs, which were open all hours. Clem had seen them both, and a verse in one of his poems reads:

> We have no solace to delight
> Our poor and hapless folk
> Only the boozer shining bright
> Where men can sit and soak.
> Whereby the worried housewife knows
> The way the money flies
> When half the scanty earning goes
> To purchase paradise.

The House of Lords vetoed the Licensing Bill, and also threw out an Education Bill which had become enmeshed in bitter religious controversies. Churchill and David Lloyd George, newly made Chancellor of the Exchequer, were not minded to allow the Lords to stop them from doing the work they had been elected to do. But would the voters support them against the Lords? Elections in the first decade of the twentieth century were unpredictable affairs, but the omens from by-elections were not good.

Newspapers were now reaching hundreds of thousands of people, and were crudely partisan, generally on the Conservative side. Every by-election turned into a bear-garden, with a propaganda battle between free-traders and Empire free-traders and a procession by the Coal Consumers' League protesting against the Eight Hours Bill affecting the mines. Every pub became a Conservative committee room; every chapel a Liberal committee room. Liberals hired undernourished East End children and showed them off as 'victims of drink'; Conservatives hired poverty-stricken old people who, they claimed, had invested their life savings in breweries and coal mines. The crudest and least edifying of the features of popular political campaigning were noisily struggling to be born, and no systems were yet in place to check their excesses. It was not a good moment for radicals to mount a general election. But they had no choice. By the time of Campbell-Bannerman's death it was clear that a clash between the Commons and the Lords could not be long delayed. Lloyd George's 1909 Budget – the People's Budget, as it became known – was designed to raise money for social reforms, for the labour exchanges which had been created the previous year, for roads and for arms; and to pave the way for sickness and unemployment insurance. Supertax was to be imposed on the very rich at the rate of tuppence in the pound, death duties were to be increased by a third to bring them up to twenty-five per cent on estates over £1 million, land was to be taxed, and income tax and duties on tobacco and spirits were to go up. It was a Budget, he told the House of Commons, for 'raising money to wage implacable war against poverty and squalidness'.

The House of Lords broke a 250-year-old convention that it should not block finance measures, and threw out the Budget. Two general election campaigns were fought in January and December 1910, on the issue of the Budget and the power of the House of Lords to frustrate the will of the elected chamber. Clem threw himself into the resulting general election campaign, believing that this was the chance for Labour to establish a real parliamentary foothold. Lloyd George launched his campaign in the heart of Clem's territory, a Limehouse pub called the Edinburgh Castle, where he told an enthusiastic cockney audience that the issue was whether Britain should be ruled by 'King and people or by King and peers'. It was an extraordinary general election, with hundreds of backwoods peers appearing on hustings for the first time. Hilaire Belloc described it:

> During a late election Lord
> Roehampton strained a vocal chord
> From shouting very loud and high
> To lots and lots of people why
> The budget in his own opin
> Ion should not be allowed to win
> He sought a specialist who said
> 'You have a swelling in the head
> Your larynx is a thought relaxed
> And you are greatly over-taxed.'
> 'I am indeed! On every side!'
> The earl (for such he was) replied.

The doctor instructs Lord Roehampton to go to bed, and not to speak until Wednesday week. But when he visits his patient on Wednesday week, an inconsolable butler tells him:

> 'Oh sir, prepare to hear the worst.
> Last night my kind old master burst.
> And what is more, I doubt if he
> Has left enough to pay your fee.
> The budget . . .' With a dreadful oath
> The specialist, denouncing both
> The budget and the House of Lords
> Buzzed angrily Bayswaterwards.

The government emerged in January 1910 with its majority over the Conservatives cut to two, and dependent on the votes of Irish Nationalists and Labour. Labour had consolidated its parliamentary base, going up from twenty-nine to forty MPs. Clem was delighted that his friend George Lansbury won an East End seat, Bow and Poplar. The Budget was passed in April 1910, a year after it had been introduced, and the government turned its attention to neutering the House of Lords. A second election in November produced a Parliament with almost exactly the same balance of power as before, and in August 1911 the House of Lords lost its right to amend or reject any financial measure, or to veto any bill if the Commons passed it in three successive sessions. On the same day, state salaries for MPs were introduced. The conditions which would eventually make it possible for Labour to govern were now in place.

In that year, Lloyd George's National Insurance Act was passed, and this provided Clem Attlee with a chance of congenial employment. The Act provided for free medical and sickness benefits for workers in certain trades paid for through insurance contributions. The government employed several temporary lecturers – 'official explainers' – to tour the country and explain what the Act was all about, and Clem's allocation was Essex and Somerset. So in the summer of 1911 he bought a bicycle and pedalled from village to village, his pipe clamped firmly between his teeth, stopping on fine days to eat his sandwiches by the side of the road and ponder why his friends in Stepney should be permanently denied such peace and beauty.

Sometimes young Conservatives sat in the front row of his meetings, jeering. One hot day he cycled over the hills to a country vicarage where the villagers were gathered to hear him, and overheard the local vicar say: 'I suspect that young man is a socialist. He wears a soft collar.' It was however only a temporary job, and his old patrons the Webbs, and his ILP friends, could easily have been offended to see him promoting a measure which they, and he, knew fell short of what they hoped and worked for. They might have suspected that, like many other official explainers, he was using the job as a path to a civil service career – which is exactly what his family hoped he was doing. But Clem, as usual, made his move so tactfully that he only cemented old friendships and loyalties. There was not the slightest chance now that he was going to settle down to a civil service career. Four years ago he had written a poem called 'The Civil Servant':

> No more the old street corner
> Where the busy traffic plies
> No more the dear old platform
> And the cause that never dies.
> I've got a government job now
> Propaganda isn't wise.
>
> No more I'll take the platform
> With my comrades tried and true
> And talk for twenty minutes
> To three men and a dog or two
> I've got a government job now
> That sort of thing won't do.

No more the old branch meeting
Where I learned and where I taught
The minutes, correspondence
And delegate's report
I've got a government job now
My silence has been bought.

I feel a sort of traitor
But who the stone can cast?
The dread of unemployment
And the workhouse at the last.
I've got a government job now
And the job has got me fast.

But when my time is ended
And my pension safe in hand
Though I be old and weary
I'll join again our band
And have just one job only
Preach our gospel through the land.

The year 1912 found Clem out of work again. In that year the London School of Economics took over and reorganised a small School of Sociology with money raised by the Webbs. The school now needed a lecturer. There were two candidates: Clem, and a brilliant young Cambridge-educated barrister called Hugh Dalton, nearly five years younger than Clem. Sidney Webb chaired the appointments committee, and, by Dalton's account, told Dalton after Attlee's appointment: 'Don't be discouraged. We thought that, if we appointed him, he'd stick to it, and that if we appointed you, you wouldn't.' Attlee however was told that the decision had more to do with his practical knowledge of social conditions and of local government. He had already favourably impressed the Webbs. Three decades later Dalton became Attlee's Chancellor of the Exchequer. The LSE job was perfect for Clem: 'The salary was small but sufficient for my wants, while the hours of work left me plenty of time for social work and also for socialist propaganda, for it was a fundamental rule of the School that no one could be restricted in venting his political opinions.'

In these years Clem became a figure in the ILP without consciously trying to do so. He took on all the humble, time-consuming jobs which have to be done, and which ambitious politicians generally consider are for lesser mortals. He cut up loaves to feed dockers' children during the 1911 dock strike, and stood at the

41

bottom of Petticoat Lane with his brother Tom holding collecting boxes during the Irish Transport and General Workers' Union strike in 1913. He carried the Stepney ILP branch banner on demonstrations through Central London. He went to court to plead mitigation when a half-starving boy was caught thieving. In 1909 he spoke at fifty-three indoor and outdoor public meetings; in 1910, eighty-eight; in 1911, sixty-three; and in 1912, seventy. He made brief notes of how they went: 'Bad meeting – competitor at pitch' (Acton), 'good but stormy meeting' (East Ham), 'meeting cancelled – no audience' (Poplar). He loved the comradeship of his fellow speakers, as well as their idiosyncrasies. Many later received honourable mentions in his autobiography. Jack Edwards, a corporation dustman, apparently used to select a word from a dictionary and use it for weeks. 'Once it was "adamant" which he pronounced "adamnant" which made it more impressive. While he was "adamnant" he opposed practically everything. Finally he "took umbrage" for several weeks, a phrase which suited his personality, and we had a gloomy time.'

'The people I admired,' Clem wrote in his autobiography, 'were those who did the tedious jobs, collecting our exiguous subscriptions, trying to sell literature, and carrying the improvised platform from one street corner to another.' He not only admired them: he was one of them. No other future Prime Minister could say with truth that, as a young man in politics, he 'had no idea of anything more than working as a member of the rank and file and perhaps getting on to a local council.'

He also, quietly, helped the ILP branch with his own money, paying part of the rent when it set up its headquarters above a funeral parlour in Galt Street; and he saw the membership rise from a dozen or so members to about seventy. The Stepney branch was not one of the ILP's most significant. It was founded only in 1907, and had no money – the need to pay the printer for an election leaflet was a serious deterrent to fighting elections. The whole of London had only three – and, briefly, four – Labour MPs. Outside Woolwich and Poplar there were not even many Labour councillors. It was a small circle. A man who was educated, intelligent, likeable, sincere and hard-working was bound to become a major figure in it. And so it happened. Clem gradually and almost accidentally became known outside Stepney, not just to the Webbs, but to the ILP hierarchy. He represented Stepney at meetings of the ILP's East London Federation. He was twice runner-up for election to the ILP's ruling body, the National Administrative Council, and after 1909 a regular delegate at the ILP's national conference. By 1914, he wrote afterwards, 'I appear to have been known by name to the heads of the Labour Party, for I remember going to a reception to the South African deportees and also to a dinner to Andrew Fisher, the Australian Prime Minister.'

He also made sure he sometimes got away from it all with trips to the continent and to the West Country. And so it was that the declaration of war in August 1914 found him on holiday in Seaton, in Devon, with Tom and Kathleen. The ILP had always declared that if war came, socialists should refuse to fight, and the Attlee brothers read that in faraway Westminster, Ramsay MacDonald had resigned the Labour leadership because he opposed the war, and was succeeded by Arthur Henderson, who supported it. What were they to do themselves? Tom and Clem had travelled a long way together. Now they chose diametrically opposite directions. Tom was certain at once that, as a Christian and a socialist, he must be a conscientious objector, making it clear from the start by joining the No-Conscription Fellowship and the Fellowship of Reconciliation. Clem enlisted in the army as soon as he could get back to London, two days after war was declared. Neither stand was easy. Pacifism was not readily understood among Tom's friends, and the Christianity which underlay it was not popular in the ILP, while joining the army was considered very suspect among Clem's ILP comrades.

These firm decisions were remarkable because external events did not force them to a decision. Conscription was still two years away. Most people thought the war would be fought by professional soldiers, and be over by Christmas. It need not yet have touched their lives. But Clem and Tom both felt forced to take a stand, one way or another. Why was Clem so keen suddenly to leave the work which he had come to love, and go to fight and perhaps die in a cause which, however much it stirred simpler men, did not stir him much? His own explanation, offered ten years later, is rather odd, and, like several of his explanations as he became more of a politician, curiously unilluminating, as though, already, he is using his reputation for shy and laconic answers to avoid giving any answers at all. Here is what he wrote for publication in the Twenties, when Labour was bitterly divided between ex-servicemen and ex-'conshies':

43

I could not accept the ordinary cry of "Your King and Country Need You" nor was I convinced of Germany's sole guilt. On the other hand it appeared wrong to me to let others make a sacrifice while I stood by, especially as I was unmarried and had no obligations . . . I realised that some people had to serve and perhaps be killed and that I was partially trained already. I had no real religious conscientious objection. Whether I was right or wrong I cannot say.

He also once wrote that he had been finally persuaded by the German invasion of Belgium. His autobiography does not refer to his reasons at all. But a private jotting written in 1918 while stationed on Walney Island, Barrow-in-Furness, in Lancashire, probably contains more of the truth:

It was not until the Great War that I fully grasped the strength of the ties that bind men to the land of their birth . . . I well remember how (as soldiers in the war) a fellow Oxonian and I tantalised ourselves amid heat and flies in a dug out with remembrances of the cool grey of Magdalen tower and the light coming chequerwise through the trees on to the water of the Cherwell.

His love was not only for 'the true England of nature, the trees, hedges, grass and the lie of the land, but even the transitory England of the twentieth century with its railways, towns and lighted streets, above all, the lit pavements shimmering and wet with rain of my own birth place, London.'

It is not a love for Britain, but for England; not even for England, but for southern England.

During my training at home I was in the south country, in Wiltshire, Hampshire and Surrey, counties well known and loved, but in 1918 it was my fate to be stationed in Lancashire, in one of the most dreadful products of 19th century industrialism . . . It was there that I realised that I was not only an Englishman but a South Country Englishman. The England that I knew and loved in peace time was all south west of the line between the Wash and the Bristol Channel.

Clem's England was

Salisbury with its mellow old red brick houses clustering round that wonderful spire . . . The little towns of Somerset and Dorset set in the gaps of the gently sloping hills half drowned in apple blossom in April . . . Dorchester in that rich green valley folded in the heath land with its clear streams and wooded slopes . . .

The towns beside the Thames, especially Oxford; Cornwall and

Devon; Dorking and Guildford; East Anglia: this was the England Clem loved, the England for which he would fight and die, not the cold north with its 'silent, slow and irresponsive' people.

Clem probably expected to enjoy the army. He enjoyed the Officers' Training Corps at Haileybury, and drilling the boys at Haileybury House, which was run on military lines. There was still a deep-seated conformism inside this political radical. He also knew he would not have to slum it as private soldier, which would be the fate of most of his Stepney comrades. His class and background would entitle him to a privileged, if dangerous, life as an officer.

Clem found it far from easy to persuade the army to let him join. First they said he was too old at thirty-one. Then they said he could not join the regular army because he held a volunteer commission with the cadets – the commission that had enabled him to manage Haileybury House. He joined the Inns of Court Officer Training Corps as an instructor and drilled new recruits for a month, and in September finally got into the regular army as a lieutenant of the 6th South Lancashire Regiment. He walked into the barracks in Tidworth at the end of September 1914, knowing no-one and consumed with shyness. He forced himself to ask someone where he could find the adjutant, who was having tea, but who made Clem feel at home and found him a room shared with another officer. The routine at Tidworth was a short route march before breakfast, then drill, musketry instruction and physical exercises for most of the day, with occasional exercises or lectures in the evenings. Clem enjoyed army life and the company of his brother officers. 'Charming fellow,' said one. 'Just going to play bridge with him – but a damned democratic socialist tub-thumping rascal.' Clem recalled with affection two colonels who would say: 'Let's have a good "strafe" tonight – have Attlee to dinner.' They would then, he says, 'discuss socialism or some similar controversial topic'.

Clem had more experience than most of the subalterns, and his superiors found him to be a quick and decisive officer. After five weeks or so he found himself in temporary command of a company of seven officers and 250 men, most of them from Wigan, Warrington and Liverpool. He enjoyed the work, and was good at it, though the food was bad and the accommodation uncomfortable. Drilling young men and getting them to trust him was something he knew how to do. He was promoted to captain early in 1915, in permanent charge of a company of about 250 men. 'We started firing on the range in awful weather,' he recalled, 'a rather tedious experience and one not altogether devoid of danger as the men were still very raw.' There he celebrated Christmas 1914, and at one of his Company concerts his commanding officer, who probably realised that Clem was shy, cruelly put him up to sing first. No record exists of what he chose to sing.

In February they moved to Winchester, where the men were billeted in church halls, while Clem and the other officers lived in lodgings in the town. He shared a room with two lieutenants. Years later he typed out a list of all the officers of the South Lancashire Regiment, with notes on what happened to them, so we can trace the fate of his two room-mates. T. H. Naylor was wounded in the Dardanelles and H. E. Voelcker was killed in France in August 1916. They then moved to Black Down, into some permanent huts erected at the time of the Boer War. In the first week in June they received maps of France and Flanders and assumed they were being sent there. But instead they set sail through the Mediterranean to Turkey. There was a long sea voyage during which Clem amused himself by writing limericks for the ship's newspaper, and in the brief stops in Valetta and Alexandria managed to get in a few games of billiards. Most of the officers played card games of chance, but Clem did not enjoy these, and instead played picquette with the commanding officer, Lt Colonel M. C. A. Green, later killed in France. He shared a tiny cabin with four other officers, which was a tight fit in a ship which was not designed for the increasingly hot climate, and Clem generally slept on deck.

A fortnight after leaving England the troopship steamed into Mudros harbour, joining 300 others at anchor there, and a few days later the battalion was sent up the peninsula on two destroyers. They went ashore about 5 pm and marched to their tents, in a vineyard by the harbour. This was the site of the Eastern front which Churchill, Lloyd George and Kitchener had demanded to take pressure off the Western front in France. It was a bold strategy and controversy still rages about whether it was a good one, but Clem never had any doubt. It gave him his lifelong admiration for Churchill as a military strategist, an admiration which contributed enormously to their working relationship in the Second World War. The strategy was ruined, Clem always believed, by lazy and complacent generals.

The next evening Clem's Company embarked on two destroyers for an overnight trip up the peninsula, and Clem spent a sleepless night on deck because it was too hot below, where his brother

officers were consuming whisky and bread and butter. They dis-
embarked in the small hours, marching quickly and silently so as
to get into the trenches and under cover before daylight. Men who
had never before seen real war found themselves in trenches facing
accurate snipers and shells from the Turks, as well as water which
tasted of sand, unbearable heat, and an endless barrage of flies;
they lived in dugouts on a diet of bully beef, biscuits, some very
salt bacon and tea without milk. There was an allowance of half
a water-bottle each per day, which was woefully inadequate in the
intense heat. The sides of the dugout were black with flies, which
filled everything they drank. The trenches smelled terrible from the
bodies of Turkish soldiers embedded in them.

Officers would amuse themselves by firing Verrey pistols to draw
the Turkish fire into harmless places, and Clem wrote a little
occasional poetry:

> The homely chirping of the birds begins
> A little wind springs up and faints and dies
> Old Akhi Baba turns from grey to green
> And rat-tat-tat, machine guns usher in
> Another day of heat and dust and flies.

Soon, to add to their troubles, came dysentery. Clem did not know
he had it at first. He assumed that his insides, like everyone else's,
were playing up because of the sandy water and the flies. When
he fainted, he was sent down to the beach, where he lay in a
tent with two other officers similarly afflicted. Next day, in the
full insufferable heat of the day, they were turned out and told
to rejoin their regiments. One of the other officers collapsed and
eventually had to be taken back to England, but Clem managed to
struggle back to his Company. He led his men into new trenches
and kept himself awake on night-duty with long talks about politics
with a sergeant-major, a shop steward in the National Union of
Railwaymen who shared Clem's views. After a few days he had to
go back to the beach, this time on a stretcher. Unconscious, was
put onto a hospital ship bound for England. But Clem wanted to
stay with his men, and when he woke up, he asked to be put off the
ship at Malta, where he was taken to a hospital on a peninsula to the
north of Valetta. It was a thoroughly comfortable hospital, though
the main treatment for dysentery was plenty of cod-liver oil.

There, so far as we know, he started his lifelong exchange of
letters with his brother Tom. He wrote to Tom regularly, at least

once a month and often several times, for the next forty-five years, never forgetting a letter on his brother's birthday, even when he became Prime Minister. The first letter, or the first which survives, was written in his tiny, spidery and almost illegible hand from the hospital in Malta. He had just heard that the South Lancs had been sent into battle at Sari Bair, and 500 of them were killed. Wounded men streamed into the hospital. First to arrive was the scoundrel of Clem's Company, who gave him an account 'whereby it seemed he had led the company with great skill.' The Company captain, a bullet in his lungs, sat up in his hospital bed, lit a cigarette, sent for maps and explained the battle to Clem.

Clem must have known, though he typically did not mention it or dwell on it, that dysentery had probably saved his life. He comments tersely but pungently to Tom: 'As usual in war the best men are among the killed.' He has, he says, been reading Carlyle's *Cromwell*, which left him admiring Cromwell and detesting Carlyle. Tom must have written describing the troubles of being a pacifist in England in 1915, for Clem writes: 'The papers as you say are vile especially *The Times* who are [bursting] for conscription for all they're [fit]. They must know at this stage conscription would not be of any service.' Tom's pacifism would have disgusted most of Clem's brother officers. He spoke regularly at street corner meetings, several times being knocked off his platform. Conscription was introduced five months later, in January 1916 – not because it was useful but, as Clem had predicted, because the newspapers had whipped up great public agitation for it.

The Maltese hospital was a pleasant place to be and he was able to get in a good deal of billiards in the neighbouring town of Valletta, but he was desperately anxious to get back to his Company, to be with them among the flies in the unbearable heat, to share their misery. A fellow officer, A. G. Calme-Seymour, remembered years later going with Clem to the commanding officer and asking whether they could not return on a transport ship they had seen in Valletta Harbour. They were told the ship was full, but they pointed out that as it was about 10,000 tons 'there ought to be room for two more'. 'Go away and don't be insolent,' was the response. In October Clem at last managed to return to the front by easy stages, the very rough sea almost bringing back his dysentery.

The commanding officer, Captain H. H. Douglas Withers (who later received the Military Cross), noted in his war diary for 16 November: 'Capt C. R. Attlee rejoined from Mudros.' For Clem 'it was really like coming home after so much wandering about and uncertainty . . . It was funny to find unpaid Lance Corporals now quite experienced sergeants.' Heat had been replaced by extreme cold, and then a great storm. On 26 November, Captain Withers wrote: 'Violent thunderstorms, very heavy rain. By 11 pm trenches were knee deep in water.' They worked through the night to drain the trenches, and the following night the temperature dropped below freezing. 'As the men were drenched this caused great distress in all ranks. The situation was however taken in hand by the officers and a serious state of affairs prevented by the immediate construction of braziers from old biscuit tins, and fires and hot meals were soon got going. No deaths from exposure occurred.' Clem was impressed by Captain Withers, who 'bustled round' and whose energy, he believed, saved several lives. Clem found himself in a trench facing a rushing torrent of water from a higher trench, and could hardly stand up. When he got out, he set his men to digging new trenches and had a foot inspection, making all men with sodden feet rub them with snow. The temperature stayed below freezing for three days. Clem remembered: 'I waded into my dugout and with the help of some men already soaked rescued my kit. We then got a rum ration issued and I think the rain slackened off . . .' He found men shivering under the trees, chased them round to make them run about, and gave them frequent tots of rum.

Soon afterwards he was invited to dine behind the lines with the commander of his battalion, Major-General F. S. Maude. Maude was one of the younger generals whose energy and decisiveness, Clem always believed, might have saved the Gallipoli campaign from disaster, if they had been given more responsibility. Maude had managed somehow to rustle up braziers from nowhere when the trenches were flooded, and now, in a nearby house, he was miraculously able to provide Clem with his first decent meal for ages. This settled Clem's stomach, which was still giving him intense pain. But what Maude had to tell him was profoundly disturbing. The government had finally decided that Gallipoli was a failure, and Clem had been allocated a key role in the retreat.

He was told that his Company had been chosen to hold the final lines when Gallipoli was evacuated, and it would be the last to embark on the ships. It was a dangerous assignment, but a crucial one, and he must have greatly impressed his superiors to be given it. It was also, though soldiers do not talk about such things, the definitive statement that Clem's men had died for nothing.

On 10 December, wrote Captain Withers, 'B Company under Capt Attlee left for Lala Baba to construct defensive works there.' These were trenches, as cover for the rest of the men to embark. On 19 December, Clem led 205 men to the beach at 5.30 pm. He disposed his men in trenches and installed himself in a dugout with a telephone. During the evening three parties of men went to the beach and embarked, silently and under the watchful eyes of Clem's Company. Captain Withers noted: 'Capt. C. R. Attlee's party after remaining in the Lala Baba defensive until the evacuation was complete then embarked his party on HMS *Princess Irene.*'

Clem was the last but one soldier to leave Gallipoli. The last was General Maude himself, who had returned to get a bag, telling the men in the last boat to wait for him. He took longer than expected, as Clem's Company waited in silence and darkness, ever fearful that the Turks would start firing. Someone was sent to look for Maude, found him trapped in barbed wire intended for the Turks, released him and brought him to the boat.

April 1916 found him camped by the Suez canal, preparing for a battle. The evening before they were due to attack, he prepared his men for an early start, then sat in the trench with his sergeant-major, who told him stories of the Boer War. Perhaps it was in the cold, quiet half-dark before he was due to charge at the enemy that he wrote this poem:

> If this dawn usher in eternal night,
> If I should die before another day,
> I shall not leave a child behind to say
> 'My father fought and died in Freedom's fight.'
> Nor has the power been granted me to write
> Books that the minds of other men shall sway,
> Keeping my name in memory alway
> To unborn generations a delight.
> I leave not books or children; thought alone,
> Sprung from my words in others' minds like seeds
> Fall'n by the wayside on the road of life.
> What harvest shall be reaped where I have sown?
> Good full eared wheat or tares or barren weeds?
> Beauty and love or ugliness and strife?

At 5 am Captain Attlee came charging out of his trench at the head of his men, carrying a flag to warn the British to lift their fire to avoid hitting their own troops. Other companies were advancing all round them. It soon became clear that the Turks had abandoned the first line of trenches. The British artillery were still firing into the trenches which the British troops were beginning to occupy. When the fire seemed to have lifted, he led the way forward to the next trench, holding his flag aloft. 'Just as I got [to the Turkish trench] and was sticking my flag in the ground, a shrapnel got me from behind, lifting me up like a big kick. I found myself sitting opposite Private O'Neill. Two lads came up and asked if I was hit. I said I did not know, but when I stood up I found that I was, and could not move.' He had lost the use of his legs.

After a painful day in a field-hospital he was sent to India and to a hospital in Bombay, from which he wrote to Tom again. The letter seems designed to be cheerful, so as not to alarm his family, but they must have seen through that at once, because the handwriting is appalling even by Clem's standards. It is written in pencil and the tiny characters clearly took great effort to shape.

There is, he says, a bullet in his left thigh, a large hole in his right buttock, another small hole and burns from the fumes.

> It is surprising how little they hurt, especially at the time. My chief trouble was with my legs as they felt just as if broken and I could not have them lifted unless they were supported all round – this has largely passed off but I still can't move them at all. Something wrong with the transmitting apparatus, I suppose, it's most absurd, I send along a direct order to my leg to lift itself and it takes not the slightest notice ... The whole upper part of me was well and happy and I have not had any shock ...

He even has a little joke for his ILP friends. 'It may interest the comrades to know I was hit while carrying the red flag to victory. I had a large artillery flag of that hue and was just planting it on the parapet when strafed. I pointed out to the CO that I thought the colour was a delicate compliment to my political persuasions.'

By the time he got home to England he could walk again, and strengthened his leg by playing vigorous games of tennis with his oldest brother Rob. He spent a year training soldiers in different parts of the country, being promoted to major in February 1917 and getting what he described as 'a sort of Cooks tour' of the western front. In Barrow he played bridge with 'some war profiteers' and served on a court-martial of a German prisoner who had tried to escape. As a barrister he was a little shocked when the presiding colonel said: 'Of course he's guilty, his CO wouldn't have sent him for trial otherwise.'

It wasn't a bad life, as a solder's life in that terrible war went: training, square-bashing, playing tennis, reading Thomas Hardy, and on one occasion conducting a class in trade union history to a group of invalids who could not go on parade. However, it did not suit Clem. He itched to be at the front and no-one would take him there, as he explained in a letter to Tom on 20 March 1918: 'The trouble with us Eastern Front men is that those who know us are at the other end of the world.' Senior officers kept telling him they really wanted a western front officer. 'It's pretty sickening . . . This soldiering business is only tolerable when one has a definite unit under one's command . . . This depot business where men pass through one's hands constantly is the acme of boredom.'

But he had something more pressing on his mind than his own frustration, and most of his letter was concerned with it. Tom was in prison. Tom had refused to be conscripted into the army. He refused even to do work which could be taken as assisting the war effort, the only sort of work permitted to conscientious objectors. In December 1916 he had been thrown off an East End platform by an angry crowd demanding to know why he was not in uniform. On 22 January 1917 he was arrested and told the court: 'I am a conscientious objector . . . I have been offered non-combatant service but I won't have it.' He was sent to Wormwood Scrubs for three months. The 'absolutists', as they were called, were treated more harshly than ordinary conscientious objectors, and the first two weeks of his stay were in solitary confinement, sleeping on a plank without a mattress and living on bread and water. Even when this was over the diet was pretty poor, and the life consisted mostly of slopping-out and sewing mailbags. His letters were both limited and strictly censored. Warders, who disliked 'conshies', watched him continually through peepholes and abused him.

Tom had a young son and another baby was on the way, and his wife Kathleen was having a difficult time coping with them and with the disapproval of their neighbours. He was released at the end of his three-month sentence, but quickly arrested again, and sentenced this time to a year. Clem was distressed, and in this, the longest and most interesting of his surviving letters to Tom, he wrote: 'I don't know what chance there is of your release. Parmoor and others in the Lords and Hugh Cecil in the Commons have made strong efforts but they break down before the mass of British stupidity which is so strongly entrenched in the cabinet.'

This is a strange, introspective letter, very unlike the Clem Attlee his friends and colleagues knew. It is a man who is fed up, frustrated, but also, for a few moments at least, deeply unhappy, probably because for the first time in his life he is cut off from the human being who has been his anchor for most of his thirty-five years. 'I find here rather a lack of people with whom to discuss things in general.' This leads to 'vain imaginings'. He writes almost as though he does not know his brother's views. He must have known that Tom was one of those who welcomed the 1917 Bolshevik revolution in Russia, yet writes a little coldly: 'The Russian debacle is rather appalling but quite explicable. Lenin and Trotsky appear to me to be of the SPGB [Socialist Party of Great Britain] type or the wilder types of the SDP [Social Democratic Party, the pre-war revolutionary socialists many of whose members ended up in the Communist Party]. I can imagine the state of the country run by the Whitechapel branch of the SDP.'

He knew too that Christianity was central to Tom's life, and wrote: 'I am becoming more and more up against the churches. I think there is very little hope in them – blind leaders of the blind . . . I think the general feeling towards the organised religious bodies especially the C of E is contempt. Certainly the mass of officers I've met don't give a damn for the churches.'

As for Tom's beloved pacifists,

I think the chief value of your movement is as a protest against the doctrine of force which is very much needed but in my view my action is also a protest against the doctrine of 'might is right' so that in different ways we are on the same side . . . I do not see how your principles can be applied in practice in the actual carrying on of the community. Don't they logically lead to anarchic individualism?

He heaped praise on Labour's pro-war faction: 'Henderson Horner and Smillie are doing particularly well I think – their attitude seems to be much the same as mine i.e. socialist pro-war.'

Every so often a little of the anguish he feels about his brother bursts through the languid philosophising. 'Being cut off from books is a great deprivation – it is absurd of me to complain when you are in so much worse a case.' Towards the end he writes with almost audible sadness: 'This letter is I fear very egoistic but I am so shut off from you that I can only tell you of my doings and thoughts.' And then suddenly, after eight large, closely-written sheets of paper, having dipped his pen again so that the new sentence appears sharper and stronger than the rest, he writes, 'I wish these damn fools in the government would let you out.' Then he signed the letter as usual 'your loving brother, Clement R. Attlee', but with an addition not seen in any other letter, before or since: 'Major, 3.S. Lan. R.' It was a statement indicating the gulf between his beloved brother and himself.

Not a man who felt the need to express emotion, Clem's emotion almost forces itself out in this letter. Tom must have sensed the anguish behind the dry phrases and wrote a long and careful answer. It has not survived, but it was probably much the same as that which he wrote to his sister Margaret:

> The prohibition of resisting evil by *physical* force is not just one of the many instructions of Our Lord's, but the central fact of his life and teaching . . . If you've a dispute with a man and honestly believe that you have the right on your side, you can either kill him (which we all rule out) or you can somehow so call out what is reasonable and just and honest in him that he will see the justice of your cause. If you really love him you will have enough insight into his point of view, enough sympathy with him, to manage it; really saintly people do. On the other hand if you fight him you weld all his qualities together into one vigorous form of opposition, you submerge for the time being all that is reasonable and righteous (in the literal sense) in him under his pugnacious, violent, self-regarding, self-protecting instincts – and when it is all over you will have to start afresh just where you left off – trying to get him to be reasonable, trying to call out his decent qualities, his better self . . .
>
> Our Lord was talking hard common sense – his way is the only chance of success. When has war ever 'settled' anything? How has the present war succeeded? We have not saved Belgium – she has been devastated from end to end. We refuse to negotiate for peace and declare that we will drive the Germans back to their frontiers . . .

Clem provided Tom with a careful, polite refutation of absolute pacifism. 'I see your position but I think your final qualification rather upsets the argument. You say "some sanitary measures demand unqualified coercion perhaps." Well this war is to my mind a sanitary measure . . . To me the present struggle is one of white against black.' But he also mentions again the other disagreements with his brother, if only to define and perhaps also limit the space between them. 'I saw a fine example of clerical fatuity in *The Times* the other day. Bp [Bishop] Weldon wrote saying that "among the most tragic incidents of the war was the German attack occurring in Holy Week." The most tragic!! as if the loss of a single human life was not infinitely more tragic . . . I am less convinced than ever of the truth of the church's teaching.'

Clem ends again with a cry from the heart: 'Well I wish they'd let you out so that I could see you again . . .' But the letter, writes Tom's daughter-in-law Peggy Attlee, 'cannot have given Tom much comfort. Apart from expressing . . . his contempt for the Church of England and for religion generally, Clem was clearly quite unable to understand or appreciate Tom's pacifism.'

In June 1918, Clem managed to get to France. There he wrote a limerick inspired by Captain Hargreaves, who persisted in sitting in the dugout and reading when some orders came through, insisting that he was improving his mind:

> Captain Reginald Hargreaves MC
> Is superior to you and to me
> You will generally find
> Him improving his mind
> While the work's left to James Gace and Lee.

He was again watching casual slaughter. 'There was Wallington a good lad,' he wrote laconically, 'but during my absence somewhere he was adjudged to have failed and was ordered to do a daylight patrol on which he was killed I thought quite needlessly.'

Clem once drew his revolver on a junior officer who was upsetting the men by weeping and saying he could not go over the top because his nerve had gone. Frightened by the revolver, the man went, but fainted, and Clem had to intercede with the commanding officer to prevent the man being shot.

Told to attack a German strong-point at midnight, Clem said that the attack would be quite impossible and suicidal and insisted on having the order in writing before he would carry it out. In fact the attack was cancelled, and Clem referred to it as 'an amusing incident'. He often told the story of the sergeant who had a knack of knowing where the shells were falling. Clem was about to lead his men round a field but the sergeant said: 'Right through the middle, sir.' The edges of the field were mercilessly shelled; had he not listened to his sergeant, Clem and his men would have been killed. Reading his notes from the front, it is not hard to see where he learned the decisive ruthlessness that later marked out his premiership.

In France he got piles. He had an operation and was shipped home where, exhausted and run down, he came out with boils all over his stomach, which the doctor used to prod with a steel instrument: 'Painful but not helpful,' he reported. He celebrated the Armistice on 11 November 1918 in a hospital on Wandsworth Common, and persuaded a friendly doctor to sign a chit that he was well so that his brother, Rob, could collect him and take him to his sister's house. There a civilian doctor cured him quickly.

Tom was less than half a mile away from the hospital, in Wandsworth Prison, and was not released until the following April. Conditions were as bad as those in Wormwood Scrubs, but the conscientious objectors were used to it now and had ways of dealing with it: passing messages in Morse code, even playing chess by means of a code, with bands of sympathisers coming to sing hymns and socialist songs outside their windows. Ellen Attlee, thinking of Tom in Wandsworth Prison and Clem in Wandsworth Military Hospital, remarked: 'I don't know which of these two sons I am most proud of.'

When Tom was released, he was disfranchised and unable to vote for five years, and his prospects of finding employment were practically nil. He was badly run down and his wife was ill. She decided that the welfare of her sons required a rural upbringing, and the family settled in as remote a place as they could find, on the south Cornish coast between Truro and Falmouth. They bought a substantial house standing by itself miles from anywhere, with neither electricity nor mains water, facing a creek from the River Fal, and that was where Tom spent the rest of his life, growing his own vegetables and slowly beginning to work, at first offering private tuition for the sons of the local gentry. The war overshadowed the lives of most young men of their generation, soldiers and 'conshies' alike. Clem emerged, by comparison, unscathed in mind and in body. Discharged from the army on 16 January 1919, he immediately set about taking up his old life. He wanted it all back: his LSE job, his small, cosy room in the Haileybury Club and the regular contact with the boys there, his old ILP branch. The East End was his home now, and no less kindly and comforting than the home he had had as a child. His old boss at the LSE welcomed him back with open arms. He was less lucky with the Haileybury Club. He found it on the decline, with the upstairs boarded up. Toynbee Hall gave him a temporary home instead.

The ILP was not what he remembered, either. In 1918 the Labour Party ceased to be a loose federation of trade unions and societies and became a political party with branches in each constituency. Before 1918 you could only join the Labour Party by joining an affiliated society like the ILP, or an affiliated trade union. Now anyone could join the Labour Party direct. It began to siphon off some ILP activists, and in the long run the changes helped destroy the ILP. That same year Labour adopted a policy which included the famous Clause 4 committing the party to collective ownership of the means of production, distribution and exchange. Sidney Webb, who together with Arthur Henderson was the driving force behind the changes, said the idea was to transform 'the Labour Party from a group representing the class interests of manual workers into a fully constituted political party of national scope, ready to take over the government of the country.'

In this it was helped by the split in the Liberal Party between supporters of Asquith and those of Lloyd George. In the East End, most of the large Irish community shifted from Liberal to Labour. Stepney now boasted a Borough Labour Party and a trades council and the two worked closely together.

Clem, like Labour, had changed, though less tangibly. He had a clearer sense of direction. The retired Major Attlee who limped back to Stepney in 1919 'to see how things are going politically', as he put it, was, perhaps without appreciating it, less of a youthful political idealist and more of a professional politician than the soldier who had left five years earlier to go to war. He was professional and calculating enough to make straight for the East End's most powerful political boss, a man he had never met before, who had not even been involved in Labour politics when Clem was last in the East End. Two days after he was discharged Clem was sitting above the Harford Street chemist's shop owned by Oscar Tobin.

3

Limehouse in Step with The Major

A Jew born in Romania, Oscar Tobin had been sent to Britain by his parents at the age of eighteen to escape persecution. He quickly earned enough money to study for a chemist's diploma and later a medical degree, and became involved with Labour politics just before the war. He possessed energy, organising ability, and an addiction to intrigue. He saw that a broad movement combining local trade unionists, ILP members and other Labour supporters could gain control of Stepney Borough Council and win its three parliamentary seats, Limehouse, Mile End and Whitechapel. But to achieve this, he saw that the two ethnic communities in the East End – the Jews and the Irish – had to put aside their mutual distrust and work together, and he carefully cultivated the friendship of the most influential Irish Catholic trade unionist in Stepney, Matt Aylward. At about the same time that Tobin launched the Mile End Labour Party Aylward launched the Limehouse Labour Party, and in 1918 the two joined forces to found the Stepney Trades Council and Labour Party. Tobin wrote in its 1918–19 annual report: 'For many years Stepney has been the black spot of the Labour movement. There has never been a Labour organisation worth speaking of . . .' It was 'the most reactionary borough in London'. He was determined to change all that.

Tobin knew at once the value of the trim little major, demobilised just twenty-four hours earlier, who now sat puffing his pipe in the tiny room above Tobin's shop. He had heard all about Clem, of course. He knew Clem was popular and well-thought-of. And he saw that as a political figurehead, Clem had four priceless assets. He was neither a Jew nor an Irishman and had been out of East End politics for five years, so he had few enemies. He had a private income and only worked part time at the LSE, which meant that he could spend more time on politics than others could afford and could contribute to his own election expenses. And he was a toff. However much socialists might have wanted workers to trust men of their own class, Tobin knew the workers would feel more comfortable voting for a man who spoke in the accent of the ruling class. For many years after that meeting Clem was always referred to in Stepney as 'the Major' which was a subtle way of telling his future constituents, not just that he was a gallant soldier, but also that he came from the class which was born to rule, because working-class soldiers did not become commissioned officers. Finally, he had volunteered to fight in the war. The voters of Stepney thought more of a man for that, and the pacifists of the ILP could take comfort from the fact that he was also active in the No More War Movement, where he quickly earned respect from men who had gone to prison rather than fight. One of these, the Movement's chairman, Fenner Brockway, found Clem 'slight in figure, modest, at first enquiring, seeking knowledge, feeling his way; then, when he had grasped our plans, he began to suggest this and this and this, a series of proposals, down to earth, practical, voiced with a minimum of words, clear and certain.' Clem, said Brockway, 'would tell quietly in private conversations of the barbarities he had seen. He was appalled by the waste of young life.'

Elections for the London County Council were due in two months' time and Tobin wanted Clem to stand for one of the Mile End seats. Clem, who by now had acquired the habit of omitting the personal pronoun from his sentences, so much a part of his image when he was Prime Minister, replied, 'Think it over.' The expansive Tobin replied: 'I already thought it over,' and Clem said: '*I'll* think it over.' He did, but decided on Matt Aylward's advice to run for one of the two Limehouse seats instead, because he had lived there for many years and had a strong local reputation. Despite an election leaflet with a picture of Clem in uniform, he lost narrowly. He was not used to losing, and it seems to have upset him, particularly since the other Labour candidate for the two-member constituency managed to get elected.

More than three decades later his autobiography notes a little smugly: 'My defeat was largely due to the intervention of a parson who stood as an ex-Serviceman candidate and took away some of the votes which I might have had. Later, when I was in the first [1924] Labour government, he sought my aid to be made a Dean. Apart from his unsuitability, I did not think his previous interposition gave him a valid claim on me.' But the defeat did Clem no harm. The powerful alliance of Tobin and Aylward still saw him as an asset, and lobbied successfully to have him adopted as parliamentary candidate for Limehouse.

Clem was making up for lost time in establishing a solid career. A young man with a full head of hair who wanted to change the world had gone off to war in 1914. A thirty-six-year-old man with a polished dome between two neat tufts, with solid and serious intentions that included changing the world, came back in 1919. He once claimed that wearing a tin-hat in the war cost him his hair, but a great many men wore tin-hats without losing their hair, and most male Attlees become bald in middle age, so no-one took this explanation seriously, and they were probably not intended to.

Young people feel immortal. Leading men to their deaths is a swift way of learning that they are not.

Clem must have sounded different: older, with more gravitas and less time to spare. He had grown a carapace. His poetry, before the war sensitive and missionary, became bouncing and escapist. He wrote a G. K. Chesterton pastiche for the end of the war, making fun of standard Chestertonian obsessions and perhaps comparing them with the reality of war, and called it 'The Ballad of Bashan'.

> So the war's done with its fury and fun –
> No more need to harry the hun –
> Still Belloc goes bluffing and bouncing,
> Chesterton's chuckles will never be done.
> What is the stimulant sets them singing?
> What is the tipple that makes them lurch?
> (Chorus! Chorus! Join in the chorus)
> Blood and beer and the Catholic Church
>
> What if America's dry as dry,
> What if the price of wine is high!
> What if the whole world, turning to cocoa
> Toasts vegetarian victory!
> What if the future looks dry and drear –
> We have these and they're here, they're here!
> (Nunc et semper, nunc et semper)
> Blood and the Catholic Church and beer.
>
> Socialists say they won't kill any more,
> Pacifists talk of abolishing war,
> Bolshevists threaten to flatten our frontiers –
> Signs of a sensible slump in gore.
> Still there's bloodshed carried a blessing –

Oh let it flow in crimson blood –
There's always the Jews and there always will be
Beer and the Catholic Church and blood.

This is the slogan that staggers the Socialist
Tumbles the pacifist off his perch,
(Chorus! Chorus! Bellow the chorus)
Blood and beer and the Catholic Church.

For this more worldly man, there were to be no more little rooms in the Haileybury Club or Toynbee Hall. He wanted a home. He bought a lease on a big, dilapidated old building in Limehouse called Norway House, in a cul-de-sac off the Commercial Road. He spent some money on it and did a good deal of work himself, in particular scraping away paint from a splendid Adam fireplace. He converted the first floor into a flat for himself, and the second floor into a flat which he rented out. The ground floor he gave to the Limehouse Labour Party for its headquarters, complete with canteen, card tables, and a three-quarter size billiard table. The next requirement was someone to look after him, for he was far too busy to cook and clean. Never the sort of socialist who thought he ought to live like a poor man, he at first hired a former batman, and then the services of a local ex-soldier, Charlie Griffiths, whom he always called Griff, of whom he wrote in his autobiography: 'He has remained a close friend of myself and my family ever since. He is a great character with a genius for making friends.' There is a slightly less guarded assessment of Griff in some autobiographical notes he wrote for his children in the Thirties: 'A cheery youth who had a fairly stormy time in the army, quite a rough lad but very faithful and did what I wanted.' So this socialist agitator, living in the East End, had a manservant or batman who called him at 7 each morning, ran his bath, cooked his boiled egg and toast, saw him off to work and had his meal ready if he returned in the evening.

But it was not a conventional master–servant relationship, as Griff recalled years later.

If he had a bit of time to spare after his tea, he'd light his pipe and say 'hundred up, Griff?' and we'd go down to the billiard table. He was very hot. He didn't like to lose. He'd have given you the shirt off his back, but when he played billiards, he played to win. He was a cunning devil; he'd never leave a thing.

In 1919 the Prime Minister was Lloyd George. In 1916 he had displaced the Liberal Prime Minister, Herbert Asquith, and had led the wartime coalition government until December 1918. The moment the war was over he called a snap election which became known as the 'coupon election' or 'khaki election', in which he asked voters to support whichever candidate, Liberal or Conservative, had the Lloyd George 'coupon', an endorsement of the popular war leader. This caught everyone else unawares. Liberals still loyal to Asquith were driven out of Parliament in droves, the Labour Party was not able to organise effectively in time, and Lloyd George returned to 10 Downing Street at the head of a massive majority provided by a coalition of Conservatives and those Liberals who followed him rather than Asquith. The government comprised 473 MPs, 332 of whom were Conservatives. Labour had fifty-seven MPs. Clem and his friends were furious. They knew that the immediate aftermath of the war was Labour's best chance, in an election fought on the issue of how to create a better society in peacetime, an election that might have been crucially influenced by men returning from the war determined that they had not fought and suffered, and seen their friends killed, to have the same pre-war injustices back again. That election did not take place. It was to fall to Clem to make sure that the chance was not missed a second time, in 1945.

With little parliamentary representation, much of the turbulent and restless demand for a better society spent itself in demonstrations on the streets, in revolutionary-sounding rhetoric, and in the campaign to keep Britain from going to war with Lenin's new Bolshevik government in Moscow. But some of it went into electing Labour councils. In Stepney, Tobin and Aylward's strategy was triumphantly vindicated in November 1919 when Labour, which had never before held a single council seat, won forty-three seats out of sixty. This time Clem was not a candidate, since the strategist Tobin wanted to save him for the parliamentary election. But the new Labour council appointed him Mayor just ten months after his return to Stepney.

The Mayor's task required real political skill. 'Our Party had a considerable number of Irish Catholics and a number of Jews, and some diplomacy was needed to get harmonious working,' Clem wrote later, with characteristic understatement.

He was proud of the council's record during his mayoral year. He was able at last to do something about the slum landlords who charged exorbitant rents but refused to spend money on keeping their property in a habitable condition. The council served more than 40,000 legal notices on house-owners to repair their property, and made sure these orders were enforced. It set up advice bureaux to advise tenants of their rights. It appointed sanitary inspectors and health visitors, started ante-natal clinics, and reduced the infant mortality rate. It created work for some of the unemployed ex-soldiers for whom the government refused to do anything. To pay for this, it did more than raise the rates. Clem, who was chairman of the valuation committee, brought in professional valuers to look at many of the pubs which had never been properly valued. The result was an additional £200,000 on the council's income, and the renewed hostility of Conservative publicans.

The fifteen London Mayors formed an association and elected Clem chairman, so that he found himself leading a demonstration to 10 Downing Street to press Lloyd George on measures to relieve the scourge of unemployment. They got nothing out of the Prime Minister, but when they came out of Number 10 demonstrators were fighting with mounted police in Whitehall. Major Attlee, who had probably drilled some of the demonstrators at Haileybury House before the war and commanded others in the war, took control at once: 'I ordered the column to halt and turn about and led them back to Stepney, thus saving some broken heads.' While Mayor, Clem, who had taught social workers at the LSE, was asked to edit a Social Service Library series for publishers George Bell and Sons, and to write the first book himself. *The Social Worker* is a dry, thorough and workmanlike textbook for professional social workers, written in a precise, slightly pedantic style. But it is something more. It is a clear statement of some of the principles which underlay the actions of his government a quarter of a century later. In particular, it attacks the idea that looking after the poor can be left to voluntary action. Charity, says Clem, is a cold, grey, loveless thing. If a rich man wants to help the poor, he should pay his taxes gladly, not dole out money at whim.

'In a civilised community,' he writes,

> although it may be composed of self-reliant individuals, there will be some persons who will be unable at some period of their lives to look after themselves, and the question of what is to happen to them may be solved in three ways – they may be neglected, they may be cared for by the organised community as of right, or they may be left to the goodwill of individuals in the community . . .

The first way is intolerable, as and for the third:

Charity is only possible without loss of dignity between equals. A right established by law, such as that to an old age pension, is less galling than an allowance made by a rich man to a poor one, dependent on his view of the recipient's character, and terminable at his caprice . . .

He quotes Robert Louis Stevenson: 'Gratitude without familiarity . . . is a thing so near to hatred that I do not care to split the difference.' Charity 'is always apt to be accompanied by a certain complacency and condescension on the part of the benefactor; and by an expectation of gratitude from the recipient, which cuts at the root of all true friendliness . . .' The rich, Stevenson had written, should instead 'subscribe to pay the taxes. These were the true charity, impartial and impersonal, cumbering none with obligation, helping all.'

Clem thoroughly approves of people doing voluntary work among the poor, as he himself had done for many years, but it must be underpinned by paid staff – and properly paid staff at that. Why should we expect that people doing worthwhile jobs for the community should not be as well paid as those whose jobs are about making money?

Well-intentioned persons will start a baby clinic and expect the doctor to give his services as an act of charity . . . When school meals were started it was suggested that the teachers should supervise them in their meal times, forgetting that the wearing nature of the work of the elementary school teacher made a good rest in the middle of the day a necessity; or again, a treat will be provided for school children on a Saturday, and it will be calmly assumed that the teachers should give up their holiday without pay 'for the sake of the little ones.' It would be just as reasonable to expect the railway to carry them for nothing or the caterer to provide a free meal. I mention the case of the teacher particularly because no class of worker, except perhaps the public entertainer, is so much exposed to this form of imposition. I repeat it is fundamentally unfair, and a form of sweating.

His advice on how to be a good social worker is full of quiet good sense and compassion. Don't start off in administration of relief; it gets you off on the wrong footing. Start, as he did, in a boys' or girls' club: 'Children are responsive and the work is interesting.' Don't treat people as 'cases'. He recalled a colleague describing a man as 'unsatisfactory', yet the man's son had written 'Give my love to my dear, dear, dear old dad.' This, wrote Clem, 'seemed to show that whatever the visitor's opinion of Mr Barnes might be, he was not so unsatisfactory to those who knew him intimately.' The book was not widely read and Clem once wrote: 'I doubt if I made more than £25 from the whole exercise' (writing the book and editing the series). But it established his reputation as a Labour intellectual, in the days when there were not many competitors.

By the end of his mayoral year Clem had almost everything an aspiring politician could want. He was the natural choice as Labour's representative on several public bodies, because his private income allowed him time to devote to them. He was parliamentary candidate for a winnable seat. He had a secure local base where he was liked and respected, and was a member of the London Labour Party executive. He had the beginnings of a national reputation within his party. He was a former Mayor, bathed in the glory of a successful first Labour local administration. He had become an alderman, able to continue on the council without the inconvenience of having to stand for election. And he was a member of the committee of the 1917 Club, founded in 1917 by Ramsay MacDonald and some other Labour and Liberal pacifists, with headquarters at 4 Gerrard Street in London's West End. This was where the political and literary left met, dined and talked the excitable radical politics of the time. Here, although not a regular at the club, he could mix socially with the ILP leaders, and could meet and talk to the great Ramsay MacDonald himself. Clem at that time admired him as much as anyone else did.

He had reached this point in twenty-two months, without any apparent effort, and – most remarkably of all – with few enemies to show for it. This was to become the pattern of Clement Attlee's career.

In the summer of 1920 his mother and his eldest sister, Dorothy, died within a few weeks of each other. Dorothy was forty-two and left seven children. The Putney family house was sold, along with its contents. All the great heavy Victorian furniture of his childhood went under a Putney auctioneer's hammer. The proceeds, and the remains of Henry Attlee's money, were distributed among the children, which gave each of them an extra £5,000.

There were just two things the rising politician now needed which he did not yet possess: an agent, and a wife.

For the former, he advertised in the *Daily Herald*, and put it about in the 1917 Club; the Club grapevine produced a visit from another former soldier, John Beckett.

Beckett, eleven years younger than Clem, was the founder and chairman of the National League of Ex-Servicemen, a left-wing alternative to the British Legion. He had been a councillor in neighbouring Hackney, where the Labour council was bitterly divided. The majority was led by the full-time secretary of the London Labour Party, Herbert Morrison, now firmly embarked on his long career as Labour's chief political fixer in London; and Beckett had led a left-wing rebel group. A former advertising copywriter, he now lived on a meagre income earned from charging small fees for addressing ILP meetings. He was tall, humorous and extrovert, with enormous energy, and specialised in a rough, knockabout platform style which was very popular on the ILP circuit.

He had heard a good deal about Major Attlee and liked what he heard. It was mutual. Waiting in Norway House to be interviewed by the Limehouse party executive, a member of it came out and told Beckett his appointment had already been settled because 'the Major wants you'. The Major was also going to pay his salary of £6 a week. Beckett told Clem they needed more money – real money, not the pennies you could raise in a poor constituency by normal party fundraising. They needed enough for propaganda, to start their own newspaper. Clem said that the only money available was the remainder of the £300 placed in the bank for Beckett's first year's salary. So they agreed that Beckett should move into the top floor of Norway House, where he would have no rent, light or heating costs to pay, and Clem would not pay him: he would raise his own salary as an itinerant ILP speaker and organiser, supplemented by freelance work for newspapers and advertising agencies, and they could use the £300 for propaganda. Beckett and his wife moved in, and their daughter was born in Norway House.

Beckett's education had ended abruptly at the age of fourteen, when his father went bankrupt. The witty, educated Clem fascinated him. He loved the long evenings they spent together, puffing their pipes, talking about God and politics and the state of the world, and compiling a complete genealogical tree of Galsworthy's Forsytes, some years before the Saga was published. This must have been Clem's project. He loved precise, detailed work and, like many of the Attlees, he enjoyed family history, his own and that of others.

Beckett set about, as he put it, 'selling Clem to the electors'. They decided to announce that the Major was there to help those in difficulties, and Beckett spent most mornings and some evenings listening to the troubles of Attlee's future constituents. 'Where I felt that help could be given I would promise to "see the Major about it." When the matter had been settled I would announce that by personal intervention, and at the cost of great trouble, Major Attlee had managed to put the matter right. If the case was hopeless it was I who scored a failure.' Beckett also founded a Labour paper, the *East London Pioneer*. It lasted two years, reached 5,000 people in Limehouse, Mile End and Bow and Poplar, and paid its own way. This was partly because of its success at attracting advertising. As Mayor Clem managed to ensure that some of the Borough Council's advertising went into it, trade union branches advertised, and some Labour supporters owned shops. A regular display advertisement urged readers to:

> Bring your Insurance Prescriptions to
> O. TOBIN MPS Qualified Chemist
> Patent Medicines, Drugs, Surgical Appliances,
> Perfumes and Toilet Articles at Store Prices

Another advertisement appeared beside the masthead in March 1922: 'SAVE MONEY AND JOIN HENRY'S TOILET CLUB'. Particulars were promised on an inside page, where all was explained:

> DO YOU WANT A HAIRCUT? Henry's Toilet Club in Harford Street will provide two haircuts and a shave and hair brush every day for a subscription of 3s per month.

Acquiring a wife could not be achieved through the *Daily Herald*, or (except in rare cases) the 1917 Club. There is no evidence that Clem cold-bloodedly went in search of one, and every reason to suppose that in 1921 he fell suddenly, hopelessly and unpredictably in love. But the timing was right nonetheless and his autobiography notes: 'I was somewhat handicapped in my work as a Mayor by being unmarried.' The death of his mother and the breakup of the Putney home left him feeling lonely and perhaps abandoned. His life and career were now clear before him. He was thirty-eight. It was time for a sensible man to think about marriage. And Clem was always a sensible man.

As far as we know, Clem never had any affairs in his life except his intense love affair with his wife, Violet, which began in the summer of 1921 and continued until her death. He told his daughter Felicity that, before meeting Violet, he once proposed marriage, but we have no idea to whom, or when. He had something of the misogyny of the comfortable bachelor; the ignorance and naiveté of the public schoolboy in whose life sexual relationships played no part; and a certain prudish voyeurism about other people's sexual relations. John Beckett wrote of him with amused affection: 'The few occasions when his humour became caustic were in his discussions about feminine methods and their effect on masculine life. Never a young woman came near a friend without his instant realisation that she was "gunning for poor old so-and-so".'

This attitude is borne out in a strange paragraph in Clem's autobiography. The former batman who looked after him for a while in 1919 soon returned, Clem writes, 'to Lancashire, where he married a widow whose pursuit of him he had sought to avoid by coming south.' Of Oscar Tobin he also wrote, in some autobiographical notes which he decided not to publish: 'He had unfortunately . . . a promiscuity in his marital relations which led to his changing the sphere of his activities from time to time in the course of his political career.'

'It was therefore a great surprise,' commented Beckett, 'when . . . [Clem] went off for a continental tour with a man friend, and returned completely absorbed in his friend's sister who, by some strange chance, had been, with her mother, on his line of route. In response to a query whether she had been "gunning", he spent some time telling me how difficult his task was, and how fortunate he hoped to be.'

What actually happened was this. In the summer of 1921 Clem arranged to holiday in Italy with a close friend from Oxford days of his brother Tom's called Edric Millar. Millar suggested that his mother and younger sister, whom Clem had met, should accompany them, and Clem agreed. Clem and Edric had been to Italy together once before, in 1912, and Clem's fascination with the Renaissance and the Risorgimento had not left him. They left in August and stayed away five weeks, travelling over the whole of the country. Clem's autobiography states in his terse way: 'As our tour proceeded, it seemed that I was more often the companion of Miss Violet Millar than of the other members of the party.' Violet told Clem's official biographer Kenneth Harris: 'I knew no Italian history and history was Clem's subject, so he and I were frequently together.' But she told her daughter Felicity that she woke from a sleep on a train to find Clem looking at her intently, and knew then that he loved her.

'I do not know whether I shall surprise you', Clem wrote from Norway House on 8 October to his brother Rob and his sister Margaret (known in the family as Mig), 'when I tell you that Violet

Millar and I got engaged today. Although we had only met twice before the Italian tour, yet we have had I think better opportunity than most of getting to know each other. I can only half believe my good fortune . . .' The writing is flowery by Clem's standards, and almost large enough to be legible to the naked eye.

'Dear Rob,' he wrote twelve days later, 'I am so very glad to know how much you appreciate Vi. I was of course sure you would like her but it is good to be assured. It will make her happy to know it.'

'She is very nice looking and fresh,' wrote his sister Mary to his brother Bernard, the vicar, 'about Clement's height and a nice voice. *He* is transformed! tremendously in love. It was such real fun to see them together.' In fact Clem was about 5 foot 6 inches, Vi some two and a half inches shorter. Clem told Bernard he was 'as mad as a March hare with joy'.

Vi, or Vio (Clem always used the two diminutives indiscriminately), was twenty-five, her husband, thirteen years older and balding, was often taken for her father. But neither of them minded. The Millars were upper-middle-class people with whom the Attlees felt entirely comfortable: the marriage created no awkward class barriers for either family to cross. They were perhaps rather more conservative than the Attlees, without the tradition of social service that had taken Clem and Tom to the East End and brought them eventually to socialism, and Vi had no understanding of Clem's politics, nor did she ever acquire any. But it never mattered in the slightest; in fact, it seems rather to have suited Clem, who, unlike most politicians, liked to switch off when he got home and practically never talked politics with her.

Vi was an attractive woman, but not always a happy one. Much of their married life was taken up with concern over her health, beginning on their honeymoon when she had to lie flat on her back on a sofa for two days after a bad attack of lumbago. She felt a little overshadowed by her twin sister, Olive, who was ten minutes older than her and was taller and more confident, and took a degree at Cambridge while Vi was working as a wartime nurse. But for Clem, Vi never stopped being magical, and he never stopped marvelling that she had chosen him, short, bald and unprepossessing though he was. For Vi, her clever and affectionate husband was a constant joy and comfort.

The engagement was announced in *The Times*, and they were married in January 1922 on, Clem wrote later, 'a lovely sunny day' in Hampstead, where the Millars lived. The wedding was performed by Clem's brother Bernard, the vicar, and a clergy-man brother of Vi's; Clem's oldest brother, Rob, a rather silent fifty-year-old bachelor, was best man, perhaps because Clem's close relationship with Tom was still smarting from the wounds inflicted by the war.

They honey-mooned in Dorset, then gave a reception in Lime-house Town Hall for Labour Party comrades. The *East London Pioneer* reported: 'Major Attlee, in replying in a brief and witty manner . . . said that in his marriage at a not very early age, he saw a happy simile for the Labour movement. The movement was waiting some time, before it came into its own, but it would do so . . .' Mrs Attlee added that she left speech-making to her husband. There was never any question of Vi moving to the East End. 'She would have hated it,' says Felicity, and Clem would not have dreamed of suggesting it. His youngest brother Laurence lived in Woodford, a respectable middle-class suburb within convenient travelling distance of Stepney, and Laurence found them a house, 17 Monkhams Avenue. Leaving the East End seems to have caused no ill-feeling at all. His election address later that year contains a curious phrase: 'For many years Major Attlee has lived among you.' Even while fighting the class system, Clem and his comrades knew their respective places in it, more clearly in these post-war years than before the war. His comrades were pleased and flattered that he had lived among them while single. To bring his 'lady wife' there was more than ought to be expected.

Their first child, Janet, was born in February 1923 after a difficult pregnancy. Vi took some time to recover physically and was told that she should not have any more children. She became very tense and was often in tears, and needed a spell in a clinic to learn relaxation techniques. Meanwhile her husband's seemingly effortless political progress continued. The 1922 annual conference of the ILP agreed a new policy, drafted by a small committee including Clem. It contained radical demands for a living wage for everyone and for workers' control in industry. 'The membership of the ILP reform committee reads curiously now,' Clem wrote in the Thirties with his usual understatement. It consisted of four people who could only have come together in the unusual conditions of the immediate post-war years. There were two ex-soldiers – Clem and John Beckett – and two ex-'conshies', Fenner Brockway and Clifford Allen. In 1922 the divide between soldiers and 'conshies' was still bitter, the wounds still raw.

Clem distrusted Allen, and Beckett felt more than distrust. Commenting on Allen's pacifism Beckett wrote later: 'I am against war because it is a blind and expensive way of weeding out the population. It takes your Rupert Brookes and leaves your Clifford Allens, and that is an extremely bad thing.' Yet the policy lasted the ILP until 1933 – and by then the four men who drafted it were in four different political parties. The Labour Party and the ILP divorced acrimoniously in 1933. Clem had by then left the ILP and was in the Labour Party. Brockway remained in the ILP. Allen had followed Ramsay MacDonald into the National Government in 1931, so that by 1933 he supported what was for all practical purposes a Conservative government. And Beckett had joined Sir Oswald Mosley, becoming his propaganda director and bringing to fascism the skills which he had used on behalf of Clement Attlee.

The general election came sooner than expected. In October 1922 Lloyd George's unstable coalition was brought down by his Conservative supporters. The new Conservative Prime Minister, Andrew Bonar Law, went to the country the following month. Clem faced a sitting Conservative Member with a 6,000 majority, yet there was a sense of victory about his campaign from the start. The Liberal split already looked terminal, and the 1918 Representation of the People Act had changed the electorate radically. For the first time, women could vote (but only if they were 30 or over) and so could many more working men. Altogether the voting roll had increased from seven million to more than twenty million.

But Clem took no chances. He engaged an additional agent, an efficient ILP man called Len Brighton, to handle the detailed work so that Beckett could concentrate on propaganda and publicity. According to Beckett, Clem needed careful handling:

> Even now [1938] he is far from being an orator, and in those days his best friends could not have called him even a tolerably good speaker. His strongest cards were his erudition and wit, both of which were over the heads of a Limehouse audience which needed fireworks and crudity. I was able to supply them with both . . .

They hired an old two-seater car. 'Look out for the little yellow car', said the election literature. Every day, with supporters clinging to it, they drove through the narrow streets. They would pull up in the middle of a street, and make as much noise as possible while supporters knocked at the doors, inviting electors to appear at windows and doors and listen to the Major.

'When an audience had gathered,' wrote Beckett, 'I would make a five minute speech and introduce Clem, who, looking extremely unhappy, would answer questions and exchange friendly greetings before we drove to the next street.'

Once we met a number of Conservative canvassers, and as one of our men rang a bell loudly to attract attention, a resident thrust his head out and asked if we were selling muffins. Like lightning a Tory woman replied 'No, mate, pups', a retort which the crowd, seeing my shy and miserable companion, were not slow to appreciate.

Beckett's view of Clem's oratorical abilities was not shared by Clem himself, but was confirmed by Fenner Brockway, who was standing for Lancaster, and for whom Clem addressed a meeting.

His speech to an audience of a thousand ... was a flop, so dull that people left before he finished. We did not speak to each other as we drove on to a village meeting, a schoolroom, crowded. Clem was a different man. He was at home with the villagers at once, laughing with them in his opening remarks, and then became absolutely brilliant, pouring scorn on the coalition with Lloyd George a prisoner of the Tories, picturing the bright hope of socialism and peace, a dazzling performance. The audience gave him an ovation. I never heard Clem speak like that again. It showed what he could do if he let himself go. Later responsibility held him in check.

His election address expressed the fury of the men who had fought the war. It was a heartfelt indictment of post-war governments, carefully broken into bite-size chunks with heavy headlines:

THE GREAT BETRAYAL

Like many of you I took part in the Great War in the hope of securing lasting peace and a better life for all. We were promised that wars should end, that the men who fought in the War would be cared for and that unemployment, slums and poverty would be abolished.

ALL THESE PROMISES HAVE BEEN BROKEN

In every way the conditions of the workers are worse than before. Wars and threats of war continue.

Your wages are still falling and many of you are unemployed.

You pay high rents and live in overcrowded hovels.

Ex-soldiers are found lining up for unemployment pay or outdoor relief.

The wounded and widows have to struggle on a starvation dole.

Men made insane in the War are sent to pauper lunatic asylums.

He ended with a categorical promise.

LIFE FOR ALL

... If you return me to Parliament to represent the people among whom I have lived and worked for the last seventeen years, I shall carry the message that they are sick and tired of the injustice which condemns them to toil long hours for low wages, to live in poverty and squalor without the certainty of where the next meal is to come from, and to see their children doomed to endure the same conditions. I shall claim that all shall enjoy the wealth that all produce.

They produced a tabloid newspaper, *Limehouse Election News*, with a front-page picture of the scene outside the Hotel Cecil when the Conservatives decided to dump Lloyd George and make Bonar Law Prime Minister:

THE ROLLS ROISTERERS

Our picture shews the parade of Rolls-Royce cars which blocked up the Strand when the Tories elected Bonar Law as their leader at the Hotel Cecil.

A Rolls-Royce costs about £2,000. This would provide £5 a week for a family of five or six workers for over seven years – Or it could be used to build four decent houses. Yet when the worker asks for a living wage or somewhere to live, the Rolls Roisterers shout: 'We can give you nothing; we are crushed by taxation.'

Inside was a strip cartoon of an ugly war-profiteer clutching his bag of gold, finally despatched by the heroic figure of organised Labour, accompanied by a rhyme which possibly came from Clem's own pen:

My name is Mr Profiteer
And talk of taxes makes me queer.
I made my millions in the war,
That's why your living costs you more.
Let homeless heroes starve in ditches,
But don't make levies on my riches.
And if the Empire needs a tax
Well – shove it on the workers' backs.
The Tory-Libs, they love me so,
They'll never make me pay, I know.
But oh! when Labour wins, I fear,
It's goodbye Mr Profiteer.

The leaflet would have caused Attlee serious trouble in today's Labour Party.

On the night of 15 November 1922 the 1917 Club was packed to capacity to hear the election results, and they cheered and cheered as news of victories came in. The Limehouse result was not announced until the next day, but it was worth the wait. Clem won by 9,688 votes to 7,789, a majority of 1,899 – a considerable achievement since the popular sitting Conservative had held the seat for sixteen years. A horse and cart came to the town hall and carried him through the streets to the cheers of his constituents. He was one of 142 Labour MPs – there had only been fifty-seven after the general election in 1918. The Liberals, now disastrously split between those who had been on the Lloyd George 'coupon' in 1918 and those who were faithful to Asquith, were decimated: Lloyd George's Liberals had fifty-three seats, Asquith's sixty-two. Labour was now the principal opposition to Bonar Law's Conservative government.

Not only were there a great many more Labour MPs; they were a very different collection of people. Before the election almost all the Labour MPs were working-class and trade union-sponsored. ILP leaders like Ramsay MacDonald had lost their seats in the 1918 'khaki election' because of their pacifism. But between 1918 and 1922 the left worked hard to ensure that ILP candidates carried Labour's banner in as many constituencies as possible. So a majority of Labour MPs elected in 1922 were ILP members; thirty-two were, like Clem, ILP-sponsored. For the first time there was a substantial number of middle-class intellectuals – though the majority was still working-class, and Clem and E. G. Hemmerde, also of University College, were the first two Oxford graduates to be elected as Labour MPs.

Labour was an unstable coalition in every possible way. The soldiers and the 'conshies' still mistrusted each other, and some of those on the Labour benches disliked and distrusted the Labour Party itself, pointing out with pride that they were only in the Labour Party at all by virtue of their ILP membership. The left-wing coalition within the Parliamentary Labour Party was also unstable, breaking roughly into three groups: the traditional ILP leaders: MacDonald, Philip Snowden; the London ILP, such as Clem and Clifford Allen, who tended to be to the left of the leadership; and the Clydesiders, led by newly elected MPs Jimmy Maxton and John Wheatley, who were what we might now call the hard left. The three groups worked together to elect ILP leader Ramsay MacDonald as Labour leader rather than the trade union nominee J. R. Clynes. It was the first time the socialists had defeated the trade unions in a party which the unions considered to be their creation. Like many victories for the left in the Labour Party, it was to acquire a very acrid taste within a decade. 'Like others, I lived to regret that vote,' wrote Clem in his autobiography.

MacDonald had been born fifty-six years earlier in Lossiemouth, the illegitimate son of a farm worker. His handsome face, his magical, musical voice and his talent for high-sounding oratory were his most valuable political gifts. His radical reputation and his claim on the loyalty of the left rested on having been a wartime pacifist, and on his socialist rhetoric. It was a cruel fraud. MacDonald seems to have had no particular beliefs at all other than a belief in his own righteousness and destiny. The lesson Clem learned from MacDonald was that the left-wing tendency to apply simple litmus paper tests of someone's socialism and sincerity was always to be distrusted.

Clem's luck persisted. First, MacDonald, anxious to mend the gulf between Labour's ex-soldiers and its ex-'conshies', looked for a Parliamentary Private Secretary with a distinguished war record, and the quiet, sensible Major from Limehouse seemed perfect. Second, Clem made his maiden speech earlier than anyone else, and did not make a mess of it. It happened when the Speaker, fed up with hearing a succession of Clydesiders in the debate on the King's Speech, told Labour's whips to find someone else in a hurry. A harassed whip was casting around for a safe pair of hands just as Clement Attlee was returning to the Chamber after his supper. He happened, discreetly and modestly, to be in the right place at the right time. He managed the same trick nine years later, when his party needed a deputy leader. According to the *Daily Herald* the new MP for Limehouse was 'a slight figure, delicate complexion, lofty brow, and gentle manners – his personality wins you from the first.'

The Parliament lasted just a year before Stanley Baldwin, who had become Prime Minister when illness forced Bonar Law to retire, took everyone by surprise by calling a general election. The election, he said, was to secure a mandate for reversing the policy of free trade and instituting protection as the only way of reducing the high level of unemployment. Bonar Law had fought the 1922 election on a promise that such a change would not be made without a further election. It was an extraordinary thing to do. Baldwin could have governed for another four years with a comfortable parliamentary majority. But protection was an excuse. The main reason was a long-term instinct, from the most relaxed and intuitive Prime Minister of the twentieth century, that Britain needed a strong two-party system, and that the sooner the Conservatives were united, the Liberals consigned to history and Labour established as the official opposition, the sooner things could get back to normal. In those frantic post-war years, getting back to normal was the great dream of Baldwin's political generation. Clem's generation knew it was neither possible nor desirable.

At the December 1923 election Clem's majority, like his party's, continued its inexorable rise. With Len Brighton installed as his agent (Beckett now had his own seat to fight) Clem defeated an ineffective Conservative by 11,473 to 5,288, a majority of 6,185. The Conservatives remained the biggest single party, with 258 MPs, but no longer had an overall majority. Labour had 191, its best result so far, and the Liberals, now reunited but too late to save their party, had 158. There was no precedent for this situation. Should Labour be asked to form a government? If asked, should MacDonald agree?

The *Daily Mail* and the City wanted an anti-socialist coalition, believing, as Winston Churchill, a defeated Liberal candidate, put it with his usual hyperbole: 'The enthronement in office of a Socialist Government will be a serious national misfortune such as has usually befallen great states only on the morrow of defeat in war.' But cooler heads in the Conservative Party agreed with Neville Chamberlain that a Labour government would be 'too weak to do much harm, but not too weak to get discredited', which was a remarkably accurate prediction. The key figure, Asquith, without whose support the Conservative government could not be brought down, said: 'If a Labour government is ever to be tried in this country, as it will be sooner or later, it could hardly be tried under safer conditions.'

So in January 1924 Labour and the Liberals combined to bring down the Conservative government, and the King sent for MacDonald. MacDonald agreed to form a government – rightly, according to Clem: 'The electors at the time needed to see a Labour government in being, if they were to appreciate that Labour was now the alternative to a Conservative administration. Refusal on our part to accept responsibility might have given a new lease of life to the Liberal Party.' Perhaps he would have been less happy if he had known that MacDonald and Snowden had already agreed that they 'should not adopt an extreme policy . . . We must show the country that we are not under the domination of the wild men.'

Clem, who had earned himself a reputation as a solid and reliable parliamentary debater, became Under-Secretary of State for War.

It was a good post for so new a Member, but he was a little disappointed. He had mentioned to friends that he would not be surprised to become Chancellor of the Duchy of Lancaster, presumably because MacDonald had given him a hint to that effect. He had yet to learn the value of MacDonald's promises. Work at the War Office did not tax him. Because of the absence of a parliamentary majority, junior Ministers were on more or less permanent duty as lobby fodder, and Labour's tenure of the War Office did not revolutionise the lives of Britain's soldiers, or indeed anyone else. Clem did his duty. He opposed a moderate proposal from some Labour Members that the right of appeal on legal grounds against army death sentences should be increased, even though he personally did not think army court-martials ought to be able to impose a death sentence at all. He lunched and dined with old army friends and earned a reputation for efficiency and for taking his responsibilities seriously.

It seems a long way from the ideals that brought him into politics. Neither he nor the government was righting any of the wrongs for which he had embraced socialism. Only Housing Minister John Wheatley, the Clydesiders' leader, produced legislation which furthered Labour's agenda, a Housing Act which gave government aid for building council houses. After all the heartache Clem's socialism had caused his family, all the mutual affection he had with the dispossessed of the East End, had he settled down to be the standard parliamentary time-server?

Not exactly. Clem's motivations were neither so pure nor so simple as they had been before the war. He was willing to take a longer term view; and he had a wife and daughter to concentrate his mind. The socialist anger was still there, underneath the discreet, accomplished parliamentarian's exterior, and it was exemplified by what he did when a gross piece of corrupt exploitation of the poor by the rich crossed his War Office desk.

During the war the Germans had discovered a new method of extracting nitrogen from the air, which was much cheaper than the British method. Nitrogen was vital in the manufacture of explosives, and important in peacetime for the production of fertiliser. The Germans used their method in a vast factory in Cologne, and the British used theirs at a factory in Billingham-on-Tees. The Armistice terms gave the allies the right to investigate German secrets, and a commission of three army officers went to Cologne for several months to report. But Clem could not find a copy of their report in the War Office; nor could anyone tell him where it was; nor was there any trace of the three officers who compiled it. He suspected what later proved to be the truth. The Billingham factory had been sold at a knockdown price to Sir Alfred Mond in 1920, when Sir Alfred was a member of Lloyd George's government. Sir Alfred had set up a company to exploit the new method of extracting nitrogen from the air. The senior officer on the Commission was made a director of this company, and the other two officers were employed by it. Sir Alfred was using his monopoly to keep the price artificially high. Here was the 'hard-faced man who has done well out of the war'. Here was the man who made a killing over the blood of Clem's comrades. Here was the wartime subject of Clem's election leaflet:

> But oh! when Labour wins, I fear
> It's goodbye Mr Profiteer

Clem's political message since the war had been that the nation had come together to defeat Germany, and must now come together to defeat poverty. Meanwhile, men like Sir Alfred Mond were asset-stripping the nation. What should he do?

While he was in the government, he did nothing. But after the general election, when Labour was in opposition, he handed over the facts to a new MP. Clem was not to be identified as the source of the story. He chose his old agent John Beckett, newly-elected MP for Gateshead. He knew that Beckett had a talent for publicity, and would feel, as Clem did, that men like Mond made a mockery of the deaths of his wartime comrades. Beckett asked parliamentary questions and received evasive answers; raised the matter on an adjournment debate; wrote a newspaper article which would have been libellous had the allegations it made been false; and watched helplessly as Mond was given £2 million of government credits. Beckett could not believe that, when these facts were known, Sir Alfred was not even damaged. It was the beginning of the road that led Beckett to black despair and eventually to fascism. Clem knew the world better. He was sure the job ought to be done, but knew also that it would achieve nothing.

Apart from this, it was a question of waiting until the Liberals withdrew their support and the government fell. Clem did not have to wait long. In July 1924, the Communist Party's weekly newspaper *Workers Weekly* published an 'open letter to the fighting forces'. It asked them to 'let it be known that, neither in the class war nor in a military war, will you turn your guns on your fellow workers'.

The editor, John Ross Campbell, was charged with incitement to mutiny but Labour's Attorney General, Sir Patrick Hastings, withdrew the charge because, he said, Campbell was a man of good character with a fine war record. The Conservatives seized the chance to level the charge that Labour helped Communists. The Liberals offered a face-saving formula: a select committee to look into the affair. Why did MacDonald not jump at this chance to save his government? Many, probably including Clem (whose admiration for MacDonald was ebbing fast), believed that the clumsy handling of the Campbell case, for which Sir Patrick Hastings took the blame, was really down to MacDonald, and that an inquiry would have revealed that. For whatever reason, MacDonald rebuffed the Liberal proposal in a speech which left everyone thinking he was shifty, and another general election became inevitable.

Four days before polling day, the *Daily Mail* came up with a manufactured story designed to frighten people by suggesting that Labour was in the pockets of the Soviet Union. Its headlines were designed to chill the blood:

CIVIL WAR PLOT BY SOCIALISTS' MASTERS
MOSCOW ORDERS OUR REDS
GREAT PLOT DISCLOSED YESTERDAY
'PARALYSE THE ARMY AND NAVY'
AND MR MACDONALD WOULD LEND RUSSIA OUR MONEY!
DOCUMENT ISSUED BY FOREIGN OFFICE
AFTER 'DAILY MAIL' HAD SPREAD THE NEWS

The 'proof' was a letter from Zinoviev (whose real name, so the paper pointed out, was Apfelbaum, which somehow made it worse), General Secretary of the Communist International. It was a forgery, but it helped secure a massive Conservative victory.

Labour lost forty seats, leaving them with 151 MPs. The Liberals were reduced to just forty, even Asquith losing his seat. The Conservatives had 419 MPs – more than twice what Labour and the Liberals could muster between them. The old Lloyd George Conservatives now loyally supported Baldwin; one of them, Winston Churchill, becoming Baldwin's Chancellor of the Exchequer. It was everything Baldwin had dreamed of. 'I did not think it would come so quickly,' he wrote to a friend. 'The next step must be the elimination of the Communists by Labour.' Labour once again set out to implement Baldwin's agenda, MacDonald implausibly claiming that Communists had brought down his government. Clem had little difficulty in winning again in Limehouse. His vote slightly increased, but so did that of his Conservative opponent, and this time there was a Liberal candidate. Clem received 11,713, the Conservative 5,692, and the Liberal 2,869. He busied himself with his duties as an opposition spokesman on War Office affairs, and on bills on rating and valuation and electricity, both of which he knew a good deal about from his local government experience. But very soon the general strike was upon the country. For Clem, this caused a crisis which almost drove him out of politics.

One of Baldwin's first acts was to provide a subsidy to the mine owners, to delay lowering miners' wages and prevent a miners' strike which might lead to a general strike. The subsidy ran out in May 1926, by which time the government was ready to face a general strike. It had set up the Organisation for the Maintenance of Supplies and had volunteers ready to take on essential work.

The TUC and the Labour Party, on the other hand, were far from prepared. There was no excuse for this. They had plenty of warning. They knew that the miners, already on starvation wages, working long hours at hard, dangerous work, were not going to accept lower wages and longer hours. They knew that the slogan offered by miners' leader Arthur Cook – 'not a penny off the pay, not a minute on the day' – had struck a chord, not just with miners, but with other trade unionists too. They knew they would face a choice: either ditch the miners, or fight for them. Yet when the time came, they did neither. They called a general strike, the call was supported everywhere, and they then scurried around trying to find any sort of excuse to call it off. Like First World War generals, they threw their troops into the front line; but unlike the generals, they then withdrew them, leaving their casualties – the miners – to be picked off by the enemy. The TUC issued a strike newspaper, the *British Worker*, which reported, a week into the strike: 'From every town and city in the country reports are pouring into headquarters stating that all ranks are solid, that the working men and women are resolute in their determination to resist the unjust attack upon the mining community . . . The General Council's message . . . is: Stand Firm. Be Loyal to Instructions and Trust your Leaders.'

But as the paper was being distributed, TUC leaders agreed to call the strike off on the basis of an informal talk with Sir Herbert Samuel, who claimed to be an unofficial emissary for the government. The miners would go back to work, on lower wages and with worse conditions, in return for which the mine owners would take them all back. There would be no victimisations. They met the Prime Minister to finalise the deal, but the question of victimisation was not mentioned until, as they were leaving, the TGWU's Ernest Bevin pressed Stanley Baldwin on whether they would be meeting soon to discuss how to ensure that striking miners would not be victimised. Baldwin replied suavely: 'I cannot say that, Mr Bevin. I think it may be that, whatever decision I come to, the House of Commons may be the best place in which to say it.' Arthur Cook, ill with anxiety and overwork – he was the miners' only full-time official – appealed desperately to the TUC General Council not to call off the strike on these wretched terms. He was right: the no-victimisation agreement turned out to be a deception. Most miners stayed loyal to Cook and stayed out when everyone else went back to work. But after seven months they were starved into returning. The mine owners then chose the ones they were willing to take back, and union activists found themselves unable to feed their families – their punishment for defiance.

The bitterness in mining areas was passed down the generations. It was at the heart of the miners' strikes of the 1970s and their last tragic stand in 1984–5. Perhaps it was destroyed after 1985 when the mining communities were themselves destroyed; or perhaps such deep ancestral bitterness can outlive its original home. To Clem, the strike was a disaster in which inept TUC leaders played into the hands of a cynical government. He was horrified to see the way in which the mine owners and the government milked their victory regardless of human suffering, but glad to see the back of the idea of a general strike as a political weapon. He told his official biographer Kenneth Harris nearly forty years later: 'I'd heard a general strike discussed for fifteen years. When it came, it collapsed, because nobody knew what to do with it, and most of them discovered they didn't really want it.' It is unlikely that he felt as blasé at the time, but he certainly agreed with MacDonald that a strike should never be a political weapon, only a means of achieving an industrial end.

His personal problems from the general strike arose from his chairmanship of the electricity committee of Stepney Council. The day the general strike was called, he convened an emergency meeting of the committee to deal with the practical problem of ensuring, without undermining the strike, that Stepney's hospitals still had power. He obtained TUC agreement that Stepney's members of the Electrical Trades Union would work in order to supply light for the borough and power for hospitals only. But factories were supplied from the same mains. The electricity committee's solution was to announce that factories which used power would have their fuses pulled, and they would be without light as well. When a factory defied the instructions and used current for power, its fuses were pulled. This company – Scammell and Nephew Ltd – suffered little inconvenience because it had its own private generating plant. But the company took a vindictive civil action for conspiracy against Clem and the other Labour members of the committee. They took no action against the Conservative members who had also agreed to the decision. The verdict in the High Court went against Clem and his fellow councillors. Damages of £300 were awarded against Clem. He appealed. He was clear in his mind that without a successful appeal he would leave politics and enter a profession where a regular and sizeable salary could be obtained, to enable him to pay damages and legal bills without causing too much hardship to his family. The appeal was not heard until 1928. An old friend who had been in chambers with Clem, Malcolm Macnaughton, by then a KC and Ulster Unionist MP for Londonderry, took the appeal at short notice out of personal friendship, and won it.

For the first time, but not the last, Clem's concern to provide a regular income for his family almost forced him out of politics. Once married and with children, Clem needed to feel financially secure. Macnaughton had saved his political career. He wrote to Tom: 'It was great news our winning the case . . . I never anticipate success in cases like these, for fear of disappointment, so the pleasure is all the keener.' Even before the court case, he worried that, without his ministerial salary, he was rather hard up, especially after a second daughter, Felicity, was born in 1925, and a son, Martin, in 1927. Vi ignored her doctor's advice in order to have them, and the births did not give her the health problems that had accompanied Janet's birth. But they did cause Clem to worry about money.

A backbench MP's salary was £400 a year, set at a low rate because most Conservative MPs earned their real money elsewhere. Clem could earn occasional additional sums from newspaper articles; and he had what he coyly calls in his autobiography 'some private means', though we do not know how much of Henry Attlee's legacy he had left: three general elections in three years had eaten heavily into it. From 1925 until 1940 we find Clem persistently anxious about money, not because he was in any risk of real hardship of the kind his constituents knew, but because he expected his family to live in the style to which the Attlees of Putney and the Millars of Hampstead were accustomed. He had a small car and took regular family holidays; he made substantial additions to the Woodford house to accommodate three children; and in 1926 he accompanied two of his brothers on an extended trip to Gallipoli, Greece and Italy.

Most of the events of the 1925–9 Parliament took place without Clem. He spent much of 1928 and 1929 in India on a parliamentary commission. The 1919 Act on India provided that within ten years Britain would send a commission to see whether more independence was desirable. The Act was a disappointment to many Indians, and there were regular outbreaks of violence, often between Hindus and Muslims; there were strikes; and there was widespread resentment and distrust of the British. Baldwin and his Secretary of State for India, Lord Birkenhead, did not believe that the country was ready for self-government; Birkenhead doubted if it would ever be ready. They feared that if they left the commission until the latest possible date, 1929, there might by then be a Labour government which would want to make India self-governing within the British Empire. So Birkenhead decided to send a commission two years early.

The members were chosen in the expectation that they would not recommend greater independence. The chairman was Sir John Simon, a veteran Liberal known to have 'safe' views on India. There were four Conservatives and two Labour members: Clem and Vernon Hartshorn, whom Clem considered 'the ablest of the South Wales miners in the House'. The two Labour men were both recommended to Baldwin by MacDonald, who seems to have shared Baldwin's hope that the result would be a safely conservative report, and thought Hartshorn and Attlee were orthodox enough. Years later, in his retirement, Clem would frequently say that the achievement of which he was most proud was giving India its independence. But the visit that started his passion to give that country justice was one he was reluctant to undertake.

He did not want to spend long months away from his wife and young family. It was not an assignment which would enhance his political career. Many of his Labour colleagues, particularly the ex-soldiers, saw India as a diversion from the real business of politics, which was to obtain justice for the British working class. Those who thought India mattered viewed the India Commission with great suspicion, seeing it, with some justice, as an excuse to avoid any real move towards independence. Labour's National Executive had been reluctant to allow anyone to go if Indians were excluded from membership of the Commission, and the ILP policy was that India should receive its independence straight away. Clem's old friend Fenner Brockway referred to Clem years later as 'Labour's representative on the hated Simon Commission'.

Clem thought the Indian problem 'particularly intractable and nearly insoluble'. He also understood the harsh political fact that, in the Westminster hot-house, the man who is not seen or heard for more than a year is forgotten. This was impressed on him when he returned from India: the Hansard index spelt his name incorrectly. It had all the makings of a political graveyard. He was sure he would be putting himself to a great deal of inconvenience for no purpose except to damage his career. In fact, he asked MacDonald for an assurance that it would not cause him to be passed over when Labour next formed a government. MacDonald gave the assurance. Giving assurances was something MacDonald was good at. He broke this one, as he broke most of them. But nothing could be more indicative of the way Clem had changed than the fact that he took the trouble to ask the question. Having asked it, he decided he must serve in the role his leader gave him and reluctantly agreed to go.

Indian politicians, it seemed, were even less willing to meet Clem than he was to meet them. The lack of a single Indian representative on the Simon Commission was understandably considered an affront, and it was seen as another attempt to foist a foreign-made constitution on India. Commission members arriving in Bombay were greeted with banners saying 'Simon Go Home', and they were boycotted by Gandhi's Congress Party as well as the Muslim League.

The commission paid two visits to India. There was a three-month reconnaissance in early 1928, and a longer trip from October 1928 until April 1929. It visited every province and heard evidence in all the provincial capitals. Clem's letters to Tom from India give little hint of the socialist egalitarian, the man who was to give India its freedom. From Poona Clem wrote on 4 October 1928 about how many Corpus Christi men he had met: 'We are quite in a Corpus atmosphere.' From Bahchistahn on 14 November he provided a long description of the splendour of the scenery and a shorter summary of Indian attitudes to democracy: 'There's nothing to choose between Hindu and Muslim on this. The Hindu professes a belief in free and open competition because he is good at exams. The Muslim believes in adult suffrage because his is the poorer community and a property franchise favours the Hindus.'

From Rangoon on 20 March 1929 he sent congratulations that Tom's eldest son was going to a top public school, for neither of these brothers, socialists though they were, ever seriously considered having their children educated in the state system. 'I am glad to hear that Chris is going to Shrewsbury and I hope that he will pull off a scholarship all right. It makes one feel a bit older doesn't it?' As to India, 'I fear it will be difficult to make people at home understand that we are not dealing with a tabula rasa but a paper that has been much scribbled over.'

Some friends had agreed to look after the three children so that Vi could accompany Clem for the first three months. She had a wonderful time, dancing and playing golf and tennis, Clem wrote to Tom, and seemed to overcome some of her shyness and low self-esteem:

> There was a huge dinner given by Victor Sassoon . . . dancing afterwards. I was bored to distraction and managed to get away by 12 o'clock. Vi enjoyed herself hugely and danced until 2 o'clock. She has another dance tonight to which, thank goodness, I'm not going . . . The trip has done Vi a great deal of good and I imagine she will never be shy of functions of any sort again . . . Vi is very well and looking very young so that people scoff at the idea that she can have three children . . . Old Lord Airedale . . . amused her by asking how her father (me) was enjoying India.

Clem returned just in time to take part in the 1929 general election. He had missed a difficult period for Labour.

The collapse of the general strike had, as Baldwin predicted, ensured that a vastly weakened trade union movement would talk to the government. He agreed to ditch a bill which would have severely damaged the Labour Party's income, sounding as though he were being gracious to a defeated enemy. The bill, which had wide Conservative support, would have required trade union members to 'opt in' to paying the political levy instead of 'opting out' as formerly. Baldwin looked on benevolently as trade union leaders and industrialists started meeting together and talking about a strategy for industry – the so-called Mond-Turner talks, named after industrialist Sir Alfred Mond and the textile workers' leader and TUC General Council chairman Ben Turner. It may have been as well for Clem's career that Mond knew nothing of Clem's part in exposing his wartime profiteering.

In May 1929 Baldwin called an election and campaigned under the slogan 'Safety First' which, with unemployment now at ten per cent, was not very inspired. It was however probably more exciting than the Labour policy statement 'Labour and the Nation'. The divisions over this policy caused a split in the Labour Party which in the early 1930s grew into a chasm.

The ILP had adopted a programme called 'Socialism in Our Time'. It called for a national minimum wage, a system of family allowances and nationalisation of the Bank of England to secure control of credit and monetary policy. As the ILP produced more and more detailed blueprints for a Labour government, MacDonald's public statements became increasingly vague and messianic. A sub-committee of Labour's National Executive was charged with writing a draft programme. MacDonald and the majority wanted a very long statement presenting vague ideals, but a minority argued for something more precise. A recruit from the Conservative Party, Sir Oswald Mosley, and a recruit from the Communist Party, Ellen Wilkinson, argued forcibly on the sub-committee for a short statement which should, they said, 'present in unmistakable terms the actual measures on which a Labour government would at once embark.'

Mosley and Wilkinson were right, and Clem learned from it. Some years later, in 1937, he made the practical point that even the summary ran to four pages and contained seventy-two proposals, with no indication as to which of them was to be given priority. MacDonald did not like his governments to be inhibited by clear promises to the electorate.

Clem's absence from the fray at a crucial time, which he thought was a political disadvantage, may have helped his career, because it allowed him to enter the 1929 Parliament as one of the few Labour MPs not marked by the battle. Had he been in Britain, even Clem's gift for avoiding making unnecessary enemies would have been sorely tried.

'Labour and the Nation' was one of Labour's periodic attempts to capture the middle ground of politics. ILP attempts to defeat the programme were routed as MacDonald's rhetoric combined with the harsh political arithmetic which ensured that the leaders of the big trade unions could in the end call the tune. MacDonald was typically apocalyptic about it. The document was 'full not only of one programme, but pregnant with programme after programme after programme'. As MacDonald got older his metaphors became more and more organic, and his wonderful voice sounded more and more like a church organ.

The election made Labour, for the first time ever, the biggest party in the House of Commons, with 287 seats, but without an overall majority. The Conservatives were reduced to 261 and the Liberals under their leader Lloyd George won fifty-nine seats. Some of Baldwin's advisers urged him to carry on in government until he was defeated in the House of Commons, and most party leaders would have done precisely that, but it was typical of this relaxed Prime Minister to take the long term view that this would look 'unsporting' and would count against him next time. He resigned five days after the poll and Ramsay MacDonald became Prime Minister for the second time. Clem was returned once again with a handsome majority, receiving 13,872 votes against 6,584 for the Conservative, 4,116 for the Liberal and 245 for the Communist.

He was forty-seven years old and had been in Parliament for seven years. He was a quietly respected MP, on terms of mutual respect with the greatest in the land and considered solid. But it must have crossed his mind that absolutely nothing either he or his party had done in Parliament had even begun to address the evils that brought him into politics. His Stepney constituents still lived dreadful lives full of grinding poverty. Yet we find in his papers not a hint of frustration, of self-doubt, of concern that he might be wasting his time. His private letters are about his immediate family and Tom's family and about the many books he was reading – in 1929 he was particularly impressed by a biography of Oliver Cromwell, a statesman who fascinated him, and quoted from it at length in his letters to Tom. Perhaps he was hoping that the second MacDonald government would begin to address Labour's reason for existing. If so he was to be cruelly disappointed.

4

The End of Innocence

After the 1929 election, the Conservatives and Liberals could combine and muster 320 votes, enough to defeat the Labour government, with its 287. MacDonald reminded Labour MPs of this whenever they asked for radical policies. The reality, though, was that nothing of the kind was going to happen. The Liberals had been wounded by their poor showing in the election and their relegation to the status of third party. Lloyd George made the complaint which every Liberal leader has made since – that it was not the electors but the system which had beaten them: 'The Conservative and Labour Parties have each secured one member for 33,000 votes. We on the other hand have obtained one member for every 100,000 votes.' No senior Liberal wanted to precipitate an early election. The longer it could be deferred, the greater the chance that they might be able to revive their fortunes. In any case the Liberals had produced a programme to deal with unemployment which involved public works on a huge scale, so they could hardly have opposed radical measures on unemployment if MacDonald had been inclined to introduce them. As Lloyd George put it during the election:

> The Labour Party could not make up its mind whether to treat the Liberal plan as a freak or to claim its paternity. Mr Thomas said it was an absurd abortion, but Mr Henderson said it was the child of the Labour Party. Mr MacDonald, as usual, tried to have it both ways. He said – often in the same speech – 'This is a stunted thing' – then looking at it fondly he said 'This is my child.'

Baldwin was in no mood to overthrow the government either. In fact he studiously avoided criticising it too much, to the irritation of many Conservatives. He explained in a speech in Sheffield in May 1930:

> I hold the view very strongly – and I know I have been criticised for it – that when a government has not got great experience, is a minority

government, it is essential if you can possibly support it that it should be able to speak with a strong voice to the countries of the world.

He also had more subtle and cynical reasons. Baldwin was sure that Labour would permanently replace the Liberals as Britain's other main party. He was not at all unhappy about this. It meant that Lloyd George, whom he loathed with all the loathing of the languid country gentleman for the clever parvenu, would never be back in power, and that instead he would be doing business with the vain, manipulable MacDonald. The economic circumstances, as well as MacDonald's own inclinations, would render Labour quite harmless. And Baldwin had internal problems – serious ones. The press lords, Beaverbrook and Rothermere, supported by some right-wing Conservatives, had committed themselves to a plan for free trade within the British Empire, which Baldwin resolutely opposed. They, along with important Conservatives like Winston Churchill, hated his willingness to contemplate more freedom for India. They hated the idea of Labour as one of the two main parties in the state, and considered Baldwin lazy and without the will to fight the socialists. In short, as a later generation of right-wing Conservatives would have put it, he was wet.

Their own more robust approach to such matters is well illustrated by a headline which appeared in Rothermere's *Daily Mail* in May 1030: 'REDS THROWN INTO RIVER WORKERS' REPLY TO STRIKE TALK URGED ON BY WOMEN'. The story was about a trade union meeting in an un-named company, a director of which told the newspaper: 'Our employees have resented these [union] meetings and I was not surprised when decent workmen thought that the speakers needed a good wash.' The combustible mixture of aggressive anti-socialism and anti-trade unionism with intense xenophobia was remarkably similar to the way the same newspapers today campaign against the European Union and the trade unions. It was not Baldwin's style, which was why the press lords wanted to bring him down.

Clem's private estimate in a letter to Tom in November 1930 was: 'I doubt whether Stanley B will last long . . . The difficulty is to find a successor.' The fact that Baldwin did survive shows that – like Campbell-Bannerman before him and Attlee after him – he concealed startling political gifts beneath an apparently unexciting personality.

The Labour government had the benefit of a divided and ineffective opposition at by-elections, because the press lords put up Empire

Clem Attlee

Free Trade candidates against official Conservatives. It had the general support of two Irish Members, two independents and some of the Liberals, and might even have survived a combined attack by the Conservatives and Liberals, in the unlikely event that such an attack was launched. It is not hard to see why, as Roy Jenkins writes in his biography of Baldwin, 'the MacDonald government, despite its many faults and vicissitudes, was left almost miraculously free from strong and sustained attack by its principal opponent.'

So, despite its lack of an overall majority, Labour had real power. What would MacDonald, Prime Minister for the second time at the age of sixty-two, do with it? His rhetoric was as windy as ever, strong on what today we might call the 'feelgood factor', weak on content. On 1 June, the day after polling day, he told an enthusiastic gathering in the Miners' Hall at Easington Colliery:

Did Labour people ever live in such an inspiring moment as this? . . . Make no mistake about it, it is not going to be all beer and skittles, especially for me. You have finished the fight. I am afraid I am only beginning to bear the burden, but I will do it cheerfully, and I know I shall have your sympathy, your support, and your backing through thick and thin . . . When I saw the women, and more particularly the young women, marching to the poll yesterday with happy faces and proudly wearing their colours, I had a vision of this result, and I knew that it was all right.

This was vintage MacDonald: the statesman reluctantly shouldering the crushing burden thrust upon him, expecting sympathy from those who did not have to bear it.

He took the train to London, where huge crowds, cheering and singing 'The Red Flag', met him at Kings Cross. *The Times* reported: 'Mr MacDonald, on passing the barrier, found himself in the vortex of a seething mass, and looked exceedingly uncomfortable.' But *The Times* knew its man better than MacDonald's own supporters. It commented a few days later, on 8 June when it heard his choice of Ministers: 'The general impression left by a study of its personnel is that it is the best that could have been designed to carry out the unprovocative policy which is apparently to mark the beginning of the new Labour regime, and which the circumstances of the moment certainly render desirable.' Arthur Henderson, who had created Labour's electoral machine, was Foreign Secretary; Philip Snowden was a very conservative Chancellor of the Exchequer; and railwaymen's union leader Jimmy Thomas was Lord Privy Seal with the task of finding a cure for unemployment.

The Times was reassured by those who were in, and even more by those who were out. The one member of MacDonald's first government who had changed anything was his Housing Minister, the left-wing Clydesiders' leader John Wheatley. His Housing Act had for the first time started to address the problems of slums. The *Daily Express* saw his omission, with some justice, as a declaration of war on the left. MacDonald's one gesture to the left was to give seventy-year-old George Lansbury the Ministry of Works. Among the younger men, Herbert Morrison became Minister of Transport, though he had little parliamentary experience, having lost his seat in 1925 and only just returned, and Hugh Dalton became Under-Secretary to his friend and mentor, Henderson, at the Foreign Office. One name was unexpectedly absent: that of Major Clement R. Attlee.

Clem felt betrayed. When he agreed to go to India he had specifically asked whether it would prevent him from getting office under a Labour government, and MacDonald assured him it would not. Not only did he and Hartshorn not have a job, but (he noted in his autobiography) 'it was characteristic of MacDonald that he did not take the trouble to inform us of his decision.' To add insult to injury, 'The Indian Commission had not yet reported, but it might be supposed that its members had acquired some useful information. MacDonald proposed to deal with the Indian question himself, but neither then nor subsequently did he give even five minutes to ascertain the view of his two emissaries.' Clem thought MacDonald was too weak to confess to ignorance.

MacDonald eventually explained himself in a handwritten note to Clem: 'I am in a fix about this Indian affair. Obviously we cannot put members on it into the Ministry. It is a terrible concern for me, but I shall not forget you. There must be changes before very long in some of the offices and both Vernon [Hartshorn] and you must be amongst my cares.' Dalton – who knew how to flatter MacDonald – wrote in his diary that at 10 Downing Street he told the Prime Minister he would be 'proud of the chance to do something for peace and to carry forward *his* work. I express sympathy with him in this business of fitting people in. "Yes" he says, "it has been terrible. I have had people in here weeping and even fainting." (I wonder who?) I said, "May it be counted for righteousness that I have kept off your doorstep."'

Clem learned from this experience. When he became Prime Minister, he never expected sympathy from people who did not have to shoulder his burdens, for he knew that they did not have the rewards of the job either. He did not suffer from self-pity, or from vanity, or from inability to listen to others, or from being hypnotised by the beauty of his own voice. He never forgave or forgot MacDonald's insensitivity (or cowardice) in leaving him to read about his omission in the newspapers, and when Prime Minister himself, he always made sure he gave bad news, as well as good news, personally. Part of the success of Labour's second Prime Minister lay in being, by nature and by choice, the opposite in every respect of Labour's first Prime Minister. During the 1929 Parliament his admiration for MacDonald was swiftly replaced by contempt.

Once the names of MacDonald's Ministers were known, Jimmy Maxton on behalf of the ILP put the demands of the left in the debate on the King's Speech.

> I am going to promise the Cabinet active hearty support and work on one condition and one condition only, that they will arrange the affairs of this country that no unemployed man, his wife or child, shall have any dread of starvation or insult.

It soon became clear that this modest demand would not be met, and by midsummer Maxton was asking the House of Commons: 'Has any human being benefited by the fact that there has been a Labour Government in office?' In October he said: 'It would be foolish to expect the government to deliver socialism but . . . the government had it in their power to stop starvation.'

Maxton was an eloquent, romantic former schoolteacher, two years younger than Clem, whose spellbinding oratory, like MacDonald's, was legendary. He was almost unhealthily thin, with long wavy black hair, and lived on his nerves and a constant supply of tea and cigarettes. He and fellow Glaswegian John Wheatley led the ILP together and made a striking contrast, Wheatley being a stout and practical businessman, not a great orator but a devastatingly exact debater. With Conservatives and Liberals pulling their punches, these two led the opposition to the government. They demanded an increase in the levels of unemployment pay, and they demanded that the government withdraw the provision which prevented benefit being paid to those 'not genuinely seeking work', under which an unemployed man had to show he had traipsed round all local factories and firms, even when he knew they had no jobs available. Unemployment pay was kept to its starvation levels. When Rothermere's newspapers printed endless horror stories of people getting a few shillings from the dole to which they were not entitled, the ever impressionable MacDonald began talking of married women turning up to collect dole in fur coats; and in 1931 the government passed an Anomalies Act purportedly to prevent abuses, which deprived many already desperately poor people of their lifeline. The ILP harried the bill unmercifully in an all night session, nine ILP MPs making over one hundred speeches and forcing forty divisions to keep the House in session from 3.45 pm until 10 am the following morning. It was a declaration of war.

Clem Attlee must in his heart have ageed with the ILP. He had become a socialist from seeing the wretched way the poor lived, and had joined the ILP and waged war on the moderation of Labour's parliamentary leaders before 1922. He knew, better than anyone, how right the TUC was to say of unemployment pay: 'Nobody can conscientiously say that ... thirty two shillings is too much for a man, wife and three children. To any thinking person it is a constant source of wonder as to how the unemployed exist on such amounts. Many of those who urge a reduction of benefit would themselves spend such an amount on a single meal or for a seat at the theatre.' He had gone into politics to change the world, not to be a tame placeman. Would he – could he – give his support to a Labour government which had real power, yet clearly intended to leave the poorest citizens of Limehouse to starve? The answer was: yes, he could. He appears not even to have considered rebellion.

What had happened to the man who drew up a radical policy for the ILP in the early Twenties? John Beckett, who had worked with him on it, wrote that in those early days 'it would have seemed impossible to me that a kind, gentle, loveable man might be so corrupted by the Parliamentary system that he could represent the people of the abyss and yet vote for two shillings a week for their children; and support the Anomalies Act, which swept them away from their meagre dole like flies.'

Had Clem forgotten what brought him into politics? No: we know, if only from the record of the government he led, that he never forgot. Though he wanted office, he was never a single-minded parliamentary careerist. He knew the government was failing the people for whom Labour existed. But he had little faith in ILP tactics. The ILP 'became more and more irresponsible under the leadership of Jimmy Maxton', he wrote in his autobiography. 'With many others

I found it necessary to part company with this organisation. This was a matter of a very great regret, for I had spent my political life in its ranks.'

That is a little convenient. Clem was one of 140 Labour MPs who entered the 1929 Parliament as members of the ILP. The ILP conference that year demanded that its MPs should vote in accordance with its policies. Labour's parliamentary whips took a dim view of this, because ILP policy was bound to conflict with the Labour government's policies. The 140 had a choice to make: the Parliamentary Labour Party or the ILP. Senior Ministers made it clear that anyone who did not support the government could kiss goodbye to their political career. Only eighteen stayed with the ILP, which from then on was effectively a separate party led by Maxton. That was when Clem found it necessary 'to part company with this organisation'. It was certainly possible for Clem to argue that he could achieve nothing by being one of the eighteen. They became known as the 'parliamentary suicide club', not just because they were destroying their own careers, but because they never looked like achieving the ends they sought. But was it necessary to be quite so loyal to the government? Did he *have* to vote for the Anomalies Act?

In a book written in the late Thirties, *The Labour Party in Perspective*, Clem says that MacDonald in 1929–31 'was greatly helped in preserving his position in the Party by the actions of the ILP, whose tactics frequently caused others to rally to the support of the government.' This looks like guilt. Is he suggesting that, but for the ILP's bad tactics, he would have come out against MacDonald? His future colleague Aneurin Bevan, first elected to Parliament in 1929, was an example of someone who avoided the ILP embrace, but nonetheless joined them in the division lobby on specific occasions rather than vote for particular measures. Nothing was being done about unemployment, which Clem knew was the greatest scourge of his constituents. It rose from 1,630,000 in June 1929 to 1,912,000 a year later. Well before the end of 1930 it had topped the two million mark and it reached three million by the time the government fell. Any constructive proposals to deal with it, he wrote in his autobiography, 'had no chance of acceptance against Snowden's pedantry and MacDonald's inability to take decisions.' Jimmy Thomas, who had been given the task of solving the problem, was disintegrating before his colleagues' eyes. A man who owed his political career to his superficial joviality, he was petrified by the enormity of the task, and was drinking too much and offering nothing but trite pieces of homespun wisdom.

Clem had the lowest possible opinion of Thomas, whom he considered not only incompetent but also dishonest. (By contrast, he thought Snowden at least had some gritty integrity.) He would like to have seen the government bring in a socialist programme and challenge the Liberals and Conservatives to bring it down; or to join forces with the Liberals, whose prescriptions for unemployment were radical and acceptable to socialist opinion. But he had no chance of persuading MacDonald and Snowden to do either. So he took the long view. The Labour Party was still the instrument by which the lives of his constituents were going to be improved, but not this time round. Clem was not a rebel. He had rebelled just once in his life, before the First World War, when he could see no alternative to the view that socialism was right and just, and capitalism wrong and unjust. This time he must have decided that rebellion was avoidable. And – though this was probably not decisive – he did want a post in the government.

This is one of the occasions in Clem's life when a diary, or thoughtful and revealing letters, or a conversation, would aid the biographer; but Clem was one of the few politicians who left no such records. He never felt the need to confide, and we are left groping for the reason why a man whose motive for going into politics was to help the poor decided to be utterly loyal to a government which did nothing at all for them and even reduced their benefits. It may have been – almost certainly was – a decision he subsequently regretted.

In 1929, he had a huge task to perform which had nothing to do with the distressing business of a floundering government. The report of the Simon Commission still had to be written, which meant that for the first year of the new government Clem's only contact with day to day parliamentary business was to vote in divisions. Most of his thoughts were on India, where he felt he could do something useful, and not on unemployment, about which, for the moment at least, he did not feel he could do anything useful at all. The Commission submitted a unanimous report which was mostly the work of Simon and Attlee. It called for more self-government for India, but stopped short of recommending full self-government or Dominion status. It was therefore considered a betrayal both by the Congress Party in India and the ILP in London, and served further to fuel suspicions that Clem's radicalism had deserted him. Full self-government, it concluded, was necessary in the long term but not yet possible, for three reasons. First, there was the tension between Muslims and Hindus. Second, Britain's obligations were not to India, but to each of the Indian states separately. The British could not hand them over to another power without their consent, even if that power was India. Third, too many of the officers of the Indian army were still British. Until its top echelon was Indianised, it was not possible to make the army responsible to an Indian government. But there should be a central legislature; provinces and their princes should have more power; and Burma should be free from India.

It was a lengthy, lucid and informative piece of work, describing in detail India's geography, its races, its political institutions and its problems. But by the time it appeared MacDonald, without a word to Attlee or Hartshorn, had announced that India was to have Dominion status and had called a round table conference in London. So Clem, having damaged his political career and sacrificed his chance of office, and made himself a target for the left of his party, found that his leader, for whom he had done all this, made the sacrifice worthless and took what Clem considered the easy and popular route.

Soon after the report was published, Sir Oswald Mosley stormed out of the government because his radical proposals for dealing with unemployment were rejected, and nothing put in their place. The start of Mosley's journey to fascism was also the chance for Clem to re-enter government, in Mosley's place as Chancellor of the Duchy of Lancaster, in May 1930, the month in which the first telephone line between Britain and Australia was inaugurated with a conversation between MacDonald and Australian Prime Minister J. H. Scullin. Clem was as frustrated as Mosley himself by the inertia and incompetence of the government, but he thought Mosley was indulging in gesture politics made worse by lordly arrogance. 'Why does Mosley always speak to us as though he were a feudal landlord abusing tenants who are in arrears with their rent?' he said to a journalist after a Mosley address to the Parliamentary Labour Party.

The Times, presumably briefed by MacDonald, said that, but for his membership of the Simon Commission, Clem 'would have been included in the Ministry when the socialists took office last May . . .' It rather surprisingly called him 'one of the smartest looking men in the House of Commons' – not the usual description of a man who cared little for clothes and, according to his family, disfigured all his suits by carrying his pipe in one jacket-pocket, his tobacco-tin in the other, and often stuffed papers into them too. Clem's new job had few specific duties attached; he was expected to put his hand to any task the Prime Minister assigned to him. In practice this meant helping MacDonald with the 1930 Imperial Conference and with economic advice, and helping Christopher Addison, the Agriculture Minister, to pilot the Agricultural Marketing Bill through the House. As well as learning a good deal about Commonwealth affairs, Clem learned how *not* to run a government. He was asked for a paper on the problems of British industry and how to put them right. 'With the help of my Private Secretary, Colin Clarke, I prepared and submitted what was, I think, within the terms of reference, a useful and constructive paper. It was circulated to the Cabinet, but, as was not uncommon in the MacDonald Government, never reached the stage of being discussed in Cabinet,' he wrote in his autobiography.

Hugh Dalton – who was growing to dislike Clem's understated style, so very different from his own flamboyant one – also remembers that paper, noting in his diary in November:

> Colin Clarke comes to see me in the afternoon and gives me a cabinet paper prepared by Attlee last July. It is not a very distinguished production, but it recommended that a Ministry of Industry should be set up to rationalise on socially sound lines – armed with considerable powers. The only result has been that Horace Wilson (of all people) has been set up as industrial adviser, to rationalise, with no powers.

Sir Horace Wilson, a civil servant, was Jimmy Thomas's chief of staff.

A further reshuffle in March 1931 gave Clem a real job at last – Postmaster General. Clem's reaction to this was unusual, and tells us a great deal about the man and his approach to politics. He felt keenly that he was short on administrative experience for someone about to run a big and important organisation. So he asked Clement Davies, Liberal MP and legal consultant to ICI, if he could arrange a crash course for him at the company's headquarters. Most politicians come to government office just as short on managerial experience as Clem, or shorter. But it does not worry them, because management expertise is not required for their core business, which is political survival and advancement. For Clem, it was central. He did not want to sit at the top of his department and let others run it. He thought of politics as a job, like any other, which you did to the best of your ability. The House of Commons was his office, fellow MPs – even political enemies – his work colleagues, which is why he found it so easy to make friends on the Tory and Liberal benches. He wanted the skills to run the Post Office himself, and to most people's surprise, he did run it. Baldwin, congratulating him on the appointment, told him: 'Your real difficulty will be Murray,' meaning the autocratic Permanent Secretary, Sir Evelyn Murray, who was used to telling his Ministers what they must do. So from his first day Clem insisted on meetings with all the managers, not just with Sir Evelyn, so that he was really in charge. Sir Evelyn showed his disapproval and was reprimanded in the Major's firm, clipped voice. 'You were bored in the meeting today. You showed it. Mustn't happen again.'

Not that he despised the pleasures and privileges of office. 'I dined with the Prince of Wales last Tuesday at St James's,' he wrote to Tom in November 1930. 'A pleasantly small and quite informal affair. It was indeed interesting to contrast the lack of ceremony there with the excess of it in some government houses in India. He is certainly a very charming person.' This was the man in whose abdication he was later to play a key part. Two months later he managed to get some speaking engagements in Cornwall so that he could stay with his brother for a couple of days, and Tom told him he was writing a novel. Back in London, he offered to help to get it published: '. . . I could also see Harold MacMillan [sic] who is in the House. I know him fairly well. He is quite a good chap . . . I have no doubt that Molly Hamilton would introduce you to her publisher . . . There is John Buchan who is a partner in Nelson's. I don't know how far they deal in novels but John would I am sure advise.' Years before Clem had himself begun a novel, and the first 2,000 words or so are still in a tiny notebook among his papers.

The relationship between the two brothers was now as close as ever, but it had been stood on its head. Before the war Tom had led the way – to socialism, to the books they both read, perhaps even to the idea of social service which brought Clem into contact with the East End. Now Tom was getting his politics, and especially his political gossip, vicariously. He was living quietly in Cornwall, still a socialist and a Christian pacifist, deeply involved in church affairs, pottering about his garden, helping to organise a playreading group, acting as a volunteer librarian every Monday for the newly formed public library service in rural Cornwall. Apart from a little tutoring, he had done no paid work since his release from prison, keeping his family on legacies from his father and mother and recovering slowly from the psychological effects of wartime imprisonment. But during the second Labour government he took a job as a lecturer with the Workers' Educational Association in Cornwall, teaching history and literature (including modern drama) as well as architecture. It was not well paid, but it suited his ruminative style as well as his political views.

Clem was Postmaster General for five months. The job came to a sticky end with the crisis of August 1931. As early as May 1930 MacDonald had taken the extraordinary step of writing to the other parliamentary leaders, Baldwin and Lloyd George, suggesting that the world financial crisis called for a meeting for the purpose of 'putting our ideas into a common pool, and seeing whether from that we could come to a measure of agreement which would enable important legislation to go through the House'.

Baldwin turned the idea down. Lloyd George accepted, but little came of the meetings. The Liberals pressed their radical proposals of public works onto the government; MacDonald and Snowden agreed in principle but said they were financially and administratively impossible.

By the end of 1930 talk of an all-party government was rife at political dinner-parties, with candidates for its Prime Minister scrawled on the backs of hundreds of menus. Lloyd George was mentioned most frequently, but almost as often the names were those of Rothermere, Beaverbrook and Sir Oswald Mosley. In the first few months of 1931 the financial situation grew worse almost by the minute, and many countries tried to insulate themselves from the surrounding chaos by putting up tariffs. British banks had taken short term loans from the Americans and the French, and lent to the Germans at higher rates of interest. When the German banks failed, they were left deeply in debt to the French and the Americans. By February, Philip Snowden was telling the House of Commons: 'The national position is so grave that drastic and disagreeable measures will have to be taken.' Labour MPs knew he meant a reduction in unemployment pay. And if, like Snowden, one rejected out of hand a Budget that did not balance, further borrowing, withdrawal from the gold standard, devaluation, tariffs, or any additional taxation, there was indeed little option left. 'This is a question', Snowden continued, 'to be dealt with by no one party, but . . . in co-operation by all three parties in the House of Commons.'

The next month MacDonald set up a committee chaired by Sir George May, secretary of the Prudential Insurance Company, to recommend 'all possible reductions in national expenditure'. In July there was a flight from the pound. On 1 August 1931 the

May Committee report was published. Suddenly, instead of Britain being seen as an innocent bystander in a world recession, Britain's problems started to be seen as her fault, because of Labour's notorious (though mythical) profligacy. It became established wisdom that Sir George May offered the only possible solution: to save £97 million of national expenditure by cutting unemployment benefit and teachers' and police salaries by twenty per cent.

MacDonald and Snowden, in a political blunder remarkable even by their standards, published the report without comment or policy statement, then went on holiday. So throughout August the drift from sterling accelerated, and the bandwagon for cutting unemployment pay, propelled by the newspapers, the banks, and the Conservatives, rapidly became unstoppable – especially after Snowden abruptly informed his colleagues that the amount needed was not £97 million, but £170 million. But did it all really have to come from the unemployed, from social services, and from the pay of public servants like teachers and policemen? Several Cabinet members, and the TUC, wanted at least some of it to come from the 'rentiers' – those who lived on investments or on property. They thought the rich ought to pay as well as the poor – including the City financiers, whose greedy strategy had collapsed, and who had then run to the government to demand that the unemployed and public servants should pay the price.

MacDonald struggled for a compromise. On the morning of Thursday 20 August he put a package to Conservative and Liberal leaders, who rejected it as not Draconian enough. That afternoon he put it to the TUC General Council who rejected it as too Draconian.

MacDonald and his closest colleagues were furious – not with the Conservative and Liberal leaders, but with the TUC. 'The General Council are pigs,' said Sidney Webb afterwards to Beatrice. 'They won't agree to any cuts of unemployment insurance benefits or salaries or wages.' But how could he have expected them to? The government was proposing the very measures that the TUC had founded the Labour Party to oppose. And the General Council believed – rightly, most people now acknowledge – that MacDonald's measures would not do the trick. It put forward alternative proposals: new ways of raising funds for unemployment benefit, the suspension of the sinking fund for the national debt, and new taxes on investments. General Council opposition ensured the resistance of the trade unionists in the Cabinet, in particular that of Foreign Secretary Arthur Henderson.

By the end of August, MacDonald and Snowden were sure that Britain's salvation depended entirely on obtaining a loan from a New York bank. The bank told Snowden that there must be a ten per cent cut in unemployment pay, or there would be no loan. The Cabinet turned this down by twelve votes to nine. MacDonald, 'looking scared and unbalanced' according to Harold Nicolson in his biography of George V, went to the Palace to advise the King to summon the other party leaders. But Baldwin and acting Liberal leader Sir Herbert Samuel (Lloyd George was ill) believed the best solution was a national government consisting of all three parties and led by MacDonald. If unpopular measures hurting Labour's natural constituency were to be introduced, it would be convenient to have Labour implicated. MacDonald put up a token resistance to the flattering idea that he was the indispensable man, and then on Monday morning, 24 August, he told the Cabinet that he 'could not refuse the King's request' to lead the new National Government.

On the previous day, Sunday 23 August, telegrams went to all those members of the government not in the Cabinet to be at Downing Steet at 2.30 pm the next day. Clem received the summons at a house in Frinton-on-Sea in Essex which he had rented for a family holiday, and arrived in time to have lunch at Odone's restaurant with Hugh Dalton, where, wrote Dalton in his diary, 'we prepare ourselves for the 2.30 meeting . . . by drinking a bottle of Sautenay [sparkling red Burgundy].' Dalton probably drank most of it, for Clem preferred a small sherry before dinner or, like his father, a small quantity of good claret during it; sparkling wine at lunchtime was not to his taste. But he was unusually vehement: 'He is hot against JRM, his indecision and his inferiority complex, especially in all economic questions, and hotter still against Snowden, who has blocked every positive proposal for the last two years,' wrote Dalton.

Dalton's is the best description we have of the meeting that followed:

> At 2.30 the cabinet room is crowded. All ministers not in the cabinet are invited, including whips. JRM sits in isolation on the other side of the table. Christ crucified speaks from the cross. He had originally summoned us he says to tell us that our salaries were to be cut (this is a lie. The summons went out yesterday evening when the National Government was already decided on.) but now he has to tell us that the government is at an end. He is very sorry. We shall curse him, and he is afraid that he has caused us great embarrassment . . . He realises he is committing political suicide. He is not going to ask any of us to do the same, or

to put our heads into the noose. But . . . perhaps some of us *would* be willing to join him. The best plan will be for him to write to us individually and enquire. He would have liked to stay longer with us but he must go to the palace. 'But I have done one thing for you' (at this stage I almost anticipate a distribution of savings certificates) 'I have made it a condition that there shall be no reprisals against those who oppose us.'

Clem's own account, though much less detailed, adds: 'He made us a long and insincere speech in which he begged us to remain with the party out of regard for our careers, but really because he had all the appointments fixed up and any adhesions would have gravely embarrassed him.'

There were a few questions, but Clem asked the only one that mattered. If social services, public servants and the unemployed were to suffer, what would happen to the rentiers? MacDonald said he could not answer that – he could not anticipate a Budget statement. Clem's contempt for MacDonald was confirmed. His leader had fumbled his chance to do something for the poor, and then stabbed in the back those who had given him that chance.

Some of Clem's colleagues were less fastidious, and took MacDonald up on his implied offer. He gently turned most of them away, but seems to have wanted Clem, because he wrote to him that same day, a three-page letter, prolix, vague, self-serving:

> . . . We were on the verge of a financial crisis which, if not dealt with within the space of a few days, would have meant not cuts of ten per cent, or anything of that kind, in unemployment pay, but would have disorganised the whole of our financial system, with the most dire results to the mass of the working class. It may take a little time for people to understand what are the issues and the alternatives to what I have done with some colleagues . . . Before this week had well begun we should have been in the midst of a crushing calamity . . . As the days go on the Party will have to stand impotently by while its work is done by others . . .

Clem replied that, while he was sure MacDonald had acted in good conscience, 'I personally must take my stand with those members of the cabinet who disagree with the course adopted.' Privately, he resented the loyalty he had given to MacDonald, and may also have felt guilty that he had supported the government for so long.

He went to say goodbye to his officials. 'We have heard the crack of the master's whip,' he told them, 'and we have all got to go. He is filling our places with other men.' With the job, of course, went the ministerial salary. Just at that time the Attlee family was going through a crisis. Vi was seriously ill.

The End of Innocence

Her constitution, never strong, had been under real strain in 1930. Their fourth and last child, Alison, was born in April – another difficult birth – a month before Clem returned to government. She was seeing very little of her husband, who was involved with the Commonwealth Conference and with a conference on India. Several nights a week she would have to put the four children to bed and go straight into town to accompany him to a dinner or a reception. One Sunday, as she walked to church, she realised she was unsteady on her feet, and the next morning she felt too giddy to get out of bed. Clem carried Alison from her cot to her mother. Over the next few days it became harder for her to walk or to concentrate, and the burden of looking after the children fell almost entirely on the young nanny, Nellie, who had been with them since 1926. A fortnight in hospital and a fortnight's convalescence did no good and Vi went into Westminster Hospital for several weeks. There they diagnosed what Clem always called 'sleepy sickness', which she probably picked up in India. Fluid was taken from her spine and she had several injections, but her recovery was slow and erratic. Clem constantly worried about her, and when at home he was always by her side. She was still not properly better when the government fell more than a year later in 1931. It is likely that she never completely recovered.

As a result of Vi's illness, they moved house, which made the loss of Clem's ministerial salary serious. They wanted a bigger house, nearer to Vi's family, so that there was support on hand when she was not well. They left 17 Monkhams Avenue in Woodford, and Vi found a fine detached house, standing in its own grounds thirty yards back from the road: 'Heywood', in London Road, Stanmore. They decided to move in June 1931 when Clem was a Minister and expected to continue as one for some time. By the time they moved, in October, he was a Minister no longer, and anxious about whether he could afford his new home. He solved the problem in the short term by increasing his journalism, and by taking a small loan from the family firm of Druces and Attlee.

There were six weeks between the formation of the National Government and the dissolution of Parliament for an election. The government secured the American loan; went off the gold standard which it had been formed to safeguard; and, of course, made the reductions in unemployment benefit and public service pay which MacDonald's Labour colleagues had refused to make. Sixty-eight-year-old Arthur Henderson became Labour leader, and left with his demoralised troops for Labour's week-long annual

103

conference in Scarborough. A few MPs had to stay in London, for Parliament was still sitting, and it is typical of Clem that he chose, or was chosen, to mind the shop. Unlike many of his colleagues, Clem never tried to electrify the faithful. His preferred place was in his office, doing his daily work; in this case, in his superiors' absence at conference, to lead Labour's attack on Snowden's Finance Bill, a job he did with the competence that everyone expected of him.

During the general election which followed, Clem was genuinely shocked by the lies and distortions used by the National Government, though by today's standards they were not exceptional. 'Our late leaders vied with Liberals and Tories in misrepresentation,' he wrote in his autobiography. 'MacDonald distinguished himself by flourishing worthless German notes, and suggested that Britain would experience what had happened in Germany, while Snowden, who knew the truth, supported Walter Runciman and others in the lying story that the Labour Government had improperly used the money in the Post Office Savings Bank to maintain the unemployment fund.'

Labour was fighting on several fronts. The ILP had tried to make peace, but this had infuriated the Labour leadership, because ILP leaders pointed out that they had been right about MacDonald and the rest of the party had been wrong. So Labour ran official candidates against ILP candidates. The split vote meant that in most of the rest of their constituencies, National Government supporters won. The Mosleyites, calling themselves the New Party, also put up candidates against Labour, but none of them got a significant vote, Mosley and his wife being ejected from Parliament forever.

The public had had a bad scare, and with some justice put it down to the incompetence of the Labour government. The fact that the two chief figures in that government were Prime Minister and Chancellor of the Exchequer in the National Government mattered little, because now they stood alongside the reassuring figures of Stanley Baldwin and Herbert Samuel. Behind the scenes in the government, all was chaos and confusion, with Baldwin in favour of protection and Samuel against it, but the electors did not know that. MacDonald's talent for finding a fine-sounding meaningless phrase had not deserted him: he called for a 'doctor's mandate'.

Labour knew it was in for a bad result, but no-one had any idea just how bad it would turn out to be. The National Government returned to Parliament with 556 seats and a majority of 500 over all opposition parties. Labour won just forty-six. Labour people scattered all over the place: Mosley and Beckett towards fascism; John Strachey and the Webbs in the general direction of communism; the remaining ILP people, including Jimmy Maxton and Fenner Brockway, to the wilderness. If there was a consolation for Labour, it was that the Liberals were clearly on the road to irrelevance. Young socialists sang a song, to the tune of 'The Church's One Foundation'. There was a rumour that Clem wrote it. We cannot know for certain, but it is perfectly possible.

> The Liberals' One Foundation
> Was recently free trade.
> 'Twas Cobden's own creation
> But now it has decayed.
> Since Sinclair backed the quota
> And Herbert joined with Mac
> The puzzled Liberal voter
> Has gone and won't come back.

The Labour leader, Arthur Henderson, lost his seat, and so did all remaining members of the MacDonald Cabinet. Only three of the forty-six returned Labour MPs had any Front Bench experience: Clem, who scraped home with 11,354 votes to the Conservative's 10,803; Clem's old East London comrade, George Lansbury; and a distinguished lawyer, Sir Stafford Cripps, who had been Solicitor-General for a year, but was very new to the party and had only been in the House for a year. There was only one conceivable leader, Lansbury, and only one conceivable deputy leader, Attlee.

The conventional theory of Clement Attlee's career is that he became Labour's Prime Minister in 1945 because of the accidental fact that he scraped back into Parliament in 1931. If any of a dozen other men had held their seats, we would not have had little Clem Attlee pottering insignificantly about Downing Street for six years. We would instead have been treated to the more prime ministerial presence of Herbert Morrison, or Hugh Dalton, Ernest Bevin, or even Oswald Mosley. Dalton in his autobiography listed twelve ex-Ministers, including himself and Morrison, any of whom, he claimed, 'had he been re-elected, would either have been chosen leader in preference to Lansbury, or deputy leader in preference to Attlee.' Looking sourly in from outside the House at men he considered his inferiors taking positions he coveted, Dalton wrote in his diary on 8 October 1932:

The Parliamentary Party is a poor little affair, isolated from the National

Clem Attlee

Executive whose only MP is Lansbury. Attlee is deputy leader of the Parliamentary Pary – a 'purely accidental position' as someone puts it – and he and Cripps, who are in close touch with [G. D. H.] Cole, sit in Lansbury's room at the House all day and all night and continually influence the old man. With none of these are Uncle's [Arthur Henderson's] relations close or cordial . . . Attlee is a small person, with no personality, nor real standing in the movement . . .

Dalton was wrong. Clem was quietly clever and ruthless, while most political leaders, especially Dalton, are noisily clever and ruthless. He suited the mood of the Labour Party in 1931 as well as that of the country in 1945.

In 1931, Herbert Morrison was senior to him in the sense that he had held a more senior post – he had been in the Cabinet as Minister of Transport. But Morrison had voted with MacDonald to accept cuts in unemployment benefit, and was thought – we now know correctly – to have actively considered going with MacDonald, if only MacDonald would give him a job. He was also thought, with some justice, to be a machine man whose skill was in the murky backrooms of politics. Dalton was better known than Clem, noisier, and gossipy, and had used all his Old Etonian charm to assist his rise. But he, like Morrison, was not quite trusted. Clem was. As for Sir Oswald Mosley, he believed for the rest of his strange life that, if he had stayed in the Labour Party, he would have led it to victory in 1945; and led his biographers to believe it too. But the party had just been betrayed by a man who was full of radical, resounding, orotund oratory and who had a weakness for aristocrats. Mosley was full of radical, resounding, orotund oratory, and *was* an aristocrat. The Labour Party never trusted Mosley. At least half the Labour Party that realised it wanted the opposite to MacDonald. And in Clem Attlee, that was what it got.

Perhaps the man who understood that best was Labour's key power-broker in those dark days, the General Secretary of the Transport and General Workers' Union, Ernest Bevin. After the 1931 crisis, much of the control of the Labour Party passed back to the unions. It seemed to TUC leaders that the intellectuals had once more made a mess of the weapon the unions had fashioned, and that the unions must once again put things to rights. The TUC ensured that MacDonald was rapidly expelled from the party he had led for a decade, and that to follow him was political suicide in the Labour Party.

The TUC General Secretary, Walter Citrine, pronounced a doctrine which was accepted without a murmur by Labour leaders:

'The general council should be regarded as having an integral right to initiate and participate in any political matter which it deems to be of direct concern to its constituents.' The TUC General Council over the next decade did exactly that. The key figure was Bevin.

Born illegitimately to a desperately poor mother, Bevin had effectively created what was then the biggest and most powerful trade union in the land, the Transport and General Workers' Union. He believed that a trade unionist must address an employer on equal terms: arrive in as big a car, come from as big an office – and that is why he built the Union's first imposing headquarters, Transport House, in Smith Square, which was opened in May 1928. That year he negotiated the last of his famous series of mergers which made the TGWU the effective leader of the labour movement for half a century, until the early 1980s. The following year he negotiated an agreement with Odham's Press, owners of the *Daily Herald*, which gave the labour movement effective control of a national newspaper, and that control was always exercised, in practice, by Bevin. In 1933 the *Herald* became the first national newspaper to reach a regular circulation of two million.

Even today occasionally trade union officials model themselves on Bevin: tough and noisy, full of bravado and a kind of simple cunning; conspiratorial and supremely egoistical, but inspired by a passion for justice; crudely bullying yet socially conservative and conformist, with a precise view of the correct behaviour for, and dignity of, a Labour and trade union leader. Bevin's political armoury was fearsome. There were his sponsored MPs; his union's block vote, which was nearly ten per cent of the vote at a Labour Party conference; and the *Daily Herald*. Ernest Bevin, though he had never been in Parliament, was by 1931 a power in the land in a way that Clement Attlee was not.

Bevin and Attlee made an odd contrast: the former big and fat, noisy and noisily working-class, the latter small and trim, quiet and discreetly public school. But they had similar instincts. Neither naturally confided in others; both liked the Labour Party's arcane structures. Both had a strict sense of propriety which had been outraged by MacDonald even before his defection. Clem noted, disapprovingly, MacDonald's 'habit of telling me, a junior Minister, the poor opinion he had of all his Cabinet colleagues', while Bevin was outraged when MacDonald said in his presence, 'You must remember the low mental calibre of those I have to work with.'

He replied, 'Mr Prime Minister, you shouldn't say that sort of thing in front of me.' Bevin, like Oscar Tobin ten years earlier, knew at once the value of the Major from Limehouse. At heart they were soulmates, and it seems likely that they discovered this when thrown into alliance in the 1930s, and never forgot it.

With friends like Bevin, Clem did not need the admiration of Hugh Dalton. Dalton was right about one thing, though. The influence of G. D. H. Cole, the academic socialist whom Clem had always admired, was increasing. Cole now took the initiative in founding two new bodies designed to take the place of the ILP as the socialist thinkers and educationalists of the movement: the New Fabian Research Bureau and the Society for Socialist Information and Propaganda (SSIP) which was to disseminate the Fabians' research. In order to avoid a repeat of the troubled history of the last few years of the ILP, neither body was to put up parliamentary candidates or seek formal affiliation to the Labour Party. The initiative had the enthusiastic support of the parliamentary leaders, Lansbury and Attlee, as well as Bevin. 'The ILP', Bevin wrote to Josiah Wedgwood soon after the 1931 election, 'became purely an emotional body, a sort of Plymouth Brethren, and the Labour Party has not taken over the early educational work of the ILP and the old SDF. I am going to devote my attention to some educational work of a practical kind.'

The ILP disaffiliated from the Labour Party in 1932, and rival factions struggled for its soul until, within fifteen years, they had effectively killed it.

> We are the peoples party, the grand old ILP
> The most amoebic Party that ever you did see
> We reproduce by splitting . . .

sang a new generation of political radicals. It was a sad end to the source of Labour's radical energy and Attlee's socialist inspiration. Its place on Labour's left was taken by the newly formed Socialist League, founded by those ILP people who did not want to follow Maxton into the wilderness, and fronted and discreetly financed by Stafford Cripps. At first Clem was a member of the League, but he slowly and imperceptibly distanced himself from it, as he had done from the ILP, and for the same reasons.

The next two years were the busiest Clem had ever known. He, Lansbury and Cripps worked well together. Clem liked and admired both his colleagues. Lansbury came from the left of the party – he had gone to prison in the early 1920s as the leader of the rebel councillors of Poplar, in defence of his borough's unemployment relief fund. Clem wrote in his autobiography that, as opposition leader, Lansbury took great trouble with 'a task which was, I think, not particularly congenial. He was by nature an evangelist rather than a parliamentary tactician. Yet during those years in which he led the small Party in the House he showed great skill and powers of everyday leadership.'

As for the wealthy, aristocratic and intellectual Cripps, Clem told Mark Arnold-Forster years later that lawyers are seldom good parliamentarians: 'The great exception is Stafford Cripps. He was a brilliant lawyer but he captured the House . . . He never put a foot wrong. He was extraordinarily good in the House. But the average lawyer doesn't, you see. He's too legalistic.' Clem and Vi often stayed in the Crippses' splendid home in the Cotswolds. The Crippses were the only people in the Labour Party whom Vi knew at all well. But Cripps was inexperienced, Lansbury was over seventy, a high proportion of Labour's forty-six MPs were elderly trade unionists from mining areas who could not contribute a lot to debates, and Clem had to shoulder much of the burden. He became an expert in all sorts of subjects he had not before studied in any depth, especially finance and foreign affairs. In 1932 he filled more columns in *Hansard* than any other MP, and he went everywhere, fulfilled every engagement, let no-one down.

'Last week was somewhat hectic,' he wrote to Tom in February 1933.

I had to speak three times in the House. Then on Tuesday afternoon . . . Frank Owen formerly Lib MP for Hereford came in to say that Aneurin Bevan had flu and could not debate with Tom [Oswald] Mosley at the Cambridge Union. I agreed to take his place. He drove me up in an open car through a succession of snow storms and we got there just in time for dinner. Mosley talked pretty fair rot to a crowded house. I laughed him to scorn pretty effectively and got a good majority. [Oxford preferred socialism to fascism by 335 to 218.] I had to frame my speech from what he said. He has not any coherent ideas. It is really Mosley and nothing more. As if this was not enough on Wednesday when I had to open a new telephone exchange in Mile End at 2.15 and speak in the House on India about 4.15 I was rung up and asked to broadcast instead of Megan Lloyd George who was ill so I had hurriedly to compose a Week in Westminster for Thursday morning. On Friday I went to Catterick to talk to the officers on self determination. I got to Darlington in deep snow . . .

At the same time the methodical Attlee was working on a way to ensure that the next Labour government did not fail as the last two had failed. 'We are hard at work on defining policy,' he wrote to Tom. 'My idea is a plan of action to be agreed on, so that when we win next time we shall know exactly what to do, how to do it.' This aligned him with the left. Henderson urged the party conference in Leicester in 1932 not to tie the hands of the next Labour government, but Clem was all for having his hands tied. By 1933 he was, as he had been in the early 1920s, on the left of his party. No doubt, as his detractors insist, Clem was very good at sensing the way the wind was blowing and going with it. But it is also true that he was now occupying the political position in which he was naturally comfortable. His mood exactly fitted that of Labour's activists in the country. There were to be no more betrayals, no more MacDonalds. The key sin of 'MacDonaldism' was vagueness. Clem wrote to Tom:

> It is difficult to get at MacDonald's mind at any time. It is I think mainly fog now. I think that while at the back of his mind he realises his own incompetence for the job which he has in hand, he sees himself in a series of images in the mirror, images which constantly fade and melt into each other. Now he is the Weary Titan, or the good man struggling with adversity; anon he is the handsome and gallant leader of the nation, or the cultured and travelled patron of art and letters . . . Despite this, however, there is some leaven of shame, hence his irritation at the existence of GL [Lansbury], which is a standing reproach to him. What I think annoys him is that GL has taken his place entirely with the masses of the people and is also obviously popular with the House of Commons which is entirely indifferent to *him*. He cannot stand the cold blast of criticism. Ceremony and respect due to his position are for him a necessity now, a shell for adulation.

Others might become tolerant to the lost leader, but not Clem. MacDonald had betrayed his trust, his supporters, his friends; he had betrayed Clem. He was never forgiven. On one occasion, when the Prime Minister passed him in a House of Commons corridor and smiled and spoke to him, Clem cut him dead. Another time he raised his voice as MacDonald passed and said to his friend Jack Lawson: 'And Esau sold his inheritance for a few pieces of silver.' Gratuitous rudeness was not Clem's style, and was reserved only for those he considered morally worthless: probably only MacDonald and Lord Beaverbrook. Years later, in his retirement, he offered Mark Arnold-Forster his first temperate judgement of MacDonald, couched in typical Attlee language: 'Curious bird. I never knew how to take him. He had a sort of Highland aloofness. I don't know what it was exactly. But you never quite knew where he was. He was always rather apt to impress on you that the whole burden of the world is on him.'

Despite his passion and hectic work-rate, most people still did not think of Clem as a future leader – and by 1933 Clem was seriously thinking about quitting politics altogether. It was the usual problem. He was worried about money. Changing the world came second to Vi and the children, and if he could not provide for them the proper standard of living as a politician, he must provide it by doing some other job. That standard of living including giving Vi the upper middle-class comfort she had known in her own family, and giving his children the benefits of an expensive education of the sort that he himself had received. Janet was ten in 1933, Felicity eight, Martin six and Alison three.

Definitions of poverty depend on expectations. The Attlees would not have seemed poor to Ernest Bevin, or to Clem's constituents. But Clem, more than other senior modern politicians, kept his home and his work in separate compartments. 'As children we never went to Limehouse,' says Felicity. 'We were never to be worried by anything.' The girls all attended a local private school in Bushey called St Hilda's, where Vi's sister taught, and where several of Vi's relatives went to school. A school friend of Felicity's once asked her: 'Why are you here when your father believes in state education?' Felicity asked Clem, and he replied: 'The man who lives in the world as though the world is the way he hopes it is going to be is a crank.'

Clem and Vi employed servants. There was Martha, a Durham miner's daughter who was cook general (she left before the move to Stanmore); a series of Welsh parlourmaids; and Nellie, the nanny, who stayed for seventeen years after Felicity's birth and became a family friend. Felicity says:

> We used to be handed down the Cripps girls' clothes. We knew we were poor, we didn't have summer holidays. It sounds strange now but we had to have a nanny, my mother had to go into town for functions. It was a sudden shock, no longer being in government, not having that salary. So in the early 30s we started looking at houses again, and looked at two in Stanmore which were not in such good condition as ours. My father told us we were looking for a house for a friend. But we knew. He almost never told a lie and couldn't dissemble.

111

Without his ministerial pay, his parliamentary salary of £400 a year, even supplemented by occasional writing, was not enough for the lifestyle he was determined his family should have. There was not much of his inheritance left, and he owed £487 to Druces and Attlee.

Clem and Vi's careful attitude towards money is well illustrated by a story Felicity still tells – it clearly reverberated throughout her childhood. Vi's twin sister had bet her a small sum of money – probably only about a pound – that Vi would get engaged before she was twenty-five. Vi did, so she gave her sister a cheque. By the time her sister paid it into the bank, Vi and Clem were going through a lean time, and thought it was a bad moment for it to be cashed. Clem was also painfully aware that his work-rate was not allowing him to give Vi enough time and care. She was still far from well, and she was not as emotionally self-sufficient as he was. 'At this time he was in the House day and night and I always think of her having her supper on a tray, and how lonely she must have been,' says Felicity. He would leave the House at midnight and take the train to Edgware, then walk four miles or so from the station to his home, creeping in at two in the morning so as not to wake the family.

These worries came to a head in December 1933 when Lansbury fractured his thigh and was told he needed a complete rest, and Clem was faced with being acting leader for several months. There was no leader of the opposition's salary in those days, and he wrote to Cripps that he could not afford to do it: 'I think that the only thing for me to do is to resign my position as temporary leader and for you to take over.' Cripps wrote to Ernest Bevin:

> . . . Clem Attlee is rather on his beam ends financially as he has no outside income and with a family his parliamentary £360 is not enough for him to live on . . . Apart from a certain amount of broadcasting (which has now ceased as account of the BBC policy changes have to be made) he has no outside income. Could the *Daily Herald* employ him to write some articles for them? Say a weekly article on parliament, or something of that sort. He has a very wide public as he has been broadcasting on events in parliament for over a year . . . I do think the movement somehow or other ought to help him in his financial difficulties, and he has such a first class brain that this should not be difficult . . . Of course don't tell him on any account that I have written to you in this vein though there is no harm in his knowing you have a clue from me.

Presumably Bevin declined to intervene, because subsequently Cripps, who was born wealthy, had married an heiress, and earned a great deal of money at the bar, guaranteed a donation to Labour Party funds of £500 a year as the acting leader's salary until Lansbury was fit to take over again. He knew – and probably Clem did too – that a recent convert to Labour as he was, with no roots in the movement, could not hold the party together in those difficult times. No wonder that, despite finding Cripps frequently irritating, Clem never changed his view that Cripps was 'a most warm-hearted and generous friend and a delightful companion'.

Acting as leader turned out to be longer than expected – nine months – and by the end, for the first time, the implausible idea that the modest Major from Limehouse might one day be Prime Minister had started to dawn on his colleagues. At first Clem was often not taken seriously. 'His general attitude is one of patient and rather bored tolerance,' commented the *Evening Standard*. 'He is small and dark and has a slight stoop.' The stoop seems to have been new: no-one suggested the Postmaster General stooped two years earlier, and it was evidence of the weight of the burdens placed on the deputy leader's narrow shoulders.

He came better equipped mentally for the job than most opposition leaders. First, there was the knowledge he started out with. He had not forgotten what he learned in Limehouse before the war. He faced a government which was doing nothing about clearing the wretched slums and replacing them with places fit for humans to live in, and nothing about unemployment; and was imposing the meanness of the means test on the poorest of its citizens. In November 1933 he told the House of Commons: 'I lived for many years in, and I represent now, a slum area, where the houses are utterly worn out. The Minister of Health reminds me of a lady who came some years ago to our district, whose object was to help the poor by showing them how to make a baby's cradle out of an old banana crate.' He rightly received some of the credit for preventing the government from lowering still further the rates of unemployment pay.

This concentration on the minutiae which make poor men's lives bearable or unbearable might have looked parochial. But Clem had made himself an expert on India, and now he played a key part in drawing up and piloting through the House the Government of India Act of 1935, which devolved a good deal of power to the provinces. Though it did not go as far as Labour left-wingers or Indian politicians wished, it was a triumph for Clem and the moderate Conservatives, like Baldwin, who saw that sooner or later India must have its self-government; and it was a bitter defeat for the Conservative 'Die-Hards', led by Winston Churchill, who believed that a British Viceroy negotiating with Gandhi as an equal was 'a nauseating and humiliating spectacle'.

The two years before he had become acting leader had also left him with a deep interest in foreign affairs, as well as the respect of European socialists and prominent American liberals and New Dealers like Felix Frankenfurter, who wrote in 1934 that Attlee 'seems to me to have real size, courage, freedom from mist and, therefore, insight and a grand simplicity . . .' In foreign affairs, Labour was at first on strong ground. It supported the League of Nations and collective security, as the only ways in which permanent peace might be secured. The government, on the other hand, showed little enthusiasm for the League, and Stanley Baldwin – in reality, if not yet in name, the Prime Minister – told a Glasgow audience: 'It is curious that there is growing among the Labour Party support for what is called a collective peace system. Well, now, a collective system in my view is perfectly impracticable. It is hardly worth considering.'

For Clem, and for Labour at that time, any alternative to collective security was too horrible to contemplate. Labour was bitterly critical of the government for conniving in Japanese aggression in Manchuria, for failing to support the League of Nations, and for apparently being ready to sacrifice Abyssinia to Mussolini. Clem wrote a satire on the Foreign Secretary, Sir John Simon:

> He saw that Mr Yen had got Mr Tael by the throat with one hand and was going through his pockets with the other. Simple Simon said: 'I wonder who is wrong' and went to consult the rest of the residents. After some time they decided that Mr Yen was in the wrong. Simple Simon went back and found Mr Tael sitting on the floor half dazed. Mr Yen had got his watch and valuables and was making himself comfortable in the front room. 'It looks to me' said Simple Simon 'that they are coming to an agreement.'

His attitude to Adolf Hitler and Germany echoed the same principle: that if force is allowed to win, then the world will not be worth living in. Hitler became Chancellor at the start of 1933, and Clem became acting Labour leader at the end of the same year. Hitler's demand for a fundamental renegotiation of the Treaty of Versailles placed British socialists in an awkward position, because they agreed that

Versailles was unjust. Clem expressed the new dilemma succinctly: 'I think this country ought to say that we will not countenance for a moment the yielding to Hitler and force what was denied to Stresemann and reason.' Privately he was deeply pessimistic. In a letter to Tom – whose pacifism must have been stony ground on which to sow the seed of collective security – Clem wrote.

> The situation on the continent is terribly serious. There is so much loose powder lying about and one cannot tell where the match will be applied. I fear social democracy in Germany is down and out for a generation, and Austria is likely to be crushed. Thus all Europe, with the possible exception of Czecho Slovakia, that lies east of the Rhine and south of the Baltic, is lost to democracy.

It was his views on collective security which resulted in Clem's first, and as far as is known his only, challenge to a duel. One Captain Fenelli, editor of an Italian Fascist weekly, considered that Clem's slighting remarks about Mussolini should be avenged. Clem replied that in Britain one enjoyed free speech and left one's statements to be judged on their merits, not on one's prowess with guns and swords.

The idea of collective security and the League of Nations was fine, but it masked the real problem. In an increasingly serious international situation, should Britain rearm? Labour's 1933 conference passed a resolution saying that it would not support any war except at the bidding of the League of Nations – not even if Britain were attacked. The pacifist element in Labour was still strong.

Collective security accorded with Clem's passionately held views, formed by the waste and cruelty he had seen in the war. But it also enabled him to advance an apparently unanimous policy, to avoid questions which he knew would divide his party, and to oppose government proposals for rearmament, as party policy demanded. 'You have got to put loyalty to the League above loyalty to your country,' he said; and 'We deny the proposition that an increased British Air Force will make for the peace of the world.'

The 1934 Labour conference saw the Socialist League taking a position of absolute pacifism and unilateral disarmament. They were fought off. But soon there were demands for the opposite – that the party should support rearmament. These demands coming from such a figure as Ernest Bevin had to be taken seriously. Lansbury, now recovered and leading the party again, had always been a

Clem Attlee

Christian pacifist, as absolute and unyielding as Tom Attlee. The stage was set for a confrontation. After the 1931 debacle, the leader of Britain's biggest union was resolved that Labour's parliamentary leaders would never again ignore the unions; and Bevin was one of the first British public figures to realise what the rise of Hitler could mean for the world.

Clem was not yet convinced on rearmament. Hugh Dalton records his argument to a joint meeting of Labour MPs, the National Executive and the TUC General Council, as 'We must relate our armaments, not competitively with any one country, but to the forces available to support Collective Security.'

But the cracks were starting to show – and in October 1935 they turned into a gaping fissure. The TUC, under Bevin's tutelage, resolved that any Italian aggression in Abyssinia must be stopped, by force if necessary. Lansbury and Cripps disagreed publicly with this view, and Bevin, furious that the intellectuals, as he saw it, had let the movement down yet again, prepared for a showdown at Labour's conference beginning on 1 October in Brighton. On 3 October Italy invaded Abyssinia – and two days later the conference debated a resolution calling for sanctions against Italy and for League of Nations intervention. Of Labour's three parliamentary leaders, Cripps and Lansbury opposed the motion bitterly; Attlee supported it. It was a difficult and emotional time for all three. Clem was parting company, in a very public way, with the two men to whom he had been closest during the previous couple of years. The pacifist tradition in the Labour Party was far older and more deep-seated than its opposition to fascism, and Clem shared with the pacifists a holy anger at the way the rich had sent the sons of the poor to slaughter in 1914. The speech to the conference had been honed over fifteen years in argument with his brother, and echoed some of his surviving letters to Tom: 'We are in favour of the proper use of force for ensuring the rule of law . . . Non-resistance is not a political attitude, it is a personal attitude. I do not believe it is a possible policy for people with responsibility.' Lansbury followed with an emotional speech restating his pacifism. He understood that disagreeing with party policy affected his leadership: 'It may be that I shall not meet you on this platform any more'; but 'when I was sick and on my back, ideas came into my head, and one was that the only thing worth while for old men to do is at least to say the thing they believe and at least try to warn the young of the dangers of force and compulsion . . .'

Labour's conference has always been a sentimental gathering – it is one of its best qualities – and the delegates gave Lansbury one of the greatest ovations it has ever produced. Lansbury was elderly and decent and idealistic, and was giving the last of his strength in his declining years to the movement, the people and the causes about which he felt passionately, and which he had served all his life. Attacking him at that moment would have been like abusing Mother Theresa. Only one man in the Labour movement could have contemplated it. Ernie Bevin waddled to the microphone and flung into this ocean of sentiment a brutal personal attack on Lansbury. 'I hope this conference will not be influenced by either sentiment or personal attachment,' said Ernest Bevin; then, looking directly at Lansbury, went on: 'It is placing the Executive and the labour movement in an absolutely wrong position to be taking your conscience round from body to body asking to be told what to do with it.' This from a man with half a million votes in his pocket. The motion was carried, and Lansbury resigned as leader on 8 October. The general election could well be only weeks away, and Labour was leaderless and publicly divided. The government, on the other hand, looked strong. Five months earlier, in May, Baldwin had replaced an ailing MacDonald, whose mental powers had started to fade with alarming rapidity, and whose natural tendency towards indecision and misty generalisation had turned almost to incoherence. Baldwin was once again Prime Minister, leading a National Government which looked more united than ever, and with the power to call the election when he chose. Taking advantage of Labour's disarray, he announced on 19 October, eleven days after Lansbury's resignation, that the election would be held on 14 November. There was little argument that Clem should lead Labour into the election, but everyone, including Clem, saw that as an interim measure. After the election, a bigger and more representative Parliamentary Labour Party could make a long-term decision.

'So the leader of the socialist opposition is to be Major Attlee,' commented the *Daily Mail*. 'I am afraid that he will not be so for long, but he deserves the success that is his momentarily.' Political prescience has never been the *Mail*'s greatest strength. Two years earlier it had hailed the foundation of the British Union of Fascists by Sir Oswald Mosley with the headline 'HURRAH FOR THE BLACKSHIRTS'.

The *Mail* was not alone in dismissing Clem. Members of his own party were finding it hard to forgive him for being unobtrusive and a little too left-wing for comfort. By 1934 Hugh Dalton could hardly mention Attlee in his diary without a sneer. On 24 January he noted: 'Attlee mentioned the possibility of resigning . . . the other day, if there was any "repudiation" which might involve him. This was mentioned at the NE [National Executive] and Dallas said audibly, "Well, let him. If he does, he'll never get anything else."' In May 1935 Dalton referred to a speech made by Attlee at Smethwick. 'They expected an important pronouncement on current issues. And he talked about – the Sino–Jap dispute! Infinitely remote from the audience both in time and space. Little man, little head, little speech . . . !'

That same month he wrote: 'A consultation between PLP, NE and GC [TUC General Council]. On the first day I speak vigorously against Hitler and state the position that one can't vote against an increase in our air force . . . Attlee reads an essay when he proposes to deliver a speech . . .'

There was no realistic chance of Labour winning the election. Unemployment was falling slowly, and though this was not the result of anything the government had done, Baldwin received the credit. Clem had no real answer to Baldwin's jibe that Labour claimed to support the League of Nations and collective security, but consistently voted against the defence estimates. What sort of collective security could you have if you did not spend any money on defence? The fear that the sight of a Labour government would cause foreign investors to make Britain bankrupt, carefully played on by the National Government, was still strong. The familiar and reassuring features of Stanley Baldwin contrasted favourably with Labour's little-known leader and the dangerous socialist policies he was said to believe in.

Clem put his heart and soul into the election. He travelled 2,300 miles and addressed forty-nine public meetings. 'The government was supposed to be formed to get the country through a crisis. The crisis cannot have been got over, for Mr MacDonald told us that he had only joined up for the duration, and he's still there,' he told a Norfolk audience.

He went straight into the enemy camp with an article in the *Daily Mail* which incidentally paid him better than anything he had written so far: fifty guineas for less than 1,000 words. The article was a clever one: the programme it offered was radical, but the language was so humdrum and everyday that it did not frighten anyone. It was a precious gift which was to serve him well.

The End of Innocence

What is it that the average reader of the *Daily Mail* wants? Not wealth or power, but just to lead the kind of life he wishes; he wants just a reasonable share of the national wealth and a feeling of security so that he can enjoy it.

Today, thanks to the conquests of science, it is possible to provide a higher average standard of life for all our people. Yet never was there so much insecurity.

The rapid changes of technique and the violent fluctuations of trade and industry make a safe job very difficult to find. Skilled, honest and intelligent workers giving of their best never know when some decision made by the big interests which control industry and finance may not throw them on the scrapheap . . .

The piece of the machine that has gone wrong is that called finance and credit. There are plenty of people willing and able to produce things, and plenty who want to consume them, but machinery is lacking to bring them together . . .

Labour therefore wants the community to plan its life . . . We must plan the country, just as a good businessman plans his works, or as a good council plans its city.

We need control of the banking system so that the credit of the country may be used where it is needed. We must obviously take control of the land if the community is not to be bled white by the landlords . . . If we want to plan our country so that we can give everyone access to open spaces and pleasant surroundings, we must have a national system of transport. If we want a prosperous countryside, we must organise agriculture properly.

I will give you an example. London people used to swelter in the summer without any place to bathe. The Serpentine was there, but unused. Mr Lansbury determined that Londoners should have their lido. Despite intense opposition he succeeded. Everyone now says he was right.

A week later the *Mail* tried to stoke up the fears which Clem had damped down:

If the socialists were to obtain a majority there would be a constitutional change in the method of forming a government . . .

There would be a meeting of the general executive of the party, which would first decide who was to be the leader, and later this body would select the names of members of the cabinet to be submitted to the King.

In 1932 the Leicester conference of the Labour Party passed a resolution that if the party obtained a majority, no matter how small, socialist measures must be introduced to Parliament forthwith.

The socialists have no 'shadow cabinet' like other political parties maintain when out of office. The socialist 'shadow cabinet' is the general executive of the Party, which includes all the trade union leaders, the strongest of whom is Mr Ernest Bevin, general secretary of the Transport and General Workers' Union.

It was a charge which Clem was to hear again, under very different circumstances, from one of his own colleagues, Herbert Morrison. In the 1935 election Morrison seems to have been staking out his claim for the leadership of the party. He too had an article in the *Daily Mail*, and several in the *Daily Herald*, where Clem only had one.

Most of the press was as determined as ever that Labour should not win, the *Mail* running a front-page headline on polling day:

VOTE FOR THE NATIONAL GOVERNMENT TOMORROW
AND KEEP OUT THE SOCIALISTS.

Philip Snowden, now a Liberal, became the first advocate of tactical voting, urging that Liberal supporters should vote Labour where there was no Liberal candidate, to keep out the Conservatives.

Labour won 154 seats against 432 for the National Government (which really meant the Conservatives) and twenty for the opposition Liberals. It was hardly a triumph, but given the low base from which they started, it was not a disgrace either. It was satisfying to see Ramsay MacDonald and his son Malcolm defeated, the only two Cabinet members to lose their seats. 'The result, if considered merely in terms of seats won, is disappointing,' Clem told the press. 'On the other hand, the total votes cast show how great and widespread has been the response to Labour's policy of socialism and peace.'

Clem had staked his claim. He had established a style of leadership. He always believed that Labour should say exactly what it wants, not trim its policies in the hope of widening its appeal. That was the true difference of approach between him and Morrison, though it did not come out into the open until the late 1940s. 'George, Stafford and I', he wrote to Tom two years before the election, 'endeavour to give them the pure milk of the word and no blooming gradualism and palliatives.'

The great men were now back – the stars of Clem's generation who, so Hugh Dalton thought in 1931, would have been preferred to Clem if only they had been available: Dalton, Herbert Morrison, the former Health Minister Arthur Greenwood. So were the fading stars of an earlier generation, including J. R. Clynes who had so nearly become leader instead of MacDonald more than a decade earlier. Now, if the theory ran true, was the time for the modest little Major to give place to better and more colourful men.

5

Leader of the Opposition

In 1935, Herbert Morrison was forty-seven. He was short and stocky, with one almost blind eye and an air of furtive pugnacity. The cockney son of a London policeman, he was now the leader of the London County Council (LCC) as well as MP for Hackney. He had come to personify the London Labour Party (LLP) which he had done more than anyone else to build. To this day the LLP is what Morrison made it. Its many strengths are Morrison's strengths, and its less attractive features are Morrison's too. From the time in the early 1920s when Morrison became its secretary, it has always been able to pull off the organisational success of which he was master – getting out the vote at elections, organising to get its way at party meetings. And it has had all the failings of an organisational and political machine in which politics is about power struggles in smoke-filled rooms.

Morrison trusted no-one and loved power. He was an organiser, a fixer, and an intriguer. Unhappily married to a shy woman with a stutter, his life was politics, his social life the bantering bonhomie of politicians. He had no hobbies and played no sports. He worked phenomenally hard and very long hours. He never forgave anyone who slighted him. As a young man he was a vegetarian and neither drank nor smoked, at a time when most people, and especially politicians, smoked either cigarettes or pipes. But when he became Minister of Transport in 1929, he abandoned this abstemiousness. 'He eats, drinks and smokes too lavishly, works his mind too hard and his body too little,' said Beatrice Webb.

In London local government he had shown himself to be distinctly unsqueamish about his methods of getting the right people into the right jobs. His biographers, Bernard Donoughue and G. W. Jones, put it like this: 'He recognised that the electoral system did not inevitably throw up as members of local councils those most fitted to discharge the responsibilities of local government, and when he first became a member of the London County Council he could see that the quality of the majority of Labour members was not such as to inspire confidence that they could be chairmen of committees.' So he protected the LCC from the vagaries of democracy by looking for people he considered possessed the right qualities, urging them to become members of the LCC, then persuading a local party to nominate them, if necessary offering a sweetener by way of an LLP grant towards election expenses. It was while engaged in this, according to Donoughue and Jones, that the mould of his relationship with Clement Attlee was set. In 1919 Morrison had set about with his usual efficiency ensuring that a City financier friend should become the LCC's first Labour alderman.

> Morrison invited him to stand and urged his claims, and he was duly selected. This decision probably was the origin of Attlee's dislike of Morrison. Attlee said that Morrison had approached *him* to sound out whether he would be prepared to be an alderman. Attlee was keen and agreed, yet the next he heard was that [the financier] had been chosen ... In Attlee's eyes Morrison had condemned himself as not being straight. This incident stuck vividly in Attlee's mind to the end of his life.

It is true that Attlee's dislike of Morrison had its origins about that time, but there was more to it than this trivial affair. George Lansbury, then the leader of Poplar Council, went to prison rather than pay the borough's precepts to the Tory-run LCC, because he wanted to use the money to help the unemployed. Morrison, leader of the council in neighbouring Hackney, publicly denounced Lansbury and 'Poplarism'. Clem had been a friend and admirer of Lansbury even before the war. He was shocked at the ferocity of the attack, and at the fact that it was launched while Lansbury was in prison. So Clem was probably not unhappy to find that in November 1935 he was the main obstacle to Morrison's leadership ambition. At fifty-two, five years older than Morrison, he still lacked the immediately recognisable personality and easy familiarity which most politicians consider vital.

Many people thought Clem dull: efficient and hard-working, certainly; intelligent, no doubt; sincere, probably; sometimes witty, in a dry way; but there was no getting away from it, dull. He made little impression on the son of his friend and future Parliamentary Private Secretary, Arthur Jenkins. Fifteen-year-old Roy Jenkins thought he 'looked and sounded like a retired major, which of course was what he was'. Thirteen years later Roy Jenkins was to write an excellent biography of the retired Major. His skills did not sound exciting, either. Clem had the sort of mind that squirrels away facts. He could always tell you the capital of any country and the names of the seven wonders of the world. He was wise enough only to display his gift with his children. But his papers are full of extraordinary examples of it. Stuffed into a book which he owned around this time is a flimsy sheet of paper containing, carefully typed out, the name of every boy in his class at Haileybury. In a file there is a full list, written in the Thirties, of every officer of his regiment during the war, with a precise account of what happened to them – 'killed Sail Dali', 'died 1920'. Then there is a full list of all soldiers from his battalion who were killed. Among his papers, at Churchill College, Cambridge, there is a sheet of paper headed 'Approximate ages of the masters at Haileybury College when I went in 1896': a list of twenty-nine masters aged between twenty-four and sixty. There is also a list of boys in Lawrence House in 1896 with notes on what they became after they left the school, and a similar list for 1901. There is a list of rowing, rugger, hockey and athletics blues produced by University College, Oxford, with a note remarking on the large number: 'It may be of interest to set these details down as they are rather unusual.' Perhaps most extraordinary of all are several sheets of typed paper proudly headed 'Boys at Northaw [his preparatory school, which he left at twelve] with me, written down from memory June 1944, 48 years after leaving.' There are eighty-five names on it.

This almost obsessive record-keeping suggests a devotion to his prep school, public school and Oxford college that goes beyond the normal. Was he perhaps compensating for his class treachery? I suspect not, or only partly. He liked to keep his memory sharp, and did it in a way that provided a pleasantly nostalgic private interlude. It gave him the gift, invaluable to a politician, of instant recall when he met people. In 1938 he met a soldier who had served under him in the war and he said at once: 'I posted you with a sten gun in Spent Trench in the last push.' 'He was much bucked,' Clem wrote to his brother Bernard, and no wonder.

His children longed for weekends, which he kept as far as possible for his family, and especially Sunday lunch. That was when they talked together, and when his four children – now aged between five and twelve – badgered him for scurrilous tales from what they hoped had been a dissolute youth. 'We longed for him to have

been a naughty child', says his daughter Felicity, 'but of course he
hadn't been. He kept a low profile at school and worked hard. So
he made up a character called Sniffkins who chewed aniseed balls
all the time and was very naughty, and he told us about his exploits.
After a while he got tired of Sniffkins, so he made him disappear
down the ventilator shaft in the dormitory, leaving behind only a
faint aroma of aniseed balls.'

He brought them jokes. In Stepney at that time, there was a series
of jokes about two traders called Ikey and Moses (there still are, but
their names have changed) with which Clem regaled his children.
Ikey went into Moses's shop and pointed out that it needed a blind,
but Moses said he could not afford one. So Ikey took a box, cut a
slit in it, and attached a notice: FOR THE BLIND. And so on. When
they tired of talking they played games. There was a game where
they all had to guess the date on a penny. If you got the date right,
you got the penny. There were general knowledge games – what is
the capital city of such-and-such a country?

At weekend bedtimes he read them poetry – often Rudyard
Kipling – or a book, often by Jane Austen, or John Buchan, or J.
B. Priestley. Felicity heard his favourite Kipling poem, 'The White
Seal', so often in the mid-Thirties that she can recite it to this day:

> Oh! hush thee, my baby, the light is behind us,
> And black are the waters that sparkled so green.
> The moon, o'er the combers, looks downward to find us
> At rest in the hollows that rustle between.
>
> Where billow meets billow, there soft be thy pillow;
> Ah, weary wee flipperling, curl at thy ease!
> The storm shall not wake thee, nor shark overtake thee,
> Asleep in the arms of the slow-swinging seas.

Apart from at weekends, the children only saw him if they woke late
at night. They would hear the rapid tapping of his typewriter after
they had gone to bed, and if they had a nightmare, the tapping would
stop and their father would appear to explain away their fears with
careful agnostic rationalism. At Christmas they hung his golf socks
on the ends of their beds, but one Christmas in the mid-Thirties
Janet told Felicity that she was sure Santa Claus was Daddy really.
Sharing a room, they pretended to be asleep and caught sight of
his bald dome. Janet said, 'You're Father Christmas,' and he just
nodded.

Clem and Vi played a lot of golf, for which he wore plus-fours.

They had a bar billiard table in the house, and she learned to play the only game he had ever been good at, becoming so good that she often beat him. He took the children for long walks, usually accompanied by the family dog Ting, a Welsh terrier provided by Vi's sister, who bred dogs. Vi's sister had named the dog Tiny, but the handwriting on the certificate was poor, and Vi's mistaken reading of it stuck. Ting ended her days in Number 10 in 1950 at the age of fifteen, and Vi's sister provided another Welsh terrier.

Clem's home life sounds almost a caricature of suburban bliss. In the evenings Vi would curl up at his feet in the living-room and he would sometimes lean down to kiss her forehead. She would hand him her wool to unravel and his eyes would gleam – 'nice to have one problem with a solution' – and he would clench his teeth round his pipe and get stuck in. She would go to bed and leave him at it, and find all the wool in a neat ball in the morning. He was what we now call a DIY enthusiast, spending his Saturday mornings repairing broken furniture, putting legs back on dolls, re-upholstering chairs, building rabbit hutches or doing French polishing (a speciality).

Vi's health gradually improved through the early Thirties. The illness never completely left her, and she was always unsteady on her feet in the dark, but she started to drive again. One of the most famous Attlee myths is that he never learned to drive. It isn't true. He drove regularly during her illness. But as soon as Vi was fit to drive, he gave it up and, as far as anyone knows, he never sat behind the wheel of a car again. He had absolute confidence in her driving. His confidence was not widely shared and stories of Vi's erratic performances became common over the next twenty years, though they were probably exaggerated. This modest method of travel was what he preferred, but later it also became an invaluable part of his image. 'Vi drove us from Stanmore', he wrote of George V's jubilee celebration, 'and we parked in a street at the back which enabled us to get away afterwards when all the great people were searching in vain for their cars.'

Many of the traits which became the stuff of affectionate anecdote during the Attlee premiership were, like Vi's driving, already present in the 1935 Clem Attlee: his devotion to *The Times* crossword puzzle, which he was good at solving – another mind game; his devotion to cricket, though he had never been a cricketer; his interest in Attlee family history – he helped the Attlees of Virginia, whose family left Brentford for the new world around 1600, trace their roots to Surrey; his strange and rather exaggerated devotion to Haileybury, where he had not received a particularly good education, and to University College, Oxford, and even to his prep school, Northaw Place, 'I should have liked to go to the Northaw dinner,' he wrote to Bernard in September 1935. 'Curious that the only three MPs from that school should all have held office in 1931.'

'Did you notice', he wrote to Tom about this time, 'that Holland is being made Bishop of Wellington, New Zealand? Our year are doing quite well one way or another.' And to his brother Bernard, three years later: 'I was pleased to see that Powell of Univ had been made a bishop. That makes two from my year and five from men of my time. When you add Professors Dodd and Greensted we had a pretty good theological output.'

Just after the election of 1935 he wrote out – then wisely filed away in a book and kept to himself – a careful list of every Old Haileyburian elected to Parliament. He visited Haileybury in 1937 and spoke to the fifth and sixth forms on Labour's policy. He was impressed that the Master was broadminded enough to employ, as he wrote to Tom, 'an excellent young master, an Etonian, who is a keen Labour man and works for the Hertford Labour Party apparently in the complete acquiescence of the Head. They are proud of young Mayhew (O. H.) [Old Haileyburian] who has been President of the Union and is the leading force in Oxford Labour.' Christopher Mayhew was to become a Labour politician whose career was carefully nurtured by his leader.

Clem would have liked his own son to go to Haileybury, but he wrote to Tom: 'Martin is not very bright at work so far and therefore I am not laying any plans with regard to him until I see how he shapes. He is . . . on the slow side,' and a few months later: 'Martin is enjoying Belmont [a private boarding school] and has quite settled down but he is woefully bad at work.' Martin had what we now know as dyslexia. Clem eventually heard of pioneering work on reading problems at Millfield School, and sent his son there.

Much as he loved his family, and they loved him, the life of the deputy leader and acting leader of the Labour Party had kept him away from them a good deal, and he was now standing for the leadership, which for the foreseeable future would ensure that his time with them was limited. We may suppose that Vi looked to the result with mixed feelings. There were three candidates: Clem, Morrison and Arthur Greenwood. Greenwood had been an economics lecturer before becoming head of the Labour Party's research department, which was where the 1926 general strike found him, and Health Secretary in the 1929 government. He was a tall, thin, intelligent man, loyal and likeable. The unions would have welcomed his election. But his parliamentary colleagues, though they liked and admired him, knew that he had a serious and deepening drink problem. In 1935, political journalists were too gentlemanly to divulge such knowledge to their readers. Snatch pictures of senior politicians stumbling into their cars were still in the distant future.

Labour's leader was to be elected at a private meeting of Labour MPs in Committee Room 14 of the House of Commons on 26 November, twelve days after the general election. Dalton told everyone who would listen that the choice was between 'a nonentity, a drunk, and Morrison' and invited a group of MPs supposedly pro-Morrison to dinner on Wednesday 20 November: 'Of course the leadership came up and we were nearly all for Morrison,' he wrote in his diary. 'Ellen [Wilkinson] pretended not to be keen. She wrote to me afterwards that she was very keen on Morrison but feared Bellenger blabbing. She turned out to be right. He is a wretched little tyke.' This was F. J. Bellenger, MP for Bassetlaw 1935–68, who had defeated Ramsay MacDonald's son Malcolm, the Colonial Secretary, in the general election.

The diary entry is remarkable for the light it throws on the elaborately conspiratorial atmosphere in which Dalton and Wilkinson operated. Ellen Wilkinson started her political life as a Communist, and until 1929 was a left-wing rebel. Distressed at being excluded from MacDonald's government in 1929, she vowed to mend her ways, and became very close to Morrison, with whom she almost certainly had an affair in the Thirties. Wanting Morrison to know she was for him, but wanting to prevent Attlee from knowing she was against him, was a stance which Dalton, apparently, wholly approved of.

That Sunday's newspapers show all the signs of heavy briefing by all sides. Dalton was sure Bellenger had leaked the *Sunday Dispatch* story:

A few days ago Dr Hugh Dalton . . . started a movement in the Party in favour of Mr Herbert Morrison being made the new leader. He held a meeting at his flat, when the movement was launched. Mr Morrison's supporters met with opposition from a large section of the Socialist Party, which contends that Mr Morrison is fully occupied with his duties as leader of the LCC. Mr Arthur Greenwood's chances of leading the Party are gradually receding although at the time he had the warm support of trade union MPs and of Mr Ernest Bevin, General Secretary of the Transport and General Workers Union . . .

Apparently Morrison refused to confirm or deny the meeting in Dalton's flat. According to the *Observer*:

> It seems probable that Mr Attlee will be asked to carry on for the time being, not because he is considered the ideal choice, but because he is the only one . . . whose election would be considered temporary. The present struggle is not between the right and the left wings of the movement since all four [Attlee, Morrison, Greenwood and Clynes] belong to the moderate section of the Party. The left wing is hardly represented in parliament at all . . .
>
> Having gained the ascendancy the right wing has no intention of weakening its position by quarrels over the leadership. Hence the present desire to compromise and to delay a final decision. The election of Mr Attlee seems the only way out. To appoint anybody else would be regarded as settling the question for a long time ahead, and would therefore involve a very bitter struggle.

The *Sunday Express* took exactly the same line – a sure sign that it was someone's briefing. Its diarist Peter Howard wrote:

> I feel sure that for the time being bald-domed close-eyed Mr Attlee will be allowed to keep it.
>
> Not because he has been an outstanding success so far. Indeed, in some socialist circles he is regarded as a failure.
>
> Not because the socialists would scruple to cast aside their leader.
>
> But because each of the rivals fears that if Attlee is unseated now somebody else harder to dislodge will jump into the saddle. So they will combine to prop poor Mr Attlee insecurely in his seat until one of them feels strong enough to thrust him out again and to hold back all other rivals as he scrambles into power.
>
> Mr Attlee interests me. He used to be called Major Attlee. Then he let it be known that he wished to drop the title of Major and become plain Mister. I am not concerned about whether he is Major Attlee, but whether he is Attlee Major.
>
> My father was at school with two Attlees. One of them Attlee Major, the other Attlee Minor. One of them is the present Leader of the Opposition.
>
> But my father doesn't know which one it was. If I can find out I shall be in a position to tell you many entertaining stories of his schooldays.

Dalton noted in his diary: 'Great activity by enemy press on behalf of Attlee. Morrison rings up (a daily occurrence now) slightly bothered about the degree of press.'

Whoever briefed the *Observer* and the *Sunday Express* – it was probably a last desperate throw by Dalton – it was rubbish. Most MPs knew they were electing the man to lead them into the next general election. Few if any of them were foolish enough to vote for Clem in the hope that they would eventually get someone else. Clem went into the leadership election sure of the support of the few MPs who had sat in the 1931 Parliament. They felt they owed it to him. Mostly undistinguished trade union officials, they could not have put up any effective parliamentary opposition without him. They had grown to like and respect him.

Morrison had much going against him. He was already leader of the LCC, and had tried to become the Labour Party secretary the previous year. He had been told that, to do this, he would have to give up his intention of returning to Parliament. He had apparently hoped the party would let him be leader of the LCC, party secretary, and an MP. Quite apart from the question of whether one man could do all these things properly, it looked greedy. He also seemed to want to launch a holy war against the left. He had just published an article in *Forward* which attacked both the left and the Lansbury-Attlee leadership: 'We ought to have done better [in the general election],' he wrote. 'It is the fault of no-one in particular but since 1931 we have failed to evolve a clear leadership. Our so-called "left" has some bloomers on record in speeches and writing. This country is not going to vote in a hurry for a first class financial crisis.'

The MPs trusted Clem, and were not sure they trusted Morrison. The votes on the first ballot were:

> Attlee 58
> Morrison 44
> Greenwood 33

On the second ballot nearly all Greenwood's votes transferred to Attlee:

> Attlee 88
> Morrison 48

A meeting at Friends House that night stood and cheered the new leader for several minutes, led by the platform party of Lansbury, Morrison and Greenwood. Morrison refused to be deputy leader, claiming that his LCC work kept him too busy. Cynical MPs noted that it did not keep him too busy to stand for leader, and elected Greenwood instead. Dalton confided in his diary: 'A wretched disheartening result. And a little mouse shall lead them!'

Dalton understood that Clem was not a stopgap. Roy Jenkins, in his biography of Clem published in 1948, wrote: 'Although many were slow to realise it, this election marked the end of his stop-gap period, which had lasted in one form or another since 1931. In future his position was insecure only in so far as he might fall down on his duties.'

No other episode in twentieth-century British political history has inspired more games of historical 'if'. Morrison's biographers, among others, are convinced that it was only malign chance which prevented Morrison from being elected Labour leader in 1935 and Labour's Prime Minister ten years later.

The theory is that if Morrison (or Dalton, or pretty well any other substantial figure) had not lost his seat in 1931, that man would have become deputy leader in 1931, leader in 1935 and Prime Minister in 1945. But it is not necessarily true that Morrison would have been preferred to Clem as deputy leader in 1931. Even if he had, it is most unlikely that he would have worked successfully and harmoniously with Lansbury, as Clem had done, and it was that teamwork which ensured the success of Clem's 1935 leadership bid.

The fact is that Clem was the man Labour wanted in 1935 – not as a substitute for someone else, not as a stopgap, but as the man the party believed it could trust to turn its dreams into legislation. He has been described as an accidental leader, but he was probably the least accidental leader in the party's history.

Both Clem's obvious rivals offered themselves, and the party preferred Clem. It was much less accidental than the accession of, say, Harold Wilson or Tony Blair, which depended not just on the unexpected death of their predecessors, but on the timing of that death.

Clem had always been a step ahead of Morrison: earlier into Parliament, earlier into government. In each of the key years – 1931, 1935 and 1945 – key sections of the party preferred Clem over his more flamboyant colleagues. Clem was the man the Labour Party thought best qualified to lead it out of the morass which MacDonald had led it into, and towards a new government which would at last start implementing Labour's agenda. And the Labour Party was right.

Politics for the next four years was dominated by foreign affairs. Almost as soon as Parliament met, the Hoare-Laval Pact leaked. It was an agreement between French Prime Minister Pierre Laval and the British Foreign Secretary Sir Samuel Hoare to hand over to Italy about half the territory of Abyssinia, and to give Italy special economic rights in the other half. It was a simple capitulation to Mussolini's army, and it made a farce of the idea of collective security. Although Baldwin sacrificed his Foreign Secretary, the fact

THE NEW SEE-SAW
'Well boys, you'll have to jump about a bit to make much
difference at this end'

was that Baldwin knew all about it, and was as guilty as Hoare. It was
an embarrassment for Baldwin, but Clem took no pleasure from the
episode. 'The foreign situation is pretty bloody all round,' he wrote
to Tom in April 1936. 'I fear that we are in for a bad time. The
Government has no policy and no convictions. I have never seen
a collection of ministers more hopeless after so short a time since
an election.'

No sooner had the British and French governments been caught
quietly handing Abyssinia to Mussolini than, in March 1936, Hitler
marched into the demilitarised Rhineland. In July, General Franco
launched his rebellion against the elected government of Spain.

These events enabled Labour's leader to effect a transformation in British politics – a transformation no less remarkable for not being remarked upon at the time.

Labour had gone into the 1935 election vulnerable on defence because it was unwilling to spend money on rearming and still had elements of absolute pacifism associated with it. Within a year, it was the Conservative-led government which seemed to be abject to foreign dictators; Labour, meanwhile, was quietly and discreetly repositioning itself. Clem knew that the international situation required it to jettison its pacifism. Another leader might have gone to the party's annual conference, made a fiery speech, and used Ernest Bevin's block vote to reverse Labour's traditional policy of voting against the annual defence estimates. It would have worked; at the 1936 conference Bevin wanted to do just that, and so did a section of the parliamentary party led by Hugh Dalton. Most subsequent Labour leaders, from Hugh Gaitskell to Tony Blair, have gone down this route when they wanted to change direction. Clem turned the chance down, saying that you could not vote for money for arms when you had a government which was not committed to support League of Nations policy. It was a line – as Roy Jenkins puts it in his biography of Attlee – which 'had a certain logical coherence, but . . . owed its adoption more to the fact that it offered a convenient transition stage to a party which was shedding a deep-seated pacifism to become a champion of resistance to fascism, and which was finding the change extremely difficult.'

If Clem had gone down Bevin and Dalton's route, he would have won his majority, but he would not have taken the Labour Party's heart with him. Labour people had suffered for their pacifism during the First World War. Clem himself had been active in the No More War movement during the 1920s, and his much-loved predecessor George Lansbury was an absolute pacifist. So Clem's approach was subtle – perhaps too subtle.

'As soon as the 1935 parliament met', he wrote in his autobiography, 'I determined to take steps to create a better understanding of defence problems in the Party . . . I . . . formed a Defence Committee which met regularly and discussed defence problems. We got able officers to address us on various points. We made a very careful study of air warfare and we employed a very able man to engage in research into this vital question . . . Some of us were acquainted with high-ranking officers in the three services. The result was seen in the far more informed contribution which Labour men were able to make in Service debates.'

Thus his colleagues started thinking seriously about the mechanics of defence, instead of engaging in sterile debates about its morality. Major Attlee quietly started writing knowledgeable articles for the *Army and Air Force Gazette*, whose editor wrote to him in May 1936: 'I think your notes on defence are really excellent.' It was a first example of Clem's way of moving the Labour Party on, and the fact that it has gone largely unnoticed is a measure of the success of his approach. He began to attack the government's appeasement of the dictators, and demand full support for the League of Nations, with credibility. 'Whatever arms are required', he told the House of Commons in February 1936, only three months after the election, they must be for the League policy, and the first condition for any assent to more arms is that the Government shall be following a League policy.'

There is in Clem's papers a remarkable ten-page private document on defence under Labour, written around this time, which he seems to have intended as an aide-memoire for himself. Undated and full of crossings-out, it was not in a state to present to anyone else. In it he says that any future war would come closer to the home front than before. There would be a need for rationing. 'Once war has broken out there is a military necessity for the closest regimentation of the whole nation.' This cloud has a silver lining: 'It affords the opportunity for fundamental change of the economic system.' In 1945 it did just that.

The division between navy, air and army was nonsense. There must, he argued, be a strong over-arching Ministry of Defence. The Defence Minister must be in the Cabinet. This would help prevent the government from taking on foreign policy obligations it could not implement. A Labour government must also 'take in hand at once the democratisation of the armed services', ensuring that officers come up through the ranks. But it must move carefully on this – Clem knew the officer class well enough to be sure they would not let their privileges go without a struggle: 'Sudden and brusque changes might bring about a coup d'etat.' And it would mean starting to pay officers properly – Britain was getting its officers on the cheap because they were rich men who did not have to live on their pay.

By November 1937 he was pressing the government for its defence plans – its air raid precautions, plans for evacuation, anti-aircraft guns, air force, and the location of industry from the point of view of defence. Few Labour leaders have shed so much ideological baggage, so quickly, with so little fuss. The Spanish Civil War helped. The position of absolute pacifism looked increasingly untenable when Franco's army was bombing and shelling Spanish towns and villages in order to destroy an elected government – especially when the military rebellion was supported by Nazi Germany and Fascist Italy.

Britain and France pioneered a policy of 'non-intervention' in Spain. This meant that they refused the Spanish government's desperate pleas for arms, while Germany and Italy poured in troops and weapons to help General Franco. Labour's 1936 conference in Edinburgh condemned non-intervention and demanded that the British government restore to the Spanish government its right to buy arms. Still Clem moved cautiously. Léon Blum and the French socialist government supported non-intervention. Clem did not want to oppose the most successful democratic socialists in Europe, nor did he want to embarrass Blum, whom he greatly admired and whose task was difficult enough anyway. But he wrote to Tom in April 1937: 'I'm afraid there's no doubt about the strong pro-Franco attitude of many of the government.'

On holiday in North Wales that summer he took time to write four closely-typed, closely-reasoned and quite unyielding pages to Tom setting out once again why he could not adopt his brother's pacifism. Tom had written a letter, which has not survived, which must have been a fraternal plea not to lead the Labour Party down the path of rearmament. 'I do not think', Clem ended his reply, 'you face the problem of how to deal with those who refuse to accept the rule of the majority and so nullify the consent of the ninety-nine by the refusal of the one.'

At the end of 1937, Clem travelled to Spain to visit loyalist territory and to take a message of encouragement to the government forces. He and his party of three Labour MPs went first to Barcelona, where they stayed with the Spanish Prime Minister. One of Clem's companions was the diminutive Ellen Wilkinson, and in his memoirs he recalled with gentle amusement her introduction to a British consular officer. 'She, rightly or wrongly, believed that he was very pro-Franco. She drew herself up to her full height (which was not great) and, looking at him with blazing eyes, repeated his name twice. She then made a very deep curtsey and turned away. It was most impressive, suggesting Queen Elizabeth receiving the French Ambassador after the massacre of St Bartholomew's Eve.'

They also went to the front line and carried out a torchlight inspection of the British battalion of the International Brigade, who had volunteered to fight for democracy in Spain, and had been smuggled across the Pyrenees to avoid French and British blockades enforcing non-intervention. One of the companies was named in his honour: the 'Major Attlee Company'. He returned with their letter: 'The people of Britain can force the National Government to abandon its policy of help for Franco. All of us have read with great interest the splendid campaign being conducted in Britain by the Labour Party . . .'

'The most dramatic scene was our visit to the international brigade,' Clem wrote to Tom. 'Arriving in the dark in a bitter cold wind and finding the men drawn up in the square of a village with torches held all round. The officers were an interesting group of very varied nationality . . . The YugoSlav officer had a very fine voice and sung the Volga Boat Song after dinner.' The visit, he thought, 'has done a lot for the movement and has also had a good effect internationally.'

Back in Britain the MPs produced an eight-page pamphlet called *We Saw in Spain*. Attlee's own contribution, 'Spain Fights For Democracy', was written in his clipped, lawyerish style, with his usual quota of saving phrases – 'In my view the policy of non-intervention is responsible to a great extent for the food difficulty' – but real passion sometimes breaks through as when he writes: 'Continued acquiescence in a one-sided non-intervention has made the British Government an accessory to the attempt to murder democracy in Spain.'

Clem quickly established a leadership style that was more low-key than that of any other Labour leader, before or since. It came across in his method of dealing with fascists and communists who barracked his meetings. Herbert Morrison would stand on the platform calling to the police: 'Out with him, officer. We pay a police rate and we will get free speech.'

A Mosleyite of the time described what happened when he and a few friends went to one of Clem's meetings at a school in Battersea, South London, in 1938: 'There were about ten people there, and six of them were ours. He started talking about Spain, so we shouted Put Britain First and other slogans. He just walked out and never returned.' He does not appear to have worried even when he read the *Daily Mail* headline 'ATTLEE CHASED OUT OF BATTERSEA '.

His media image does not seem to have bothered him, though he did complain when Labour papers ignored the Parliamentary Labour Party. Dalton records in his diary a difficult meeting he and Clem had with the then editor of the *Daily Herald*, and in May 1937 Clem sent a private letter to *New Statesman* editor Kingsley Martin:

A colleague in the House made the following remark to me last week which is perhaps worth passing on with some comment. He said: 'Why does the *New Statesman*, which professes to stand for democracy against fascism, hardly mention Parliament and never the Parliamentary Labour Party?' I think there is substance in this . . . I think it would be a pity if the NS got so highbrow that it entirely ignored the existence of parliamentary institutions.

Clem played a low-key, but crucial, part in the events leading to the abdication of King Edward VIII in 1936. Baldwin briefed him before the King's wish to marry the divorced American, Mrs Wallis Simpson, became public. There was a temptation for Labour to side with the young, handsome, popular king – especially since Edward had been shocked at the conditions of the South Wales miners, saying: 'Something must be done.' The party might even have won a general election fought on the issue. But Clem chose at once to support Baldwin in his determination that the King should either give up Mrs Simpson or abdicate. He told Baldwin that, if the King asked the leader of the opposition to form an alternative government, he would refuse.

He took the decision on the spot, without consulting his colleagues. He reported what he had done to Labour's NEC, forestalling protests with a long memorandum. Labour must not encourage the King to ignore the advice of his Ministers. A victory for the King against his Ministers was very dangerous – that way, he wrote, lies fascism. He could not have known that the leader of the British Union of Fascists, Oswald Mosley, was in touch with the King through intermediaries, trying to persuade him to ignore the advice of his Ministers. Clem added that many Labour supporters, especially women, were quite conservative enough to object strongly to Mrs Simpson. It was not just her divorce, but the circumstances of her divorce. Characteristically, he thought 'we should settle for a humdrum and respectable monarchy'.

Then he persuaded a reluctant and sceptical Ernest Bevin to deliver the support of the *Daily Herald* – the only popular newspaper to support Baldwin on the issue. 'My dear Ernie,' he wrote when it was over, '. . . everyone says that [the *Herald*] was among the two or three papers that kept its head and dealt with the matter in a statesmanlike, not merely a sensational, manner. I know this was largely due to you.' Who 'everyone' was, and whether it was good for a popular left-wing newspaper to be 'statesmanlike', were questions which, no doubt wisely, he did not address.

Though Clem held radical political views and eventually became the most radical Prime Minister of the twentieth century, he was in his social attitudes the most conservative and conventional of men. And he was a firm monarchist, loyal to the institution of the monarchy in a way that is hard to understand today. Clem thought the King's action would damage the institution of the monarchy – and that mattered dreadfully to him. In this, as in many things, he was in tune with the Labour Party. Anyone who thinks that a party with trade union roots is likely to be naturally rebellious, or tolerant of sexual peccadilloes, has never seen the unions from the inside. 'I found that I had correctly gauged the Party attitude,' Clem wrote in his autobiography. His reasons for supporting Baldwin do not sound convincing today. Of course, constitutionally, the King must accept the advice of his Ministers on affairs of state. But must he always accept any advice they may choose to offer in deciding whom he should marry?

Clem was a monarchist, and did not want the King to do anything that might damage the monarchy. His attitude to Edward VIII may have been summed up by a poem by Osbert Sitwell, Rat Week, unpublished because it was libellous, but privately passed around top politicians; for Clem typed it out on his own machine and put it with his own poems:

Where are the friends of yesterday
That fawned on Him
And flattered Her
Where are the friends of yesterday
Submitting to His every whim
Offering praise of Her as myrrh
To Him?

They found her conversation good,
They called His Majesty 'Divine'
(consuming all the drink and food,
they burrow and they undermine),
And even the most musical
Admired the bagpipes horrid skirl
When played with Royal cheeks out-blown,
And Royal feet tramping up and down.

Where are they now, where are they now,
That gay, courageous pirate crew,
With sweet Maid Mendl at the Prow,

Clem Attlee

Who upon Royal wings oft flew
To paint the Palace white – (and how!)
With Colefax – in her iron cage
of curls – who longed to paint it beige;
With John McMullen at the Helm
Who teaches men which way to dress?
These were the mighty of the realm –
Yet there were others less!
That nameless, faceless, raucous gang
Who graced Balmoral's Coburg towers,
Danced to the gramophone and sang
Within the battlemented bowers
Of dear Fort Belvedere;
Oh, do they never shed a tear?

Oh, do they never shed a tear
From swollen lids and puffy eyes,
For that, their other Paradise?
How far it seems from here, how far –
Now home again
In the Ritz bar.

Oh, do they never shed a tear
Remembering the King, their martyr,
And how they led him to the brink
In rodent eagerness to barter
All English history for a drink?

What do they say, that jolly crew?
Oh . . . Her, they hardly knew,
They never found her really *nice*
(and here the sickened cock crew thrice);
Him they had never thought quite sane,
But weak, and obstinate, and vain;
Think of the pipes! That yachting trip!
They'd said so then ('say when, say when!')
The rats sneak from the sinking ship.

What do they say, that jolly crew?
So new and brave, so free and easy;
What do they say, that jolly crew
Who must make even Judas queasy?

A few months later he was sending Tom a rhyme his daughter
Felicity had brought home from school (he called it, rather quaintly,
'a ribald rhyme'):

138

Leader of the Opposition

Hark the herald angels sing
Mrs Simpson's pinched our king.

He gained nothing from his stand except the distrust of the left in the party, but he was acquiring that anyway: it went with the job.

In that year, 1936, a Popular Front government, an alliance of socialists and communists, was elected in France, led by Léon Blum. In Britain, the three groups to the left of the Labour Party started to work together to create a United Front 'against Fascism, Reaction and War'. The three were the Communist Party; the remains of the declining ILP; and the Socialist League, led by Stafford Cripps, which had been formed to provide a refuge for those who broadly supported ILP views but did not want to leave the Labour Party.

At the party's 1936 conference in Edinburgh, Clem and the National Executive had firmly resisted pressure to join these three. In January 1937 the three groups issued a 'unity manifesto' which cited Attlee's support for Baldwin over abdication as an example of 'class collaboration'. The Labour Party, guided more by the heavily centralist Bevin than the consensus-seeking Attlee, not only refused to reconsider admitting Communist Party members into membership; it banned Labour Party members from participating in the Unity Campaign. Cripps challenged this at the 1937 party conference in Bournemouth in October but was heavily defeated, and the Socialist League wound itself up. By this time Clem was firmly anti-communist. It was not an ideological stance. It was, like the anti-communism of many of his contemporaries, directly a product of the unrestrained abuse the Communist Party aimed at Labour people during its 'Class Against Class' period of the late 1920s and early 1930s. Stalin had instructed Communists worldwide to call all social democrats 'social fascists' and to break up their meetings, contributing heavily towards the already poisonous atmosphere of the 1931 election. By the time, in the mid-1930s, that the Communist Party started to abandon Class Against Class, the damage was done, and socialists like Clem were bitterly alienated for life.

It was at this conference that a first small step was made to loosen the grip of the block vote on the Labour Party. The view that the ordinary party member's voice was drowned by the block vote of the big unions was now so widely held that something had to be done. Bevin, typically, wanted to tough it out, but Clem persuaded him and the other union chiefs to make a concession. Labour's

139

National Executive includes some representatives of constituency Labour parties, but until 1937 they were chosen by the whole conference, which in effect meant that the seats were in the gift of the big unions. At the 1937 conference, constituency delegates were given the right to elect their own representatives. Bournemouth 'was remarkably successful' Clem wrote to Tom the following week. 'The decision giving the right to local Labour Parties to choose their own reps on the Executive made all the difference. I have been pressing for the change for ages.'

This was as far as Clem wanted to move his party. The conference left the trade unions still essentially in control. Clem liked it that way. Many other Labour leaders – MacDonald, Wilson, Blair – have veered between seeing the unions as a weight round their necks, and as the cavalry to be used when the left is attacking the leader. Only Clem liked dealing with their political power.

He explained why in his 1937 book *The Labour Party in Perspective*, which established Clem as one of that small band of eccentrics who enjoyed Labour's arcane structures.

> In the Labour Party the trade union element serves as the solid core of disciplined membership. The loyalty to majority decisions, which is the foundation of industrial action, takes the place of what is called among Conservatives the team spirit . . . Those who make the greatest song about the block vote are significantly silent when it happens to be cast in accordance with their own views.

This was a remarkably percipient comment; for the Labour left, having railed against the trade union block vote for decades, suddenly came to regard it as the bastion of their liberties in the early 1980s when, briefly, the unions inclined to the left. Labour's 'basis in organised Labour must remain. The complaint that the Labour Party is bossed by a few trade union officials is untrue,' he wrote.

Unlike almost every other leader of the Labour Party, he claimed to welcome internal dissent, 'especially from those whose enthusiastic desires make official policy appear too slow', or to put it another way, the left. 'Self-criticism is a healthy thing so long as it does not lead to paralysis of the will.' But 'there is a danger that the party may be so concerned about its own health that it becomes a political valetudinarian, incapable of taking an active part in affairs. It may discuss its own internal condition to such an extent that it disgusts all those with whom it comes into contact.' Did he foresee the sterile, destructive debates of the 1950s and the 1980s?

The careful, lawyerish title of the book and its sometimes unappealing prose style concealed a set of policies and beliefs which had not changed fundamentally from his days as an East London councillor.

The newly elected Labour government in New Zealand, he wrote, had shown the way for a Labour Party which knew what it wanted. In its first year it had nationalised the banks, given generous old age pensions, decreed a forty-hour week, and taken over the export of dairy products, by far the nation's biggest industry. So there is no point in compromising on socialist principles. 'I find that the proposition often reduces itself to this – that if the Labour Party would drop its socialism and adopt a Liberal platform, many Liberals would be pleased to support it. I have heard it said more than once that if Labour would only drop its policy of nationalisation everyone would be pleased, and it would soon obtain a majority. I am convinced it would be fatal for the Labour Party . . .' People who say socialism curtails individual liberty

> belong invariably to the class of people whose possession of property has given them liberty at the expense of the enslavement of others . . . A far greater restriction on liberty is imposed on the vast majority of the people of this country by poverty . . . The poor man cannot choose his domicile. He must be prepared at the shortest notice to . . . remove himself elsewhere, if economic circumstances demand it . . . How little would those who so easily recommend this to the workers appreciate being transferred from their pleasant homes in Surrey or Buckinghamshire to Whitechapel or the Black Country.

There is no point in 'watering down Labour's socialist creed in order to attract new adherents who cannot accept the full socialist faith. On the contrary, I believe that it is only a clear and bold policy that will attract this support.'

The Labour Party in Perspective, published by Victor Gollancz and the newly formed Left Book Club, sold well – between 50,000 and 60,000 copies – and, Clem noted carefully, it netted him more than £600. A careful man with four children at private schools does not ignore such things. A list of his publications, which he typed himself in retirement, notes in 1935, 'I got the largest payment I have ever had for an article. 50 guineas from the *Daily Mail* at the time of the general election.' The same year, editing a series of books for Methuen called *The Will and The Way* was much less satisfactory: 'I probably got about £80 altogether.' In 1936 he started to write a monthly article for a French syndication agency, bringing in fifteen guineas every month. 'They pay quite reasonably well,' he wrote to Tom.

In 1937 he became the first leader of the opposition to have a salary – an extra £2,000 a year. 'I lunched with Clem at the House yesterday', wrote Rob, his oldest brother by twelve years, to Bernard, the vicar, who was ten years older than Clem, 'and found him in capital form, partly I think because his £2,000 is now a fait accompli.' For the first time since his first child was born, Clem was not worried about money. At the same time, a pension was provided for ex-Prime Ministers and Clem, in his autobiography, says in his almost comically down-to-earth way: 'This was, I think, a desirable step, for in these days a Prime Minister may have little or no private means and it is not easy for anyone who has held the post of First Minister of the Crown to take up other work.'

Clem was becoming a good parliamentary debater. He was never going to be one of the century's great orators; but he wrote to Bernard, evidently pleased with himself: 'I had a good press this weekend for a speech on defence which rather took the fancy of the House. It's a curious thing how when one prepares very little it sometimes comes off.' Only a year earlier, in 1935, the *Daily Mail* had described his speeches, rightly, as 'too tied to notes'.

His letters to Tom are those of a man increasingly at ease with himself and with the world, aware that the world was not that of his youth, but comfortable with many of the changes. In the early Thirties he stopped signing these letters in the formal Edwardian manner, 'Your loving brother, Clement R. Attlee', and replaced it with 'Your loving brother, Clem'. He was approaching his mid-fifties, Tom was three years older, and details of their ailments start creeping into their correspondence. Tom had to have an operation for piles and Clem wrote in May 1937: 'I have an acute recollection of my own op for the same thing.' By November of that year he was writing: 'Sorry your hydraulics are not good. These defects seem to come to our family when its members reach the fifties. My export is slow and I was examined by Morson of Thomason a few months ago. He thought that I was all right for a bit.' 'A bit' turned out to be two years: in 1939, at the worst possible moment, Clem's 'hydraulics' caused the surgeon Clifford Morson to rush him into hospital for an operation.

Tom was still living quietly in deepest Cornwall, lecturing for the Workers' Educational Association and doing some private tutoring for children facing examinations. He was also active in the church. His two sons left their public schools for Oxford in the mid-1930s. Clem stayed with him again in September 1936, addressing meetings in St Austell and Falmouth on behalf of the local Labour candidate. He must have found Tom's house, Leory Croft, set by itself among empty fields, woods and streams, spartan after the suburban comfort of Stanmore: it had one tiny bathroom and a limited supply of water, and lighting came from candles and flickering gas jets. Books, papers, boxes, tins and shoes were piled everywhere. The place was full of cobwebs, cracked crockery and candle-stumps. Tom and his wife Kathleen, whom Clem thought a rather strange woman, pottered about their home in old clothes, looking – so some visitors remarked – like a pair of tramps. Tom generally wore two hats in the summer to protect his balding head, saying he needed both because the holes were in different places. He had just bought himself his first car, a thoroughly temperamental second-hand Morris 8. Vi was always appalled by the way they lived but Clem appeared not to notice anything odd. Perhaps Clem found the pace of life in Leory Croft a little slow after the hectic round of a top politician.

But on the few occasions when he could get away, Clem seemed to like a complete change of pace. He was not a workaholic, a politician who lives and breathes politics, as Morrison was. In 1937, 1938 and 1939 the family took their holiday in the last week of August and the first two weeks of September on a farm in Nevin, North Wales, eating substantial meals cooked by the farmer's wife. From here he wrote to Tom in September 1937: 'We are having a great time here. Good weather and most beautiful scenery and pleasant people at the farm where we stay. Martin and Alison are constantly in and out of the great old farm kitchen. They milk cows and assist in all kinds of farming operation.' Vi's improvement was maintained – they had climbed Cader Idris and Snowdon, not by the easy route, and 'it is really remarkable that Vi can now do this, as a year ago she could not have stood the height let alone the walking.' The two older girls went with them, wearing sandals which they took off half way up. His oldest daughter Janet, fourteen, 'is now an interesting companion. She has quite a good knowledge and conception of history. She realises the importance of ideas and not merely of knowing facts. Felicity is very bright and imaginative and will be very entertaining soon.' He had to go to London for the National Executive and 'by skilful arrangement I left at 3 on the Sunday and got back by breakfast on Tuesday.' But he returned from his holiday to a rapidly darkening international situation.

By then the political transformation was complete. The government, now headed by Neville Chamberlain, stood for appeasement, and the Labour opposition for standing up to the dictators. Clem denounced Britain's failure to take strong measures against Japan for its attack on China. He had received a direct personal appeal from Mao Tse Tung, then chairman of the Chinese Military Council: 'The Chinese people, like the people of Spain, stand now in the vanguard of the International Peace Front.' Chamberlain accused Clem of warmongering.

In February 1938 the Foreign Secretary, Anthony Eden, resigned over the Prime Minister's appeasement policy. It must have been about then that Clem sat down and wrote two versions of a verse about Chamberlain's crumbling government; this extract includes the leaking of the Hoare-Laval Pact, the disgrace of Jimmy Thomas, the ennobling of Baldwin, the death of MacDonald and the resignation of Eden:

> Ten little Neville boys sitting in a line
> Hoare met with Laval and then there were nine.
> Nine little Neville boys governing the state
> Jimmy proved a leaky tub and then there were eight.
> Eight little Neville boys with a Liberal leaven
> Baldwin was sent upstairs and then there were seven.
> Seven little Neville boys journeying to the Styx
> JRM crossed it and then there were six.
> Six little Neville boys still were left alive
> The serpent entered Eden and then there were five . . .

The next month, March 1938, Hitler's troops entered Austria. Clem ranged himself alongside Eden and Winston Churchill – with one important difference of emphasis. To the Labour Party, Eden and Churchill were wrong to ignore Spain – the one place where something could be done. Simply letting the Spanish government buy arms would transform the situation.

He was fortified in this conviction by a visit from the last commander of the Major Attlee Company in Spain, Jack Jones, later to become the most powerful trade unionist in Britain. Jones and three or four colleagues came to get Clem's signature for a public appeal to help volunteers who had been wounded in Spain, and the families of those who had been killed. Jones, then a Liverpool Labour councillor and a product of the Liverpool working class, took to the reserved public schoolboy at once. Middle-class recruits were still unusual in the Labour Party, and trade unionists sometimes regarded them with suspicion, but Jones knew at once that this one was 'with us but not of us – a man of tremendous integrity'. They met at Labour Party headquarters at the time of Munich. 'He was such a humane man that I had no need to try hard and Clem agreed to associate himself with the appeal.' He was, says Jones, full of the dangers of Chamberlain's appeasement policy, 'very apprehensive about what was going on, gave the impression that he thought the world was going to tumble around us'. Clem did think that. He wrote to Tom:

> This government is leading the country into war . . . The Government will I think continue to allow all the smaller democratic states to be swallowed up by Germany, not from a pacifist aversion to war but because they want time to develop armaments. There is really no peace policy at all. Chamberlain is just an imperialist of the old school without much knowledge of foreign affairs or appreciation of the forces at work.

In September Hitler demanded that the Czechoslovak government should grant autonomy to the German-speaking Sudetenland. Labour called on the government to defend Czechoslovakia, if necessary by force, but neither they nor Hitler knew that Chamberlain's mind had been made up five months earlier, when he noted privately: 'You have only to look at a map to see that nothing that France or we could do could possibly save Czechoslovakia from being overrun by Germans if they wanted to do it . . . I have therefore abandoned any idea of giving guarantees to Czechoslovakia . . .' Clem and Arthur Greenwood saw Chamberlain on 21 September, and told the Prime Minister that if Eastern Europe were overrun by Hitler, Britain would be to blame. Six days later Chamberlain was broadcasting over the radio: 'How horrible, fantastic, incredible it is that we should be digging trenches and trying on gas masks here because of a quarrel in a far-away country between people of whom we know nothing.'

The next day, while he was speaking to the House of Commons, a note was passed along to the Prime Minister. Chamberlain read it and announced that Hitler had invited him to a meeting in Munich the next day which Mussolini and French Prime Minister Edouard Daladier were also to attend. Clem had to respond at once. 'Everyone in this House', he said carefully, 'will have welcomed the statement of the Prime Minister that, even at this late hour, a fresh opportunity has arisen of further discussions which may lead to a prevention of war.' At Munich, Chamberlain agreed to give Hitler most of Czechoslovakia, and returned bearing his famous piece of paper. There was no Czech representative there, and no representative of the Soviet Union, which had offered its support to help defend Czechoslovakia.

'It is a tremendous victory for Herr Hitler,' Clem told the House of Commons. 'Without firing a shot, by the mere display of military force, he has achieved a dominating position in Europe which Germany failed to win after four years of war . . . He has destroyed the last fortress of democracy in Eastern Europe which stood in the way of his ambitions.'

As Clem was speaking, Hitler was increasing the supply of arms for Franco; and Spanish Prime Minister, Juan Negrin, was pondering a message from Chamberlain telling him to send home the International Brigades which Clem had visited the previous year, and which, Chamberlain had been told, were irritating Hitler and Mussolini. Negrin was looking into the abyss. His Cortes (Parliament) was meeting in the dungeons of the Castle of Figueras and Franco's armies were closing in on him. He lived in daily dread of being captured, or handed over to Franco as his troops defected to the winning side. Refugee camps were building up on the French side of the border. His only peace terms were that there should be no reprisals, and Franco refused those terms. He had nothing to negotiate with, and knew that his only hope was a general European war. So he did what Chamberlain asked, in the hope that Chamberlain might then ask Hitler to stop arming Franco. It did not, so far as anyone knows, ever occur to Chamberlain to raise the matter with Hitler. In February 1939, Chamberlain recognised the Franco regime as the legitimate government. He wrote in his diary: 'I think we ought to be able to establish excellent relations with Franco, who seems well disposed to us.'

Most people in the Labour Party recognised the urgency of ending the policy of appeasement, but there was a sharp division on how to do it. The left – headed again by Stafford Cripps – wanted to construct an alliance of all parties and individuals, including dissident Conservatives like Anthony Eden and Winston Churchill, against Chamberlain and appeasement. This United Front, said its supporters, would range 'from Churchill to Pollitt' (Harry Pollitt, leader of Britain's Communist Party). In January 1939, Cripps presented detailed proposals to Labour's National Executive. It turned them down, and decreed that Labour Party members must not advocate them. Cripps, Bevan and five others were expelled from the party for continuing to do so. The party conference in June confirmed the expulsions and rejected the United·Front. The idea was dead.

Expulsion is an extreme way of dealing with dissent in the Labour Party, only rarely used even under its most intolerant leaders. So why was it used now, under its most tolerant leader, and against Cripps of all people, who had been Clem's friend and ally, and whose personal generosity had sustained him just five years earlier? Clem could have been expected to agree with Bevan, who wrote to the Executive. 'If every organised effort to change Party policy is to be described as an organised attack on the Party itself, then the rigidity imposed by Party discipline will soon change into rigor mortis.' Surely Clem Attlee, who had preached in *The Labour Party in Perspective* a degree of toleration, could have ensured that the disagreement did not lead to hounding valuable people out of the party? True, some of them had used particularly insulting turns of phrase. The Labour Party always goes over the top in internal disputes. True, their campaign tended to blunt the leadership's campaign, but that, as Clem had often explained, was the price of being a democratic party. True, they were putting forward a point of view which did not square with the real world; privately Dalton, with Clem's authority, had made overtures to the potential Conservative rebels, confirming that they were not ready to come out openly against Chamberlain.

For whatever reason, the leader who managed to get most rebellions in proportion allowed this one to get under his skin. 'I don't much like direction from those who have entered our movement from the top,' he wrote to Tom. Cripps, 'like all the Potter family' (Cripps was related to Beatrice Webb, née Potter), 'is so absolutely convinced that the policy which he puts forward for the time being is absolutely right and will listen to no arguments.'

In February Clem wrote an article for the *Daily Herald* complaining of Cripps's 'apparent conviction that the inability of others "all to turn when father says turn" is due to blind obstinacy and narrowness of the mind.' His swift conversion 'from the advocacy of a rigid and exclusive unity of the working classes to a demand for an alliance with capitalists . . . is a remarkable phenomenon.'

The United Front, Clem argued, would ensure that socialism had no future.

A desire for unity on the left has been a constant feature of Liberalism. Thirty years ago socialists were accused of splitting the progressive vote. Amiable radicals have often put the plea to me 'if only you would drop socialism and join with us'.

It is assumed that the Labour Party cannot win a majority for its immediate programme. I do not accept this, although I admit that disruptive tactics and the preaching of defeatism has made that task more difficult . . . It is assumed that a majority can be obtained by Labour allying itself with Liberals, Communists and mugwumps on a non-socialist programme. I believe that any alliance with the Communists would be electorally disastrous . . .

In 1939 as in 1931 I reply to those who ask me to change my faith because times are difficult that socialism is not a fancy fair-weather creed but a faith.

Coming from Clem, this is tantamount to being incandescent with rage. He allowed a poem to be published, anonymously, in the *Daily Herald*. To the tune of 'The Red Flag', it went:

> The People's Flag is palest pink
> It's not blood red, but only ink.
> It's sponsored now by Douglas Cole
> Who plays each year a different role.
>
> Then raise our pallid standard high
> Wash out all trace of scarlet dye
> Let Liberals join and Tories too
> And socialists of every hue . . .
>
> With heads uncovered swear we all
> To have no principles at all
> If everyone will turn his coat
> We'll get the British people's vote.

In March 1939 Hitler occupied what remained of Czechoslovakia, which he had undertaken not to do, and immediately began threatening Poland. Chamberlain, cured too late of the notion that Hitler could be appeased, pledged protection to Poland. The next month, Mussolini invaded Albania. Attlee and Dalton met Chamberlain on 13 April and pressed him to announce a guarantee to Romania that day, and to draw the Soviet Union into the guarantee. Chamberlain claimed that the Poles and Romanians did not want to risk the Russians coming to defend them for fear they might not go away again. In the House that afternoon Labour Members pressed a reluctant Prime Minister on the question of working with the

Soviet Union. Chamberlain was furious, feeling apparently that Clem should have controlled his MPs, since the situation regarding the Soviet Union had been explained to him: 'Attlee behaved like the cowardly cur he is.'

Before the month was out Chamberlain had managed to wrong-foot Labour by introducing conscription. Clem thought this was of doubtful military value, and military conscription might pave the way for industrial conscription. But his opposition made it look as though Labour wanted to will the end but refused to will the means. 'I think we were probably wrong then,' he told journalist Mark Arnold-Forster, years later. 'But you must remember the hangover from the last war. The generals were given far too many men. They sacrificed men because they wouldn't use their brains. Didn't happen in the second war.' A few days later the Soviet Union proposed a triple alliance with Britain and France to guarantee the smaller states of Eastern Europe. Chamberlain sat on the Soviet proposal for three weeks, then refused to send anyone above the status of Foreign Office official to talk to the Russians. The reality – that Britain was going to *have* to work with the Soviet Union if it was to defeat the Central European dictators – had still not penetrated through to him, despite constant Labour pressure throughout May and the obvious unhappiness of many of his own side.

During this crucial period Clem's 'hydraulics' finally let him down and he had to be rushed to hospital. He had been unwell for most of the year. He was ill and off work for much of March and April – 'an annoying sort of flu which took a lot of time to shake off', he told Tom, but he had probably already been told his prostate trouble required an operation. By the time he arrived at Labour's conference in Southport on 29 May, he was in serious pain and could not appear at the conference until the Thursday, when, still obviously in pain, he made a short speech in which he insisted that you cannot have one policy for foreign affairs and another one for home affairs. 'I want us to devote ourselves to making people realise that if they want peace abroad they must have social justice at home.' He knew that his operation could not be delayed any more. Tom read that he was ill and dashed off a concerned letter: he had had a prostate operation himself the previous year, and suspected that Clem had the same trouble. A swift response, on 4 June 1939, confirmed his fears:

You are right in supposing that it is the family trouble. I had been wanting to get it dealt with for some time but could not find a quiet period. I had arranged to go into a clinic this week anyway but a spot of trouble at Southport precipitated matters. I got a chill on the bladder which induced a temperature and considerable pain in the JT. I am being done by Clifford Morson of Thomason who is one of the leading experts in this direction and am going into the London Clinic which is I believe very convenient. I shall hope to be fit to convalesce by the time the House rises and shall go with the family to Wales. Southport went off very well, an excellent tone.

At once there was an almost comical attempt to topple him. Ellen Wilkinson, who had taken so much trouble to ensure that her support for Morrison in 1935 was secret, wrote an extraordinary article for the *Sunday Referee*, a lively paper mostly concerned with the romantic entanglements of film stars. She began by mourning the foolishness of Cripps in getting himself expelled from the party: 'Stars are as necessary to a political party as to a film . . . A debate in which it is known that Chamberlain, Churchill, Lloyd George, Herbert Morrison and Stafford Cripps will speak fills the House.' In 1931, she reminded her readers, all Labour's stars lost their seats.

Mr Attlee was a quiet London member who had been Postmaster General. After Lansbury, Cripps was the biggest figure in His Majesty's Opposition. When Mr Lansbury broke his thigh and was in hospital for months the leadership was offered to Cripps, a fact few know . . . He persuaded Mr Attlee to take it instead – a decision which has altered subsequent history.

Thousands are watching Cripps and saying 'what next?' I shall astonish them if I say that Cripps is a bad leader but a magnificent lieutenant. But serving with a leader who has just that background, whose fingers are on the pulse of the real political life of this country, one who can use Cripps' dynamic enthusiasm to drive the engine instead of blowing up the boiler – then Labour would find in him a great asset.

I wonder what Mr Chamberlain would think if he were informed that in future he would have to face daily a Herbert Morrison, that superb political organiser, at last induced to give to the Front Opposition Bench the gifts that have made him such an administrative success in the LCC, and with him a corps of lieutenants like Dalton, Greenwood and the brilliant, hitherto erratic Cripps, now welded into a working team.

She wrote a further article for *Time and Tide* anonymously which attacked Clem much more directly:

If Labour will not give a lead through the Popular Front, then who will give a lead to the country through the Labour Party? Mr Attlee was unfortunately on a sickbed through most of the conference. The news of his illness was received by the delegates with due sympathy. Clearly no one expected his absence to make the slightest difference to the conference. Nor did it.

Now this is serious . . . The man who led the Conference on all the main issues – the Popular Front, ARP, National Service – was Mr Herbert Morrison, with Dr Hugh Dalton as an able lieutenant. Mr Morrison is Labour's biggest personal asset. He has great achievements to his credit. His work in London is known all over the country . . . Mr Attlee does not command that authority. It would be doing no service to Labour to pretend, for the sake of politeness, that he does . . .

If Labour, more united now within itself than for a long time, is prepared to give the country a leader it trusts, then the country – thoroughly disillusioned by the Chamberlain fiascos – may turn its way.

The editor of the *Daily Herald*, Francis Williams, took the same line, though rather more circumspectly, as befitted a man who must answer to Ernest Bevin:

Can the Labour Movement bring to the political scene during the next few months before the General Election the vigorous urge which will rouse the nation to a new political awareness and a new determination? I believe, after the Southport conference, that it can . . . Internal dissensions are at an end . . . Even those who voted for the popular front recognised after the debate that they had participated in the burial of a ghost.

This was because of 'the masterly statement of the case against the Popular Front by Herbert Morrison and Hugh Dalton's superb reply to Cripps'. But still the nation needed to be convinced of Labour's capacity to lead. And leadership 'is at this moment shown pre-eminently in the commanding position in public respect which has been achieved by Herbert Morrison through the great qualities of courageous and imaginative leadership he has brought to the control of London.' Attlee was not mentioned. The message was clear.

Greenwood decided this could not be ignored. The next week at Labour's Executive he complained that, while the leader was ill, a Labour MP had cast doubts on his capacity. Wilkinson made a poor show of defending herself; Morrison said he had nothing to do with the article and would have opposed it had he known about it, and the NEC passed a vote of confidence in Clem, Ellen Wilkinson

151

abstaining. Clem, at home ill, seems to have taken his usual casual approach. His family had no idea anything was going on. It is hard to think of another senior politician who switched off at home so easily, and who in similar circumstances would not have been eaten up with worry. He told Kenneth Harris years later: 'Dalton wouldn't have backed Morrison, Morrison wouldn't have backed Cripps, and Cripps wouldn't have backed Dalton. The PLP wouldn't have let Greenwood go, and Greenwood was loyal to me.'

Though Morrison's love affair with Wilkinson was more or less common knowledge, Clem did not think Morrison had put her up to it: 'He talked a lot about how well he could do things, and younger people sometimes thought he talked that way because he was encouraging them to try and make him leader. But he talked that way because he was vain. He liked the sound of his own voice.' He was not short of reassurances from colleagues, with the usual mixture of genuine affection and loyalty and a natural desire to be on the right side of a man who might soon have ministerial jobs to hand out. 'The one thing I want to let you know', wrote Emanuel Shinwell, who had defeated Ramsay MacDonald to become MP for Seaham in 1935, 'is that some of us are quite capable of looking after your interests while you are away. There is nothing you need worry about, keep that in your mind all the time.'

John Jagger confessed to 'a very real personal regard and respect for you . . . It's not the kind of thing one says to a colleague under ordinary circumstances.' Jagger was a much respected trade union MP ten years older than Clem and, more significantly, Ellen Wilkinson's closest friend in Parliament after Morrison. He was also the one person who had spoken in her defence over her recent articles. 'May you soon be back in your old place at the head of the movement,' wrote George Lansbury, while Neville Chamberlain, a strange, stiff man, wrote a strange, stiff note: 'Although we differ on politics I hope that does not exclude sympathy on other subjects . . .'

Clem went to convalesce on the farm at Nevin in North Wales where they had enjoyed recent family holidays. He was sitting on the Nevin sands with his children when, on 23 August 1939, Hitler and Stalin signed a non-aggression pact. He was on the golf course when, on 1 September 1939, Hitler sent armoured divisions and planes into Poland; and he was back on the beach the next day when a shocked House of Commons heard the Prime Minister talk about offering Hitler another time limit to stop bombing the Poles.

Clem told Greenwood to protest furiously that Britain had not yet fulfilled its obligations to Poland, and after the debate Greenwood followed the Prime Minister to his room to tell him the House of Commons would not tolerate a delay in declaring war beyond the next day.

Greenwood was taking no steps without consulting his leader. Consulting his leader, was, however, not as simple as you might imagine. There was no telephone in the farmhouse. In the midst of these great events, the leader of the opposition was calmly convalescing in a farmhouse with no telephone. He was reading John Buchan's *Greenmantle* to his children, and giving no sign that he had anything at all on his mind. His daughter Felicity knew only that the postman kept arriving with telegrams, to which he sometimes sent a reply. One telegram was eaten by Ting the family dog before Clem could get to it. The children rescued it from Ting's mouth and pieced it together so that their father could read it. It said: 'War imminent. Arthur.' Felicity also noticed that he occasionally slipped out quietly, and speculates that perhaps he was going to the public telephone in the little town of Nevin, a few hundred yards away.

Clem was on the beach again when, on 3 September, Britain declared war on Germany. That evening he carried on reading aloud to his children – he wanted to finish *Greenmantle* before going back to work. 'He was always amazing at not showing he was worried,' says Felicity. They discussed how the war would change their lives. They would have to go back to Stanmore the next day, and then the children would have to leave London, because they expected London to be heavily bombed. Vi sent a telegram to St Felix's in Southwold, which the oldest daughter Janet already attended, to say that Felicity was to start there at once, and told Felicity how exciting it would be to go to boarding school. Martin was sent back to his Sussex prep school, and the youngest, Alison, stayed in Wales with one of Vi's sisters, who lived ten miles from Nevin.

Chamberlain brought Churchill and Eden into the government, but Clem and Greenwood were clear that Labour would not serve under him, because Chamberlain was the wrong man to lead the country through the war. Some of their colleagues saw things differently. Herbert Morrison had a strange talk with a Foreign Office official who summarised it in a memorandum for his superiors that probably reached the Prime Minister. He said that an opposition could only be dispensed with if 'those who composed it could bring exceptional and valuable gifts to a coalition government. Frankly, this was not the case with the present opposition and he [Morrison] doubted whether there were half a dozen members of it who could add anything in strength or decision to the present government. Most of the Labour Front Bench, he said, were frightened of power and few were capable of drive . . . He thought [Chamberlain] could carry it through and doubted whether there was a better man.'

It sounds like MacDonald complaining to Bevin of 'the low mental calibre of those I have to work with'. Morrison seems to have hoped that Chamberlain might bring him, rather than his leader, into a senior position in his government.

On 17 September Stalin invaded Poland from the east. On 20 September Clem returned to work, though still not completely fit, and a week later advocated in the House of Commons that there should be a small War Cabinet whose members were free of departmental responsibilities. Before the month was out Poland had effectively ceased to exist, carved up between Hitler and Stalin. By mid-December, Britain was having to contemplate war against the Soviet Union as well as against Nazi Germany. Clem supported the government in its decision to send troops to defend Finland against Stalin, but Finnish resistance collapsed in March 1940, before British and French troops reached the country.

By the beginning of 1940 Clem was fully fit again, which was fortunate, because 1940 was to test him as he had never been tested before. He started the year by visiting the British Expeditionary Force in France, flying to Amiens and picnicking with British officers in the snow on one of the coldest days of that very cold winter. Tom's son Patrick was commanding an anti-aircraft battery nearby, and he was invited to dinner with his increasingly famous uncle.

Clem found that there was no adequate reserve to reinforce whatever sector of the line the Germans might attack. And because Belgium still hoped to remain neutral, it was not possible to dig in on Belgian soil. What was to happen if, as in the First World War, Germany decided to march through Belgium? His next trip to France the following month was equally disturbing. This time he went to Paris with Dalton and Philip Noel-Baker for a meeting at Léon Blum's apartment. He found most of the French socialists – though not Blum himself – were either pacifists or believed that defeat was inevitable.

He came back with renewed determination that Chamberlain must go and that a government must be installed which had the energy and imagination to fight and win a war. Prime Minister and opposition leader seldom talked, partly because Clem was waiting his moment to pounce, partly because they never liked each other, and Clem found Chamberlain uncommunicative and irritated by criticism. So Labour's impatience in this 'phoney war' period frequently found expression on the floor of the House.

How, Labour wanted to know, could Britain still have 900,000 unemployed after eight months of war? What was being done for the Danes and Norwegians? To Clem this was more than a political question. 'Just at the moment I find it difficult to think of anything except the tragic plight of the Danes and the Norwegians,' he wrote to Tom; 'I hate to think of the decent civilised kindly Scandinavians being in the hands of the SS men. I have no doubt that the Danes will be cruelly plundered of everything worth taking just as the Czechs have been . . . Our garden is very jolly with daffodils just now. I have handed over our field to allotment holders whose president I am. They are digging earnestly every evening.'

Many Liberals were also convinced that Chamberlain must go. A leading Liberal, Clement Davies, convened several secret meetings between Labour leaders and dissident Conservatives aimed at a joint initiative to replace him. The moment to do the deed came in May, with the fall of Norway. Clem delivered an attack on the whole conduct of the war. The message was harsh and uncompromising. Chamberlain must go.

'People are saying that those mainly responsible for the conduct of affairs are men who have had an almost uninterrupted career of failure,' he told the House.

> . . . They see everywhere a failure of grip, a failure of drive, not only in the field of defence and foreign policy, but in industry. The government are not organising the resources of the country . . . I say that there is a widespread feeling in this country, not that we shall lose the war, that we will win the war, but that to win the war we want different people at the helm from those who have led us into it.

Even more wounding for the Prime Minister was to find that many Conservatives agreed. Leo Amery famously echoed Oliver Cromwell: 'You have sat here too long for any good you have been doing. Depart, I say, and let us have done with you. In the name of God, go!' After the debate Clem recommended to the Parliamentary Labour Party that it should force a division the next day. He told them that it must clearly be understood as a vote of censure, and that if Labour forced a change of government, Labour would have to help create a new one.

Thirty-three Conservatives voted against the government and sixty abstained. The government majority had been cut from 200 to eighty-one. Chamberlain still seems to have hoped that Labour would make it possible for him to carry on as Prime Minister by agreeing to serve under him. Clem and Greenwood went to Downing Street to talk to him the next day, Thursday 9 May, and swiftly disabused him of this notion.

Chamberlain, his Foreign Secretary, Halifax and Lord of the Admiralty Winston Churchill sat on one side of the table and the two Labour men on the other. 'It was not a pleasant task to tell a Prime Minister that he ought to go, but I had no option but to tell him the truth,' Clem wrote in his autobiography. Would Labour serve under another Prime Minister? 'I said that I thought they would, but that as the Party was holding its annual conference at Bournemouth I would go down and ask the delegates. It was accordingly agreed that I should put to them two questions: (1) Would they enter a Government under the present Prime Minister? (2) Would they then come in under another Prime Minister?' To some Labour leaders, the idea of asking the conference what to do at a moment of national crisis would have seemed weak. But Clem knew his party. He did not ask questions until he was sure of getting the right answer. It was worth a few days' delay, because having their endorsement in his pocket made him much stronger.

That day Germany invaded Holland and Belgium, and on Friday 10 May Clem took a train to Bournemouth and met the National Executive at the Highcliffe Hotel. As he expected – he would have been horrified to receive any other answer – they unanimously gave him a 'no' to the first question and a 'yes' to the second. Chamberlain telephoned. Clem gave him the answer, and returned to London at once. Chamberlain had anticipated the answer. Clem's attitude at their meeting had the intended effect. Before his call to Bournemouth, he had summoned Halifax and Churchill – the only possible alternative Prime Ministers. Winston Churchill wrote:

> He told us that he was satisfied that it was beyond his power to form a National Government. The response he had received from the Labour leaders left him in no doubt of this. The question therefore was whom he should advise the King to send for . . . As I remained silent, a very long pause ensued. It certainly seemed longer than the two minutes which one observes in the commemorations of Armistice Day. Then at length Halifax spoke. He said that he felt his position as a peer,

out of the House of Commons, would make it very difficult for him to discharge the duties of Prime Minister in a war like this . . . He spoke for some minutes in this sense, and by the time he had finished it was clear that the duty would fall upon me – had in fact fallen upon me.

Was it really as simple as that – that Halifax felt that a peer could not do the job properly? Nothing in politics is ever that simple. The movement to get rid of Chamberlain had been going on ever since the declaration of war, nine months earlier, and there had been plenty of time for plotting and gossiping. Chamberlain preferred Halifax, and among Chamberlain's friends grew the rumour that Labour, too, would prefer Halifax, because they had never forgiven Churchill for ordering troops to fire on striking Welsh miners in the early 1920s. But this was quite wrong, and Clem had, in his discreet way, made sure that key people knew it was wrong. Clem preferred Churchill – not because Churchill had been right about this war, but because Churchill had been right about the last war. Major Attlee, the Gallipoli veteran, believed that Churchill's Gallipoli plan had been a brilliant strategic concept, frustrated by stupid generals unable to think beyond the idea of flinging millions of men out of Flanders trenches and into hails of German bullets. He believed Churchill was the man to win the war. He could not say so publicly. He could not insist that Churchill got the job, and he would have served under Halifax. But what little could be done by discreet conversation, he had done. 'Queer bird, Halifax,' he said in one of those asides which his colleagues started to treasure; 'very humorous, all hunting and Holy Communion.'

Clem arrived in London from Bournemouth at 9 pm. There was a message for him at Waterloo station to go straight to Admiralty House and meet the new Prime Minister. Churchill and Attlee had never worked together, but now these two very different men had to learn to do so quickly. Both of them wanted to announce the membership of a War Cabinet and the Service Ministers at once. France might fall at any moment, and Clem was determined not to hold things up by bargaining over offices; for Major Attlee, First World War veteran, remembered how vital decisions were delayed during the Dardanelles campaign while Conservatives and Liberals bargained for places in Asquith's coalition of 1915. They talked well into the night. The War Cabinet, they decided, should consist of three Conservatives, Churchill, Chamberlain and Halifax, and two Labour men, Attlee and Greenwood. Only Halifax, the Foreign

Secretary, should have a departmental responsibility, though Attlee was to be Lord Privy Seal, and Churchill took the additional title of Minister of Defence. Throughout Friday night and Saturday they settled the other appointments. Churchill proposed, and Clem at once agreed, that Labour should have a little over a third of the posts in the government.

On Monday, Labour's conference officially began, and Clem had to convince delegates who had not been a party to these great events that he had done the right thing. By Clem's standards it was an emotional and almost ornate speech. 'Life without liberty is not worth living. Let us go forward and win that liberty, and establish that liberty for ever on the sure foundation of social justice.'

Listening to the debate that followed, one might have had the impression that the vote was on a knife edge. But, as so often at Labour conferences, the debate gave no clue as to the real result. Labour's leaders knew that the big trade unions were going to cast their block votes in favour of going into the government, and that when the House of Commons met that afternoon, Clem Attlee would be sitting beside Winston Churchill on the Treasury Bench.

6

Mr Attlee has a Word with the PM

The war brought to the surface the iron in Clem Attlee's soul. It is doubtful if more than half a dozen people in the whole country were aware of it at the time, but Cabinet papers reveal a ruthlessness which had not been evident before.

Three weeks after Labour joined the government, Britain was frantically scooping up its exhausted and demoralised army from Dunkirk's beaches. A fortnight later, on 17 June 1940, the new French government of Marshal Pétain asked Hitler for an armistice, and Britain faced a summer of German bombing and the near certainty of invasion. It was a shock. For nine months after the declaration of war, not a lot had seemed to be happening. All people saw of the war were restrictions and regulations in anticipation of air raids which never came. The resulting black-out doubled road deaths in the winter of 1939, and brought fines for the odd chink of light which could not have been of the slightest use to a bomber, even if there had been any bombers. Schoolchildren were evacuated from cities in September 1939, but by January 1940 half of them had been sent home. Appeals to dig trenches, and to put on the gas masks issued by the government, fell on deaf ears.

Now, suddenly, there was mortal danger, and Britain did not feel equipped for it. People talk about 'the Dunkirk spirit' as though it was one of unalloyed heroism: 'Men of the undefeated British Expeditionary Force have been coming home from France . . . Their morale is as high as ever. They are anxious . . . to have a real crack at Jerry,' announces the newsreader.

The reality was quire different: soldiers felt let down, both by the French army and by their own leaders. They had not been trained or equipped to withstand being shelled, dive-bombed and machine-gunned by low-flying aircraft, night and day. Civilians looked sourly at the sacrifices which were to be demanded of them, and asked whether the rich would this time be making the same sacrifices. John Betjeman captured the public suspicion in his portrayal of a wealthy woman praying in Westminster Abbey in 1940:

> Gracious Lord, oh bomb the Germans.
> Spare their women for thy sake,
> And if that is not too easy
> We will pardon thy mistake.
> But gracious Lord, whate'er shall be
> Don't let anyone bomb me . . .
>
> Think of what our Nation stands for,
> Books from Boots' and country lanes,
> Free speech, free passes, class distinction,
> Democracy and proper drains.
> Lord, put beneath thy special care
> One-eighty-nine Cadogan Square.
>
> Although dear Lord I am a sinner,
> I have done no major crime.
> Now I'll come to evening service
> Whensoever I have the time.
> So, Lord, reserve for me a crown,
> And do not let my shares go down . . .

Mass Observation took the temperature of civilian morale. Its reports were full of verbatim quotes such as 'If France and Britain can't do it together, I don't see what we can do alone'; 'It looks as though all we can do is give up. It's no use throwing away lives when there's no hope.' The reason for going to war was to defend Poland, and Poland had fallen. Hitler had swallowed Denmark, Norway, Holland, Belgium, Luxembourg and France, and Britain was next on his menu. The undignified scramble from Dunkirk's beaches did not suggest that Britain was going to be able to do much about it. The new Prime Minister was bitterly resented by most of his Conservative colleagues. That first day, with the Labour leader sitting beside him, when Winston Churchill promised the House of Commons 'blood, sweat, toil and tears', only Labour MPs cheered. The Conservatives remained sullenly silent behind him for nearly two months. The new government had to turn round civilian morale. Churchill was not a man of the people. He was sixty-eight, a Victorian, the scion of dukes. He went on the radio and sounded like a man from another age and another class. He called the Nazis 'a monstrous tyranny never surpassed' (shur-parshed) 'in the dark, lamentable catalogue of human crime'. And everyone loved hearing Churchill say it.

But morale alone was not going to win the war. Most of Britain's weapons had been left behind in France. In that desperate summer, Churchill went outside the political circle, appointing men to two key jobs, one of whom had never even been a Member of Parliament. The newspaper proprietor Lord Beaverbrook became Minister of Aircraft Production, and Ernest Bevin, General Secretary of the Transport and General Workers' Union, became Minister of Labour and National Service.

Bevin had been ill and was on the point of retirement (he would be sixty in 1941). He had said of Churchill in 1929: 'It is not safe to leave the destinies of millions of people in the hands of a man with an unstable mind.' But Churchill knew what he was doing. Bevin had none of the inhibitions of his Conservative predecessor in demanding power to direct all the country's labour. To him, the rights of private business had never been sacrosanct. He wanted power to turn strategic decisions into production programmes, and allocate labour accordingly. And in order to make the workers' sacrifices palatable, he demanded that the Cabinet should guarantee to restore pre-war arrangements when peace came, to raise wages for agricultural workers, and to improve the Unemployment Insurance Scheme.

Beaverbrook and Bevin, together with Herbert Morrison who was Minister of Supply, led a race to equip the fighting services, and especially the air force, before Hitler invaded or the bombing began. When Ernest Bevin demanded that workers should give up the few hard-won advantages they had gained in the last twenty years, he was listened to as no-one else would have been. They gave up holidays, bank holidays, days off, and worked twelve-hour shifts. And when Beaverbrook, the most strident and dogmatic free marketeer of his time, brusquely commandeered privately-owned factories, the complaints of industrialists could be safely ignored; for once they were unlikely to get into the newspapers. That was part of Beaverbrook's value to Churchill – he could nip 'unhelpful' press coverage in the bud. The former Foreign Secretary, Sir Samuel Hoare, who had been sent to Madrid on a special mission to reassure General Franco, complained to Churchill that newspapers were attacking him and Franco. Churchill sent him a telegram in July: 'Do not be disturbed by attacks mentioned. Am consulting Max [Beaverbrook] about best way to deal with papers.' The message came back from the Ministry of Aircraft Production: 'It is Lord Beaverbrook's view that these attacks on Sir Samuel Hoare are unwarranted and cause a great deal of injury. He proposes to discuss the matter with some of the other newspaper proprietors.' He instructed the *Daily Express* editor not to run any more 'unfriendly and trouble-making' articles about General Franco.

He also had to keep his own indiscretions out of the newspapers. A few weeks before he joined the government, 'the Beaver', in his restless search for amusement, had invited to dinner the three remaining ILP MPs, led still by Jimmy Maxton, and now the only group in Parliament opposed to the war. He had a proposal. The three main parties had agreed not to contest by-elections during the war. The Beaver offered the ILP £500 per by-election and plenty of space in his newspapers, if they would fight *every* by-election. One of them told the story publicly, and questions were asked in Parliament, but not a word appeared in the press. When Beaverbrook's *Evening Standard* printed an article by Fred Copeman, who had fought for the Republicans in Spain, Beaverbrook sent the editor of the *Express*, E. J. Robertson, to read the riot act in the *Standard* office to his rather wild young men there, including the youthful Michael Foot. 'There will be no more articles by Copeman,' Robertson reported back grimly.

The *News Chronicle* incurred Beaverbrook's and Churchill's wrath by speculating on the views of Cabinet Ministers. Its editor wrote a grovelling letter of apology to Churchill, receiving this magisterial rebuke in reply: 'It is always a mistake to attribute particular attitudes to individual ministers in respect of their secret discussions in the cabinet . . .'

Beaverbrook revelled in the use of his great power for its own sake, and could generally bring to heel not just his own papers but those of Lord Rothermere as well. He was opposed to censorship, and with him around it was hardly necessary. As Aneurin Bevan jeered: 'You don't need to muzzle sheep.' And indeed, only the Communist *Daily Worker* was actually suppressed.

With Beaverbrook looking after the press, Churchill turned his attention to the radio, a medium on which he has had a lasting impact. 'Should the invader come,' said Churchill in a broadcast of 14 July, 'there will be no placid lying down in submission before him as we have seen in other countries. The vast mass of London itself, fought street by street, could easily devour an entire hostile army and we would rather see London laid in ashes and ruins than that it should be tamely and abjectly enslaved.'

Mr Attlee has a Word with the PM

Whether the invasion would come by sea, by air, or by dropping parachute troops, no-one knew. Dunes and cliffs were implanted with concrete gun emplacements, huge rolls of barbed wire covered the coast, and no-one was allowed within ten miles of it. Summer holidays were unknown in 1940. Rumours abounded. German fifth-columnists were supposed to be everywhere, and not only British fascists but also continental refugees – many of them Jews who had fled from Hitler – were rounded up and interned. Yet if there was a fifth column, it was remarkably ill-informed. Hitler never realised how ill-defended Britain was. If he had, he would surely have invaded.

At the height of the summer of 1940 – a glorious summer, as sunny as anyone could remember – the cloudless sky was suddenly darkened by German fighters. Britain's planes fought them in the skies above southern England throughout that month. Even Churchill later admitted that there were days that summer when he awoke 'with dread in my heart'. But the Germans were losing two aeroplanes for every one British loss, and on 17 September Hitler postponed the invasion indefinitely. Instead, the Luftwaffe was to bomb Britain's cities and civilians into submission. The blitz lasted from September 1940 until May 1941 and left huge swathes of many of Britain's cities in heaps of rubble.

Where was Clem Attlee while these great events were going on? He had almost dropped from public view while his colleagues – Churchill and Beaverbrook, Bevin and Morrison – were ever more visible. Clem's official title was uninspiring: Lord Privy Seal. But in all but name he was deputy Prime Minister. While Churchill busied himself with the war, and travelled constantly, Clem looked after the shop. Behind the scenes his voice was often crucial, and never more so than just before the fall of France. French Prime Minister Paul Reynaud wanted Britain to try to negotiate a general peace with Hitler. The War Cabinet met in the Prime Minister's room in the Palace of Westminster. Halifax and Chamberlain saw it as the only way to avert disaster, and pressed Churchill strongly to agree. Churchill's response, though determined, hardly had the ring of confidence: '[Hitler's] terms would put us completely at his mercy. We should get no worse terms if we went on fighting, even if we were beaten, than were open to us now.' Greenwood and Attlee opposed a negotiated peace. Attlee spoke first. If negotiations began 'we should find it impossible to rally the morale of the

163

people'. Greenwood followed, calling the idea a 'disaster'. The idea was dead.

Clem never once allowed for the idea of a negotiated peace. He spoke for the government when the ILP called for one, sharply rebuking his old friend Jimmy Maxton whom he now considered to be thoroughly irresponsible. He led the pressure within the War Cabinet for a statement of war aims, fearing that without them there might be renewed agitation for a negotiated peace. It was he – with Churchill's support and Greenwood's help – who reorganised the machinery of government, doing away with dozens of committees which he considered had been used by lazy and indecisive Ministers as a means of passing the buck. In an unpublished fragment of autobiography he wrote that the machine was infected with the all-pervading influence of Sir Horace Wilson. 'We proceeded to scrap most of the committees.' It was Clem, more often than not, who took Prime Minister's questions, who arranged day-to-day House of Commons business. He instituted the Lord President's Committee, which took decisions on home front matters which did not have to go to the Cabinet. He insisted that there should be a reconstruction committee to make sure that life after the war really was going to be better – even at the moment when it looked as though life after the war might not be the concern of any elected British government. He even brokered an uneasy peace between an angry and suspicious Prime Minister and the *Daily Mirror* – the one paper in which Lord Beaverbrook's writ did not run. This soon broke down, and in any case did not stop Churchill from secretly instructing Scotland Yard to find out who had ultimate financial control, so that he and Beaverbrook would know whom to pressurise.

Only Attlee and Churchill were in the War Cabinet from start to finish, and Clem did the nuts-and-bolts work required to keep the government together. There was a constant need to reassure Labour people that Labour had not sold its soul, its principles and its future for a few seats in the War Cabinet. There was a need to reassure Conservative backbenchers. There was a need to manage the temperamental Churchill – not an easy task at any time, and supremely difficult when Churchill had the burden of the war on him. A typical example of this burden is reflected in the Prime Minister's papers for July 1940. Two conscientious objectors had taken their protest so far as to refuse even to register as objectors. Bevin, as Labour Minister responsible, decided they were harmless enough, and took the initiative and registered them, rather than see them go to prison. The Prime Minister got to hear of it, and Bevin received a furious missive: 'Why should men who have taken the most contumacious attitude . . . receive special consideration and special favour . . .' Two days later, a relieved civil servant sent the papers back to the Ministry: 'I understand that Mr Attlee has had a word with the Prime Minister as a result of which no further action is called for.' Clem was the administrator, the conciliator, the greaser of wheels, the reassuringly commonsense figure at the heart of government, and there were many times in the next four years when it was necessary for Mr Attlee to have a word with the Prime Minister. (And he understood conscientious objectors from his brother Tom: he once intervened at his brother's request and an internee was released.)

Right from the start – as a Churchill aide told Hugh Dalton – 'if CRA digs his heels in he will win'. Dalton was the first beneficiary of this. He was desperately anxious to have the role of Minister of Economic Warfare, for which Clem recommended him, but Brendan Bracken, a close crony of Churchill's, disliked Dalton and raised several objections. Dalton waited in desperation and hope for the call that never came. At last Clem told him he would beard the Prime Minister about it yet again. Dalton wrote to the First Lord of the Admiralty, Labour's A. V. Alexander: 'Clem says he will stand firm tomorrow. I hope you will back him up. Clem stood firm and Dalton got the job.

But Clem used his influence selectively. When necessary he dug his heels in. On lesser matters he was as likely just to drag his feet a little, or simply to do things the way the right-wingers around Churchill wanted them done. Sir Samuel Hoare wrote to Churchill in November 1940: 'Some time ago you invited our Labour friends to moderate the *Daily Herald* attacks on Neville Chamberlain. I have to some extent taken his place . . . You might think it wise to make our Labour colleagues do something about it.' There is no record of what, if anything, was said, but the *Herald* line on Spain seems to have softened a little.

Hoare also had strong views about the presence of Juan Negrin in England. In September 1939 the former Prime Minister of Republican Spain had fled for his life from Franco's victorious armies to Paris, from where he sent a handwritten letter to a fellow social democrat, the only senior British politician he felt he knew well enough to approach:

Dear Mr Attlee,

Upon the declaration of war my first thought is to serve the democratic countries in their struggle with Germany and I have learned something in doing so [sic]. I have no desire to be in the public eye or to occupy any position. I want to embarrass no one. But as a Spanish Republican and in the interests of my country I wish to do my best against totalitarianism. I would appreciate a word from you on this matter.

When France fell, Negrin fled again, this time to London. Within days, terrified that Franco might enter the war, Sir Samuel Hoare was writing to the Foreign Secretary: 'Great harm is being done in Spain by Negrin's presence in London. I assured [one of Franco's ministers] that Negrin as an alien would be under close supervision, would be prohibited from political activities, and would leave England in about a week. May I rely on you to see that these conditions are fulfilled?' Halifax came up with the happy notion of suggesting that Negrin might like to spend some time in the USA – and that the best person to make the suggestion was Clem Attlee. Clem met Negrin, and Negrin agreed reluctantly to apply for a US visa, writing to Clem: 'I consider the decision taken not only morally wrong and unfair, but what is much worse, as being a tremendous political mistake . . .' Personally, Clem probably agreed, and if his role in the affair became known, it would cause major problems with the Labour Party.

The USA refused Negrin a visa, and he seems to have spent the next few months helping the Admiralty, which was run by Clem's Labour colleague A. V. Alexander, with some experiments in which his scientific training may have come in useful. Perhaps this was Clem's answer to Negrin's request to be given an unobtrusive role in the war effort. He lived quietly in Bovingdon in Hertfordshire, and wrote the occasional friendly letter to Clem. But in November Halifax himself met Negrin and put pressure on him to go to South America or New Zealand. It seems likely that Clem was asked to make this suggestion, and declined. Negrin made it clear that he had no wish to visit either place, and stayed in Britain throughout the war, to Sir Samuel Hoare's constant irritation. Negrin's letters congratulating Clem on each and every allied victory are still in the Negrin file kept by Clem. So too are his letters each time Franco captured another of his former colleagues, and copies of Clem's own letters to the Foreign Office asking for a protest to be made. In one case, an irritated Sir Samuel Hoare wrote back to the Foreign Secretary that he was assured the man was not in Spain: 'If this be so it shows once again that Dr Negrin has been attempting to spread rumours for his own purposes.' Hoare, of course, was the Foreign Secretary who in 1935 had signed the Hoare-Laval Pact agreeing that Italy could carve up Abyssinia, and Clem must have realised that Hoare had 'gone native' in Franco's capital.

In 1942 Negrin wrote to Clem inviting him for lunch in his London flat to discuss a matter which 'can not be put in writing'. Clem asked the Foreign Secretary, by now Anthony Eden, who advised against the meeting because news of it might leak and feed Franco's paranoia about British intentions. So Clem wrote Negrin a polite letter declining. A week later he left for Canada and his private secretary wrote again to Negrin. Clem's real reason for not seeing him, he said, was the trip to Canada: 'For security reasons Mr Attlee was unable to explain fully at the time.' No doubt Clem found out what Negrin wanted to say, but sadly, as with many other episodes, he left no record of it in the file. Negrin stayed in England until France was liberated, and then returned to Paris. He resigned as Prime Minister in exile in 1945, hoping that his resignation would unite the exiles, and died in Paris in 1956.

Like Churchill, but to more mundane purposes, Clem broadcast to the nation. He wrote to Tom that it was 'no easy thing, to follow such an artist. I eschew embroidery and stick to a plain statement.' When the government took to itself potentially dictatorial powers, in the 1940 Emergency Powers Act, which gave Ernest Bevin authority 'to direct any person in the United Kingdom to perform such services' as he might require them to perform, Clem presented the measure, first to Parliament, then to the British people via the radio.

'Today, on your behalf,' he told radio listeners

> Parliament has given to the government full power to control all persons and property . . . This does not mean that everyone must give up what he is doing, or that everyone's property will be seized . . . It has power to control any business, factory, mine, shop or bank. It can take property of every kind . . . Excess profits duty will be at the rate of 100 per cent . . . These very wide powers will be exercised by the competent authority, the appropriate minister . . . The central direction for persons to perform services will be under the Minister of Labour, Mr Ernest Bevin . . .

Clem Attlee

In the sonorous tones of a Churchill this might have sent shivers down the spine, but not coming as it did from Clem's rather precise, schoolmasterish tones. A man who pedantically pronounces the name of the Soviet leader as 'Marshal Sta-leen' and from whom the word 'retrospect' comes out as 'ree-trospect' could not, one felt, be a potential tyrant.

With the Labour leader in the Cabinet, someone had to lead the Opposition. In his autobiography Clem describes the solution: 'In making my recommendation to the Prime Minister I had thought it necessary to leave out some of our older leaders. They were therefore available to lead the Party in the House.' Those who think Clem did not have the ruthlessness to run a government should read those words again and contemplate their cruel, understated finality. The undistinguished H. B. Lees-Smith became leader of the opposition, and asked mostly undemanding questions of Ministers.

Early in the war Clem moved into 11 Downing Street, the traditional home of the Chancellor of the Exchequer, the Prime Minister's closest colleague in peacetime. The Chancellor continued to occupy the ground floor. Clem had an office on the first floor, overlooking the Prime Minister's garden, with a desk, a large conference table, and maps all over the walls. One floor further up he had a bedroom which Felicity thought rather severe, with a miserable-looking single bed in it. But at least he did not live like the workaholic Herbert Morrison, who slept each night on a camp bed in the bomb-proof basement of his Ministry, and ate his 1940 Christmas dinner at his desk.

Clem lived a busy bachelor life, rising at 7.30 am and walking across St James's Park to breakfast at the Oxford and Cambridge Club, which he had joined in the late Thirties. He would be back at the club for dinner at around 8.30 or 9 pm before returning to work, to listen to the midnight news bulletin, and to go to bed. He kept up his old interests, for even at his busiest Clem was not a Morrison, with no life outside politics. 'Thanks to a Tory MP', he wrote to Tom in 1942, 'I have contacted a young South African cousin Dennis Attlee great grandson of Uncle John now serving as an AB in the South African navy, a pleasant lad with a considerable family look about him. I am about to take him to dine at the Club.' He saw less of his family than ever, only getting to Stanmore for an occasional weekend, and even then generally only seeing Vi, because the children had been sent out of London to boarding schools. They spent these few evenings as they had always done, Vi curled up at his feet as Clem read, or sitting opposite him, or handing him her wool to unravel. But these evenings were rare. At the start of the coalition government, Vi was suddenly alone, with neither Clem nor the children about her. The cat had just had kittens which helped relieve her loneliness, and she became the local Red Cross commandant, and was out regularly on night-duty during the blitz. Clem worried about her. 'She is rather tired', he wrote to Tom, 'as owing to our only domestic help getting married and our old gardener falling ill she has the whole burden of domestic affairs external and internal in addition to war work.'

By chance Clem was at home during the weekend in mid-October when a bomb dropped 200 yards from the house. 'Vi assisted some of the casualties,' he told Tom. 'I have had a refuge erected in the garden in which we shall be able to sleep.' He did not add that Vi refused to enter it because, she said, it gave her lumbago. The previous weekend they had stayed with Churchill at Chequers – Clem's first visit there. They were delighted with the house, and even more with the magnificent Elizabethan four-poster bed in which they slept.

Clem found the children constantly entertaining. 'The great word for everything is super, spelt sooper by Alison, which is the equivalent of the ripping of our time,' he wrote to Tom. His wartime letters to Tom were chatty, offering bits of political gossip as well as the little jokes of Clem's metropolitan circle. 'Have you heard the story of the chauffeur who went to the Palace to receive a decoration accompanied by a highly respectable grande dame who employed him. "Is this your wife?" "No, sir, she's my mistress."' And later, after his trip to the USA: 'Have you heard the story of the Negro soldier who was in a plane to practise parachuting but was reluctant to jump. His excuse was "It don't seem sensible to done practise something which you must get right first time."'

Tom seems to have decided that there was no alternative to war this time, and was even employed occasionally by the army to teach classes for Cornwall-based soldiers. His two sons, now grown up, both joined the army, though the older, Chris, soon left to work for the Colonial Office, and sent a stream of letters to his distinguished uncle about its failings and how it ought to be run. Tom kept up his WEA classes, teaching 'Some Modern Poets' at St Agnes and 'Modern Architecture' at Camelford, among other things. He did not hesitate to ask his influential brother to intervene on behalf of a pacifist friend in prison, and once to pass on a request from his friend, the retiring vicar of Truro, that the next vicar should be a man with experience as a leader of men's work and youth organisations. 'Mr Attlee has promised his brother that the representation will be considered in the proper quarter,' reads a dry civil service note. 'Churchwardens have nominated a Rev Leslie Stevenson.'

In the summer of 1940, Clem went away for a week's holiday in the Cotswolds with Felicity, staying in the Swan Hotel, Bibury. But on the second day of their holiday the blitz started, and they heard that Stepney had been bombed and many people killed. Clem fell silent. The village had only a manual telephone exchange, and a call to London might take hours to get through, so Clem told his government driver to take them to University College, Oxford, where the elderly college porter was delighted to see him and to undertake the task assigned to him, swelling with pride as he said into the telephone: 'I want a priority call for the Lord Privy Seal.' Clem was briefed by phone on the damage and was then driven straight to Stepney, where they were still digging people out of the rubble.

The blitz did not achieve its object of destroying Britain's war effort, and by the end of 1940 the mood of the country had changed. People believed in victory. The idea of a negotiated peace was dead, and this seemed to be symbolised by the departure of the 'men of Munich' from the War Cabinet. Chamberlain was diagnosed as having cancer and resigned at once, dying two months later. Halifax became Britain's ambassador to the USA. Anthony Eden replaced Halifax as Foreign Secretary, Herbert Morrison became Home Secretary, and Beaverbrook and Bevin entered the War Cabinet. Greenwood was given responsibility for post-war reconstruction.

Belief in victory was fortified by victories over the Italians in North Africa. But the German counter attack expelled British forces from most of Libya, and from Greece and Crete, and German forces occupied the Balkan peninsula. Even the British navy was finding the line hard to hold, trying hard to protect trade routes in the Mediterranean and the Atlantic. By the end of 1941 nine million tons of shipping, both allied and neutral, had been sunk, either from the air by the Luftwaffe or from under the sea by submarines and mines. The raids were having a serious effect on food supplies and on the supply of war materials.

But it was in 1941 that the two great powers entered the war whose forces were ultimately to decide the issue: the Soviet Union and the United States. With the USA it began gradually. In March the Lease-Lend Act authorised President Franklin Roosevelt to put American resources at the disposal of any nation whose defence he considered essential for American security. This enabled Roosevelt to supply Britain, regardless of Britain's ability to pay in dollars. In December the Japanese attacked the US navy at anchor in Pearl Harbor. The USA declared war on Japan, and Germany and Italy declared war on the USA. With the Soviet Union it began suddenly. Stalin had despaired of being able to reach any arrangement for common defence with Britain and France, and had signed a non-aggression pact with Hitler. But in June 1941 Hitler invaded the USSR, and Churchill at once promised all possible aid to Stalin. 'A poisoned Russia, an infected Russia, a plague-bearing Russia' was how Churchill had described the USSR just two decades earlier, and his views had not changed. 'A Russia of armed hordes ... accompanied and preceded by swarms of typhus-bearing vermin which destroy the bodies of men, and political doctrines which destroy the health and even the soul of nations.' War makes strange alliances.

Clem found himself sandwiched uncomfortably between the prototype Cold Warrior in Downing Street, and the many Labour people who believed Britain should do much more than the government was doing to help the USSR. Already, a month before Hitler invaded Russia, he had had to defend the government against attacks from Labour Members, as well as some Conservatives. He won a comfortable majority in the House of Commons, and soon afterwards at the Labour Party conference, but he must have known that he had won more votes than hearts. The feeling was strong in Labour circles that Labour Ministers, and especially Attlee himself, were becoming ciphers in a government where the only voice that counted was Churchill's; that they were letting Churchill dictate both the military strategy and the domestic policy.

In home affairs, the charge was unfair. It was, after all, the Labour leaders who were making the running in the preparation for reconstruction after the war, and for war aims which ensured that Britain was not just fighting for the old status quo, but for a new and better world. Arthur Greenwood had been placed in charge of making plans for reconstruction, but for the moment, Clem told Labour's 1941 conference, uniting to win the war had to come first. Nonetheless, the immediate implementation of a few Labour policies would have helped Clem's position, and just before the party conference he asked Churchill to repeal the 1927 Trade Disputes and Trade Union Act, brought in to shackle the unions after the general strike. It 'was imposed on the Unions as a kind of Brest-Litovsk peace and the memory rankles. I should have thought that agreement might be reached on certain specific amendments. Alternatively a commission might be set up . . .' This would have blunted the arrows of Clem's critics. But Churchill would have none of it.

Clem also had to resolve regular rows resulting from distrust between Labour and Conservative Ministers. Brendan Bracken, Churchill's Minister of Information, had not given up on his running feud with Hugh Dalton, Minister for Economic Warfare, who was also in charge of the Special Operations Executive, whose purpose was subversion and sabotage overseas. Like Beaverbrook, Bracken was one of Churchill's newspaper proprietor friends. He had deserted humble Fenian origins and his Catholic faith, owned the *Financial Times*, and was resentful of the Old Etonian who had become a socialist. He attached himself to Churchill years earlier, and his political star had risen and fallen with Churchill's.

Bracken and Dalton were supposed to be working together on

propaganda, but Bracken was conducting one of those guerrilla wars which frequently erupt in Whitehall (and in every other office, great and small). He was telling anyone of any importance who would listen that Dalton was not up to the job, and that the Chiefs of Staff and senior civil servants would not work with him. He intended making Dalton a figure of fun in Whitehall; he even took tables in restaurants so that he could insult his enemy sitting close by, in a loud voice, while apparently in conversation with someone else. Dalton was forced to appeal several times to Clem for help. 'Bracken was abusing me loudly in the Carlton Grill at lunch,' he wrote at one stage. Clem talked to Churchill, Churchill talked to Bracken, Bracken explained that he had called Dalton 'the biggest bloodiest shit I've ever met', and Churchill laughed.

Dalton wrote that Bracken was violently anti-Labour, and 'takes the view that, though we were necessary last May in order to bring about a change in government, we are not really necessary any longer and should be gradually pushed out of the picture'. Later he wrote again:

> The game is to discredit some of us by whispering campaigns and to reduce to a minimum our influence upon the conduct of the war. I believe that I am only one of several who are now the objects of such a campaign. If this goes on, the time must come when each of us must seriously reconsider his position. The Labour Party are not in this government as poor relations of the Tories. Nor will our Party in Parliament or in the country tolerate our being so treated.

According to one of Professor Peter Hennessy's MI5 contacts, Churchill was told that Dalton was using SOE facilities to spy on his Labour colleague, Arthur Greenwood. Churchill may have been told this, but whether it was true or part of Whitehall's internecine warfare is another matter.

But it was not a question of the party tolerating it, but whether Bracken could succeed in undermining Dalton's confidence and standing sufficiently to make it impossible for him to do the job. Clem raised the problem with Churchill several more times. Each time the situation eased, only to flare up again. In the long run the only solution would be to get rid of Bracken, and Clem knew it was beyond his powers to persuade Churchill to do this, so Dalton was eventually promoted out of the situation, to run the Board of Trade.

A more serious row erupted between Beaverbrook and Bevin. In February 1942 Churchill made Beaverbrook Minister of Production, proposing to give him control of manpower. That was Bevin's patch, and Attlee believed that labour had to be in the hands of someone whom the workers and the unions trusted. If the plan went ahead, Bevin would resign. If it did not, Beaverbrook would resign. Once more it became necessary for Mr Attlee to have a word with the Prime Minister, and this was one of those occasions when he dug his heels in. Clem loathed Beaverbrook. Young left-wingers including the rising Labour star Michael Foot worked on Beaverbrook newspapers, and Clem believed Beaverbrook corrupted them with his money, and pursued his cynical exploitation of the world for his own amusement. If Bevin had resigned, it is hard to see how Clem could have stayed. This was a battle which he had to win, and he did win it. Bevin kept manpower. Beaverbrook resigned, calling Attlee 'a miserable little man'.

Churchill seems not to have resented Clem's power to get his own way when it mattered. The two men were never soulmates, but they had grown comfortable with each other and developed a mutual respect. The new Chief of the Imperial General Staff, Sir Alan Brooke, noted with approval his calming influence on Churchill. Clem in his autobiography put it this way: 'Churchill does need men around him who, while ready to support a good idea, however novel, are prepared on occasions to take an emphatic line against a bad one.' They shared a rather cavalier attitude to religion which was unusual in those days. Clem, an agnostic or an atheist all his life, once asked Churchill if he were a pillar of the Church, and was delighted with the answer: 'Not a pillar, a buttress. I support it from outside.'

After they bade a 'cordial farewell' to Soviet Foreign Minister Molotov, Clem quoted to Churchill Lewis Carroll's 'The Hunting of the Snark':

> He would joke with hyenas, returning their stare
> With an impudent wag of the head:
> And he once went a walk, paw-in-paw, with a bear,
> 'Just to keep up its spirits,' he said.

Churchill replied that he would walk paw-in-paw with the Russian bear, just to keep up its spirits.

Later that year, over dinner in Downing Street, Clem suggested a passage from Milton's 'Samson Agonistes' which Churchill might like to use in a speech. Churchill, with an instinct for popular culture which Clem did not have, knew it would not work.

Mr Attlee has a Word with the PM

O how comely it is, and how reviving
To the spirits of just men long oppressed
When God into the hands of their deliverer
Puts invincible might,
To quell the mighty of the earth, the oppressor,
The brute and boisterous force of violent men,
Hardy and industrious to support
Tyrannic power, but raging to pursue
The righteous, and all such as honour truth.

In February 1942 Churchill at last gave in to pressure – notably from the more broadminded Conservatives, especially Anthony Eden – to give Clem the title of Deputy Prime Minister. Clem also became Dominions Secretary, which brought him back once again to the problems of India. Stafford Cripps, who had just returned from a mission to Moscow with a much enhanced reputation, replaced him as Lord Privy Seal and became Leader of the House. The other main change was the departure from the government of Arthur Greenwood, who took over the leadership of the Labour Party in the House. Clem knew that he was not really up to the job any more, but Greenwood had been firmly loyal to him for six years, had protected his back and faced down threats to his leadership, and perhaps had deserved better of Clem than to be sent to join 'some of our older leaders' on the constitutionally necessary opposition Front Bench. There is no record that Greenwood was resentful, but Clem, not a man to waste time questioning his own actions, felt a little uneasy. 'These questions [of loyalty] are the very devil,' he wrote to Tom.

The next month Churchill's simmering distrust of the *Daily Mirror* again boiled over, and this time Clem could not defuse the row. The paper first made fun of generals. 'All who aspire to mislead others in war', it said, 'should be brass-buttoned boneheads, socially prejudiced, arrogant and fussy . . . An indispensable condition for employment as a brass-boy in the back rooms of Whitehall is a profound knowledge of the last war but two . . .' A few days later it printed the famous Zec cartoon showing an exhausted sailor lying on a raft in a stormy sea with the caption, 'The price of petrol has been raised by a penny (official).'

Churchill and his Home Secretary, Herbert Morrison, decided that this cartoon implied that British sailors were sacrificing their lives for petrol companies to make excessive profits. Petrol companies were, as a matter of fact, making profits from petrol shortages. Morrison threatened to suppress the paper, telling the House of

175

Commons that the cartoon was 'one example, but a particularly evil example, of the policy and methods of a newspaper which, intent on exploiting an appetite for sensation and with a reckless indifference to the national interest and to the prejudicial effect on the war effort, has repeatedly published scurrilous misrepresentations, distorted and exaggerated statements and irresponsible generalisations.' He did not regard this statement as an attack on press freedom, though it is hard to see how it could have been anything else.

It caused a nasty row. F. J. Bellenger – Dalton's 'awful little tyke' who had leaked details of Morrison's leadership bid to the press in 1935 – pointedly remarked that he had fought for his country in the last war while Morrison had not, and quoted devastatingly from a pacifist leaflet Morrison had written at that time: 'Go forth, little soldier. Though you know not what you fight for, go forth. Though you have no grievance against your German brother – go forth and kill him. Though you may know he has a wife and family dependent on him – go forth and slay him; he is only a German dog.'

'I say,' Bellenger told the House, 'that a man who could write that stuff in the last war, when many of us were defending our country and he was not, is not the man to be the judge of subversion on this occasion.' The old First World War resentment between servicemen and 'conshies' was not dead.

None of this helped Clem when he came to convince the party conference in May that Labour should stay in the government, and he only narrowly won endorsement. Socialists were being elected to Parliament as Independents and Common Wealth Party candidates in by-elections, while Labour was in the ridiculous position of supporting unsuccessful Conservatives against them. The most spectacular example was the June by-election in Maldon, Essex. A Conservative majority of 8,000 was overturned by Tom Driberg, a socialist standing as an Independent. Driberg was one of Lord Beaverbrook's young men, employed at a considerable salary to produce pamphlets criticising the way the government was running the war. Clem probably thought Beaverbrook and his papers a worse menace than the *Mirror* could ever be, but he stood no chance of persuading Churchill, so he kept his peace.

At about the same time as Driberg's victory, Tobruk surrendered to Rommel. Four days later a Conservative MP, Sir John Wardlaw-Milne, tabled a motion that 'This House . . . has no confidence in the central direction of the war.' Wardlaw-Milne later offered to withdraw the motion, and the offer might have been accepted with some relief. But Clem chose this moment to make one of his decisive interventions. The time, he was sure, had come to face down the critics – the Conservatives who disapproved of the war strategy and of the alliance with Labour; the Labour people who complained about government tardiness on aid for Russia and on social reform; and Beaverbrook and his circle who complained about anything it amused his lordship to complain about.

Clem insisted that the government refuse to allow the motion to be withdrawn, and pointedly told his Labour colleagues that at the time of Tobruk, Churchill had been in the USA; if anyone was to blame, it was their own leader. This was stretching the truth, because Churchill had always been the guiding hand, sometimes forcing his generals into attacks they thought unwise. Whips of all three parties were instructed to pull out all the stops for the government, and the debate was an anti-climax. The movers of the censure motion made a terrible hash of it, Wardlaw-Milne saying that Churchill interfered too much with his generals and his Conservative seconder saying that Churchill intervened too little. By the time Labour's Aneurin Bevan rose to speak for the censure, the cause was already lost. The government, he said, had 'sent British soldiers onto the battlefield with improper weapons' and it had refused the aid to Russia that it had promised. No-one was prepared to call for Churchill's removal: the people really in the front line were his lieutenants, and especially Clem, whom less well-informed MPs thought could easily be dispensed with if a scapegoat were needed.

The government had a huge majority – 475 to 25 – but once again it was votes rather than hearts and minds which had been won. Bevan's biographer Michael Foot quotes an unnamed MP as saying: 'Never before have so many Members entered a division lobby with so many reservations in their minds.' The vote was a victory, not for Churchill's oratory, but for Attlee's strategy. Meanwhile, Foot writes, 'Bevan and the seven other Labour MPs who had voted for the Censure motion were "carpeted" by the Deputy Prime Minister, Mr Attlee.'

That episode was bad enough, but not perhaps as damaging to Labour's leader as the less public complaints of Harold Laski and Stafford Cripps. Laski, one of Labour's leading intellectuals, who had known Clem since they were both at the London School of Economics, was an increasingly popular figure on the left of the party. He wanted to have Clem replaced as party leader by Ernest

Bevin. For the first and not for the last time, Bevin found himself being invited to plot against Clem and to replace him. It says a great deal about Bevin and Attlee, and their relationship, that Bevin never seriously considered taking up the invitation.

Cripps, now inside the government and in the War Cabinet, wanted even more fundamental change. He was pressing for a new military planning agency which would take strategy out of the Prime Minister's hands. This was a direct assault on Churchill himself, and Cripps said he was prepared to resign over the issue. Eden and Attlee persuaded Cripps to accept the post of Minister of Aircraft Production without a seat in the War Cabinet, while Attlee told him he would never be forgiven if he provoked a crisis on the eve of the Anglo-American landings in North Africa.

Cripps was still outside the Labour Party, but Laski was an increasingly important figure inside it, re-elected each year to the National Executive with increased majorities. He seems to have felt strongly that Clem was the wrong leader. This attitude may be explained in part by an incident the previous year. Laski had been invited to the USA by the President's wife, Eleanor Roosevelt, to speak to an international student conference, and wrote to Churchill asking for his agreement to attend: 'Deeply as I differ from your conception of the meaning of the war, I am too keenly aware that you are the necessary leader of the nation at this time to be willing to add to your burdens by pushing a point of view about the political strategy of the war which, alas, you do not accept.' Churchill did not want him to go, but, according to a civil service minute, 'was anxious that heavy weather should not be made, feeling that the worst solution would be for L to say that the PM had prevented his coming, and he suggested that L should be seen personally and asked to give some conventional reason for non-acceptance.' Unfortunately, the minute continued, 'we know from Censorship that L telegraphed yesterday . . . saying that Downing Street disapproved . . . According to our information L is regarded as a contentious personality in the US. This impression derives from his active intervention in a big police strike in Massachusetts, and has since been confirmed by speeches.' Mrs Roosevelt pressed Laski's case, and Churchill wrote to Roosevelt's confidant Harry Hopkins: 'Laski has been a considerable nuisance over here and will I doubt not talk extreme left-wing stuff in the US. Although I liked his father and have maintained friendly relations with the son he has attacked me continually and tried to force my hand both in home and war politics. Unless therefore Mr Roosevelt makes a personal point of it I should be glad if the invitation were not pressed.' FDR overruled his wife, much to her irritation.

Laski was an enemy Clem could have done without, though it does not seem to have worried him. Neither did a public opinion poll in April 1942 which showed that if anything happened to Churchill, thirty-seven per cent of respondents would choose Eden to replace him and thirty-four per cent would choose Cripps. Only two per cent would choose Attlee. His war work was done in the dark corridors of Whitehall, and, as Roy Jenkins put it, 'He carried his loyalty to the government almost to the extent of endangering his position with his own Party.'

Clem was a strange man, especially for a politician. It seems genuinely not to have worried him that he appeared to many people to be in the shadow of other much better and greater men. Clem cared only for what is real. His shyness concealed a great, calm pride. He was so serenely certain of his own worth and judgements that he did not greatly need the approval of others. He never had any doubt that Churchill's leadership was crucial to winning the war. Having formed that judgement, he concentrated his efforts on making sure Churchill's position was secure, and if sometimes he cut a rather poor figure while doing it, he did not care.

The task of defending Churchill became easier when the war news improved in 1943. The British won back North Africa, the Red Army turned back the German advance in the East, Italy collapsed, the battle of the Atlantic was won, and plans were made for the invasion of France. Churchill's frequent absences left Clem in charge more often than before. In the winter of 1943–4 Churchill fell seriously ill in Tehran, and required a long convalescence in Marrakesh, which left Clem responsible during a vital part of the preparations for D-Day. The burden was increased by the need to keep the Prime Minister's illness secret. The Chiefs of Staff told Clem: 'The enemy, on learning that the Prime Minister was sick and in the Mediterranean area, would be led to infer correctly that the homeward journey, when it took place, would have to be by sea, and would thus much increase the risk . . .'

Clem, too, had a few trips abroad, describing them in letters to Tom which have some of the vaulting lyricism of his poetic youth, now usually kept firmly in check.

179

The Azores are attractive islands with one lofty peak which looked rather wonderful at dawn rising out of a dark sea of cloud faintly lit by a golden streak of dawn, [Our seaplane] plunged down through the cloud to take the water where night still reigned ... Washington ... is infested with motors. There are hardly any garages and every street is lined with cars at night on both sides ... I had a very jolly trip down the Potomac on the President's yacht, the banks are well wooded, brown with many scarlet maples ... I flew in a little seaplane from the Ottawa river to the St Lawrence beyond Montreal over fierce and desolate country ... I had a most interesting trip to Newfoundland and Canada crossing by bomber on each occasion. Fortunately we did not go very high so that it was not too cold, but it may be compared to a long night journey in a third class compartment six a side ... St Johns is a shabby and slummy town ... The people of the island are very simple and even more individualist than your Cornishmen ...

Clem and Churchill tried to ensure they were never out of the country at the same time. It only happened once, briefly, when they were in Italy in 1944 and Churchill said to Clem, 'That's all right, we can leave it for a day or two to the automatic pilot,' meaning Sir John Anderson. Anderson was one of those solid figures who earn the trust of politicians of all parties. A former senior civil servant who had been Permanent Under-Secetary at the Home Office, he entered Parliament in 1938 at the age of fifty-six, notionally supporting the National Government, and representing the Scottish Universities, which insulated him from the normal political rough-and-tumble. He had become Chancellor of the Exchequer in 1943. Clem thought him the ideal civil servant.

Churchill, abroad, would send back a constant flow of ideas. In London, Clem and Foreign Secretary Anthony Eden quietly buried the ones they disliked, and made the rest workable, while publicly defending everything the government did, whether or not they privately thought it defensible. Increasingly the two were seen as a team in the Cabinet – 'the sensible tendency', we might call it today.

They gave no quarter to those, like Labour MP Richard Stokes, who thought 'the indiscriminate bombing of civilian centres' was 'both morally wrong and strategic lunacy'. Clem told Stokes that there was no indiscriminate bombing, which he must have known was quite untrue. As the policy of turning German cities into rubble and massacring thousands of German civilians carried on into 1944, critics were told by the deputy Prime Minister to 'turn their attention to those who began it', which sounded as unconvincing then as it does now. Years later Clem confessed that he had doubts about the policy at the time, and no doubt he did, but there is no record of his having mentioned them, even privately. This was partly because of his exceptionally harsh view of Germany. For him, it was the German people – and not just the Nazis – who had, for the second time in living memory, shattered the peace of Europe. The destruction of Dresden, though it must have saddened him, was justified if it was necessary for the defeat of Germany and the destruction of German militarism. For him, the key post-war task was to make sure that Germany could never make war again, and to achieve that, Germany must be cleansed by the victorious powers. The task could not be left to the Germans themselves. In 1943, three Cabinet committees were set up to consider post-war reconstruction, and Clem chaired them all. Occupation of Germany must be total, he told them. Germany's military spirit must be broken, and its arms industries destroyed. Nazi influence must be rooted out, and an end made to the historic power of the Prussian junkers and the Ruhr industrialists. Germany should be divided into three occupied zones, governed by the three victorious powers, Britain, the USA and the USSR. The occupying forces must provide the police forces – no German finger was to have access to a trigger.

There was a danger of so weakening Germany, he told his colleagues in a memorandum, that the Soviet Union would be able to dominate Europe; and the solution was to persuade the Americans to involve themselves deeply in European security. He added, almost as a postscript, that German soldiers should not have the status of prisoners-of-war, because this would put pressure on food supplies. This bleak, bureaucratic phrasing can be translated as: it may be necessary to refuse to give German soldiers sufficient food to keep them alive.

Most of all Clem wanted the United Nations: a supra-national authority with the will, the power and the resources to contain international bandits like Hitler – a sort of international police force. The League of Nations failed, he said, but the idea was right. Individual nations must give up some of their sovereignty so that the UN could be effective. This had been near the top of his mind ever since 1933, and was to stay there for the rest of his life. In retirement he became a keen advocate of world government. In power, he restlessly pursued a policy of getting nations to give up some of their autonomy to the UN. On 1 January 1933 he had tried out privately, on Tom, a revolutionary idea:

I am being forced to the conclusion that nothing short of a world state will be really effective in preventing war. As long as you rely for security on a number of potential armaments you will have the difficulty as to who shall bell the cat . . . I want us to come out boldly for a real long range policy which will envisage the abolition of the individual sovereign state . . . If one could get an alliance of [Britain, France, the USA and Russia] I think the smaller neutrals would all fall in and the outlaws Japan and Germany would find that they could not compete and so come in too.

The UN was to be the basis of a new world order based on democracy. On 11 May 1943 Clem circulated a paper to the War Cabinet on how democratic principles could be applied in different parts of the world. It is worth another look now, not just for its later impact on policy, but because it identified problems which the world, to its cost, was not to take sufficiently seriously until decades later.

The British model of democracy is not the only one, he said. 'The desirability of giving India a Constitution as close as possible to our own is held most strongly by those whose knowledge of the subject is least . . .' But for democracy to work, minorities must be willing to accept the will of the majority, in the hope of becoming a majority themselves. Race divisions can make this impossible. One such was the conflict between British and Boers in South Africa – and 'behind this quarrel looms the much greater menace of the struggle between a white ruling minority and a black majority'. That was a remarkable prediction to make in 1943. 'Ireland, north and south, provide together one of the most intractable problems in the empire . . . How long it will be possible to deny full political rights to the West Indian Negroes, and how the two communities will then manage the affairs of these islands, admit of wide conclusions . . . A parliamentary system in Palestine would be a prelude to civil war', because neither Jew nor Arab would be governed by the other.

In all these places, and many others he identified, 'the difficulty is that no community will trust the other to play the game without a referee . . . The difficulty in a country inhabited by more than one community is to find some way of avoiding giving ultimate power to the majority community which is ex hypothesi distrusted by the minority . . .' He suggested, for such countries, an external referee appointed by their own governments, and different legislatures elected in different ways to reflect the different groupings. 'Suppose such a system applied to Palestine, Jews and Arabs would probably be able to agree on a Christian, preferably from a country which had no Moslem subjects and no, or a negligible, Jewish population. If they preferred it they might choose a Chinaman. Applied to Ireland, Catholics and Protestants might agree on a high-minded Gallic.'

Clem's intervention in Churchill's French policy had long-term consequences. Churchill and Roosevelt both found General de Gaulle extremely difficult, and considered – as Roosevelt put it – 'whether de Gaulle should now be eliminated as a political force'. So they went cold on de Gaulle's plan for a single Committee of National Liberation which would take over French territory as it was liberated. Instead, they suggested setting up local Free French regimes in each liberated locality. They also wanted to agree to General Eisenhower's request to bomb France in advance of D-Day, which could kill many civilians. It fell to Attlee and Eden to rescue de Gaulle from the wrath of Churchill and Roosevelt, despite what Clem later called de Gaulle's own 'complete political ineptitude', and to try to rescue France from Eisenhower's bombs. They persuaded the Cabinet, with Clem in the chair, to squash the idea of dismembering France, and hold out against bombing her, both on humanitarian grounds and because the allies could hardly bomb the French people one day and ask for their help and co-operation with the invading armies the next. Attlee and Eden managed to delay the bombing and to reduce its extent.

In these ways Clem Attlee laid the foundations of Britain's post-war foreign policy. But amid all these great affairs, did Clem remember what had brought him into politics? Or was he content to pull strings in the shadow of a Conservative Prime Minister? Did he briefly forget his socialism as perhaps he had during the 1929 government in the pleasure of just 'doing something'?

Certainly some of his party saw it that way. Late in 1942 Aneurin Bevan wrote a bitter and damaging attack on Attlee's record in the wartime coalition government, for *Tribune*, the left-wing Labour weekly which he and Stafford Cripps had helped found in the late Thirties. Attlee, he wrote, had failed to get anything more than a miserable increase in old age pensions, or to nationalise coal; had left the financial structure of the privately owned railways untouched; and, worst of all, had collaborated in a Churchillian policy on India which included putting Indian leaders in prison when they undertook a campaign of civil disobedience.

'Mr Attlee,' wrote Bevan, 'is loyal to the point of self-effacement

183

– but Mr Attlee is no longer the spokesman of the movement which carried him from obscurity into the second position in the land . . . He remains loyal, but only to Mr Churchill. If Mr Attlee has gained some of the toughness which comes with high position in politics it has been reserved for the members and policies of his own party.' Harold Laski said the same sorts of things in private, on Labour's National Executive.

They were both right, as far as it went. Answering Laski at the National Executive, Clem more or less admitted it. He did not, he said, think it right to try to bring in socialism under the guise of winning the war, and if he pushed Labour's ideas any harder he would force Labour out of the government. 'I am sufficiently experienced in warfare', he added, 'to know that the frontal attack with a flourish of trumpets, heartening as it is, is not the best way to capture a position.' But he also knew that some of the planning required for war could be made a permanent feature after the war; and that he could take the chance now to lay the foundations of a new and better society. He played a weak hand with quiet skill, slowly increasing Labour representation in the government far beyond what its parliamentary strength justified. In 1940 Labour held eight ministerial posts; by 1945 it held seventeen.

Clem was not a Ramsay MacDonald. There was never the slightest chance of him remaining in the coalition in peacetime. 'I am sorry you suggest that I am verging towards MacDonaldism,' he wrote to Laski. 'As you so rightly point out, I have neither the personality nor the distinction to tempt me to think that I should have any value apart from to the party which I serve.' Clem meant something specific by 'MacDonaldism'. MacDonald after 1931 used to talk as though all good and well-motivated men ought to agree on things, and Clem thought that was the slippery slope to fascism, so he was rather sensitive to the accusation. Apart from that one acerbity, it was a thoughtful, private four-page letter designed to secure understanding, not to alienate Laski. 'We have got to work with the House of Commons which we have got.' True, the government had not nationalised the mines or the railways, but 'we cannot get this until we have a House of Commons ready to pass the necessary legislation.' Clem was 'only a working politician' while Laski was 'a theorist'. The modesty of this statement was skin deep, if that.

This letter concealed that, in August 1942, Clem could hardly have cared less what Harold Laski thought of him. His usual detachment was increased by an agonising worry from home. His youngest daughter Alison, now twelve, had been cycling in Stanmore with her sister Felicity, and fell off her bicycle while travelling fast downhill, landing hard on her head. She was taken to a nearby first-aid post while Felicity cycled home fast to fetch her mother. Vi brought Alison home – and a few hours later she lost consciousness. Vi, terrified, had Clem fetched out of a Cabinet meeting for the first time ever to tell him. An eminent brain surgeon was brought back from his holiday to operate the next day. 'It was found that she had a fracture which had torn an artery so that there was blood pressing on the brain,' Clem wrote to Tom.

> Fortunately they secured the services of one of the best brain surgeons in the country and he operated successfully late last night. Today she is much better and has regained consciousness, but it will be a few days before she is out of danger. Vi has been staying at the hospital and took the whole thing with great courage and calm. I got over to be with her while the operation was on. Alison kept saying on the first day before she lost consciousness how sorry she was to cause so much trouble to Mummie and to have given Felicity such a start though it was not her fault, poor soul.

Alison was out of danger after a few days, and by October was apparently 'in enormous form riding ponies with great vigour and success', staying with Vi and Vi's mother in Cambridge. That month, Clem managed a rare and precious weekend alone in Stanmore with his second daughter Felicity, now seventeen, who had finished school and was taking a year out before training to be a teacher at Rachel MacMillen College. She had a temporary job teaching in a kindergarten in Rickmansworth, which was a bus ride from Stanmore. They talked mostly about poetry, Clem extolling to his daughter the merits of George Meredith and reading her his favourite Meredith poem, 'Love in the Valley':

> Under yonder beech-tree single on the greensward,
> Couched with her arms behind her golden head,
> Knees and tresses folded to slip and ripple idly,
> Lies my young love sleeping in the shade.

'I found her a very charming companion', Clem wrote to Tom. He asked her what her old headmistress was like, and was delighted with the answer he got: 'Logical but not psychological.'

Clem and Vi still had a rather touching, slightly suburban awe of Clem's celebrity and the importance of the people they knew. After a service of thanksgiving in St Paul's that year Clem wrote to Tom: 'Vi and I still marvel at times that we should sit in the seats of the mighty on these occasions with a row of kings etc nearby all of whom are personally known to us.'

Early in 1943, Clem's children asked if they could meet the great Winston Churchill. They thought their father sounded surprised at the request, but he took them to 10 Downing Street, and Mrs Churchill took them to the bunker from which her husband planned the war. 'And there was Winston in his boiler suit,' says Felicity. 'He gave us some orange juice and showed us round, showed us all the maps.'

Clem dealt with Churchill on home affairs with the same care and tact as on military matters, trying hard to convince him that reconstruction was just a matter of doing things which any government must do, regardless of politics. 'I doubt', he wrote to him, 'whether in your inevitable and proper preoccupation with military problems you are fully cognisant of the extent to which decisions must be taken and implemented in the field of post-war reconstruction *before* the end of the war.' He was also aware of Churchill's failings – and of the sense of relief around Whitehall when it was known that Attlee, not Churchill, would be in the chair at Cabinet, for everyone knew that the meeting would be far more efficiently conducted and would last half the time.

Churchill was one of the least efficient chairmen a British Cabinet has ever had. Clem was one of the most efficient. It was during the war that he developed the style which his post-war Ministers were to know so well. He was sharp with any Minister who spoke too long or was not properly briefed, and he kept debates as short as possible. Meetings, in Clem's view, were for taking decisions, not for talking. Democracy relies on discussion, he once said, but it doesn't work unless you can stop people talking. When he sat in a Churchill Cabinet, he grew quietly impatient. Once, instead of his habitual doodling, he wrote a poem about the prolix debate he was hearing, in tiny writing which his neighbours could not see, and put it away. Without knowing the exact context it loses some force, but we know that a report by Lord Cherwell was under consideration. Cherwell tended to be despatched by Churchill to stop the Labour Ministers getting up to mischief, and Clem called him Old Man River after the River Cherwell. A Conservative known as 'Shakes' Morrison was also closely involved.

Mr Attlee has a Word with the PM

I need no ceiling if a floor be laid
In this Serbonian bog which Cherwell made.
Its turbid, muddy surface heaves and quakes
Moved by the struggles of unlucky 'Shakes.'
While anxious Woolton mid the growing murmur
Tries hard to drag him back to terra firma.
Ernest plunged in with a tremendous flounder
Resolved to extricate him ere he founder
But fails in his attempt to pull him off
Entangled in the figures of the Prof.
Herbert essayed a method rather subtler
But bumped into Rob Hudson and Rab Butler.
Crookshank stretched out for aid a slender plank
To bring his worried colleague to the bank.
But Anderson called in Sir Malcolm Eve
Who sank poor Shakes's raft beyond retrieve
And Lyttleton as in the mire he settles
Says this is stickier than non ferrous metals.

Churchill – or at least the part of him that listened to Brendan Bracken and Lord Beaverbrook – believed that he was surrounded by clever, scheming socialists intent on using their position in his government to introduce revolutionary change behind his back. Churchill knew he could not be everywhere, chair every committee, attend every Cabinet. He had a war to fight. He suspected, rightly, that his Foreign Secretary Anthony Eden was not above conspiring with Attlee against him. So he planted Beaverbrook and Bracken on most of Clem's committees to try to spike any dangerous ideas that seemed to come out of those which had Clem and Ernest Bevin sitting on them. 'When they [Beaverbrook and Bracken] state their opinions,' Clem wrote to Churchill, 'it is obvious that they do not know anything about it. Nevertheless an hour is consumed in listening to their opinions.'

The key to the Labour Ministers' strategy was the Beveridge Report, published on 1 December 1942 and written by another of Clem's old colleagues from the LSE, now a distinguished civil servant, William Beveridge. Beveridge turned what could have been a dry bureaucratic task into a 200,000-word government report which sold 100,000 copies within a month of publication (plus a cheap edition for the armed services) and inspired a generation. It even percolated to deepest Cornwall, where Tom Attlee began a WEA course on 'The Beveridge Report' in Liskeard and another on 'National Reconstruction' in Troon, as well as 'Christianity and the New Social Order' at Falmouth and at Newquay.

It was a detailed plan for universal social security, the triumphant reincarnation of the 1909 minority report of the Royal Commission on the Poor Law by Sidney and Beatrice Webb – that report which the young Clem Attlee had welcomed so enthusiastically, as had Beveridge himself. It was the reason Clem was a politician.

The Beveridge Report was, quite simply, a detailed plan to slay what Beveridge called the five giants: want, disease, ignorance, squalor and idleness. To do this, he said, Britain needed a comprehensive welfare system based on three things: a free national health service, child allowances, and full employment.

Churchill welcomed the Report with a phrase which is now freely mocked by Conservatives (who probably think it was coined by a socialist): 'We must establish . . . national compulsory insurance for all classes for all purposes from the cradle to the grave.' But Churchill insisted there should be no attempt to implement Beveridge during the war, nor any guarantee that it would be implemented after the war, because it might not be affordable. Labour Ministers were unable to shake this resolve. It was a question of putting up with it, or leaving the government. Clem decided to put up with it. This provoked the most serious parliamentary crisis of the war. Only twenty-three Labour Members supported the government on the issue in the division lobbies, and twenty-two of them were Ministers. One hundred and nineteen voted against.

What was Clem to do? He could hardly discipline the overwhelming majority of his own parliamentary party for voting against the government, though Ernest Bevin angrily urged this course of action. Arthur Greenwood, now leading Labour in the House, and Clem papered over the cracks as best they could, saying that the vote was not intended as a vote of censure, simply as a way of helping Labour Ministers to argue Labour's case in Cabinet by putting pressure on the government from outside. But the vote was not a one-off incident. It was a symbol of growing discontent in the Labour Party. Labour MPs knew there was a public mood for radical change, for social justice. They knew that now was the moment when Beveridge-type reforms would carry public support. Aneurin Bevan was simply the most fluent and outspoken of those who thought Clem was letting socialism's one big chance slip through his fingers. Roy Jenkins put it this way: 'It is a heavy sacrifice for a party which has known long years of adversity to allow years of potential prosperity slip by without taking from them a substantial profit.'

Bevan wanted Labour Ministers to insist, as the price for staying in the government, on the essentials – better old age pensions, a national health service. He believed that the likely result of this – a breakup of the coalition, with Labour Ministers returning to opposition – was a risk worth taking. Clem thought it would destroy Labour's chances at the next general election, because the voters would feel that Labour Ministers had abandoned their posts when things looked bleak. As long as the war lasted, Labour must support Churchill, and be content with whatever concessions it could gain within a Churchill government. He was in a stronger position to gain concessions after a government reorganisation in September 1943. The Chancellor, Kingsley Wood, died and was succeeded by Sir John Anderson. Clem gave up the post of Dominions Secretary to succeed Anderson as Lord President of the Council – the key position for dealing with the home front. Shedding his departmental responsibility again made him more powerful, not less, and he must have anticipated this. It enabled him, as he had done before, to operate right across the government: discreetly taking an interest in the affairs of every major department, creating committees, chairing them, and guiding their work. The powerful committee was this discreet administrator's natural working environment. At once he started to turn the heat up, telling the Cabinet that decisions about post-war planning could not be postponed. Churchill, unable to give his full attention to these affairs because of his heavy involvement with international conferences, reluctantly found himself giving ground, inch by inch.

Clem turned the attention of the Lord President's Committee to Beveridge's proposals on pensions and unemployment assistance. The Conservatives on the committee, the Minister of Health, Ernest Brown, and the Chancellor of the Exchequer, Sir John Anderson, argued rather forlornly that an increase now would lead to a demand for further increases. Clem dispassionately and bureaucratically summed up the committee's views for the Cabinet: 'We have reached the conclusion that the adoption of the rates now recommended by the Assistance Board will not result in any demand, which would have to be conceded, for a re-opening of the recent settlement of the rates of War Pensions.' But in a separate note to the Cabinet, Sir John Anderson put an argument with which we have become very familiar in the 1990s: 'The burden of old age is rising progressively. In 1941 there were 7.5 persons of 15 to 66 for every one over that age. By 1971 this figure will have fallen below 4; i.e. the burden of the old on the workers will approximately double itself in the next 30 years.'

Lord Cherwell turned on the warning light for the Prime Minister. The proposals, he said, 'promise much more generous payments to the people (mainly old age pensioners and unemployed) who are helped by the Assistance Board in cases of need ... There are dangers here of all sorts of political trouble and I suggest that the important thing is to make sure that the scales be fixed so as to avoid this.' Duly alarmed, Churchill wrote to Eden: 'This does not look well. Three of our representatives were absent [from the Lord President's Committee] and the Chancellor is obviously extremely uncomfortable. I shall not be able to deal with this before I leave. I trust you will make sure it is thoroughly reviewed by the war cabinet ... I will speak to Mr Attlee myself sometime tomorrow.' At the War Cabinet Attlee stuck to the grim bureaucratic line he had chosen. The proposed rates, he said, 'would not lead to any irresistible demand for a re-opening of the recent settlement of war pensions rates.' Anderson made unhappy noises, Bevin made approving ones, and, no-one being able to produce a really good reason why not, the improved rates were agreed.

Much the same thing happened to Bevin's proposal that the government must set reasonable unemployment pay rates while the war was on, because there would be unemployed ex-servicemen to look after when it ended. Churchill also reluctantly accepted that the government must plan to provide employment for ex-servicemen. Thus Clem and Bevin ensured that the streets of London after the war would not be full of limbless and broken former soldiers begging for their bread, as they had been in the first years after 1918. Clem also insisted on a Cabinet reconstruction committee and held out strongly against the appointment of Beaverbrook as Minister of Reconstruction, persuading Churchill to appoint Lord Woolton instead. Churchill felt strongly that Labour Ministers were pushing him too hard. He prepared – but did not send – a note of complaint for Attlee about the reconstruction committee: 'A solid mass of four socialist politicians of the highest quality and authority ... all working together as a team, very much dominates this committee ...'

Half a century later, it seems extraordinary how radical were some of the proposals Clem persuaded Conservatives to take seriously. 'I had Rab Butler [Conservative Education Minister] in to see me last week', he wrote to Tom in 1941 to talk about the future of education, particularly the future of the public schools. My idea is that like most of our institutions, they should not be killed but adapted . . . Some of them which are essentially local could be absorbed into the county secondary schools. Others which are national should be brought under control without killing their individuality. They should of course have a large proportion of scholars from the elementary schools . . . If you have been thinking out anything on the future of education, let me know as Rab is quite impressionable.

Clem's beloved Haileybury would have not have liked this. Clem was still delighted whenever an Old Haileyburian crossed his path, and at the busiest times of the war found time to go and talk to the older boys.

'Our Education Bill will be out in a day or two,' he wrote to Tom two years later. 'I think it a good bit of work reflecting great credit on Rab Butler and Chuter Ede [Butler's Labour Under-Secretary].' But for Aneurin Bevan, the behaviour of Labour Ministers in government was symbolised by Ernest Bevin's reaction to a series of localised miners' strikes during the winter of 1943–4. Bevin drafted an amendment to the Defence Regulations giving the government power to deal with incitement to strike in an essential service. This caused another internecine clash in Labour's ranks. In the House of Commons, Bevan flayed Bevin, and twenty-three Labour MPs followed him into the division lobby against the government, with another eighty-six abstaining and only fifty-six supporting the government. The rebellion was not the biggest of the war, but the words spoken were far and away the bitterest.

The debate had been preceded by dire threats of what might be done to rebels, mostly from the grim tank-like Ernest Bevin. The Labour parliamentary leadership, with Clem's blessing, decided that Bevan should have the whip withdrawn, which would almost certainly lead to expulsion from the party. Bevan announced that if they expelled him he would still fight 'to retain Ebbw Vale for socialism'. But the Parliamentary Labour Party narrowly rejected expulsion, and Labour's National Executive demanded an assurance that Bevan would not do it again, which Bevan unwillingly gave. He returned to the attack a week after D-Day, when Bevin introduced a white paper on employment which Bevan considered inadequate. Privately, Clem and Bevin thought so too, but it was the best that they could get past their Conservative colleagues. To Bevin the trade union leader, who had spent months working on a deal, and come back with the best he could get, it was

intolerable to find himself under attack from some windy politician who could not negotiate his way out of a paper-bag. To
Bevan the Welsh socialist, it was intolerable to watch a cynical
old trade union leader stitching up yet another grubby compromise with the class enemy. Only the Old Haileyburian could
talk to both sides and keep his temper. The tightrope Clem was
walking looked increasingly precarious. The longer the war went
on, the harder the balancing act was getting. Soon, said Bevan,
'the Labour Party will have to abandon either its principles or its
leaders.'

Bevan was sure that if a general election were held, Labour would
win, while Morrison and Dalton, and probably Clem too, believed
Labour could not win a general election against a Conservative
Party led by Winston Churchill. On this, Bevan was probably right:
in those war years he was more closely attuned to what ordinary
people were thinking than Labour's Ministers who were deeply
enmeshed in the workings of government. But Clem's caution had
some justification. 'A silly speech by someone like Aneurin Bevan
might easily be used to stampede the electors from Labour,' he
wrote in notes for a speech probably intended for the National
Executive. Nonetheless, Labour Ministers were preparing Labour for
an election and discreetly disentangling themselves from Churchill's
huge embrace. Dalton had assiduously encouraged bright young
men from Oxford and Cambridge with left-wing views, and made
them into temporary wartime civil servants. One of Dalton's protégés
was Hugh Gaitskell. Another was Gaitskell's closest friend, Evan
Durbin, and on 26 November 1944 Clem introduced Durbin, by
then his personal assistant and a member of the War Cabinet staff,
to the voters of Edmonton as their Labour parliamentary candidate.
Clem said at the town hall meeting: 'It may well be that, in a time not
so far ahead, the electors will give Labour a majority in the House
of Commons. I have no fear that when the time comes Labour can
form an effective government.'

As a civil servant Durbin could not speak at the meeting, and
the *Daily Express* made fun of Labour's silent candidate. Two days
later Clem wrote a note to the War Cabinet saying he thought it
wrong 'to apply to war temporary civil servants the full rigour of the
1927 Order in Council which is designed for peace conditions . . .
A production engineer working for Vickers is free, but a production
engineer in the service of the Ministry of Supply may not stand . . .'
What about

the rights of the citizen, and the damage to the State by depriving it of the possibility of the service in Parliament of well qualified persons. Now that political parties are making selections for the next general election it is not fair that thousands of citizens, some of whom have been parliamentary candidates in the past, should be penalised for serving the state.

He was concerned not so much with principle, but because he knew that these bright young men were crucial to Labour's chances next time. Labour Ministers – Attlee, Dalton, Morrison, Bevin – were all of the generation born before the turn of the century, the generation which fought the First World War. To win an election, Labour must modernise. In a draft of a speech intended for a restricted audience in 1945 Clem wrote that many people were now property owners: 'In face of this it is time that the Labour Party ceased to mouth Marxian shibboleths about the proletariat having nothing to lose but their chains.'

Clem and Aneurin Bevan both wanted an election, but Bevan wanted it immediately, and Clem was happy to delay. How could he engineer that delay? A later Labour leader, John Smith, was described by a rival as like a crustacean camouflaged in the sea bed: 'For a long time he keeps so still that you almost forget he's there; then when he makes his move, he moves very quickly indeed.' Clem Attlee was similar. He let speculation and rhetoric about Labour's possible attitude to an election float around him for months – the angry Bevan view in public, the Morrison and Dalton calculations in private – and no-one was sure what he was thinking. Then, suddenly and unexpectedly, without consulting any of the Labour Ministers, he sent to Labour's National Executive a draft document advising that Labour should stay in the government for another year.

Ernest Bevin was furious. Clem's purpose was to get a decision prior to the Cabinet on 27 September, where he and Churchill proposed continuing the coalition for another year. It worked. The Labour Party and the Cabinet both having agreed an extension of the coalition, it was not going to be easy for anyone to reopen the question, unless the war ended. Whatever Aneurin Bevan thought, it did not mean that Clem was happy to be subservient to Churchill. Bevan's view might have been different if he had seen the private letter Clem wrote to the Prime Minister in January 1945 about 'the method or rather lack of method of dealing with matters requiring Cabinet decisions'. Churchill had set up several committees, he said, and overworked Ministers made enormous efforts to reach an agreed decision in them. After a long and unnecessary delay, the proposals would reach the Cabinet.

> When they do come before the cabinet it is very exceptional for you to have read them. More and more often you have not read even the note prepared for your guidance. Often half an hour and more is wasted in explaining what could have been grasped by two or three minutes reading of the document. Not infrequently a phrase catches your eye which gives rise to a disquisition on an interesting point only slightly connected with the subject matter. The result is long delays and unnecessarily long cabinets imposed on Ministers who have already done a full day's work and who will have more to deal with before they can get to bed.

Churchill, he continued, often assumed that agreed proposals were 'due to the malevolent intrigues of socialist ministers who have beguiled their weak Conservative colleagues. This suggestion is unjust and insulting to Ministers of both Parties . . .'

And so it went on: unemotional, precise, and merciless. Churchill's Private Secretary, Sir John Colville, told Kenneth Harris years later that the Prime Minister was thunderstruck, dictated a lengthy and furious reply, but withdrew it after his wife told him: 'I admire Mr Attlee for having the courage to say what everyone is thinking.' Instead he sent a terse note: 'I have to thank you for your private and personal letter of January 19. You may be sure I shall always endeavour to profit by your counsels.'

By that time allied armies were liberating Italy and France and Clem was intensely depressed at the damage done by the retreating Germans. 'I fear that the Boche have wrecked San Gimignano, otherwise up to the present my Umbrian and Tuscan favourite towns have been spared. I fear for Florence and Pisa,' he wrote to Tom in July 1944. The next month, after his visit to Normandy, he wrote that while Bayeux and Caen were in good shape, St Lo was utterly destroyed and its cathedral finished: 'I am glad we have that watercolour of its previous condition.' And the next month again: 'Poor Cassino, a complete ruin.'

But he saw a silver lining in the fate of bombed Stepney.

> Instead of the packed masses of buildings there are wide open spaces with willow herb growing on them and one sees wide vistas with trees in the distance which were formerly concealed in back gardens. The old nucleus of Stepney, the church and the High Street and Durham Row

is almost an isolated village again as the area to the north is cleared . . .
While one regrets the loss of an integral part of one's experiences, there
is the gain in the disappearance of big slum areas.

In the first few months of 1945, Clem travelled around much of
liberated Europe enquiring into relief questions and looking at the
damage. He also played a part in the formation of the UN, as a
member of the British delegation to the founding conference in
San Francisco. By that time, feelings on the Labour benches about
his supposed subservience to Churchill were so strong that there was
even a row about the fact that he was going to be second-in-command
to the Foreign Secretary, Eden. Ernest Bevin did not like it at all;
Aneurin Bevan called it Clem's 'crowning blunder', and *Tribune*
said that he was going to 'affront his own followers and demean
the status of the whole Labour movement by agreeing to serve as
lieutenant to Anthony Eden', adding that he 'seems determined to
make a trumpet sound like a tin whistle . . .'

Clem was in San Francisco when, on 8 May 1945, Germany
surrendered. Brendan Bracken and Lord Beaverbrook at once urged
on Churchill an immediate election to capitalise on Churchill's
wartime popularity. But both Attlee and Churchill wanted to keep
the coalition going, if possible, until the end of the war with Japan.
It was not possible. Four days after Germany's surrender, on the
eve of Labour's annual conference, its National Executive met in
Blackpool. Herbert Morrison, now chairman of the party's campaign
committee, put up a strong case for going to the country at once. The
mood for change was now, he believed, and should be grasped. The
NEC agreed, and Clem at once wrote to Churchill that Labour would
stay in the coalition only until October. Churchill chose to go to the
country at once, fixing the general election for 5 July.

The old game started anew. Morrison shone at Labour's conference, and Ellen Wilkinson, that year's party Chairman, privately drew
the attention of anyone who would listen to the contrast between
Morrison and the unexciting, un-charismatic leader. Would it not
be better, she said, if Attlee were now to step down in favour of
Morrison? At the end of the conference her successor as Chairman,
Harold Laski, immediately wrote a long letter to Clem explaining
why, in his opinion, Clem ought to resign for the good of the party.
Clem replied: 'Dear Laski, Thank you for your letter, contents of
which have been noted. C. R. Attlee.'

7

The Prime Minister Disposes

On 25 July 1945, Clem flew home from Potsdam, where Churchill was negotiating the post-war settlement with President Truman and Marshal Stalin. Churchill had taken Attlee, now once again the leader of the opposition, with him, against the unlikely eventuality that Labour might win the election. That same day, Clem's daughter Felicity, now nineteen and training to be a teacher, had come home from Rachel Macmillen College of Education in Deptford, for the start of the summer holiday.

Two days earlier he had been visiting the German countryside. 'My dearest love,' he had written to Vi, '. . . We got off the beaten track a bit and went into some villages in the Russian zone, still pleasant places with old buildings . . . A little boy of 8 told us he was one of a family of 11 evacuated here when the Russians invaded Silesia. His father was left behind working for the Russians . . .'

The next morning Vi drove the three of them from Stanmore to Stepney in their small Hillman Minx family saloon, to see the votes counted – 'never realising', she said afterwards, 'that at night I might be driving a Prime Minister home.' The country had voted three weeks previously, but the count had been held up so that the Forces votes could be brought home. Vi was one of Labour's scrutineers in Limehouse, and she had been there the previous day to see the Forces vote counted. She had no idea where to eat in Limehouse, and was grateful when Clem's Conservative opponent, A. N. Woodard, offered to take her to lunch. Vi saw her husband comfortably re-elected as an MP, then drove to the Great Western Hotel, whose owner, Clem's friend Lord Portal, had offered them lunch and the use of his telex machine to keep in touch with the progress of the count.

Clem, Vi, Janet and Felicity had started lunch by the time Vi remembered that Alison was due at Waterloo in half an hour. Their youngest daughter Alison, aged fifteen, was at a boarding school, the

Godolphin School, in Salisbury. It was the last day of the school term, and she was travelling to London on the school train. Felicity offered to meet her sister, and left for Waterloo by underground. The two girls decided to do some shopping in Oxford Street, and as they came up the escalator they saw a man reading the *Evening Standard*. It had a huge picture of their father on the front page and an enormous headline: 'THE NEW PM'. For the first time the idea seemed real, and they danced all the way down Oxford Street before taking the underground to Paddington, joining their parents at the Great Western at about 4 pm. They found Clem and Vi in a private room, watching the results come off the telex and sipping tea while photographers perched on the tables and jumped around the room. As the girls went in, a photographer called out, 'Could you pour another cup of tea please, Mrs Attlee?' and their mother poured what was at least the twentieth cup.

It was a landslide. Labour was returned with 393 seats. The Conservatives had 213, the Liberals 12. With two Communist Members, one Commonwealth Party Member and nineteen others, Labour had an overall majority of 146 – its first ever overall parliamentary majority.

Felicity and Alison went on their postponed shopping expedition while Clem and Vi set off for Labour's headquarters in Transport House. There, though few people knew it, there was a secret drama to be played out.

Clem, Bevin, Herbert Morrison and the Labour Party Secretary Morgan Phillips met in Ernest Bevin's room. Bevin had called the meeting, in a cryptic note the previous day. 'I note in the press you are coming home. I think an opportunity should be taken for a talk with a few of us. We shall know better how we stand. It would be difficult to go to the Administrative Committee [the new Labour MPs] with no clear mind between us . . .'

Morrison had also written to Clem: 'Whatever the result of the election may be, the new Parliamentary Party is bound to include many new members. They should, I think, have the opportunity of deciding as to the type of leadership they want . . . I have decided . . . I should accept nomination for the leadership of the Party. That I am animated solely by considerations of the interests of the Party, and regard for their democratic rights, and not by any personal unfriendliness towards yourself, I need hardly assure you.' Both letters were waiting at Stanmore when Clem returned from Potsdam, so he knew what to expect, but he had calmly gone

197

about his business all day as though he had not received them, and mentioned them to no-one, not even Vi.

Clem reported that Churchill would go to Buckingham Palace at 7 pm to resign and advise the King to send for him. Morrison said he must not accept an invitation from the King to form a government. Morrison claimed, wrongly, that the rules of the Parliamentary Labour Party required Labour MPs now to elect a leader. If Clem tried to form a government, Morrison could not undertake to join it. This was a threat to split the party. Morrison, Harold Laski, Ellen Wilkinson and Maurice Webb had been preparing for this moment for weeks, spreading the word that Clem was not fit to lead the party or the country. 'Nature intended for [Attlee] to be a second lieutenant' was the way Laski had been expressing it. Bevin protested that it would be outrageous to go into a general election with a leader whom voters believed would be Prime Minister if Labour won, and then to substitute a different leader. Morrison had had his chance in 1935, when the party preferred Attlee.

Clem said nothing, but he knew where he stood. 'Morrison had some idea that he ought to be Prime Minister in my place,' he wrote in an unpublished fragment of autobiography. '. . . The idea was fantastic and certainly out of harmony with the feeling of the Party . . .' His published autobiography makes no mention of the incident. As they argued, Morrison was called out to take a telephone call. While he was out, Bevin said: 'Clem, you go to the Palace straight away.' Morrison returned. The call, he said, was from Stafford Cripps, to say that he supported Morrison's view. Nothing more of substance was said, and soon the four men left the room. Clem told Vi nothing except that they must now go to Buckingham Palace to keep his 7.30 appointment with the King.

At the Palace, Vi, with that instinctive humility which both of them possessed, waited outside in the Hillman, just as Churchill's chauffeur had waited outside in the Rolls Royce half an hour before, 'but I was later invited to wait inside when it was discovered that I was Mrs Attlee', she wrote in a private diary. Clem is said to have told George VI, 'I've won the election!' and the King replied: 'I know, I heard it on the six o'clock news,' adding: 'You look more surprised than I feel.'

'I gather they call the new Prime Minister Clem,' the King said afterwards to his private secretary, Alan Lascelles; '"Clam" would be more appropriate.'

According to the King's diary, Clem 'was very surprised his Party had won & had had no time to meet or discuss with his colleagues any of the Offices of State.' So the King took the opportunity to try to influence his new Prime Minister. Alan Lascelles recorded immediately afterwards: 'Mr Attlee mentioned to the King that he was thinking of appointing Mr Dalton to be his Foreign Secretary. His Majesty begged him to think carefully about this, and suggested that Mr Bevin would be a better choice.'

Clem knew that Dalton wanted the Foreign Office, for which he was well qualified; and that Bevin wanted the Exchequer, and confidently expected to get it. Clem probably grunted non-committally; the King thought he had agreed to the swop. From Buckingham Palace, Vi drove Clem to a victory rally at Central Hall, Westminster. There, a huge crowd was singing community songs lustily: 'John Brown's Body', 'Three Blind Mice'. Felicity and Alison were already in the vastly excited audience. A man in front of them was waving a golf-club in the air, for no apparent reason, but that night no Labour supporter needed a reason to do anything. When their father appeared – a small, unassuming figure in a three-piece suit, looking like an accountant – they joined in the convulsive cheering that swept through the hall.

When he could be heard above the din, Clem Attlee said: 'I have just left the Palace.' Some were sure he said, 'I have just left the King,' but Felicity insists it was 'Palace'. It was the moment everyone had been waiting for. The cheers, the shouts, the joyous hysteria, became deafening and made it impossible for him to say anything more, but he did not need to say anything more.

There was a small group in the room to whom the news of his visit to the King was both surprising and unwelcome. Herbert Morrison and his friends were still canvassing to remove Clem. Morrison had just muttered to a Labour MP, John Parker, standing beside him in the gentlemen's lavatory: 'We cannot have this man as our leader.' Parker said it was too late. But for the rest of the country, knowing nothing of these manoeuvres, it was a moment of great rejoicing and, in some quarters, of terror. I am told, by a friend who was ill in a military hospital in India, that when the news came through, men confined to bed got up and danced in the wards. The playwright Trevor Griffiths described the equally apocalyptic view held by the other side in *A Tory Story*, making his top industrialist say:

Today, Thursday 26th July, the people of this country have declared war on us . . . Before the year's out, we may all be living in the West Indies on such capital as we've been able to muster from the expropriation of our possessions the socialists have been elected to effect . . . I have a copy of the socialists' election manifesto . . . Or, as Winston would have it, the Thieves Charter.

Before the speeches ended, a Labour Party organiser led Felicity and Alison out by a back door to meet their parents. The crowd outside was huge, excited and almost impenetrable. The family were helped to the Hillman, shaking hands with everyone and being patted on the back all the way, and when they got in, the crowds hammered on the roof and swayed the car, singing and shouting. 'Good old Clem' was a constant refrain. It was friendly but, says Felicity, frightening too. They drove back to Stanmore. No-one said much in the car. Clem's private secretary Joe Burke followed in another car and sat up all night answering the telephone so that Clem and his family could get some sleep. It had been, Clem remarked afterwards, 'quite an exciting day'.

Neither then nor at any time in the next hectic six years as Prime Minister did Clem feel the need to tell anyone just *how* exciting: how in his moment of triumph he had to face down one of Labour's most powerful politicians, and risk civil war in his party. Nor did he mention the hideous dilemma he faced after his conversation with the King. He was not a man to confide his troubles. He slept well, as always. Even after such a day, he could clear his mind and be asleep the moment he put his head on the pillow. And the next day he did his Cabinet-making characteristically. There was no MacDonald-style hand-wringing, no letters to those left out telling them they must be 'among his cares'. Some old friends would be disappointed, others angry; it went with the job. Bevin got the Foreign Office and Dalton the Exchequer. The next day, Clem flew back to Potsdam with his new Foreign Secretary. That same day, with the swift despatch of decisions which became such a mark of his premiership, he also decided to sell the family house in Stanmore. The family had never discussed it, but later he wrote to Tom that it would be too big 'if, as is possible by the time we return, some of the children will be living away from home.' Janet was in the WAAF, Felicity taught in a nursery school in Bermondsey, and Martin was a cadet in the Merchant Navy. Alison was still at school, and wrote to her father: 'If I am writing a letter to you both do I put The Right Honourable C. R. Attlee CH MP and Mrs Attlee or The Right Honourable C. R. and Mrs Attlee CH MP or don't I put it at all?'

Clem had originally intended to give Bevin and Dalton what they wanted, and had told them both so. But he changed his mind. Both men were disappointed. On the face of it, it seems an extraordinary decision. Hugh Dalton had been a Foreign Office minister under Arthur Henderson during the 1929–31 government. He was an acknowledged expert in foreign affairs. Bevin's only experience of foreign affairs was sitting on committees during the latter part of the war about post-war world reconstruction. Bevin's wartime contribution had been to make the labour market work well. He declared: 'They say that Gladstone was at the Treasury from 1860 to 1930. I'm going to be Minister of Labour from 1940 to 1990' (and in the sense he meant it, he lasted until 1979). The Exchequer would have given him the chance to consolidate what he had done: to ensure that the peacetime economy was geared towards the needs of those who produced, rather than those who lived on shareholdings.

Why did Clem switch them? In his autobiography he wrote: 'Various reasons impelled me to my final decision, which was, I think, justified in the event.' The first draft of the autobiography is slightly more revealing: he 'was not sure that Dalton's temperament really fitted him for the Foreign Office'; and since Bevin loathed Morrison – a fact which was obvious to everyone who had worked with the two of them – he did not want them both on the home front, where Morrison had to be.

Morrison was still trying to persuade Labour MPs to insist on an election for leader. At the same time he was telling Clem he wanted the Foreign Office for himself. A less confident leader might have been tempted to do the deal that was clearly on offer: the Foreign Office in return for an end to the manoeuvring. Clem does not seem to have been tempted for a moment. But this meant that he must offer Morrison something senior on the home front, and he decided on the posts of deputy Prime Minister and Lord President of the Council, with the key role of overseeing economic planning and nationalisation. Morrison swallowed his pride and took it. If Clem was not to have Bevin and Morrison working together on the domestic economy, Bevin must now go to the Foreign Office.

The reasons Clem gave were part of the truth, but not all of it. The King, despite Clem's denials, did play a part, for Clem, conservative about everything except socialism, believed, as he once put it, that 'a conscientious constitutional monarch is a strong element of stability and continuity in our constitution.' If the King felt strongly that he wanted one Foreign Secretary rather than another, this was not to be lightly ignored.

The King did feel strongly. Back in 1871 Queen Victoria had appointed Dalton's father, Canon John Dalton, as tutor to her grandson, the future George V, George VI's father. Canon Dalton became a lifelong friend to George V, closer to him in many ways than he was to his own children. His son's conversion to socialism was, Hugh Dalton believed, never forgiven at court. Dalton's biographer Ben Pimlott believes that Dalton had unintentionally offended George VI by disposing of some royal gifts left to Hugh by his father, and by his generally dismissive attitude towards royalty. The King was not the only member of the establishment who disliked Dalton. Foreign Office mandarins thought – rightly – that Dalton had strong views on most issues of foreign policy, and little respect for the Foreign Office. He was strongly Zionist and anti-German. They put it about that Bevin was 'sensible' and 'broad-minded', which meant they thought they could manipulate him.

The Conservatives reserved a special hatred for Dalton. It was partly a gut-feeling against an Old Etonian who had betrayed his class. But Eden and Churchill, constantly wound up by the egregious and omnipresent Brendan Bracken (who had lost his seat in Parliament but not his influence with Churchill), also thought him untrustworthy. Both the Conservative leadership and the Foreign Office made sure Clem knew their views. Before the election, Churchill had invited Clem to see all the papers relating to Potsdam and to accompany him there. A draft letter from Churchill to Clem reads: 'This arrangement would carry with it the opportunity for conversations between you, Mr Bevin, the Foreign Secretary and myself whenever necessary.' Then there must have been a discussion between Churchill and Clem, because Churchill crossed out on the draft the words 'and Mr Bevin' and sent a handwritten note to Clem: 'Of course if you wish to associate Mr Bevin with you in this arrangement, I should be very glad.'

Clem was clearly avoiding the implication Churchill was making: that in the event of a Labour victory, Bevin was headed for the Foreign Office. Churchill was displeased. A memo from his private secretary, summarising Churchill's instructions, reads: 'Mr Bevin was not to be included in the arrangement. If Mr Attlee had any comments on any of these papers he would be free to communicate them to the PM but he should not be encouraged to do so too frequently.'

The Foreign Office was the senior job and Bevin carried more political weight. Dalton was a trained economist. It seems as though the arguments stacked up until the way forward seemed clear to Clem. And there was Dalton's personality. Hugh Dalton was the opposite of Clem Attlee in every way. He was very tall – at 6 feet 3 inches he was almost a foot taller than the Prime Minister. Where Clem was taciturn, he wore his emotions on his sleeve. Where Clem was quiet, he was noisy. 'He reminded me of a pantomime king with that huge laugh,' says Felicity. During the war Churchill once heard a booming voice from an ante-room and an aide told him: 'It's Mr Dalton speaking to Glasgow.' 'Why doesn't he use the telephone?' growled Churchill.

Where Clem was the most discreet politician imaginable, one colleague said of Dalton's failure to get the Foreign Office: 'What a pity. That would have put an end to secret diplomacy.' Where Clem never lost a night's sleep worrying, Dalton's worries – about his responsibilities, about whether other and lesser men were displacing him – deprived him of sleep night after night and brought on stress-related illnesses such as boils. Clem had roots: from his childhood in Putney to his life now in an ordinary suburban family in Stanmore. Dalton had a more-or-less loveless childhood with parents who seemed to him to care more about their royal connections than about their children. Dalton was a politician who thought he had a talent for intrigue, and was sufficiently fluent to persuade others of this error. So he had the worst of both worlds: neither the glory of being considered above plotting, nor the success which attends effective plotters. He was known, perhaps unfairly, as 'the man who slaps you on the back and calls you by someone else's Christian name'. Beatrice Webb described 'his curiously deferential and ingratiating method of address with persons who are likely to be useful to him'. He cultivated obscure trade unionists who had block votes at their disposal, offering his impressive contacts, sophisticated knowledge and extensive intelligence in return for their influence inside the party, laughing a little too loudly at their jokes. Intending to leave them feeling grateful, he often only left them feeling patronised.

He had been scarred, even more than most of his generation, by the First World War. His closest friends, one of whom was the poet Rupert Brooke, had all been killed. 'People have sometimes asked, since then,' he wrote in his autobiography, 'why I had so few men friends of my own age. The answer is the war. Before that I was very rich in friendships.'

Something even worse happened to him. His four-year-old daughter died of nephritis. Dalton and his wife Ruth never had another child. Their marriage did not recover, and by 1945 they seemed to have little to say to each other. In his massive diary, which has been a rich source for historians on every other subject, he recounts Helen's death and there is no further reference to her, except once, seven years later, when he writes: 'Of Her, for fear of tears, I never speak.' He should have spoken of her, and tolerated the tears. Not to speak of her must have felt like pretending she had not existed, and that must have felt like betrayal. It did not help Dalton to like himself. Denis Healey believes that, from the moment of his daughter's death, 'an essential part of his personality ceased to develop. Peter Pan was never far away. His capacity for human feeling withered, though he tried to revive it by a series of sentimental attachments to younger men. Many politicians attempt to develop a persona for public show. With Hugh Dalton the persona came to replace the personality.'

By 1945 he was very much alone. His social life partly revolved around the younger men whose political careers he was advancing – Hugh Gaitskell, Evan Durbin, James Callaghan, Denis Healey, Anthony Crosland. He wrote that they were a substitute for the friends he had lost in the war, that he had always stood for youth against age, and no doubt it was all true, but he was also, probably, a repressed homosexual whose young male friends fulfilled both an emotional and a psychological need.

For Clem, the act of disappointing Hugh Dalton carried few political risks. Disappointing Ernest Bevin carried considerable risks, especially with Morrison still plotting. Bevin was Clem's key political ally. Several contemporaries, and several historians, have concluded that Bevin was the real power. But this is to mistake appearance for reality, and Clem showed who was in charge right at the start. Bevin might have wanted the Exchequer, but he would work where Clem Attlee told him to work. Oddly, given the King's role in his appointment, one of Bevin's first jobs was to suppress documents which would have gravely embarrassed the royal family. On 13 August 1945 he wrote urgently to Clem about the need to ensure the destruction of files relating to the Duke of Windsor, the former Edward VIII, and his stay in Spain in June and July 1940. 'They describe the efforts of the German government to retain him in Spain with a view to a compromise peace,' wrote Bevin, 'and contain second and third hand reports about the Duke's attitude derived from agents in contact with him ... A disclosure would in my opinion do grave harm to the national interest.' 'I entirely agree,' minuted Clem. The material was shown secretly to Churchill, who also agreed, and Bevin mentioned the matter to the King, reporting that George VI was 'much distressed'.

Another appointment stamped Clem's mark unmistakably on the new Cabinet. Just the previous year Aneurin Bevan had come within an inch of being expelled from the party, after being a thorn in Clem's side throughout the life of the coalition government. Under most Labour leaders this would have meant banishment from the government, as Ramsay MacDonald banished John Wheatley. Bevan himself expected nothing better, and was amazed to be offered the Ministry of Health.

Why did Clem choose Bevan? Bevan's biographer Michael Foot writes: 'For a full unravelment of the riddle the world had to wait until Mr Attlee produced his autobiography. "For Health" he wrote "I chose Aneurin Bevan, whose abilities had up to now been displayed only in opposition, but I felt that he had it in him to do good service."' Foot would not have been much more enlightened if he had seen the unpublished draft, which just added: 'He had the ability, but he might not have the judgement.' Since Clem will not explain himself properly, others have to try. Foot says: 'Some [of Bevan's friends] suspiciously noted that [Bevan] had been given one of the toughest jobs in the Government.' It was probably much less devious than that. Clem wanted the most powerful potential left-wing rebel inside the government rather than outside it, and realised that to get Bevan inside, he must give him a real job. But he also seems to have valued Bevan's intellectual gifts, restless energy, and determination, and believed that these qualities would be put to good use in the building of the National Health Service. It is worth adding – because Clem is often quite wrongly presented, not least by Foot, as having been little more than a spectator in Nye Bevan's achievements – that under any other Labour leader, Bevan would probably not have had the opportunity offered by Clem.

The Ministry of Education, with the huge task of implementing the 1944 Education Act, was expected to go to Chuter Ede, the former teacher who had worked with Butler on the Act. But Clem wanted Ede for the Home Office, and Education went to Ellen Wilkinson, partly because Clem wanted a woman in the Cabinet. She had been a left-wing rebel in the Twenties and had spent most of the previous five years scheming to get Clem replaced by Morrison. Under most Prime Ministers, this would have severely damaged her chances of promotion. Clem had originally considered her for Health, which went to Bevan. This is clear from the sheet of paper on which he planned his Cabinet, where her name is scratched out beside 'health' so that it is only just legible. Bevan does not seem to have been included in his first draft. Ellen Wilkinson instantly discovered hitherto unsuspected qualities in the new Prime Minister. A biography of Clem published in 1946, *The Man from Limehouse*, by an American academic, contains an introduction by Ellen Wilkinson which must be one of the most lavish eulogies any Prime Minister has received:

> I have seen him at a stormy Party meeting, when men of great emotional force were making passionate speeches . . . Mr Attlee is seated at the platform table, apparently concentrating all his attention on drawing an exquisitely accurate geometrical design on some odd scrap of paper . . . Mr Attlee gets up rather slowly and casually, and in a quiet, reasonable voice he will make one of his unemotional, sensible speeches, which brings the question of the moment from heights of passion and fury to the level of sensible party colleagues discussing the best way of meeting a given situation. I have seen 200 angry men, after such a speech, leave a room wondering what they had been making such a fuss about.

No doubt this was the same phenomenon which caused Aneurin Bevan to say: 'He brings to the fierce struggle of politics the tepid enthusiasm of a lazy summer afternoon at a cricket match.'

These decisions – all surprising, all imaginative, all carrying potential political risks – were a clear indication of how Clem proposed to run his government, of the sort of man he was and the sort of Prime Minister he would be, judged by what he did, and not by the little he said.

The shy schoolboy, who turned a bright shade of purple at the slightest embarrassment, was now a man of sixty-two with a stronger inner certainty than any of the superficially more confident men around him. The shyness had not gone away. It had been harnessed and put to work. Other Prime Ministers waste time and energy glad-handing their backbenchers in the corridors of the Palace of Westminster. Clem told his new MPs not to feel affronted if he failed to greet them when he met them in the corridors: 'It's only because I'm shy.' 'Before he was Prime Minister,' Roy Jenkins told me, 'his conversation-stopping remarks and the fact that he was difficult to talk to seemed like deficiencies.' He was known for terseness, so no-one expected him to explain himself very much. He said in retirement in 1960: 'People who talk too much soon find themselves up against it. Harold Laski, for instance. A brilliant chap, but he talked too much.' Much more cruelly, he said of Dalton: 'Perfect ass. His trouble was he *would* talk. He always liked to have a secret to confide to somebody else to please him.'

People say that Attlee never had an image: he just loved cricket, Haileybury and University College, Oxford, spoke very little and only in monosyllables, and did not give himself the airs and graces expected of a Prime Minister. But that *was* his image. Are we to suppose that he never realised the way in which the Attlee stories which developed around him dictated how he was perceived, then and for decades afterwards?

Clem Attlee turned suburban mannerisms and staccato, pronoun-less sentences into precious political assets. 'Very sensibly', says Roy Jenkins, 'he somewhat cultivated [his mannerisms], and enjoyed being just a little of a caricature of himself.' More privately – perhaps because they contributed less to the image – he loved poetry, the Italian Renaissance and *The Times* crossword. Back in 1918, when Oscar Tobin wanted him to stand for the Mile End Council, Clem had said: 'Think it over.' Tobin replied: 'I already thought it over' to which Clem took his pipe from his mouth and said: '*I'll* think it over.' Now, instead of driving Oscar Tobin mad, he was driving political journalists mad. One of them, James Margach, recalled one of his few press conferences. Scheduled to last an hour, it was flagging within ten minutes. The replies Margach remembered were: 'Nothing in that'; 'You're off beam again'; 'I've never heard that, have you' and 'That idea seems bonkers to me – the Cabinet's never looked at it.' At last Ernest Hunter, political correspondent of the *Daily Herald*, asked: 'Prime Minister, we're all stumped. What's number twelve across, two words, seven and six letters?' For the first time Clem took his pipe out of his mouth and laid it on the table. He said: 'Your parents wasted their money sending you to college, Hunter. You've forgotten anything you ever knew about the classics.' He then spoke for more than ten minutes, reports Margach. 'Didn't the lobby know that the first oblique reference was to Homer, that the fellow who set the puzzle that day liked to pop in Latin and Greek hints to put you off the scent. Indeed the chap had a perfect flair for Biblical affairs as well: where he slipped in the passing reference to something being well marked, it was a clear pointer to St Mark's guidance . . .'

Harold Wilson probably cared too much for what newspapers printed about him. Clem Attlee perhaps cared too little. When his press secretary, Francis Williams, brought him a particularly unpleasing reference to himself he would grunt, 'That so? Suppose they've got to write something. Circulation slipping, you think?' He did not read newspapers nor look at the cuttings. He read *The Times* each morning, as his father had done, but only for births, marriages and deaths and appointments; he completed *The Times* crossword; and he read the *Daily Herald* to keep him in touch with what his party was thinking.

He had – rather typically – appointed as press secretary the former *Daily Herald* editor who had wanted to replace him with Herbert Morrison. Francis Williams explained to his boss that Downing Street must have a telex machine so that he would know straight away what stories the press agencies were sending out to the newspapers. Clem resisted. What good could it do? Williams had his answer. It would keep the Prime Minister up-to-date with the lunchtime cricket scores. A week after the machine was installed, Clem looked into Williams's office with what, in Clem, passed for extreme concern. 'Francis, you know my cricket machine at the Cabinet door? When I checked it just now for the lunchtime score at Lords, it was ticking out the decisions and subjects discussed at the Cabinet meeting this morning. How can it do that?' Williams explained that he routinely briefed the political correspondents. 'OK, Francis, I'll leave the show to you. Good work.' Throughout his time as Prime Minister there was never a television in Downing Street or Chequers.

Yet Margach, a lobby correspondent from the Forties to the Seventies, says: 'I have never known the press so consistently and irresponsibly political, slanted and prejudiced' as during the years of Clem's government. The Prime Minister himself was a figure of fun in the press throughout his six years in office. If it did not upset him, it upset his colleagues. Herbert Morrison's day began with the press cuttings, and he always wrote or telephoned if he did not like what he saw. As early as 1946 the Attorney-General, Sir Hartley Shawcross, was attacking 'the campaign of calumny and misrepresentation which the Tory Party and the Tory stooge press' had directed at the Labour government. 'Freedom of the press does not mean freedom to tell lies.' In October 1946, Parliament set up a Royal Commission on the Press, which eventually forced the Press Council on the industry.

Most politicians go home and talk politics, and could not easily

New public relations office at 10 Downing Street

live with a partner who did not share their politics. But Violet Attlee might have voted Conservative if she had not been married to the leader of the Labour Party, and none of Clem's four children became socialists. There was no political talk at home. When he went home he left his work, as it were, in the office. He had the immense strength of a self-contained man.

Most politicians would be upset if the adjective 'unknown' were constantly applied to them. Not Clem. Whoever coined the term 'a modest little man with plenty to be modest about' was wrong. Clem had a total egoism – more so than Bevin, more so even than Churchill. It made him certain enough of his judgements not to feel that he had to explain or justify them to anyone, which is why his explanations, when he gave any, seem inadequate to the occasion. (The phrase is usually attributed, almost certainly incorrectly, to Churchill. *Daily Worker* journalists of the time have claimed it, quite plausibly, for one of their own, Claud Cockburn.)

What *is* true is that he *behaved* modestly. Soon after the election he insisted on travelling from Westminster to his constituency by train and bus. He boarded a bus and started rooting in his pocket for the fare, as he had done dozens of times before. By the time the bus got to the East End it was overrun by photographers clambering over the seats, and in Stepney the police begged him to send for an official car for his journeys to and from Downing Street. He agreed reluctantly, protesting that he could not justify taking his official car when petrol was rationed.

At first, before the Attlees moved into Downing Street, he carried on taking the train home to Stanmore, travelling by himself, a detective following discreetly a few paces behind just in case. Generally he went unrecognised. He had to change at Baker Street, where a woman once approached him and said: 'Have you ever been told you look just like Mr Attlee?' 'Frequently,' he replied, and boarded his train. Most mornings Clem, Vi and the dog Ting would slip out of the back door of Number 10 for a walk in St James's Park, and would always stop for a while to watch the ducks. He lived modestly. He and Vi did not want to live, as their predecessors had done, in the state rooms on the first floor of Number 10, amid the panoply of the premiership. They wanted a small self-contained flat and arranged for eight rooms at the top of the house, which had been turned into a flat for servants by the Chamberlains, to be converted for their own use.

Throughout his time there, Clem always finished his papers in the Cabinet Room before retiring to the flat. Even as Prime Minister he refused to take his work home. 'You don't want to come home and find a spouse who wanted to argue about the Education Act,' says Felicity. 'When my father came up in the evenings she made it home so that he could shut off completely.'

When not out at an official function in the evenings, Clem's habit was to come down to the Cabinet Room from the Downing Street flat at 9 pm and ring a buzzer for his papers. A private secretary would take them in and he would light his pipe and get to work. He worked very fast, usually taking a decision, rarely asking for more information or for people to be consulted. He wrote quickly, generally in blunt blue or red crayon, so fast that it was almost illegible. Fortunately the recipient was normally only required to distinguish 'yes CRA' from 'no CRA'. At about 11 pm he would ring the buzzer again. 'I've finished all those. Nothing else in? Good night then.' These long evening sessions would come on top of a full working day, normally spent in the Cabinet Room unless he had a speech to prepare, in which case he would retire to a small study on the first floor and beat on his, by now very ancient, typewriter.

Clem and Vi loved Chequers. Tom, approaching seventy and the chairman of the Cornwall district of the Workers' Educational Association and a member of many local committees, was one of the first weekend guests there. At Christmas 1946, Clem brought to Chequers, as he wrote to Tom, 'quite a considerable party, [including] Edric [Vi's brother and Tom's oldest friend], Margaret [Clem's sister] . . . We were lucky to have all the children here also . . . A fine children's party on Boxing Day with games, a Christmas tree and cinema. We had some 30 children complete with parents . . .' There he found time for his family, sitting with them, telling them parliamentary anecdotes (but never discussing serious politics). 'Ever tell you about Nancy Astor?' She had once, he assured them, told the House that Italy could not raise its birth rate despite the personal efforts of both Mussolini and the Pope. 'Hear about the people I once showed round the House?' He said he had warned his tour party that, as the Speaker passed, a policeman would shout, 'Hats off strangers' and they were to remove their hats. But a fellow MP saw a colleague he wanted to speak to and shouted 'Neil!' Clem's party knelt.

Tom's son and daughter-in-law were among the first lunch guests in Downing Street. Mary, Clem's oldest sister, a missionary, came to Downing Street direct from the ship that brought her back, after many years, from South Africa.

Like any pipe-smoking man from the suburbs, Clem was happiest with the familiar. Wishing to choose a Parliamentary Private Secretary from among the new Labour MPs, he writes in his autobiography, 'There was a wide choice, but, other things being equal, I saw no reason why I should not select someone from my old school.' For the first time there were Old Haileyburians in the Labour Party in the House of Commons . . . I chose Geoffrey de Freitas, who had had somewhat the same background as myself – as barrister, social worker and municipal councillor – together with war experience, scholarship and athletic distinction; he was an air officer and a Cambridge man.' He wrote to Tom: 'My young Haileyburians in the House are an able lot. Whiteley [the chief whip] selected one for a whip, Morrison another for a PPS.' (Morrison's choice as PPS was Christopher Mayhew.) Later he told Tom of his discovery that the Air Council was soon to have a majority of Old Haileyburians.

'He evidently seeks me out and wants to talk,' wrote Mayhew in his diary. 'The truth is – our old school tie is a very strong link for him Years and years of working-class contacts make him feel entitled to this strong, secret loyalty to Haileybury and Oxford. If Geoffrey de Freitas or I ever let him down I think he would feel it more of a blow than if anybody in the Cabinet did. Massigli [the French ambassador] whispered to me the other day, "Ush! Is it not true you are an 'Aileyburian too?"' But Haileybury took a long time to return his affection. The day after the election, the Master, Canon E. F. Bonhote, slipped unobtrusively into the chair always reserved for him at lunch, beside the head boy, Bill Tyrwhitt-Drake. 'Tyrwhitt-Drake, you know Clement Attlee's an old Haileyburian?' he murmured. 'It might be a nice gesture if you wrote him a note of congratulation.' Tyrwhitt-Drake, who, like most of his schoolfellows, had canvassed vigorously for the local Conservative candidate, and felt keenly that the nation had shown appalling ingratitude to Mr Churchill, replied stiffly: 'I'd rather not, sir, if you don't mind.' The Master said he entirely understood, and took on the onerous duty himself. Years afterwards, in 1962, Clem went to watch an Old Haileyburian cricket match and was introduced to Tyrwhitt-Drake. Tyrwhitt-Drake confessed that he had refused to write the letter of congratulation seventeen years earlier. Clem laughed heartily and said: 'My boy, in your position I'd probably have done the same.' Then they talked easily of their shared enthusiasms for cricket and the school.

Haileybury was for many years ambivalent about its most distinguished alumnus. He may have been Prime Minister, but he was a socialist. Today, however, it has an Attlee Room and a huge portrait of Clem hangs on the dining-room wall, right behind the place at which Bill Tyrwhitt-Drake sat in 1945 and refused to write and congratulate him.

In 1945 Clem was at the peak of his powers, with a sureness of touch which most party leaders going into an election would give their right arms for. The mood for a Labour victory had been created in 1940–41. Those months, when an invasion was expected any moment, brought a real sea change. If the nation was to pull together to fight Hitler, it had to be one nation – not two nations of conspicuous affluence and desperate poverty. Evacuation had given the comfortable middle classes their first real knowledge of slum life. A Women's Institute report, 'Town Children Through Country Eyes', noted:

In practically every batch of children there were some who suffered from head lice, skin diseases and bed-wetting . . . some children had never slept in beds . . . The state of the children [from Liverpool] was such that the school had to be fumigated after reception; we have never seen so many verminous children . . . Bread and lard are a usual breakfast for a number of [Walthamstow] children when at home . . . Most of the [Fulham] children had never sat down to a cooked meal.

The feeling was widespread that there should never again be one class which could dine at the Ritz, and another which could not afford proper food for its children. Labour's membership increased from 2.0 million in 1939 to three million in 1945, the Communist Party's numbers went from 15,000 in 1938 to 56,000 in 1942. The Beveridge Report sold half a million copies.

Yet Clem's private prediction in 1945 was a hung parliament in which he would form a government with the Liberals. Labour leaders feared that Churchill would be able to present himself as the man who united the nation and could lead a government which was above mere party. Churchill himself told 20,000 people in Coventry that they should not 'run away with the idea that you can vote [against the Conservatives] without voting against me'. Clem pottered in a few days later to address a much smaller audience. 'He looked like a businessman and obviously middle-class,' says Jack Jones, who chaired the meeting. 'He didn't make much of a speech, but then he never did. But what he had to say was sharp and clear, not the woolly-minded oratory you got from some of them. And that was what people wanted. He was a great electoral asset.'

Churchill was back in the rough-and-tumble of the hustings, which he enjoyed, and in which party leaders from time immemorial have made extreme accusations and extravagant claims, with scant regard for truth. And so, in his first election broadcast, Churchill said: 'No Socialist Government conducting the entire life and industry of the country could afford to allow free, sharp or violently-worded expression of public discontent. They would have to fall back on some form of Gestapo, no doubt very humanely directed in the first instance.'

Another Labour leader might have angrily denounced the dishonesty. Clem's broadcast the next day began: 'When I listened to the Prime Minister's speech last night . . . I realised at once what was his object. He wanted the electors to understand how great was the difference between Winston Churchill the great leader in war of a united nation' – here he dropped his voice from its grave tone so that he sounded suddenly casual and dismissive – 'and Mr Churchill, the party leader of the Conservatives.' He paid generous tribute to the Conservatives and Liberals, Labour's partners in the wartime coalition, and to 'our great leader in war, the Prime Minister'. He had politely thrown Churchill's bomb back in the Prime Minister's face, where it helped to destroy its creator.

He then outlined the difference between the parties.

> The Conservative Party believes that the basis of our economic activities must be what they call private enterprise, inspired by the motive of private profit. They seem to hold that if every individual pursues his own interest, somehow or other the interest of all will be served ... The country has been run on those principles for years, yet a great number of people in this country have always been badly-housed, badly-clothed, and deprived of the opportunity of work. The Labour Party believes that if you want certain results you must plan to procure them. In peace as in war the public interest must come first ...
>
> We need well-planned, well-built cities and parks and playing fields, homes and schools, factories and shops ... We do not want our beautiful country destroyed by haphazard development dictated only by profit ... We must have no more distressed areas.

He said with real feeling:

> There was a time when employers were free to employ little children sixteen hours a day. I remember when employers were free to employ sweated women finishing trousers at a penny halfpenny a pair ... It was freedom for the rich at the expense of the poor.

It was a remarkable broadcast. Just a month earlier, broadcasting about the United Nations, he had been hesitant, coughing and audibly turning the pages of his script, and had sounded like a Latin master at a minor public school, with pedantic pronunciations: 'problems' became 'prob-*lems*' and 'repair' became 'repayah'. But this election broadcast was different. Perhaps Williams had taken him in hand. Now he sounded like the family solicitor. No-one could imagine the mild-mannered, dignified Mr Attlee running any sort of Gestapo.

The *New Statesman* turned the theme into a limerick which, with Hitler only just defeated, had a nasty sting in the tail:

The Prime Minister Disposes

One empire; One leader; One folk
Is the Tory campaign master-stroke.
As a national jest
It is one of the best
But it's not an original joke.

For years afterwards Clem enjoyed telling the story of an old Stepney woman who wanted to vote for Mr Churchill. At the polling booth she found to her disappointment that Mr Churchill's name was not on the ballot paper, but fortunately she saw the name of Mr Attlee, and he had been Mr Churchill's deputy, so she happily voted for him instead. None of the usual buttons worked for Churchill this time. After the 'Gestapo' broadcast he tried claiming that a Labour government would really be run by the chairman of Labour's National Executive, Professor Harold Laski, that extreme left-winger with the sinister foreign-sounding name. Then he tried telling people that socialism was un-English because it had been invented in Europe; but Attlee's retort was to name Churchill's new guru, for Churchill had been much influenced by a book published in 1944, *The Road to Serfdom*, by an Austrian academic, Friedrich von Hayek, which was to have a spectacular revival after 1979 under another Conservative Prime Minister.

Clem noted Churchill's floundering with some satisfaction and produced a remarkable Attlee aphorism: 'Trouble with Winston. Nails his trousers to the mast. Can't get down.' He wrote to Tom: 'Winston keeps slogging away at the silly Laski business, but I don't think he gets the better of the exchanges with me.' He added: 'I always liked old Isaac Foot' (a long-standing Liberal MP), 'a good type of old puritanical Radical. He has a lively brood of sons of varied views.' One son, Labour candidate and soon to be MP for Devonport, was Michael Foot, Nye Bevan's friend and biographer.

Churchill travelled the country in a cavalcade, arriving at each meeting in style amid great clamour to address huge audiences. Clem travelled in the passenger seat of the Hillman, with Vi at the wheel, an atlas on his knees if they were unsure of the route, *The Times* crossword when they knew the way. The difference in style was noticed. Clem was certainly the last major party leader ever to campaign that way, and it was considered eccentric even in 1945. To the new intake of the 1945 election, the young men and women who were to dominate Labour politics for the next forty years, it was part of the slightly antique puzzle that was Clement Attlee. For the

215

1945 Labour MPs were very different from all their predecessors. For the first time, they were not dominated by trade unionists. More than half of Labour's MPs in 1945 were very able, highly educated young men (and one or two women) who were new to Parliament. From these men came all Labour's leaders after Clem right up to 1983: Hugh Gaitskell, Harold Wilson, James Callaghan and Michael Foot.

To these people, Clem Attlee was a very strange fish indeed, and few if any of them ever understood him. Those new MPs are now old men and women themselves, many of them with distinguished careers behind them, but they still struggle to understand the enigma who led them in their first Parliament. And they have largely dictated our view of him, so that we often see only the terse, pedestrian figure, without passion or poetry, whom they knew. Barbara Castle told me that his socialism was of the kindly but mild Toynbee Hall type. But Clem had disliked Toynbee Hall socialism, feeling that it was about doing kind things for the poor instead of transforming society. 'I think the key to him', she added, 'was that he was a conventional military man. They obey orders: and he had a detailed manifesto, so he carried it out. He had no real ideas of his own.' She added, with real puzzlement: 'How could he bear to be married to a Tory? What could they have talked about?' In fact Vi had joined the Labour Party in the 1930s, 'by my own wish, not through my husband's influence' she once told a newspaper interviewer.

Barbara Castle wrote in her autobiography that he was 'a decent man who wanted to build a decent society'. But 'his clipped laconic sentences could dry up conversation within minutes.' Yet she got on well with him: 'Everyone else gave up hope of getting a word out of him. He was grateful to me because I made the conversation and he never could.' She was rewarded with a mildly vulgar joke which the Clem of ten years before would not have dreamed of telling in front of a woman. It was about a tom-cat who ambled seductively into the midst of a group of female cats. He invited one of them for a walk on the roof, and when she returned, her friends crowded round eagerly to hear the full story. 'It was boring,' she said. 'All he could do was talk about his operation.'

Michael Foot thought Clem 'the beneficiary of a victory he had done little to contrive . . . He remained ill at ease on the platform or in Parliament, often giving an exhibition of feebleness or reducing great matters to the most meagre aspect. [But] . . . his light shone best under a bushel. Behind the scenes his sharp, cryptic manner assisted the despatch of business within both the Cabinet and the whole administration.' Attlee, adds Foot, 'bore his immense individual burden with an amazing, almost carefree, fortitude.' But 'was it a wiry toughness or just lack of imagination which kept Attlee cool to the point of obliviousness in a crisis?'

Foot told me that Clem 'tried to diminish the contribution of the left. Harold Laski built up the party during the war. Attlee did not treat Laski properly. Laski was terribly hurt, you know. He'd given his life to the Labour Party.'

But the man who became Nye Bevan's Parliamentary Private Secretary, Donald Bruce, says Foot is wrong: 'Michael is more interested in ideas than in power. Attlee was interested in power. We were lucky to have Attlee. The more you look back, the greater he becomes. He certainly wasn't given to over-long conversations. If you wanted to engage his attention, you had to talk about cricket.' Unless, of course, you had been at Haileybury, like another 1945 arrival, Christopher Mayhew. With other Cabinet members Mayhew could only talk politics, but 'Clem Attlee would quickly turn the conversation to other topics.'

> Australia would surely lose the Ashes . . . Haileybury seemed to have a good fifteen this year. Did I remember those wonderful tries my brother Pat scored in the 'varsity match at Twickenham in 1937? Attlee was notoriously taciturn, but on these occasions he would talk for pleasure instead of making conversation. He seemed to be coming up for air.

So. Here was a man who talked freely and happily about cricket, about Haileybury, about *Times* crossword compilers and, with his family, about poetry and Renaissance literature: about anything in the world except his job. Yet Denis Healey, who has as wide a set of cultural interests as any living politician, could write: 'Attlee's only interests outside politics were cricket and his public school, Haileybury.' Healey retails with approval a colleague's comment that a conversation with an ordinary man is like a game of tennis, but 'a conversation with Attlee was like throwing biscuits to a dog – all you could get out of him was yup, yup, yup.' Healey started to tell me that Attlee was 'rather colourless', then checked himself and added: 'But with very strong black and white shades.'

No-one, says Healey, really knew him; and it is true that no-one of Healey's generation ever really knew him. For example, Healey told me Clem 'found Labour's National Executive a bit of a bore' while Roy Jenkins said the opposite: 'Attlee may have been the only

Labour leader who actually liked Labour's National Executive. He was imbued with the spirit of the Labour Party.' Jenkins is right. Clem liked all Labour's arcane structures. It was one of his most unusual eccentricities.

Jenkins's father, Arthur Jenkins, had been Clem's PPS for ten years and Clem was a frequent visitor to the teenage Roy's family home. Yet Roy Jenkins 'was never at ease in his presence. I did not know how to talk to him, or, more importantly, how to make him talk.'

An odd misjudgement came from Woodrow Wyatt, who years later could still write that for Attlee 'dangerous foreigners began at Calais and didn't stop until you reached Bombay.' He was talking about Attlee the internationalist, the man who loved Brittany and Italy and translated Italian literature into English for pleasure.

Part of the reason the newcomers had difficulty in understanding him was that, whereas Clem had written two books, they only read one of them. They all read *The Labour Party in Perspective*. But they had not read *The Social Worker*. If they had, they might have understood their leader rather better. To the new boys in 1945, most of them in their twenties and thirties, the sixty-two-year-old Prime Minister was inevitably something of a fossil. The idea that he might be more radical than they were – and he was more radical than most of them – was not only absurd, but damaging to the self-respect of youth.

The 'new boys' made their presence felt at once. The Commons chamber was being repaired after bomb damage, and the new Parliament met in the chamber of the House of Lords, which was much too small. Excited young men who were sure they were about to change the world overflowed into the corridors. 'They were very assertive to begin with,' says John Boyd-Carpenter, a Conservative MP in 1945. 'They were creating a new world and we were relics of the past. Gradually the influence of the House of Commons began to assert itself and by the end of the Parliament they were as well behaved as anyone. They were civilised by the institution.' As the Speaker opened the new parliamentary session, a mining MP, led his new colleagues in a spirited rendering of 'The Red Flag'. 'Tories were horrified,' writes Michael Foot, 'and the officials of the House went on with the ceremony, much as a polite host continues the conversation after his guest has upset the soup.' Four future Labour leaders, two of them future Prime Ministers, joined in lustily with the rest.

In Potsdam, Stalin and Truman at first underestimated Clem as much as his own backbenchers. To the Russian and American delegations, it seemed that Clem Attlee was a small figure in Ernest Bevin's shadow, and that Britain's foreign policy had not changed from three days before when it had been conducted by Churchill and Eden.

That impression is wrong. Right from the start the new Prime Minister set about trying to create a new foreign policy which brought him into direct collision course with his Foreign Secretary, the Foreign Office, the defence establishment and the previous Conservative administration. That odd, grey little man with his bourgeois, commonplace expressions and exaggerated affection for his not-especially-distinguished public school, had for a decade dreamed of a new world order. Instead of the League of Nations, he wanted to see a United Nations with real power to coerce an aggressor. Secretly he wanted world government, and said so when he retired, but as Prime Minister he was willing to strive for what might just be attainable. He wanted to see nations giving up a substantial slice of their sovereignty to this international policeman, and giving it control over armed forces.

During the war he had encouraged Churchill's discussions about the proposed UN, using every excuse to insert his views into the debate. As Dominions Secretary he had written a detailed paper on the way in which the British Dominions could be represented at the UN. 1945, if ever, was the moment, he believed, when war between nations might be abolished.

Today this sounds like some unworldly idealist's dream. In 1945 it was a sober estimate from one of the great realists of politics. He told the United Nations Association in October 1945: 'I wish to say quite simply that it is the firm intention of His Majesty's Government to make the success of the United Nations the primary object of their foreign policy.' He told the opening session of the UN in 1946: 'In [Britain] great nobles used to practise private war in disregard of the authority of central government. The time came when private armies were abolished . . . What has been done in Britain and in other countries on a small stage has now to be effected throughout the whole world.'

Clem believed the Cold War was avoidable; and Bevin and Churchill believed it had already started. Bevin was said to think that the Soviet Union was a breakaway from the Transport and General Workers' Union. Churchill is credited with announcing the start of the Cold War in a speech in Fulton, Missouri, in March 1946, but in fact he announced it, as Prime Minister, in a private letter to President Truman as early as June 1945, talking of 'the descent of an iron curtain between us and everything to the Eastward'. Like all Churchill's best lines, his iron curtain speech of the next year went through at least one early draft.

Anthony Eden was appalled at Clem's view, answering an Attlee memo just before the election with the tart response: 'We cannot unfortunately assume that Russian policy has developed to the point where they are prepared to participate in a genuinely international security system rather than pursue their own national interests.' The First Sea Lord, Admiral Andrew Cunningham, wrote in his diary: 'Atlee [sic] has apparently written what appears to be a damned silly letter to the PM saying we ought not to oppose a great country like Russia having bases anywhere she wants them. What an ass!' To Cunningham's horror the ass was Prime Minister just weeks later, and by the end of August was staking out the new ground in a memo to the Cabinet. He was not, he said, satisfied with the arguments of the Foreign Secretary that Britain should take over Italy's former colonies so as to defend the British Empire:

> The British Empire can only be defended by its membership of the United Nations Organisation. If we do not accept this, we had better say so. If we do accept this we should seek to make it effective and not at the same time act on outworn conceptions. If the new organisation is a reality, it does not matter who holds Cyrenaica or Somalia or controls the Suez Canal . . .

He continued: 'Cyrenaica will saddle us with an expense we can ill afford . . . British Somaliland has always been a dead loss and a nuisance to us. We only occupied it as part of the scramble for Africa. If we now add Ogaden and Italian Somaliland we shall have a troublesome ward with an unpleasant neighbour in Ethiopia . . .'

Admiral Cunningham noted: 'The PM . . . practically preaches unilateral disarmament and advocates not putting in our claim for trusteeship of Cyrenaica and greater Somalia.' Alanbrooke, Chief of the Imperial General Staff, wrote later: 'We were . . . shocked by Attlee's new Cabinet paper in which apparently the security of the Middle East must rest in the power of the United Nations!' But Clem nonetheless prevented Britain from taking on the trusteeship of Cyrenaica and Somaliland. The difference between Attlee and Bevin was summed up by Edward Stettinus, the US representative at the UN: 'Attlee had his heart in the UN . . . Bevin thought that the emphasis would be more on power politics of the world in the immediate future than anything else.' Bevin's ideal foreign policy would not have differed from that of his predecessor, Eden. Listening to a Bevin speech, Rab Butler once remarked: 'Hasn't Anthony Eden got fat!' Aneurin Bevan thought Bevin was 'a big bumble bee caught in a web and he thinks he's the spider.'

Clem foresaw the end of the power of Empire a full decade before the myth collapsed around Anthony Eden's ears at Suez, but in 1945 his view was far too realistic for Bevin or for the Chiefs of Staff. He knew, and Hugh Dalton knew, that Britain simply could not afford the scale of military commitments which the Foreign Office and the Chiefs of Staff were demanding – especially when, just one week after the Japanese surrender, in August 1945, without any warning, the Americans ended Lease-Lend. From that day, Truman declared that Britain would have to pay for everything supplied by the USA.

Lease-Lend had been offered for the duration of the war, and the war was over. But no-one had imagined that it would be withdrawn so abruptly. It was a devastating blow, leaving Britain in what the Chancellor, Hugh Dalton, called 'an almost desperate plight'. Without Lease-Lend Britain could not feed its population or pay its debts. It would, eventually, starve. Clem, for the first time but not the last, appealed to the Dunkirk spirit. He told a rally in Trafalgar Square: 'Until better times come to us our duty is to save all we can and to devote these savings to reconstruction and peace.' People might think their wartime sacrifices were enough but 'such thoughts are wrong and dangerous . . . Look at our wartime achievements not as an end but as a beginning . . . I have a special word of praise . . . for the workers in the savings movement . . .'

He told the TUC in September 1945: 'We are a games-playing people, and you all know what I am talking about when I stress the value of team work . . . It is just the kind of spirit that makes a good football or cricket team, that makes a good regiment, a good air crew, a good ship's company, or a good industry. It is equally necessary if one is to have a good government . . .' He was the first Prime Minister to address the TUC and, accepting General Secretary Walter Citrine's invitation, he suggested a general talk 'as I want to have the closest co-operation between the TUC and the government and between us personally.'

But no amount of emollient words passed between government and TUC, no amount of team spirit, even the spirit of Dunkirk, could cushion the blow that President Truman dealt the government.

The withdrawal of Lease-Lend did indeed require a Dunkirk-type effort. 'I doubt', Clem wrote years later, 'if the American administration realised how serious was the blow which they struck.' Truman was new to the job. He had become President on the death of Franklin Roosevelt after less than three months as Vice-President. He had no experience of international affairs and Roosevelt had not kept him in touch with them. He signed the paper put in front of him without thinking about its implications. Clem had rather taken to the new President. Harry Truman 'had good instincts and his judgement was sound'. What the President thought of Clem is unclear. Dean Acheson told Kenneth Harris that Truman 'recognised Attlee as someone like himself, a man with his feet on the ground, who spoke in simple, direct terms and as briefly as possible', but the homely President from Missouri confided to his diary: 'Attlee is an Oxford man and talks like the much overrated Mr Eden.' Either way, the fact was that Truman had let Clem down badly – and not for the last time.

What was to be done? The stark truth was that Britain must have a loan, and there was only one place it could come from: the USA.

Maynard Keynes, by 1945 Lord Keynes, Britain's leading economist, was sent to Washington to negotiate it. ('Have I told you the pleasant slogan of the city?' Clem had written to Tom the previous year. 'Bankers of the world unite, you have nothing to lose but your Keynes.') Back in May, Keynes had sent to the Cabinet a survey of Britain's economic position at the end of the war, full of hope that Britain could survive without being totally at the mercy of the Americans, despite overwhelming debts, and that the Americans would behave generously. 'The President', he wrote, 'has often used words implying that he accepted in some sense the principle of equal sacrifice.' But 'if the hostile forces in the US overwhelm the forces of light and friendship . . . then the whole situation is changed . . . We should have to retire, as Russia did between the wars, to starve and reconstruct.'

There was 'not much doubt that the Americans would be prepared to lend us large sums *on their own terms.*' These terms would include unfettered conversion of dollars in the sterling area, and 'would place us in a worse situation than Germany.' The US had to be persuaded not to insist on convertibility, and the question was 'how to persuade Uncle Sam, who might be under the conviction that he was Uncle Sap.' It proved impossible. Keynes found a US government under heavy pressure to withdraw from Europe and not to appear to subsidise socialism in Britain. If there was to be a loan at all, the terms would be very tough. And there would be implied conditions which would make Britain subordinate to the USA on foreign affairs. While Keynes was negotiating, the US Secretary of State, James Byrnes, presented Ernest Bevin with a list of places around the world where the Americans would like to have bases, with the clear expectation that Bevin would support him in obtaining them. Thus Britain's financial problems merged with its foreign policy, and the two have remained in unholy alliance ever since.

The relationship was further strained after Truman authorised the dropping of the atom bomb on Japan, which seemed to Clem to make his central foreign policy objective – an international authority far more urgent. He was shocked by the reports he received of its horrific effects, shocked that Truman had used it without consulting Britain and shocked that atomic secrets had not been shared with Britain as the wartime agreement stipulated. He at once fired off a telegram to Truman:

> . . . There is widespread anxiety as to whether the new power will be used to serve or to destroy civilisation . . . I consider, therefore, that you and I, as head of the governments which have control of this great force, should without delay make a joint declaration of our intentions to utilise the existence of this great power, not for our own ends, but as trustees for humanity in the interests of all peoples in order to promote peace and justice in the world . . .

But there was no answer, and Clem and Bevin realised that something was badly wrong. So far from handing over the secret to the UN, it looked as though the Americans might refuse even to hand it over to the UK, though all the initial work had been done in Britain, and had been given to the USA in 1943 on the understanding that the research would be shared. Clem flew to Washington to sort it out in November 1945, with Sir John Anderson, who chaired the government's committee on atomic energy. During the flight Clem advised Anderson to read Wisden to settle the mind, and drew what must have been a dreadfully strained analogy between choosing a Cabinet and selecting a cricket team.

In Washington he found a serious problem. The American administration had never made public its agreement to share atomic secrets, and dared not do so now. The best Truman could offer was a general statement that there would be 'full and effective co-operation in the field of atomic energy'. Privately, Truman said secrets would be shared. While in Washington, Clem tried to help

Keynes by allaying the suspicions of the American people that their loan was going to help finance socialism. He told a joint session of Congress: 'There is, and always will be, scope for enterprise; but when big business gets too powerful, so that it becomes monopolistic, we hold it is not safe to leave it in private hands. Further, in the world today we believe, as do most people in Britain, that one must plan the economic activities of the country if we are to assure the common man a fair deal.'

'What a good speech you made in Congress,' Vi wrote to him. It was one of the many long, loving, untidy, unselfconscious letters she always wrote when he was away, and one of the few that has survived. 'Directly you finished John Wilmot [Minister of Supply] rang me up to say what a wonderful speech it was – wasn't it nice of him? Everybody has been complimenting me on your wonderful speech. I had a very nice cable from Mr Mackenzie King [Canadian Prime Minister].

'Clemmie [Churchill] came to tea with me and I showed her the flat – she liked it very much . . . I shall have some sandwiches and Bovril when I come in.' Vi was learning French and had given a tea for Cabinet wives. 'I've also had a long letter from Griff [Clem's old batman]. He doesn't seem to have had the framed photograph of you yet.'

A few days later she was writing about how she had held a seance at Downing Street with Felicity and some of her friends. 'At dinner this evening our talk got psychic . . . After dinner we tried table-lifting. Afterwards we tried "dear kind friend" with a glass – but it didn't spell anything sensible.' But one of the women went into a trance. 'Now, was she acting – unconsciously? I think that it was too well done to be acting. It was really most uncanny.' Clem's reply has not survived, but it must have contained a strong dose of scepticism.

Two days later she described her mishap on the way to the Cenotaph on Remembrance Sunday. 'We were just going through the archway . . . when I felt that I was losing my nether garments! There was only one thing to be done, to say hurriedly to our guide that I must go back to hold up my garments through my dress. I dived into one of the back rooms at Number 10 and did up the buttons and once more sallied through to our guide – I can't think what he thought of my hasty retreat.'

Clem was to bring back some two-ply white vest wool, a pink bed-jacket ('something light and pretty') and some pink bedroom slippers. Clem no doubt brought back from the USA exactly what he had been commissioned to bring, which is more than can be said for Lord Keynes, who emerged the next month with a loan of $3.75 billion, not the $5 billion he had hoped for, and on very harsh terms indeed.

Britain had to agree to convertibility. Within a year of the loan being granted, Britain must make sterling convertible to dollars on demand, which could easily lead to a run on the pound and a financial crisis of 1931 proportions. Repayment was to begin in December 1951 at two per cent interest over fifty years. 'If best American offer is large loan at 2 per cent interest,' Dalton had telegrammed to Britain's negotiators in October, 'we would not accept it. We remain firm that we will not accept obligations which we do not see reasonable certainty of discharging.' But they accepted it. The decision was effectively taken by the 'inner cabinet' – the 'big five' in the government: Attlee, Morrison, Bevin, Dalton and Stafford Cripps, now President of the Board of Trade. During the negotiations these five met most weekday evenings, from about 9 pm to about midnight, anxiously reviewing every telegram from the Washington negotiators and sending them instructions.

They then had to watch for months while Truman battled to persuade the Congress to agree the loan even on these harsh terms. Clem, Dalton and Bevin had to bite their tongues as they were depicted, day after day, in Congress and in the American press, as sponging socialists crawling to Uncle Sam so that they could feather-bed their people. Clem told Parliament with characteristic understatement but uncharacteristic bitterness: 'If the role assigned to us had been to expand our exports, we should, of course, be in an immeasurably stronger position than we are today.' Bevin wrote to Cripps: 'When the PM made his statement in the House on Lease-Lend, we were met with headlines in the US calling us "cry babies" . . . the world must realise that though we have paid such a terrible price in this war we are not down and out.' Today, fifty years later, that American view has been revived on this side of the Atlantic, with British historian Correlli Barnett writing of Keynes being sent to 'cadge' American 'handouts'.

Churchill helped the government by talking to his friend Bernard Baruch, an influential politician who had warned Congress not to help foreign countries 'to nationalise their industries against us'. Churchill telegrammed to Clem that Baruch and Secretary of State James Byrnes had visited him in his US hotel room and Baruch had put his well-known objections to the loan. 'I rejoined that failure of the loan at this stage would bring about such distress and call for so much privation in our island as to play into the hands of extremists of all kinds.' Churchill also gave an off-the-record press briefing in Washington, where he said that failure of the loan would strengthen two extremes in Britain: Communists on the one hand, and Imperial Tariffites on the other. He asked Clem to keep this telegram secret 'but of course Bevin and Chancellor should see it if you think it worthwhile and I should like to give Anthony a copy.' Clem, a connoisseur of Churchillian insults, would have enjoyed the delicate difference in the way he referred to Bevin, Dalton and Eden. The hated Dalton is only referred to by his office. Clem cabled back: 'I am sure you will have done much good . . .'

The House of Commons also had to be persuaded. Without the loan, Dalton told the House of Commons, '. . . we should have to undergo greater hardships and privations than even during the war; and all those hopes of better times, to follow in the wake of victory, would be dissipated in despair and disillusion.' So they swallowed the loan, and its accompanying harsh terms and bitter insults. They also had to swallow an astonishing rebuff over atomic energy. By April 1946 it was clear that, no matter what Truman had said in Washington, information on atomic secrets was not going to be shared. Clem cabled a protest to Truman followed by a 2,000-word summary of the agreements which the USA had, undeniably, broken. Truman did not answer. That summer, Congress passed the McMahon Bill which forbade the administration from passing any atomic information to any foreign government.

The turn of events in the USA denied Clem his hope that a powerful UN would be established quickly. If the USA would not even share nuclear secrets with its closest ally, the ally which had provided all the initial research on the understanding that the results would be shared, then the chance of getting it to cede any significant amount of power, sovereignty or armed capability to the UN must be rated zero. But this, to Clem, was no reason to suppose that Britain could or should police the world. Even with the loan, Dalton told the Cabinet at the start of 1946 that 'he was very much worried by the very large expenditure overseas . . . Could we possibly afford to continue in this way?' Clem backed him: 'There was no doubt that the nation could not afford either the manpower or the money for forces of the size suggested by the Chiefs of Staff.'

Unfortunately, the Foreign Secretary shared the Foreign Office's (and Churchill's) inflated and unrealistic view of the proper place of the British Empire in the world. In March 1946 Churchill delivered the final, fully-rehearsed version of the overture to the Cold War in Fulton, Missouri: 'From Stettin in the Baltic to Trieste in the Adriatic, an iron curtain has fallen across Europe.' Clem had been given a rough idea of what Churchill would say, and had written to him blandly: 'I am sure your Fulton speech will do good.' The next month his own Foreign Secretary was writing privately to him: 'The Soviet Union is no doubt war weary and wants a prolonged peace to build up her strength. But she is practising the most vicious power politics in the political, economic and propaganda spheres and seems determined to stick at nothing short of war to obtain her objectives.' Yet just one month later he made Britain's new ambassador to Moscow the bearer of a friendly personal letter to Stalin. Stalin told the ambassador he understood Britain's position in the Middle East and did not wish to dispute it, but complained of Churchill's speech in Fulton. The ambassador pointed out that Churchill did not speak for the government.

Clem also talked to Hugh Dalton, who, unlike Bevin, was excited by his ideas and wrote in his diary: 'Attlee is pressing on the Chiefs of Staff and the Defence Committee a large view of his own, aiming at considerable disengagement from areas where there is a risk of clashing with the Russians . . . This is a very fresh and interesting approach, which appeals to me.' Clem was not a man for looking back on his decisions, but perhaps even he had a moment's private regret that Dalton was not at the Foreign Office. But for public consumption, at home and abroad, Bevin and Attlee were two of a kind: Cold Warriors determined to build a cordon sanitaire round the Soviet Union and maintain a world role fitting a great power with a great Empire. In November, fifty-seven Labour MPs tabled a motion in the House of Commons calling for a 'socialist alternative to an otherwise inevitable conflict between American capitalism and Soviet Communism.' Throughout the year Attlee had constantly to defend a foreign policy to which he hoped soon to have an alternative.

Clem pointed out to the Chiefs of Staff that 'it was becoming difficult to justify our staying in the Middle East for any reason other than to be prepared for a war against Russia' and vetoed military exercises there because Stalin would realise that the manoeuvres assumed war against Russia. He resisted demands from the Chiefs of Staff, the Foreign Office and Bevin to endorse a policy of maintaining Britain's position in Greece and Turkey. Bevin, frustrated, wrote to Clem: 'The policy of the Government has been based hitherto on the assumption that Greece and Turkey are essential to our political and strategical position in the world ... Am I to understand that we may now abandon this position? I really do not know where I stand.' Clem replied: '... Of course it is difficult to tell how far Russian policy is dictated by expansion and how far by fear of attack by the US and ourselves. Fantastic as this is, it may very well be the real grounds of Russian policy. What we consider merely defence may seem to them preparations for an attack.'

Dalton was telling the Cabinet Defence Committee that Britain could not afford its generously-staffed Middle East bases. The Chiefs of Staff were telling the committee that Britain must afford it. 'By holding the Middle East we shall obtain defence in depth for East and Southern Africa, and may also secure the through-route of communication via the Mediterranean, Suez Canal and Red Sea.' A decade later, in 1956, it became suddenly clear to everyone that this was overblown nonsense, but at the time this was apparently clear only to Clem Attlee, Nye Bevan and a few firebrands on the left of his party.

Not the least of the absurdities was the proposal that there should be a permanent military base in Palestine – as though Palestine were to be a British dependency forever – when the only real question was whether Britain could leave in good order. Clem, in his May 1943 paper, had written that 'a parliamentary system in Palestine would be a prelude to civil war' because neither Jew nor Arab would be governed by the other. The Foreign Office believed that allowing unrestricted Jewish immigration would incur bitter hostility from the Arab states, which provided oil for the whole British Empire. But the Labour Party was committed to giving the Jews a Palestinian homeland, allowing all Jews to settle there. Labour backbenchers pointed out that in Poland, for example, Jews were still being persecuted, and of more than three million Jews, only 230,000 survived the war. Their mood was reflected in a private letter to Clem from Party Chairman Harold Laski: 'All the news I have is that the agony of the Jews all over Europe goes on unbearably. I do beg you, from the bottom of my heart, to give them the right to hope once more.' Clem arranged for Laski to meet him and Bevin to talk it over, but the harsh fact was that one of the Foreign Office's priorities, once Bevin moved in, was to persuade him to abandon Labour's line. They succeeded quickly, and he persuaded the Prime Minister, even though Clem did not accept the strategic importance of the Middle East. As early as September 1945 Clem sent a dusty Foreign Office-drafted brush-off to Jewish Agency leader Dr Chaim Weizmann, who had heard a rumour that the line might be about to change, and begged for a meeting before it was too late. The response to the change of line was a series of attacks on British installations in Palestine. President Truman publicly called on Britain to let in another 100,000 immigrants to Palestine, though Clem begged him not to, at length in two letters. But Truman replied tersely: 'I am aware of the complications from your point of view. It also makes difficulties for us.'

Clem and Bevin believed that Truman's interventions were dictated throughout by the exigencies of mayoral and congressional elections in New York. Bevin was indiscreet enough to tell Labour's conference that the Americans wanted more Jews in Palestine 'because they did not want too many of them in New York'. He also told the House of Commons: 'We must also remember the Arabs' side of the case – there are, after all, no Arabs in the House.' Bevin has been considered anti-Semitic by generations of Jews, beginning with Harold Laski, who wrote in a private letter: 'I am not sure EB hates Jews more than Communists, it must be a near thing.' Clem confined himself to the privacy of a letter to Tom in which, after describing a briefing from Bevin on a trip to the USA, he wrote: 'It appears that Zionism has become a profitable racket over there. A Zionist is defined as a Jew who collects money from another Jew to send another Jew to Israel. The collector I gather takes a good percentage of his collections.'

Clem told Parliament that if the Americans wanted to call the shots in Palestine, they must share the cost and put in troops; that Truman could not dictate the policy and leave British soldiers to carry it out. When the Irgun blew up the King David Hotel in Jerusalem, Clem restrained his Chiefs of Staff and his Foreign Secretary from launching an all-out hunt for terrorists and weapons, and from attempting to impose a £500,000 fine on Palestinian Jews, but could not restrain Truman from at once endorsing a plan for the partition of Palestine which had been put to him by Jewish leaders. Dalton wrote to Clem:

> I am quite sure that the time has almost come when we must bring our troops out of Palestine altogether. The present state of affairs is not only costly to us in man-power and money, but is, as you and I agree, of no real value from the strategic point of view – you cannot in any case have a secure base on top of a wasps nest – and it is exposing

our young men, for no good purpose, to most abominable experiences, and is breeding anti-Semites at a most shocking speed ... It is high time that either we left the Arabs and Jews to have it out in Palestine, or that some other Power or Powers took over the responsibility and the cost. I have been coming to feel more and more strongly on this subject, but at present I address this minute to you only.

A joint Anglo-American mission in 1947 seemed like a way of getting the Americans to take some responsibility, but it solved nothing. The British Resident in Amman wrote a paper to it which the government kept under wraps until 1997, saying that if Jews were allowed in, the Arabs would drive them into the sea; and that displaced European Jews should 'go to countries other than Palestine, particularly the USA'. He feared, he said, 'perhaps centuries hence, the final liquidation of the Jewish bridgehead, after a pogrom of dimensions hitherto unequalled in Jewish history.'

Bevin told the Cabinet Defence Committee that 'the retention of Palestine was strategically essential to the maintenance of our position in the Middle East' and a solution would therefore have to be imposed on both Jews and Arabs which neither would like. But Britain did not have the military power to do this, and on 18 February he announced that the government was not going to sacrifice any more British lives, and was handing the problem over to the UN. The birth of the state of Israel a year later was accompanied by massive bloodshed, testimony to the Attlee government's greatest failure; but also to the fact that Britain, as its Prime Minister knew, no longer had the power to control world events.

Clem held up the adoption of a thoroughgoing Cold War policy until January 1947, the month of the abortive Palestine conference. On 5 January he was still writing to Bevin: 'Unless we are persuaded that the USSR is irrevocably committed to a policy of world domination and that there is no possibility of her alteration, I think that before being committed to this [Middle East] strategy we should seek to come to an agreement with the USSR ...' He still believed that ultimately the UN would be given the power to create a new world order; and that you could negotiate with the Russians. Bevin believed neither of these things. He wrote to Clem on 9 January:

It would be Munich all over again, only on a world scale, with Greece, Turkey and Persia as the first victims in the place of Czechoslovakia ... If we speak to Stalin as you propose, he is as likely to respect their independence as Hitler was to respect Czechoslovakia's and we shall get as much of Stalin's goodwill as we got of Hitler's after Munich.

The reply did not move Clem. His mind was still made up, and he told Bevin so. Then, suddenly, four days later, he changed it, and he never told anyone why. He met the Chiefs of Staff on 13 January and endorsed their strategy for holding the Middle East. He rejected Dalton's urgent demands for huge-scale withdrawal from overseas commitments. He agreed a compromise figure for the defence estimates which Dalton considered to be £150 million more than the economy could stand, because, said Clem, of 'the importance of preserving an armed strength sufficient to support the foreign policy which the government has undertaken.' As with all his decisions, he took it silently, by himself, never confiding in anyone, and never making a note which could help us to understand his state of mind.

In the same month, January 1947, he took the momentous decision to develop what became known, euphemistically, as Britain's independent nuclear deterrent. It was a classic Attlee manoeuvre. He and Bevin had decided to treat everything to do with the atom bomb with the greatest secrecy, with no Commons debates, practically no references to Cabinet, and a secret committee for the purpose known only as Gen 75. In November 1946, Cripps and Dalton were telling Gen 75 forcibly that Britain could not afford its own atom bomb. Bevin arrived, late after an excellent lunch and a short nap, just in time to stop them taking a firm decision against it: 'No, Prime Minister, that won't do at all. We've got to have this thing over here, whatever it costs . . . We've got to have a bloody Union Jack flying on top of it. I don't mind for myself but I don't want any other Foreign Secretary of this country to be talked at by a Secretary of State in the US as I have just had in my discussions with Mr Byrnes.' The decision was deferred until January. When Clem decided to go down the Bevin route, he seems simply to have stopped calling meetings of Gen 75. A new secret Cabinet committee, called Gen 163, without Dalton and Cripps among its members, met on 10 January and decided to go ahead. Parliament and the public were not told until more than a year later. In 1952, by which time Churchill had replaced Clem, more than £100 million had been spent without Parliament knowing.

These two decisions in January 1947 have a certain sadness about them. They mark Clem's final acceptance of the inevitability of the Cold War, the moment when he became what most people thought he had always been: a Cold Warrior. Why did he change his mind? The likelihood is that things just stacked up, the way they had when

Clem switched Hugh Dalton for Ernest Bevin, until the decision seemed inevitable.

The Chief of the Imperial General Staff, Field Marshal Montgomery, writes in his memoirs that he and the other Chiefs of Staff threatened to resign if Clem continued to oppose them over the necessity of holding onto the Middle East. 'We heard no more about it,' writes Montgomery smugly. He overestimated his influence with Attlee. Clem told Sir David Hunt that Monty was a First World War-style general who boasted too much. When Monty left the job, Hunt heard Clem tell him his successor was Sir William Slim. 'I'm sorry, Prime Minister,' said Monty, 'but that's out of the question. I've already told Sir John Stopford he is to be CIGS.' 'Well, un-tell him,' replied the Prime Minister, and wrote in an unpublished autobiographical fragment: 'The outgoing Chief of Staff generally has his man, but he is not necessarily the right man.'

So while the Chiefs of Staff's threat was probably a factor, it was only one. More important, probably, was the fear that next year's US election would bring in an isolationist Republican President, leaving Britain facing the might of the Soviet Union alone. One by one between 1945 and 1948, Eastern European nations were being manoeuvred into the Soviet Union's sphere of influence: Bulgaria, Hungary, Romania, Poland, Yugoslavia, Albania, and finally Czechoslovakia. Stalin and his Foreign Minister Molotov were sounding less and less like men you could do business with.

And there was Bevin. Bevin was Clem's most important political ally and his closest political friend. 'My relationship with Ernest Bevin was the deepest of my political life. I was very fond of him and I understand he was very fond of me,' wrote Clem after Bevin's death. 'Ernest was the living symbol of loyalty . . . once he gave you his trust he was like a rock.' Their partnership extended over the whole range of government. Often after Cabinet meetings, Clem would ask Bevin to stay behind and they would discuss how to proceed. It cannot have been easy to have this secret strategic disagreement lying between them. Clem appeared far less interventionist in foreign affairs than Churchill or Chamberlain. He told Kenneth Harris: 'You don't keep a dog and bark yourself – and Ernie was a very good dog.' Bevin for his part, according to his biographer Alan Bullock, 'took no step without first making sure he had the Prime Minister's support, and if he did not hear from him regularly when he was abroad, became restive and disturbed.' Still, there were times when Clem's attitude prevented Bevin, as he saw it, from getting on with the job.

In January 1947 Clem's reputation was at its lowest ebb. There was the great freeze and the fuel crisis, and he must have heard about the mutterings among Labour MPs and senior Cabinet Ministers which were to lead to two rather farcical attempts later that year to replace him with Bevin. Had Bevin been willing to go along with these plots, they might have succeeded (though they might not: the plotters badly underestimated Clem). If they had succeeded, Clem's foreign policy objectives would have been dead anyway. Among the big five, the only one who agreed with them wholeheartedly was Hugh Dalton, and he, as we shall see, was not to be relied on as an ally.

Is it possible that the sphinx was, after all, capable of feeling the tiniest bit insecure, and of doubting, just for a moment, whether he could rely on Bevin's loyalty forever? We shall never know. Other Prime Ministers wrote diaries, or revelatory private letters, or great, compendious treasure-troves of memoirs, or occasionally confessed something of how they felt to close friends, or colleagues, or family. Not Clem.

Clem's idealism in foreign affairs did not sink without trace in January 1947. He had kept the size of the armed services below what the Service Chiefs demanded, and annually for the rest of his time as Prime Minister he insisted on further rundowns, against the trumpeting of the Service Chiefs and the Foreign Secretary. He had ensured British withdrawal from Greece and Turkey, and the Americans took over the job of supporting Greek and Turkish anti-communists. This was the end of the US drift towards isolationism, and the genesis of Marshall Aid. The new US Secretary of State, General George Marshall, believed that the USA should take a more active part in rebuilding and defending Europe. The Marshall Plan, announced on 5 June 1947, was an offer of US help to all European countries which were 'willing to assist in the task of recovery'. Bevin, who heard the announcement on the radio, lumbered into the Foreign Office, rejected swiftly his Permanent Under-Secretary's advice to send the ambassador to ask what General Marshall had in mind, and swiftly organised the European countries to put up specific plans for reconstruction. Marshall's speech was the cue Bevin had been waiting for.

The Marshall Plan, and Bevin's rapid and energetic response to it, ensured that the Americans were now deeply and inextricably involved in the reconstruction and defence of Europe, as Clem and Bevin had always wanted. But the Cold War had passed a point of no return, dashing Clem's most cherished foreign policy dream. Molotov denounced the Marshall Plan as 'an imperialist plot for the enslavement of Europe'. The plan roused the suspicions of Labour's left, which still believed the Cold War was avoidable. In April 1947 a pamphlet was circulated called 'Keep Left', drafted by Nye Bevan's PPS Donald Bruce and supported by many of those who were later to be known as 'the Bevanites'. Bruce remembers, soon after its appearance, hearing an Attlee speech in the Commons chamber which sounded much less hawkish than his other recent statements. Afterwards, meeting by chance behind the Speaker's chair, the Prime Minister said: 'Well, Bruce, what do you think of that?' 'It's a lot better, sir,' replied Bruce. But the behind-the-scenes reality was that Clem's fellow Old Haileyburian Christopher Mayhew, now Bevin's PPS, was already lobbying for an ideological offensive against communism, aimed at the third world. The result was the setting up of the Foreign Office's Information Research Department.

In finance, as in foreign affairs, the year 1947 was when the world started to look bleak and unfriendly, especially to the Chancellor of the Exchequer. Until then Hugh Dalton's star had been in the ascendant. He was – and was seen to be – a powerhouse of radical energy. The left transferred to him the loyalty that had once gone to Stafford Cripps, whose radicalism had been severely diluted by the experience of office. Dalton was popular with the 1945 intake partly because he did not have the fusty primness of the rest of the big five. But 1947 started with the worst and coldest winter of the century, which was followed by a potentially disastrous financial crisis. By February, Britain was covered with several feet of snow. The Thames froze at Windsor and ice-floes formed in Folkestone harbour. In Norfolk, parsnips had to be dug out of the ground with pneumatic drills. There were thirty-foot snowdrifts and widespread flooding. Mines were unable to function, and coal, the vital fuel without which few industries could operate, ceased to be produced. Emanuel Shinwell, the Minister of Fuel and Power – who had assured the Prime Minister that there would be no fuel crisis – now had to tell his colleagues that all electricity would have to be cut off from all private homes everywhere, and from industry in vast tracts of the country.

In freezing temperatures, families were without heat, and food was scarce. Railways were at a standstill and there was no petrol for road transport. Nearly two million people lost their jobs, though most job losses were temporary. The US loan was running out fast, but with its industry closed, Britain was not producing much that it could sell abroad. 'I want to talk to you tonight about the critical position of our fuel supplies,' Clem told radio listeners on 10 February. 'I am sure you will all do your bit as you did in the war . . . We should have been able to get through the winter unless we had exceptionally bad weather. But you all know what the weather has been like in the last few weeks.' Mines cannot work; ships cannot move. 'We face an emergency of the utmost gravity. Electrical power is therefore being prohibited for all but the most essential services . . .'

Fuel restrictions were not removed until 12 March, and the damage had been done. It was as though, in January 1947, the elements combined with the Cold War to smother the optimism and idealism of 1945 under a frozen shroud.

The summer saw the convertibility crisis, the bitter price Britain had to pay for the American loan. Clem, on holiday in North Wales, received a letter from his Chancellor: 'We are running out of foreign exchange, and if this goes on much longer, we shall not be able to go on buying anything. We must reduce the tremendous import stream . . . We must reduce the armed forces . . .' Convertibility was suspended, food and petrol rations were reduced, rationing was extended to more types of food, clothing coupons were restricted, finance for overseas travel without official sanction was abolished.

People with an ideological aversion to the welfare state look at the 1947 crisis and say: 'Told you so, all these state benefits, no good can come of it.' A New Right prophet, John Charmley, wrote in the *Daily Telegraph* on 29 December 1996: 'In an island built on coal and surrounded by fish, socialist planning had managed to engineer a shortage of both products.' (Dr Charmley's message was: don't vote for Tony Blair.) The Conservative propaganda slogan in 1947 was 'Shiver with Shinwell and starve with Strachey' (John Strachey was the Food Minister). But the crisis was caused by convertibility and the worst winter this century, not Labour's programme. As Dalton told the Prime Minister: 'If we had done *nothing* good at home, our external difficulties would be no less.' That is not to say that the government was blameless. Shinwell had certainly been complacent about fuel stocks, so much so that both Dalton and Cripps thought the Prime Minister should fire him. Clem defended Shinwell publicly but was merciless around the Cabinet table, allegedly at one point reducing his Fuel Minister to tears.

Dalton had begged for serious cuts in military spending overseas, and complained with some justification that Clem was not giving him the support he ought to have had against Bevin. His boils started to reappear and he told a friend that watching the seepage of Britain's reserves was 'like watching a child bleed to death and being unable to stop it.' He was coming back from Cabinet meetings – according to George Brown, who became his PPS in 1947 – seething with rage about 'the incompetent little Prime Minister'. It was in this mood of black despair that Dalton helped launch yet another plot to replace Clem Attlee. Brown and another Member of the 1945 intake, Patrick Gordon Walker, began collecting signatures in the Tea Room on a petition to replace Clem with Ernest Bevin, believing that more positive and forceful leadership was needed. Brown told Dalton, and Dalton, rather foolishly, gave the plan his qualified approval – and even more foolishly, mentioned it to Bevin when they happened to share a car on the way back to London from the Durham Miners' Gala. It is a measure of the extent to which the Chancellor was no longer thinking clearly, for if Bevin were to become Prime Minister, his opposition to defence cuts, instead of being formidable, would be insuperable.

The plot petered out, leaving Bevin, and probably Clem too, confirmed in the view that Dalton was not trustworthy. As for George Brown, he was roasted first by the Foreign Secretary and then by the chief whip; when he was summoned to see the Prime Minister himself, he thought his political career was doomed. With a lesser Prime Minister it might have been. From Clem he got promotion, to Under-Secretary of State at the Ministry of Agriculture. Clem at one stroke removed a promising but volatile and impressionable young MP from Dalton's baleful influence, and made him feel grateful.

'By the end of July', records Ben Pimlott, 'the Chancellor of the Exchequer was close to breaking point . . . At night, bitterness at colleagues and anxiety about the future robbed him of sleep.' By the time Stafford Cripps turned up in Dalton's office with yet another proposal for replacing the Prime Minister, the Chancellor was ill with worry. Cripps explained, according to Dalton's diary, 'that CRA was no use as PM in this crisis' – and that planning was beyond Herbert Morrison and should be done by Cripps himself. The solution, said Cripps, was to persuade Attlee to resign and hand over to Bevin. Attlee could become Chancellor; Dalton would go to the Foreign Office; Cripps would take over Morrison's planning role as Lord President of the Council; and Morrison would get a few empty baubles: deputy Prime Minister, Leader of the House, Lord Privy Seal.

Of course, the plan was a mess, feverish dreaming from a couple of overstrained Ministers. If Bevin had become Prime Minister he would have made his own appointments; Morrison would not collaborate in his own demotion; and Clem knew he did not have the economic skills to be Chancellor. But Dalton encouraged Cripps to try the idea, first on Morrison who, despite wanting Clem out, could see that Cripps's idea would do him nothing but harm; and then on the Prime Minister himself. On the evening of 8 September Cripps went to put the proposal to Clem and tell him that, unless he agreed, Cripps would himself resign, at a most embarrassing time for the government. Clem listened politely, then picked up the telephone, asked for Bevin, and said: 'Ernie, Stafford's here. He says you want to change your job. No, thought not.' And he put the telephone down. Perhaps Clem and Bevin had planned this piece of theatre in advance, for Cripps's mission cannot have come as a surprise to either of them. Dalton's famed voice had been at work – 'the loudest whisper in Westminster' as one of his friends once called it. There had even been speculation in the *Daily Mail* under the headline 'ATTLEE RESIGNING SOON—BEVIN TO BE PM'.

As Clem put the telephone down he calmly offered Cripps what he wanted for himself – the job of economic planning which Morrison had been doing. Afterwards he wrote a careful, conciliatory letter to Morrison, who was on holiday, telling him what he had done in such a way that it was hard for Morrison to take offence. It was similar to his response to George Brown's visit, only more generous. His visitor left with more than he could have hoped for; the plot, such as it was, was finished; and Clem took the opportunity to strengthen the government, bringing in one of the brightest of the 1945 intake. Bevin was lost in admiration of the way Clem had handled it. 'Bevin was sensible enough to know that he'd have split the party,' says Jack Jones, who knew Bevin well and years later came to occupy his place at the head of the TGWU. 'He didn't have Clem Attlee's precise brain. He ran the Union as a one-man band. You couldn't have done that with politicians.'

It was a stronger and a younger government, but the crisis did not go away. The press decided it was all Dalton's fault, and he had to put up with some thoroughly unpleasant and unfair abuse, especially from the *Economist*, which was owned by his old tormentor Brendan Bracken. His November Budget was to be the beginning of the policy of austerity. On his way into the chamber to deliver it, Dalton stopped for a brief word with an old friend, John Carvel, political correspondent of the London evening paper, the *Star*. In a sentence he told him the essentials of the Budget he was about to introduce. Carvel went straight to the telephone and the information went into the 'stop press' section of the next edition while Dalton was still on his feet.

No general reader of that brief news story would have realised how authoritative Carvel's unnamed source was. But the paper's two rivals saw that Carvel's predictions were so accurate that there must have been a leak, and primed a Conservative MP to ask a question in the House. Dalton owned up at once. Dalton had to offer his resignation, but Clem could easily have refused it. No damage was done. The stock market was unaffected. No-one even realised that a leak had occurred until the next day. Many Chancellors have survived worse indiscretions. Clem at first appeared undecided, but later accepted Dalton's resignation. Why? It seems likely, again, that the arguments just stacked up.

First, the leak must have seemed a symbol of Dalton's growing uncertainty of touch. A top Cabinet Minister should know better than to give a journalist a scoop and then expect him not to use it. Clem never understood the fascination which journalists hold for many politicians. His first reaction when told Dalton had talked to a journalist was: 'Why on earth would he want to talk to the Press?' Second, the Conservatives, after a little hesitation, decided to call for an inquiry. It was mid-term and any stick would do to beat the government. And Churchill loathed Dalton. Third, Dalton had not exactly earned his Prime Minister's loyalty in 1947. There had been two rather farcical attempts to get rid of Clem, and the only common factor between the two was Dalton. He knew that Dalton made a habit of running him down in private. Bevin had by then decided that Dalton was a scheming fellow who was not to be trusted, and Geoffrey de Freitas has said that Clem thought him devious. Fourth, the mood which elected Labour in 1945 consisted of many elements: idealism; a rage against injustice; and a little Puritanism, especially on financial affairs. The government had been elected partly to stop rich men lining their pockets at the public expense, and any hint of financial irregularity was alien to the mood which had swept Labour to power. Clem sensed this mood. He was the perfect Prime Minister for it, with his modest lifestyle. It was a little unfair to force a Chancellor to resign when he had done nothing corrupt, but perhaps it was preferable to the climate in which Ministers can extract financial benefit from their office with impunity.

Dalton's resignation brought a nightmare year to an appalling end. Yet Clem always looked back on 1947 with affection – despite Palestine, despite the destruction of his hopes for world peace, despite the financial crisis. The reason can be stated in one word: India. Because of his time on the Simon Commission, Clem understood the problem better than most. He decided to handle it himself, leaving nothing to chance or Ernest Bevin, and that India was to have her independence. But which India? The Congress Party, led by Gandhi and Nehru, had for a long time been seen to speak for all Indians. But no longer: now the Muslim League, led by Mohammed Ali Jinnah, was demanding a separate Muslim state – Pakistan. Congress was implacably opposed to a separate Pakistan. Clem thought it was not viable, and disliked the idea of a state based on religion: there were bound to be minorities in both states. But he was faced with the problem he had posed in that remarkable 1943 paper: how do you create a democratic system in which one determined minority, in this case the Muslims, will not accept the will of the majority?

He was sure, as he wrote in 1943, that 'the desirability of giving India a Constitution as close as possible to our own is held most strongly by those whose knowledge of the subject is least.' But what sort of constitution would enable these factions to live together? Clem's 1943 paper was not a lot of help here. The idea of some sort of external umpire had looked fine in 1943 on paper, but no-one, not even Clem, seems to have thought it worthwhile trying the idea on Gandhi and Jinnah.

'We must recognise that we cannot make Indians responsible for governing themselves and at the same time retain over here the responsibility for the treatment of minorities and the power to intervene on their behalf,' he told the House of Commons. The US offered to help with a statement of approval for Britain's handling of the situation, perhaps to try to smooth ruffled British feathers, but Bevin told them not to bother after receiving Clem's reaction: 'It looks like a pat on the back to us from a rich uncle who sees us turning over a new leaf. I doubt it would do any good in India with Congress while it would irritate the Moslems.' Clem decided that Lord Wavell, a Victorian style imperialist whom Churchill had appointed as Viceroy, was an obstacle to progress. He fired Wavell and replaced him with Admiral Louis Mountbatten, telling Wavell it was time 'to change the bowling'.

'Dickie Mountbatten stood out a mile. Burma showed it,' he

told Kenneth Harris. In Burma, which had been separated from India in 1935 on the recommendation of the Simon Commission, Mountbatten, as Supreme Allied Commander in South-East Asia, had come rapidly to the conclusion that self-government would have to come soon, and that Aung San, leader of the nationalist forces and one of Churchill's pet hates, was the man to back. Sir Reginald Dorman-Smith, the Governor, disagreed, and froze out Aung San. Clem agreed with Mountbatten, describing Aung San in a letter to Tom as 'very impressive, quite young, very straightforward, honest and broadminded'. He fired Dorman-Smith and replaced him with Mountbatten's assistant, Brigadier Sir Hubert Rance, whom he took to at once, perhaps because Rance also liked cricketing metaphors: his first report to Clem from Burma said he had had friendly letters from Burmese friends 'so that I start on a fairly good wicket'.

Rance brought Aung San in at the top in government, and by January 1947 an agreement for Burmese independence had been reached. 'If Aung San can control his wild men we may make a success there,' Clem wrote to Tom the next month. Alas, that summer gunmen burst into the Burmese Cabinet Room and killed Aung San and all his Cabinet.

Clem regretted that he had not been quicker to follow his own instinct, and Mountbatten's, in supporting Aung San. He believed this might have kept Burma in the Commonwealth, and perhaps the history of that unhappy country might have been different. Clem would perhaps have seen it as a vindication of his judgement that Burma's best hope today, in 1997, is Aung San's daughter.

He was determined not to make the same mistake with India, and gave Mountbatten unprecedented powers to negotiate without referring back to the Cabinet. No-one had been given such powers in the twentieth century. But they were both sure that the Indians had to see decisions being made in India, not in London, and they were right. Soon after Mountbatten's arrival Pandit Nehru, noticing how fast decisions came, said to Mountbatten: 'Have you, by some miracle, been given plenipotentiary powers?' 'What if I have?' Nehru replied, 'In that case you will succeed.' They were also sure the Indian politicians had to be convinced that the British were really going to leave on the date they set. A serious deadline was the only way to make them agree on something.

Ernest Bevin seems to have realised the far-reaching implications, and mourned them. 'You cannot read the telegrams from Egypt and the Middle East nowadays without realising that not only is India going, but Malaya, Ceylon and the Middle East is going with it, with a tremendous repercussion on the African territories . . .' It was true. The unthinkable was happening. The British Empire was breaking up. Clem did not say as much, but it seems certain that he, too, could see it – and that, unlike his Foreign Secretary, he had come to accept and even welcome it. 'I can't bear the shame of a scuttle, without plan or dignity,' wrote Bevin to the Prime Minister, but Clem got his way, announcing in February 1947 that independence would come not later than June 1948. Churchill was appalled, calling it 'operation scuttle'. Clem explained that everyone's knowledge of India becomes out of date:

> I quite recognise that I am out of date. I ended my time on the Simon Commission nearly 18 years ago . . . In this, I admit, I differ from the Leader of the Opposition. I think his practical acquaintance with India ended some fifty years ago. He formed some strong opinions – I might almost say prejudices – then. They have remained with him ever since.

Arriving in India in March 1947, Mountbatten found a situation close to civil war. He decided quickly that the 1948 deadline, far from being too close, was too far away. There could be civil war by then. He quickly agreed with Nehru and Jinnah a plan for partition which would allow the provinces to vote to join either India or Pakistan. The Cabinet reluctantly but swiftly abandoned hope of one unified Indian state and endorsed the plan at once. Then Mountbatten caused a flap in Whitehall by suggesting that the withdrawal should be brought forward, and occur in just five months' time, on 15 August 1947. Impossible, said the civil servants: what if Parliament kicks up rough about it? But Clem wrote an instruction in his own hand – 'Accept Viceroy's proposal' – and that was that.

The deadline was met, and Clem Attlee and Louis Mountbatten had achieved what virtually no-one else, in any country, has achieved, before or since: to withdraw in good order from a vast slice of Empire and leave it ready to start governing itself with moderate efficiency. Mountbatten wrote to Clem: 'The man who made it all possible was you yourself. Without your original guidance and your unwavering support nothing could have been accomplished out here.'

But India was a one-off example. The Foreign Office and Bevin still believed in the Empire, and in other parts of the world this belief stored up trouble for future governments. Newly released documents show that in the Falkland Islands Britain's policy in

1946, as laid down by the Foreign Office, was to 'take all possible steps to strengthen our title . . . The occupation upon which we have embarked should be such as to afford evidence of the exercise of sovereignty.' A mapping exercise was devised, simply to strengthen a rather flimsy claim, and to pre-empt any similar venture by the Argentine or Chilean governments, despite unmistakable signals that Argentina considered the Islands her territory. A task force was sent in December 1946, and a haughty, imperial Foreign Office reply was given to a Chilean protest; while Britain's delegation to the UN was briefed, if the matter was brought up, to say it had been sprung on them and they had no instructions. Amid his other troubles, Clem may not even have known. If he had, one feels that he would have put a stop to it, and saved the lives of young men who were not even born in 1947.

8

Building Jerusalem

Everyone called the 1945 government 'socialist'. Churchill called it Socialist with a capital S and a whiff of foreigners and gulags. Dalton called it socialist, as he put it more than once, 'with a song in my heart'. Clem just called it socialist. What did they all mean? They did not mean Marxist. Nor did they mean it implemented the now-celebrated Clause 4 of the Labour Party constitution, written by Sidney Webb a quarter of a century earlier. The government had not the smallest intention of bringing in 'the common ownership of the means of production, distribution and exchange.' It wanted what would become known as a mixed economy: 'Two great sectors of industry – one sector nationalised, the other in private hands,' as Clem put it.

Herbert Morrison once famously remarked, 'Socialism is what the Labour government does.' What the Labour government did was to mount a serious assault on Beveridge's five giants, Want, Disease, Ignorance, Squalor and Idleness; and to narrow the enormous gap between the very rich and the very poor. The main instrument was the welfare state. Beveridge had designed the building. Clem and his Ministers set themselves the task of erecting it, to a deadline of 5 July 1948. On that date the five giants were to be buried.

Clem gave the task of slaying Want to Social Security Minister Jim Griffiths, an able and kindly former Welsh miner in his mid-fifties. When Clem first went to the East End at the start of the century, poverty was considered to be evidence of weakness of character. If the jobless man and his wife and children were to be prevented from starving to death, the scale of benefit must be the most meagre, delivered in the most humiliating conditions. Clem never forgot the philanthropic clergyman who told him that the porridge handed out to the children of the unemployed should always be burnt. Relief was only to be administered in the workhouse. The children of the poor might be saved from absolute starvation, but not from the many diseases, like rickets, resulting from undernourishment; and not from misery and humiliation.

The Liberal administration of 1906–14 under Campbell-Bannerman and Asquith paid the first-ever old age pensions, and provided for unemployment insurance in certain industries. But the greatly-feared workhouse still existed for the many who did not qualify for insurance, or whose insurance had run out. The workhouse was not abolished until 1935, when relief in the home was allowed, though still on harsh conditions. The essential difference after 1945 was that government policy, in tune with the mood of the times, was now to ensure that benefits were universal, and that when people fell on hard times, they should not be driven to despair and humiliation.

For Griffiths, as for Clem, it was a chance to do what he had entered politics to do. His first move was the Family Allowances Act. 'The Chancellor, Hugh Dalton,' he wrote, 'gave me the money "with a song in his heart" as he told our conference.' The first family allowance day was August Bank Holiday 1946, and 2.5 million families took it up. Next came the Industrial Injuries Act, which spread compensation for industrial injuries to the whole workforce and increased the rates substantially. But the crucial piece of legislation was the 1946 National Insurance Act which for the first time insured every single person in the land for sickness, unemployment and retirement, as well as providing widows' benefits, maternity benefits and death grants, with allowances for dependants. Finally, the National Assistance Act was passed to catch those who, for whatever reason, fell through the system.

Jim Griffiths, with the unwavering support of the Prime Minister, had effected a quiet revolution in the lives of their poorest fellow citizens, though not without several Cabinet battles. Griffiths was warned that his scheme was open to abuse, just as in 1929–31, when Parliament was considering cutting unemployment pay, some argued that the dole went to the undeserving. The difference between this Prime Minister and MacDonald was that Clem was clear that it was more important to have a scheme which prevented the misery he had seen in the East End of London than to have one which was entirely fool-proof against abuse. So Jim Griffiths found he had prime ministerial support for resisting proposals to water down the scheme. If the system worked as it was supposed to do, no-one would ever again fall below a basic subsistence level. It was, of course, only a subsistence level. The irresponsible generosity of

THE UNIVERSAL UNCLES

the Attlee government, much derided by the New Right in the 1990s, simply ensured that no-one should be left to starve.

Ellen Wilkinson, Minister of Education, was given the task of slaying Ignorance. In education, the plans had been drawn, the foundations laid, even the skeleton of the building erected, by the coalition government in its 1944 Education Act, the work of the Conservative Education Secretary, Rab Butler, and his Labour deputy, Chuter Ede, with crucial if discreet support from the deputy Prime Minister. The Act turned the old Board of Education into a Ministry, with power to impose duties on local education authorities, and it specified that education should be free and universal.

But it did not touch public schools. Clem's suggestion to Butler – that 'some of them which are essentially local could be absorbed

245

into the county secondary schools. Others which are national should be brought under control without killing their individuality. They should of course have a large proportion of scholars from the elementary schools . . .' – came to nothing. Neither did the Act implement the 1942 Labour Party conference resolution in favour of what we now call comprehensive schools. It created a three-tier system of grammar schools, technical schools and secondary modern schools, and the eleven-plus examination to decide which of the three a child should attend.

Given Ellen Wilkinson's radical past, many on the left of the party hoped that she would move to rectify these two deficiencies in the Butler Act. She was personally appalled by the idea of dividing children at age eleven into successes and failures. She saw it as denying real education to most children: 'Give the real stuff to a selected twenty-five per cent, steer the seventy-five per cent away from the humanities, pure science, even history.' But she did not do anything about it. Her priority was to implement the 1944 Act, especially that portion of it which required the school leaving age to be raised to fifteen. For that she needed a huge school-building programme and a plan to train 35,000 new teachers in a hurry. She also needed a rapid expansion of university places, which increased from 50,246 in 1938–9 to 76,764 in 1947–8.

Achieving these things required every ounce of imagination and political will she could muster. Even the song in Hugh Dalton's heart could start to sound a little flat as spending Minister after spending Minister came to him for more money. Perhaps an Aneurin Bevan might have taken on the education establishment (over comprehensive schools) and the political establishment (over public schools) as well, and the subsequent history of our education system would have been very different. But Ellen Wilkinson's achievements were nonetheless considerable.

The 1906 Liberal government had allowed local authorities to provide free school meals, though this required visits to ensure that the family really was destitute. The young Clem himself had made such visits, arguing afterwards with sceptical officials that such-and-such a family was in sufficiently dire straits for its children to get a meal from the state. Clem had also, as a volunteer, supervised school meals. But free meals provided nationally on a mass basis could not rely on volunteers, and Ellen Wilkinson extended the scheme, insisting that it was part of a teacher's duties to supervise school meals.

She introduced free school milk, and Dalton found money for it in the 1946 Budget. 'Free milk will be provided in Hoxton and Shoreditch, in Eton and Harrow. What more social equality can you have than that?' she told the 1946 Labour Party conference. But of course, it mattered much more in Hoxton and Shoreditch. In places where children did not get an adequate diet, or left home without breakfast, it contributed enormously to the defeat of childhood illnesses resulting from bad diet. Generations of poor children grew up stronger and healthier because of this one small and inexpensive act of generosity by the Attlee government. Free school milk was the first of the Attlee government's measures to be clawed back by Mrs Thatcher, who abolished it when she was Education Secretary in Edward Heath's 1970–74 government.

Before the war, private school children were noticeably taller, better built, healthier and stronger than state school children, because they were properly fed. Contemporaries could see the difference, and social scientists, including the young Clement Attlee, could measure it. In the Fifties this was so no longer, due to the provision of free school meals and school milk. By October 1946 more than ninety per cent of all school children were getting their third-of-a-pint of free milk, in those funny little bottles which became a part of the childhood memories of those of us who are now in our thirties, forties and fifties.

After a year in the job, Ellen Wilkinson wrote to Clem to say 'how utterly grateful I am to you for having put me in charge of education . . . I feel as though my life had all led up to this work.' Six months later, in January 1947, she fought a furious Cabinet battle to be allowed to keep to her timetable and raise the school leaving age on 1 April. She was opposed by the economic Ministers, Dalton, Morrison and Cripps. But, crucially, the Prime Minister backed her, and the timetable was agreed. The next month she died, at the age of fifty-five, from heart failure following bronchitis. Just a month earlier she had written to Clem: 'I have collected a cold – no complications, but . . . my doctor is insisting on at least 3 days C.B. . . . Some day please take a few minutes at the Cabinet to lecture us on "How I keep well" . . . You, with the heaviest burden of all, remain healthy and cheerful, shouldering others' burdens as well.'

She died after an overdose of the medicines prescribed for her asthma. It was probably an accident, though Herbert Morrison's biographers insist it was suicide. The BBC agreed to delay the news of her death until Morrison, to whom she was still very close and who was himself seriously ill, had been told. According to the doctor who told him, Morrison 'did not say anything, but he suddenly looked years older'. Ellen Wilkinson's admiring biographer, Betty Vernon, notes that Morrison sent no flowers to her funeral: 'To the end he remained – selfishly – discreet.'

Ignorance outlived Ellen Wilkinson, but it was badly battered. Disease and Squalor were to be confronted by Aneurin Bevan.

With Bevan's record as a thorn in the side of the coalition government, Clem told him: 'You start with a clean sheet with me.' He proved it early on. His Permanent Secretary, Sir Arthur Rooker, took rough notes on what sort of a health service he wanted, and returned a few weeks later with something very different and, in Bevan's view, quite inadequate. The next day Rooker took Bevan's PPS, Donald Bruce, to lunch at the Reform Club. He sensed his new Minister did not trust him, and asked what he should do. Bruce explained that Bevan expected his Permanent Secretary to make Bevan's own ideas work, not try to water them down. But it was too late. 'Nye picked up the phone to Clem and said, I want him shifted. And he was shifted,' according to Bruce.

Bevan's relationship with the Prime Minister who had given him this wonderful and unexpected chance to change the world is much disputed. Donald Bruce claims he admired Clem and valued his support. But Bevan's biographer Michael Foot disagrees, saying that Bevan expected more support than he got and was maddened by his leader's prosaic style. 'Attlee would stress the need for teamwork in some excruciating cricketing metaphor, or he would seek to rally the Parliamentary Party with the moral uplift of a public school speech day,' writes Michael Foot. 'Affinities with Bevan could be ruptured in a matter of seconds by these prissy exhibitions. Attlee could reek of the suburban middle-class values which Bevan detested.'

Foot illustrates this with a revealing story. Invited to a royal banquet for which the invitation said 'Dress, Dinner-Jacket', Bevan, who 'considered a dinner-jacket to be the livery of the ruling class', turned up in a lounge suit. There was a good deal of hostile newspaper comment, which he must have expected. What he did not expect was that the Prime Minister would have a quiet word with him after a Cabinet meeting, telling him to wear a dinner-jacket next time. Bevan discussed it with his wife, the Labour MP Jennie Lee, who said to him: 'It seems impossible for the Attlees of this world to understand just what we do and why we do it in our own way.' They agreed that, reluctantly, a dinner-jacket would be purchased, and Bevan informed Clem of this. Unfortunately, a few days later Jennie Lee met Violet Attlee in a House of Commons corridor. Mrs Attlee gleefully announced that she could not wait to see the great Nye Bevan in a dinner-jacket. In a rage, Jennie Lee reported the interview back to her husband, and the dinner-jacket was never worn.

Clem never discussed 'real' politics with Vi. The story of the dinner-jacket was exactly the sort of lightweight political gossip he would pass on to her – and she might well have asked for, after reading about it in the newspapers, for she had an acute sense of the proper thing to do on social occasions. Felicity says: 'My father did not talk politics in the family, but told stories about politics.' That Mrs Attlee's clumsy approach should so outrage two such sophisticated politicians as Aneurin Bevan and Jennie Lee – and that the question of the dinner-jacket should have occupied their serious attention – tells us more about the Bevans than the Attlees. Years later Clem reflected on the relationship between Aneurin Bevan and Jennie Lee: 'He needed a sedative. He got an irritant.'

Aneurin Bevan and Jennie Lee had entered Parliament in 1929, the Parliament which saw most of Labour's left-wing energy fritter itself away in bitter recrimination. Bevan's name appears on a list compiled by the ILP of fifty-three Labour MPs who had voted against the government, but he carefully avoided too close an association with the ILP, whose leaders thought him lazy and comfortable and called him 'the armchair revolutionary'.

They were wrong. He was neither lazy nor comfortable, simply more shrewd than they. He knew, as he once told Jennie Lee, that it was the Labour Party or nothing. You could rail against its complacency, but nothing serious could be done outside it. He courted expulsion often, and even flirted with Oswald Mosley and the New Party in 1931, but unlike Mosley and James Maxton, he always stopped short of putting himself right outside the party. Jennie Lee was in the ILP, stayed loyal to it after 1931, and was driven out of the Labour Party along with the other ILP MPs. In 1931 she was by far the better known of the two. She left the ILP in 1944 and returned to Parliament as a backbench Labour MP in 1945, but by then she seems to have taken the conscious decision to subordinate her own political career to his. This may not have been good for either of them. She was far too strong and positive a personality, and had too many ideas of her own, to live her political life vicariously.

In 1945 Aneurin Bevan was forty-seven, the son of a miner, born and brought up in the mining town of Tredegar, Monmouthshire. He had gone to work in the pits at the age of fourteen. He had already proved that he was a great public speaker, a great raconteur, a fund of ideas, a great conversationalist and storyteller, who could turn a chronic stutter and an inability to pronounce the letter 'r' into precious oratorical gifts. No-one ever doubted the power of his intellect or the strength of his convictions. But could he do a real job, or was he best sitting in The Ivy, the famous theatrical restaurant in the West End which was one of Bevan's favourite haunts, talking about how it *ought* to be done? Clem Attlee decided he could do a real job, and gave him two of Beveridge's giants to slay.

In Health, there was something to build on, but not much. Lloyd George had introduced the National Insurance Act in 1911. It meant that workers could obtain medical treatment paid for by their insurance premiums. But wives and dependants were excluded, the treatment available was restricted, and there was an income limit for participation in the scheme. Most people still could not afford the cost of treatment if they were seriously ill. Every day, people died when treatment which could save them was available, but beyond their means. Hospitals lived largely on charitable donations. Some areas were desperately short of doctors and hospitals.

The wartime coalition government had produced a health scheme, but nothing had been done about implementing it, and in any case the scheme itself was inadequate. Even so, it had already aroused the wrath of the British Medical Association (BMA), and the Conservative Health Minister had started making concessions which would render it unworkable.

By January 1946 Aneurin Bevan had outlined what became the National Health Service, a scheme which imposed on the Health Minister a duty to provide a comprehensive health service, free of charge, paid for not by insurance but by taxation. To do this, the hospitals, which were run by local authorities or voluntary organisations, were to be nationalised. Bevan insisted that if the nation did not own the hospitals, the Minister could not provide a National Health Service – he could only exhort others to do so. He could not spread the best consultants around the country unless he could offer them interesting jobs and a secure financial future. And he could not guarantee the right of a sick person to a hospital bed. In any case, local authorities could not run hospitals effectively, and private benefactors should not. 'The benefactor tends also to become a petty tyrant, not only willing his cash but sending his instructions along with it,' said Bevan. 'It is repugnant to a civilised community for hospitals to have to rely on private charity . . . I have always felt a shudder of repulsion when I see nurses and sisters who ought to be at their work . . . going about the streets collecting money for the hospitals.'

Bevan was certain that leaving hospitals with their present owners and buying in their services would make the NHS unworkable. Already between eighty and ninety per cent of voluntary sector hospitals' money came from public funds, so why should they not be accountable? It was a brave decision, adding local authorities and the voluntary sector to the list of his enemies.

For general practitioners he proposed a small basic salary, set in 1946 at £300 a year, plus fees based on the number of patients on a doctor's list. He proposed to abolish the GP's right to buy and sell practices. All of this was intended to make it easier for young doctors starting out in the profession, without capital, to obtain a practice, and to help the Minister to ensure that medical services were spread reasonably evenly throughout the country, not concentrated in wealthy areas. The Bill's first hurdle was the Cabinet. Herbert Morrison had spent years in local government and did not like seeing hospitals taken away from it. Others feared the political consequences of offending local authorities, or were concerned at the cost.

Bevan started to realise the crucial, if often silent, force of the Prime Minister, as even Michael Foot grudgingly recognises: 'When he needed Cabinet backing for his own biggest decisions, he soon learned to appreciate Attlee's leading virtue. The mind, however unadventurous, was usually open and unprejudiced; a case presented with close argument and detailed facts had a good chance of winning on its merits. On all the matters affecting his own department, Bevan went to the Cabinet well briefed. Attlee could be won as an ally.' It would probably be truer to say that Clem was won from the start. Bevan's sentiments on charity quoted above are remarkably similar to those of Clem twenty-five years earlier in *The Social Worker*.

The BMA was outraged. It said the proposals 'could lead sooner rather than later to doctors becoming a branch of the Civil Service'. Its leaders were amazingly unrestrained in their abuse of Bevan. Former BMA Secretary, Dr Alfred Cox, wrote that the proposals 'look to me uncommonly like the first step, and a big one, towards National Socialism as practised in Germany. The medical service there was early put under the dictatorship of a "medical fuhrer". This Bill will establish the Minister of Health in that capacity.'

'We shall become West Indian slaves,' said another influential BMA figure, Dr Roland Cockshut. 'They had complete security – subject only to two disadvantages. They could not own property and they could not move from their plantations . . . The Bill can be written in two lines: I hereby take power to do what I like about the medical service of the country, signed Aneurin Bevan, fuhrer.' Today, in the Nineties, New Right historians make the same point, if less offensively. Correlli Barnett calls Bevan's plan 'a plan of military organisation produced by a general staff for a great offensive, commencing with the role of the supreme commander: "General responsibility for the service will rest with the Minister of Health . . ."' It is hard, however, to see with whom else it should lie.

'Large numbers of doctors', records the BMA's official history, 'seemed to belong to a section of society which regarded the advent of a Socialist Government as a national disaster almost as catastrophic as a defeat by Hitler.' If doctors refused to work in the NHS it was doomed. The Chairman of the BMA Council, Dr Guy Dain, told a special BMA assembly that it could say to the Minister: 'You want the doctors. We have the doctors.' The assembly rejected by huge majorities every item in Bevan's plan. The Conservatives opposed the Bill tooth and nail. They saw it, as David Eccles MP put it, as part of the government's 'concerted attack upon the middle class'. Mr Eccles added: 'If the Minister is determined to fight, we on these benches will not leave the doctors to fight alone.' 'The doctors' stand', according to a *Daily Graphic* columnist, 'is the first effective revolt of the professional classes against Socialist tyranny . . . There is nothing that Bevan or any other Socialist can do about it in the shape of Hitlerian coercion . . . The state medical service is part of the Socialist plot to convert Great Britain into a National Socialist economy.'

But on 6 November 1946 Bevan's Bill received the royal assent. It was to come into operation in July 1948. There were some bad-tempered meetings between Bevan and BMA leaders which came to nothing. The BMA declared that the Act 'is so grossly at variance with the essential principles of our profession that it should be rejected absolutely by all practitioners.' It told doctors not to work in the NHS. Bevan's and the government's nerve

THE PATIENT'S DILEMMA
'Can't you bend a little in front?'

held. Bevan made two minor concessions to enable the BMA to climb down gracefully. The scheme was massively expensive, for a country which – as American politicians never stopped reminding the government – was on its uppers and had to take its begging bowl across the Atlantic in order to feed its people. But the NHS was so popular that fairly soon both the BMA and the Conservative Party were claiming that they had been in favour of it, in principle at least. They were not. It was carried in the teeth of their opposition, and would never have come into existence at all without an exceptional Minister, backed to the hilt by a Prime Minister who understood exactly what was being created, and who had dreamed of it just as much as his Health Minister had done. The National Health Service came into being, bang on schedule, on 5 July 1948, along with Jim Griffiths's social security measures and free school meals. By that day, three-quarters of the population had signed up with doctors under the scheme. By September the figure was ninety-three per cent. Nine out of ten GPs participated from the start. Clem Attlee was the last person ever to show his feelings or talk about them, but it was possibly one of the proudest days of his life. In the broadcast he made the previous day, his voice sounds, if not ecstatic – it would not have had the tempo to express ecstasy – deeply contented:

> Tomorrow there will come into operation the most comprehensive system of social security ever introduced into any country . . . When I first went to work in East London, apart from what was done by voluntary organisations and by private charities . . . the only provision for the citizen unable to work through sickness, unemployment or old age was that given by the Poor Law . . . The Poor Law was designed to be, and indeed it was, the last refuge of the destitute.

Four Acts, he said, were to come into force: the National Insurance Act, the Industrial Injuries Act, the National Assistance Act, and the NHS Act. They were all based on a new principle: that 'we must combine together to meet contingencies with which we cannot cope as individual citizens.' They were 'part of a general plan and they fit in with each other . . . They are comprehensive and available to every citizen. They give security to all members of the family.' The NHS 'gives a complete cover for health by pooling the nation's resources and paying the bill collectively.'

On the same day Bevan made a speech in which he talked about the misery caused by the means test and of 'a deep burning hatred for the Tory Party that inflicted those experiences on me. So far as I am concerned they are lower than vermin.' Clem sent him a handwritten letter: 'It had been agreed that we wished to give the new Social Security scheme as good a send-off as possible and to this end I made a non-polemical broadcast. Your speech cut right across this . . . Please, be a bit more careful in your own interest.'

Bevan was less successful in providing housing to a country where thousands of homes had been destroyed in all major cities; where thousands of people still lived in the inhuman slums which had shocked the young Clement Attlee; where a market-led housing boom in the Thirties had produced hundreds of thousands of middle-class homes for sale, but nowhere for slum-dwellers to move to; where there was a chronic shortage of building materials; and where the post-war baby boom was just starting. In 1939 Britain had twelve and a half million houses. Nearly one in three was damaged or destroyed during the war, and no housing repairs had been done for six years. Labour had promised to build four to five million houses in the first decade of peace. Clem had said in an election broadcast: 'The housing problem is not a new one. The housing problem could have been swept away a long time ago, if the inventiveness and organisation that produced a Spitfire had been applied in this direction.'

Bevan had strong views about the sort of houses he wanted to build and the sort of communities he wanted to create – views which were in full accord with those of his Prime Minister. Both of them had seen enough of the mean little developments which industrial workers had lived in for 100 years, with no green space around them. Bevan hated the ribbon development of the inter-war years – long arterial roads with row upon row of prim semis. He wanted a decent size house for everyone. The standard minimum size house for a family was 750 square feet; he raised it to 900 square feet, and insisted on lavatories upstairs and downstairs. (Before Labour lost office in 1951 these standards were reduced by Bevan's successor.) Bevan supported the use of local material, even if it meant greater cost; and he decided to make local authorities the engine of his housing policy. Clem was worried about this because he knew that some local authorities did not have the expertise to deliver a massive house-building programme, and in April 1946 he insisted that Bevan establish a Housing Production Executive. The only real alternative to local authorities was the private sector; and that meant a repeat of what had happened before the war – that houses would not be built for those in the greatest need, but for those with the deepest pockets.

Bevan increased the Exchequer subsidy to local authorities for council-house building from two-thirds to three-quarters. The Treasury sharply turned this down at first, but he saw Dalton about it and Dalton reversed his officials' decision. Bevan rejected a proposal to give private builders the same subsidy: 'The only remedy the Tories have for every problem is to enable private enterprise to suck at the teats of the state.'

He gave priority to repairing damaged homes. Local authorities were told to requisition unoccupied housing, and conversion of homes to offices without local authority approval was banned. But houses were not being built sufficiently fast in 1945 and 1946. Faced with devastating shortages both of building materials and of labour in all the building trades, Bevan could only manage 15,000 new houses in Labour's first year of office. Young families were still crowded into parents' front-rooms and other inadequate accommodation.

In July 1946, forty-eight families moved unannounced into disused army camps in Scunthorpe. The idea caught on at once, and within weeks 45,000 people had occupied vacated army camps. From there the squatting movement spread to blocks of flats. Many Conservative local authorities had chosen to leave some blocks of flats empty, rather than follow Bevan's instructions to requisition them. In September, the word went out that people living in bad conditions should turn up on a certain day in Kensington High Street, carrying bedding. Hundreds came, not knowing what was to happen – only that their situation could hardly be made worse. Tubby Rosen, a Communist councillor in Clem's Stepney constituency, led them to an empty block of flats called Duchess of Bedford House. He went in through a back window and opened the door and as people streamed in, he took their names.

Clem demanded stern action from Ministers. He issued a statement saying the government took 'a serious view' of squatting, and that it was 'instituted and organised by the Communist Party'. It was, in London at any rate; but it was caused by the miserable condition in which thousands of people were living. But Clem disliked Communists, and direct action of any sort offended his deeply conservative instincts. The mood in government circles is illustrated by a memo to Downing Street from a senior Foreign Office official. He had, he wrote, seen an article in the *Daily Telegraph* saying that none of the squatters in Duchess of Bedford House was allowed to speak to reporters; and a child had been told by his companion to clam up when the *Telegraph* reporter tried to pump him. Only 'authorised spokesmen' could speak for the squatters. The FO official suggested how this could be used: 'It does appear to me that there is considerable capital to be made out of it, if as I assume, the official line about these squatters is to regard them as dupes of the Communist endeavour to use them for their own political ends . . . The first type of furnishing to be installed in the building is the iron curtain . . .' A Downing Street official replied that this grubby little idea had been handed to press secretary Francis Williams who had agreed to 'mention it to one or two of his press friends'. Bevan announced that no action would be taken against squatters who left voluntarily, and they would not lose their places on the housing queue. The implication was that squatters who did not leave would lose their places. The Communist Party knew that this would be enough to spoil the strategy. Telegrams went out from Communist Party headquarters that very evening: 'No more squatting – explanation follows.'

Bit by bit, the housing programme grew: 55,400 completions in 1946; 139,690 in 1947. Instead of arguing that Labour was not building enough houses, the government's critics now complained that it was diverting manpower, materials and American money into housebuilding when these ought to be going on investment in industry. Squalor, like Ignorance, was not slain, but it was damaged.

'Where are all the people I need for my [housing] programme?' Nye Bevan once rhetorically asked the Cabinet. 'Looking for houses, Nye,' answered the Prime Minister. The fifth giant, Idleness, or unemployment as it is more commonly known, had been slain for the duration of the war, but would demobilisation bring it back? After the First World War the streets had been full of former soldiers who had given their health for their country, and whose country could not even offer them the chance to work and feed their families.

It did not happen after the Second World War. 'We got about ten million people out of wartime jobs without unemployment ever going above three per cent,' says Denis Healey with justifiable proprietorial pride. Later the government, on the urging of Ernest Bevin and the Chiefs of Staff, introduced conscription for only the second time in peacetime (the first was 1939). This removed young men from the productive economy for a year, making labour a seller's market and crippling production, so much so that in March 1946 Clem broadcast an appeal, once again, to that rather overworked Dunkirk spirit: 'We have a shortage of labour . . . You remember how, during the war, we had a wonderful team spirit in the nation? . . . I want everyone . . . to recapture the spirit that brought us through the war . . . You are not just working for wages or profit, you are working for the nation.' He appealed to women to go back to work, although he added, 'I am not asking anyone to ignore that vital national service, work in the home.' Older people; disabled people; they were all needed, and employers must make use of them. 'We shall come through 1946 just as we came through 1940.'

But ensuring that the Idleness of the Thirties did not rise from the grave – that was at the heart of Dalton and Morrison's economic policy.

The long months of uncertainty in 1945, after Lease-Lend was ended and before the American loan was agreed, did not stop the government from setting in hand the policies for which it was elected, and in October 1945 Dalton produced his first Budget. It reflected the triumph felt on the Labour benches, the spirit of 'we are the masters now'. Dalton had, according to Michael Foot, 'the panache which the government so much needed . . . Dalton at the Treasury provided the resources and no small part of the drive behind Labour's great reforming measures.' Dalton reduced the very high wartime level of taxation, but the tax cuts were strongly in favour of the worst-off. He took two and a half million people in the lower income groups out of tax altogether, and substantially increased tax for the wealthiest – at its highest level, income tax reached 19s 6d (97.5p) in the pound. He introduced a profits tax and significantly raised death duties, making provision for the handing over to the community of land in lieu of death duties. 'One of the most important of all the causes of great inequality of income is the inheritance of great fortunes by a small minority,' he said. He resisted pressure to dismantle the tax structure which had been erected to meet wartime needs. It was, quite simply, a Budget designed to take from the rich and give to the poor.

Once the US loan was agreed, Dalton was able to produce another Budget, in April 1946, increasing substantially the sum spent on education, beginning the payment of family allowances, and putting £10 million into Development Areas which suffered from high levels of unemployment, a measure which gave Dalton particular pleasure. 'I have told my colleagues', he said in his Budget speech, 'that I will find, and find with a song in my heart, whatever money is necessary to finance useful and practical proposals for developing these areas, and bringing them to a condition which they never had in the past, of full and efficient and diversified activity.'

Herbert Morrison also started work before the loan was agreed. Nationalisation, whether the Americans liked it or not, was going ahead. Morrison had overall charge of the nationalisation programme, though each nationalisation was the work of an individual Minister. 'Herbert held their hands,' wrote Christopher Mayhew, Morrison's PPS for the first two years of the government. 'For example [Alf] Barnes [Minister of Transport] asked Morrison what to do and how to do it . . . And that went for a lot of nationalising ministers.' Barnes, not the brainiest of Ministers, probably relied more heavily on Morrison than most. Morrison had both the necessary administrative skills and the necessary experience, for he had brought London's buses and underground railways under a single authority. Clem had given him, as Lord President, a role both as economic overlord and as the overall Minister in charge of nationalisation. He interested himself in all the details, particularly the task of recruiting members of boards for newly-nationalised industries.

Hugh Dalton was the one nationalising Minister who required no help from Morrison. He swiftly accomplished the first and easiest nationalisation, that of the Bank of England, in November 1945, the month in which he produced his first Budget. Civil aviation followed the Bank of England into public ownership in January 1946. Three publicly-owned corporations were established: British European Airways, South American Airways, and British Overseas Airways Corporation. The same year saw the nationalisation of cable and wireless communications, and of the mines. Parts of civil aviation, gas, electricity and telecommunications were already publicly owned at the end of the war, but had the Conservatives been elected, they would probably have returned to private hands.

Coal, as Peter Hennessy writes, 'never lost its symbolic, almost romantic place in the Labour movement as the industry where the excesses of capitalism had left blood in the seams.' The task of nationalising it was formidable, and because the industry was so run down and yet so important, it had to be done quickly. The Minister of Fuel and Power, Emanuel Shinwell, complained that despite having talked of nationalising the mines for years, Labour had prepared no blueprint for how it was to be done. It had to be devised from scratch – and by a Minister trying desperately to cope with the fuel shortages at the same time. Clem decided that Shinwell needed one of his brightest young men to help him, and sent for Hugh Gaitskell, recently recovered from illness, for one of those characteristically terse interviews: 'I understand you are now well. I wish to have you in the government. Will you take mines? This doesn't mean going down mines all the time; there's gas and electricity, and the Bills coming along.'

So it was Gaitskell who was to make sense of the most resonant nationalisation of all: the industry which symbolised the Labour movement in defeat, in 1926 and again in 1984; and the Labour movement in victory, in 1946 and 1974. He steered nationalisation through its tortuous Committee stage, obstructed bitterly by Conservatives to whom it was just as great a symbol as to Labour. Brendan Bracken, now back in Parliament, loathed the Bill, and loathed Gaitskell for being one of Hugh Dalton's protégés. 'I have to sit in a committee of the House', Gaitskell wrote, 'opposite Mr Brendan Bracken, listening to every kind of taunt and insult and not being able to reply because it would prolong the debate.' He also wound up the final debate, and was the unlikely hero of coal nationalisation.

In 1947 the government nationalised inland transport – railways, canals, and road haulage – and the great utilities, electricity and gas. Transport was a huge task. There were 3,800 road haulage companies. Railway companies did not own just railways. They owned the harbours in Southampton and Hull, hotel chains, Thomas Cook the travel agents, and much more, and all of it was dreadfully run down at the end of the war.

Iron and steel were not nationalised until 1949. This was the most fiercely-opposed nationalisation of the lot, and Clem and Morrison laboured to produce a compromise plan, but the demand for full nationalisation, both among Labour MPs and in the Cabinet, was very strong. Nationalisation was finally achieved after Clem fired one Supply Minister for failing to stand up to the steelmasters.

All these industries with the exception of road haulage and iron and steel fitted the test Clem had told the US Congress he would apply to nationalisation. Was an industry a natural monopoly? If so, it was 'unsafe' to leave it in private hands. A private company which owns and controls all the means of delivering a vital commodity such as electricity or rail travel is in an immensely powerful position. It can demand any price it wishes, exploit its workers as much as it chooses, and even dictate the policy of the elected government. By the time it lost office, Clem's government had brought about twenty per cent of the economy into public ownership. The economic policy, nationalisation and above all the welfare state, were the means of dealing with the evils which had brought the Prime Minister into politics, and which had been listed and codified by William Beveridge. But could Britain afford them? In particular, could it afford the welfare state? Churchill's government thought not – in 1945 or any other time. Churchill's Chancellor, Sir Kingsley Wood, pointed out that the future cost of a welfare state as demanded by Beveridge was incalculable. No-one could calculate how much illness or unemployment there would be. All that anyone knew was that when it came, it would have to be paid for. If a government wanted to spend its money on something else, or if it wanted to cut taxes, it would be committed first to meeting the costs of the NHS and social security.

It is fashionable now to denigrate the welfare state created by the 1945 government on the grounds that it saddled Britain with a long term expense which the country could not afford; and that all it did was to give a much later government in the 1980s the trouble of dismantling it, so that Britain could once again live within its means. Bevan has been roundly attacked for failing to cost the NHS in the long term with any accuracy. The figures in his plan, as he freely admitted, were little more than educated guesses, and they proved optimistic. He has also been attacked for extracting more money from the Treasury for house-building than private industry was putting into building factories. Griffiths has been criticised for an open-ended commitment which, if there was high unemployment, could easily cost the nation more than it could afford. Was all this not the grossest sort of complacency, saddling the nation with such liabilities? Clem gave his answer to the House of Commons in 1946:

> The question is asked – can we afford it? Supposing the answer is 'No', what does that mean? It really means that the sum total of the goods produced and the services rendered by the people of this country is not sufficient to provide for all our people at all times, in sickness, in health, in youth and in age, the very modest standard of life that is represented by the sums of money set out in the Second Schedule to this [National Insurance] Bill. I cannot believe that our national productivity is so slow, that our willingness to work is so feeble or that we can submit to the world that the masses of our people must be condemned to penury.

It is, of course, all a matter of priorities. You cannot have a universal welfare state *and* low taxes, and the voters knew that in 1945.

Sir Kingsley Wood was right to say that the welfare state demanded an open-ended commitment. It did not allow a government to say: we will treat so many people on the NHS, give so many people unemployment pay – and that is that. A society has to pay for those who actually fall ill or lose their jobs, not the number budgeted to do so. It can be done. But everything else in the economy – profits, tax cuts, investment, everything – must stand in the queue behind, waiting to see how much is left over.That is the price to be paid. In 1945 the government thought it a price worth paying, to stop people dying of treatable diseases, to get rid of slums, to ensure that even Britain's poorest citizens had enough to eat.

But could Britain afford it *then*, in 1945, in a war-wrecked economy? Correlli Barnett calls it 'self-indulgent folly', claiming that Britain's manufacturing base was ignored in order that its people should be feather-bedded. If the welfare state was right at all, it was right in 1945. It is perfectly true, as Keynes pointed out when Lease-Lend was withdrawn, that Britain in 1945, her money and her export markets all gone, could not afford a welfare state without an American loan. This is what Correlli Barnett means when he sneers at the Attlee government for building a New Jerusalem 'on foreign tick', and complains that the USA wanted its money used for building industry, not for welfare schemes of which US public opinion did not approve. Clem believed that it was reasonable for Britain to ask the USA for a loan, but to reserve to the British government the right to decide how the money was spent. After all, Britain had drained her treasury and torpedoed her export market to hold off Hitler until the USA was ready to come into the war, while the USA had conserved its money and built up its exports.

If Winston Churchill had been Prime Minister in 1945, he would have faced the same crisis. He too would have sent emissaries with begging bowls to Washington. The money would simply have been distributed differently. There has not been a time, since 1945, when the British economy has not been to some extent in hock to the USA. If the fact that the government needed American cash meant that it had no right to institute welfare schemes of which Americans disapproved, then whatever the wish of the British people as expressed in elections, there could *never* be a welfare state. Any Labour government would inevitably end up, as MacDonald's did in 1931, abandoning the poor whom the party was created to help, because key bankers and congressmen in Washington and New York do not agree with those policies. The alternative is for a potential Labour government to abandon Labour's constituency before being elected.

In 1945 the electorate spoke, much more clearly than in any election since then. It said: if we were one people when we were all in mortal danger and Hitler was about to invade, then we are one people now, 'all our enemies having surrendered unconditionally or being about to do so,' as Churchill put it. In such circumstances, Churchill was understandably hurt that 'I was immediately dismissed by the British electorate from all further conduct of their affairs.'

The electors knew that Churchill had united them in war. But they believed his party would divide them in peace, as it had done throughout the inter-war years, into the haves and the have-nots. In 1945, as never before or since, people wanted the government to make Britain into one nation, to put an end to conspicuous wealth in the midst of desperate poverty. It was a moment when even many of those who were comfortably-off would concede that the community as a whole had a duty to those with nothing. You have only to listen to the discussion in any comfortable middle-class suburb in the 1990s to realise how rare such a time is, and to know that it has long gone. The war had brought the nation together and broken down class barriers. The end of the war was the time for a new beginning.

After the First World War there had been the same chance, but the essentially Conservative government under Lloyd George missed it. Clem, Dalton, Morrison, Griffiths and Bevan all knew that if they blew the chance in 1945, it would not come again. If they believed in anything they had advocated, they could not throw away that chance.

Perhaps unsurprisingly, the same commentators who consider that the welfare state was not affordable also think that it was a bad thing in itself. Correlli Barnett maintains that the welfare state idea springs from the public school do-gooding tradition of the nineteenth century – of which Anthony Eden and Winston Churchill were products just as much as Clem Attlee and Hugh Dalton. All of them, in 1945, constituted what he calls a 'liberal establishment' with illusory ideas about the state creating a better and fairer society. Conservative leaders were fellow-travellers. If Attlee and Dalton were red advocates of a New Jerusalem, Churchill and Eden were 'pallidly pink New Jerusalemers'.

It is a convenient argument, if you oppose the welfare state, to suggest that it is part of a public school tradition, and that the sturdy working class have no desire for such molly-coddling. But it's nonsense. The public school tradition of do-gooding was what first took the young Clement Attlee to Haileybury House in the East End, wearing his lawyer's clothes and his silk hat, to spend his spare time helping the deserving poor. It was the tradition of the Charity Organisation Society. Clem broke with it when he joined the ILP, and hitched himself to another tradition, a working-class tradition in which the hosts were people like Ernest Bevin and Nye Bevan, and the parvenus were the Clement Attlees and Hugh Daltons. This was the working-class tradition, made by people who knew what life for the poor was like without a welfare state and who did not want anyone to have to live it.

In *The Social Worker* Clem condemns charity as cold, loveless, and manipulative. If a rich man wants to help the poor, he should pay his taxes gladly, not dole out money at whim. The state should take on the task of looking after its poorest citizens. Conservatives believed this should be done mostly by private and voluntary philanthropy. They are two fundamentally different traditions, and lead to two fundamentally different styles of government. The myth has grown up that there was a post-war consensus, and that a Conservative government after 1945 would have pursued similar policies. But we now know, from research by Professor Howard Glennester among others, that Conservatives were very worried by the welfare state (and terrified by nationalisation). They hated the idea of universal benefits, feared for its tax implications, and worried away at the idea that the state was providing help which the voluntary sector ought to be engaged in.

Their alternative was to make home-ownership the aim for most families, with private rented housing for the rest; and to provide means-tested benefits alongside a growing private pensions industry. Instead of the NHS, they wanted an extension of the 1930s health insurance schemes. They did not want a state pension scheme which would provide for everyone, but a society in which individuals anticipated and looked after their own pension requirements. Conservative governments after 1951 worked steadily towards these goals, and the pace quickened after Margaret Thatcher became Prime Minister in 1979. Just as there was no real post-war consensus, there was no sudden break with that consensus in 1979.

But Churchill and Eden did not quarrel, in principle, with the idea that it is better to ensure that people have enough food and medical attention than not to do so. It was not until the 1990s that respectable historians began to deride the idea, as Correlli Barnett put it in 1995, of making people 'compulsorily dependent on state charity'. Today the whole concept of the welfare state brings out a sort of loathing and derision, of which Correlli Barnett provides another example: 'This liberal establishment, latter day White Knights, rode out to combat social evils with the flashing sword of moral indignation, and quested in simple faith for the grail of human harmony and happiness . . . Security from want from the crèche to the coffin . . .' And so on.

It did not seem at all strange in 1948 to hear the Prime Minister say: 'We must combine together to meet contingencies with which we cannot cope as individual citizens.' It would have seemed very strange to hear any leading politician declare, as Margaret Thatcher did, 'There is no such thing as society.' That is the measure of the distance we have travelled.

The welfare state and a better life for ordinary people were the major achievements of Clem Attlee's government, and he was, privately, fiercely proud of it. Years later when an interviewer asked what his government would be remembered for, he grunted: 'Don't know. India perhaps.' But what he felt, under those gruff layers of terse nonchalance, was probably expressed in this passage from the first draft of his autobiography (which, like most passages that expressed human feeling, he ruthlessly expunged from the published version):

> Contrast the conditions [in the distressed areas] today with the dismal record of the inter-war years. See the new spirit of hope. See the number of works in operation and planned, and you can see what a Labour government means for the workers . . . Contrast the steady carrying out of Labour's programme in agriculture with the betrayal of the countryside, of farmers and agricultural workers alike, after the first world war . . .
>
> Nor have we neglected the cultural side of life. The Education Act has been implemented, not whittled away as was the Fisher Act. The problem of betterment has been tackled and the National Parks Bill has gone through. New planned towns are to be built . . . Old abuses have been swept away and the foundations of a new order well and truly laid.

Peter Hennessy puts it this way: 'The transformation in life chances for those at the bottom of the heap was quite dramatic.' In York in 1936, thirty-one per cent of households lived in poverty. In 1950 the figure was under three per cent.

Labour's other big idea, nationalisation, did not have the same resonance. Churchill attacked it in his usual vigorous way, claiming in Parliament that it divided the nation. Clem replied: 'The burden of the Right Honourable Gentleman's speech is this: why, when you were elected to carry out a Socialist programme, did you not carry out a Conservative programme?' Clem's friend Anthony Eden, who avoided attacking the welfare state, was pressed into service to denounce nationalisation, following one of Clem's all-in-this-together, Dunkirk-spirit broadcasts in March 1947, as the worst winter of the century was starting to dissipate: 'Our difficulties are too great to indulge in party political scores,' said Clem. '. . . The difficulties we face are the same as those in your families . . . Ask yourself whether you are doing the work the community requires. Your work may bring you in more money but is it what the nation requires? . . . You may be an employer of labour but are you attracting labour into useless work? . . . We shall win in peace just as we did in war.' Then came one of those metaphors which so enraged Nye Bevan: 'We understand team work from the games we play . . .'

Eden responded on air. His voice sounded rather like Clem's. 'The Prime Minister appeals for support for the Government on national grounds, but unfortunately the Government seeks policies which divide the nation.' He put forward the rather peculiar constitutional theory that, because in 1945 nearly half the voters had voted for parties that rejected Labour's policies, Labour should not implement them.

> I say to the Government: stop galloping ahead down Nationalisation Avenue and pay attention to the things that matter now . . . not whether electricity should become a state monopoly in 1948 or not . . . I'm more than ever convinced that great state monopolies offer no cure for our national ill . . . Let the Government face their difficulties in the national spirit . . . I am confident that your democratic answer will be against state regimentation and in favour of a system of free enterprise.

'Free enterprise' is a wonderful expression. The mixture of being 'free' and being 'enterprising' is irresistible. 'Nationalisation', on the other hand, carries the taste of state bureaucracy. But in 1945 it was not at all obvious that free enterprise was anything like as good as it sounded. Keynes blamed British free enterprise management for most of the problems of British industry:

> The hourly wage today in this country is (broadly) 2s [10 pence] per hour; in the United States it is 5s [25 pence] per hour . . . Even the celebrated inefficiency of British manufacturers can scarcely (one hopes) be capable of offsetting over wide ranges of industry the whole of this initial cost-difference in their favour, though admittedly, they have managed it in some important cases . . . If by some sad geographical slip the American Air Force . . . were to destroy every factory on the North East Coast and in Lancashire (at an hour when the Directors were sitting there and no one else), we should have nothing to fear.

Forty years later it became established wisdom that free enterprise worked, that Britain's lack of competitiveness was caused entirely by the high wages paid to its greedy employees, and that unemployment was caused by their failure – as a future Employment Secretary, Norman Tebbitt, put it – to 'get on their bikes' and look for work. But these things were far from self-evident in 1945.

9

The Winston Would A-Wooing Go

Hugh Dalton's departure was a turning point. The big five became the big four, and started to look distinctly elderly: Clem (65), Bevin (67), Cripps (59) and Morrison (60), in that order of importance. The average age of the Cabinet was well over sixty. By contrast, Labour's backbenches were unusually young. For sixteen years, from 1929 until 1945, there were practically no new Labour MPs. Labour's ranks had been decimated in 1931, and the 1935 election only saw the return of 're-treads' from the 1929 Parliament. Then there was a new influx in 1945. There was a missing generation between Aneurin Bevan, first elected in 1929, who had been fashioned by the First World War; and Hugh Gaitskell, first elected in 1945, who had been fashioned by the Second World War.

The big four had failing health. Ernest Bevin had started to suffer from heart attacks. Morrison had a thrombosis in January 1947. Cripps was beginning to waste under the effects of the intestinal illness which had been with him for much of his adult life.

Stafford Cripps had been born with a silver spoon in his mouth, and it remained there. His father was a successful barrister and Stafford, educated at Winchester, was quickly recognised as an out-standing lawyer, becoming the youngest King's Counsel of his day. He inherited one fortune from his father and married another in the shape of the granddaughter of the founder of Eno's Fruit Salts.

His political views owed more to his aunt, Beatrice Webb, than to his father who was a Conservative MP, and who became a peer and a Minister in the Labour government of 1924. In 1930, before Cripps was even an MP, he became Solicitor-General when the incumbent resigned owing to ill health. A vacant constituency for a by-election was speedily found for him – and it turned out to be one of the few that could be held in 1931. So he had been an MP for less than a year when he joined George Lansbury and Clem Attlee's collective leadership.

Intellectually, no-one doubted that he was telling the exact truth when he said: 'If you gave me the papers of any case I have fought in the last 20 years for one hour, I could go to court and fight it again,' and then corrected himself: 'No, I would not need the papers.'

After the 1935 election he became a left-wing rebel and got himself expelled from the Labour Party in 1939. But his days as a rebel ended with the war, during which he benefited from Churchill's need to bring the left into his government.

By 1948 Cripps, tall, thin and ascetic, wore small round spectacles on his nose and his Christianity on his sleeve. 'There but for the grace of God, goes God,' said Churchill. The time was past for optimistic socialist Budgets delivered with a song in the Chancellor's heart, and few hearts appeared to be less inclined for melody than the one which beat beneath the austere chest of the new Chancellor.

Bevin's foreign policy, for good or ill, was set in concrete. Altering it would mean pushing aside the immovable object of the Foreign Secretary. Bevin was as much feared as admired, for he was both unforgiving and vindictive. The 'Keep Left' group had, he told Labour's 1947 conference, 'stabbed him in the back' by calling for an alternative foreign policy: 'I grew up in the trade union, you see, and I have never been used to this kind of thing.' 'Herbert Morrison is his own worst enemy,' someone reputedly once said to Bevin. 'Not while I'm alive 'e ain't' replied the Foreign Secretary. (He may have said it about Bevan. Or he may have said it about both, or someone else entirely. No one is sure any more.)

He was the only man who was allowed occasionally to waffle in Cabinet, even to turn up for a meeting rather drunk. He was Clem's friend and confidant, joining him at Chequers on several weekends, briefing him on foreign affairs, reminiscing about strikes in the past, and drinking quantities of brandy. Anecdotes about him abounded. 'I want a bottle of Newts,' he told a waiter, his lunch companion translating this as Nuits St Georges. Clem's own favourite, which he often told, was of a discussion between himself, Bevin, Hugh Dalton and Dai Grenfell. 'Bevin summed up: "Right, we'll leave it to . . ." But did he say, "Hugh and I", "You and I", "Hugh and Dai" or "You and Dai?"'

He handled foreign statesmen with the confidential camaraderie of a trade union leader doing a deal. There is a delightful photograph of Bevin with Marshall and Schuman. Bevin has manoeuvred his German and US counterparts into a small corner of a splendid state room. The large hand holding his cigarette is also holding Schuman's reluctantly patriarchal arm. It looks like a discreet caucus of power-brokers at the TGWU conference.

Herbert Morrison's star was on the wane. He was still the great machine politician, with enormous talent for exercising power through his many committees. He lost his responsibility for the economy to Cripps in the wake of the attempted putsch of 1947, but he was still deputy Prime Minister and Leader of the House, co-ordinated the non-economic side of the home front, and chaired many key Cabinet committees, and he was given overall responsibility for social services. This was part of Arthur Greenwood's job as Lord Privy Seal. Clem decided that the endlessly loyal Greenwood must now retire from ministerial office at the age of sixty-eight. Clem's unpublished autobiographical notes reveal that in 1945 he had felt the need to give Greenwood something because of his status in the party, his popularity and his loyalty, but by 1947 Greenwood was 'losing grip'.

'Dear Arthur,' wrote Clem, 'I am making some changes in the Government. It is in my view essential to look to the future of the movement and to bring on some of the younger members of the Party. This necessarily involves the retirement of some of the older men who have given long service to the movement. I have very reluctantly come to the conclusion that I should include you among the latter.' Then much about his respect and affection for his loyal colleague. Greenwood made the best of it: 'My dear Clem, I have your letter of September 26 and thank you for the generous terms in which it is couched . . .' As Labour Party Treasurer he was a key organisational figure, and devoted the rest of his career to it.

Most Prime Ministers are squeamish about firing old friends and colleagues, but not Clem. At least one old colleague asked why he was being fired and was told 'Afraid you're not up to it.' The name of this Minister has always been a secret, but a source tells me it was John Parker, whom we last met standing beside Herbert Morrison in the gents at Central Hall, Westminster, on election night 1945, declining to take part in Morrison's plot to oust Clem. Another equally good source claims it was Richard Stokes. It is perfectly likely that it happened to them both.

James Margach describes Clem sacking an unnamed Scottish Secretary: 'Good t'see you. I'm carrying through Government changes. Want your job for somebody else. Sake of the party, y'know. Write me the usual letter. Think of something as the excuse. Health, family, too much travelling, constituency calls. Anything will do. Good fellow. Thanks.' Pressed for a reason, Clem said: ''Cos you don't measure up to your job.'

Curiously, it was also a Scottish Secretary, Joe Westwood, whom Clem often cited as the man who took his dismissal best. He said: 'Morning, Prime Minister, I know what you're after, you want my job.' Clem said: 'Well, Joe, as a matter of fact, you know, you are getting on a bit and we have to make room for the young ones.' Westwood said: 'That's all right by me. You'll find I shall be just as loyal on the backbenches as on the Front Bench.' Margach's Scottish Secretary must have been Arthur Woodburn, who took over from Westwood in 1947 and lasted until the 1950 election. Clem's draft autobiography reveals that he was dissatisfied with Woodburn's performance.

Five senior Ministers lost their job in that 1947 reshuffle, including the War Minister, F. J. Bellenger, whose dismissal was urged on the Prime Minister by Dalton. Both Dalton and Cripps were free with their advice, and it was sometimes taken. But they failed to persuade him to jettison Shinwell. In deference to Dalton and Cripps he removed him from Fuel and Power and refused him the Commonwealth Office, after Cripps protested strongly, partly on the grounds that 'To put a person of that race into that position at this moment would I think be most unfortunate especially as regards South Africa.' But he made him War Minister, succeeding Bellenger, and later brought him into the Cabinet as Defence Minister.

Clem 'was the best butcher since the war', said Harold Wilson. 'He'd send for a man and say: "Well, you've had a good innings; time to put your bat up in the pavilion." And that was that.' For Clem, it was simply something a Prime Minister had to do. 'It is a most distasteful thing to have to say to an old friend and colleague that it is time to make room for a younger man.' But 'you have to send for the man and tell him so yourself. Ramsay MacDonald used to get someone else to do it.'

In 1950, when Stanley Evans, after forty five days as PPS at the Food Ministry, announced that 'no nation featherbeds its agriculture like Britain', he was out of the door before he knew what had hit him. And when Ministers let the government in for allegations of what we have now come to know as sleaze, Clem was swift and merciless, as he had been with Hugh Dalton.

In the winter of 1948–9 John Belcher, who assisted Harold Wilson at the Board of Trade, was found to have had an unwise relationship with one Sidney Stanley, whose wealth rested on his ability to convince businessmen that he had good government contacts and could therefore obtain concessions on such matters as building permits and export and import licences. Clem at once set up a tribunal to investigate that and other rumours surrounding Mr Stanley, telling the House of Commons: 'Democracy cannot thrive in an atmosphere of suspicion and mistrust.'

Belcher had been foolish but not corrupt, the tribunal decided. Nonetheless, Belcher resigned, first from the government, then as an MP. Clem replied to his resignation letter: 'I am certain that you have taken the right course in offering to resign your office.' If he had not resigned, Belcher would have been sacked, a victim of what Barbara Castle, then PPS at the same Ministry, describes as 'the austere morality which dominated Clem Attlee's government'.

He typed up, on his battered typewriter, his harsh judgements on some of his colleagues, on 5 September 1950, and put them away, safely out of sight. They make bleak reading. 'Ben Smith who was not a great success . . . Grenfell and Tom Smith who were not much good at the Mines department . . . Wilmot failed to come up to expectations and had to go . . . Hynd was not a success . . . On bad advice I made Bellenger . . . Secretary of State for War. He was not up to the position and had to go . . . [five Under Secretaries] were found wanting . . . Creech Jones . . . had not appeared to have a real grip at the Colonial Office. He was bad in the House and contributed nothing to the Cabinet . . . Noel-Baker . . . did not inspire much confidence. He was talkative but not illuminating in Cabinet . . .' And so on, pages of it, stark, spare and rather cruel.

Part of the purpose of the carnage was to give young politicians their chance, and in 1947 this meant promotion for the next three leaders of the Labour Party. Hugh Gaitskell replaced his boss Shinwell as Minister of Fuel and Power after another of those terse Attlee interviews. 'I am reconstructing the government. I want you to be Fuel and Power. It is not a bed of roses.' Harold Wilson became President of the Board of Trade at thirty-one, replacing Cripps. Wilson had been given his first government job immediately after his election to Parliament in 1945 in a terse telephone call: 'Forming a Government. Want you to be Parly Sec to the Ministry of Works. George Tomlinson is your Minister; raised no objection to you.' James Callaghan was in and out of the Cabinet Room in a minute and a half. The Prime Minister said he was to be

Parliamentary Secretary at the Ministry of Transport. 'Remember you will be playing for the First Eleven in future. If you intend to negotiate with someone tomorrow, don't insult him today.'

In the summer of 1948 the Attlees left for a holiday in County Mayo on the beautiful west coast of Ireland. They played golf, sailed and fished. At the end of their holiday they motored across the border for a courtesy visit to the Northern Ireland Prime Minister, Lord Brookeborough. At the Sligo border the customs officers insisted that Vi should stop the car while they searched it, even though the Prime Minister was in the passenger seat. As he stood beside his car, a young reporter from the *Belfast Telegraph*, John Cole, showed him a cutting from the previous day's *Observer* which said that he was seeing Lord Brookeborough to discuss the end of Irish partition. Clem read the cutting, then took the pipe from his mouth and barked: 'Got your notebook?' Cole nodded eagerly, and the Prime Minister swiftly dictated a rebuttal of the story, point by point. When Cole rang to dictate his story, he found that the quote fell naturally into paragraphs.

As soon as his holiday was over, Clem had to go into hospital, where a duodenal ulcer was diagnosed. He had to shed most of his duties for three months. One of his 'get well soon' letters came from Cyril Sladden, recently-retired schoolmaster at Eton: 'My dear Prime Minister, I had a letter recently from my friend and old Eton colleague George Tait in which he told me of the talk he had had with you a few weeks ago, and from which I learned the rather surprising fact that you had not forgotten our close association of a few weeks' duration in that most dreadful rest camp in 1915 . . .'

Clem's memory could still perform remarkably. He needed little sleep and seemed unaffected by long hours of work. This was partly because he knew how to relax, and partly from that enviable habit of never worrying about decisions once he had taken them. It was partly, too, because he was probably the most economical of effort of any Prime Minister to occupy Number 10. He did not allow his time to be wasted. Harold Wilson said: 'You'd think twice before asking to see him.' He expected his visitors to know why they had come, and to put their points tersely, then leave. According to Arthur Moyle, who became his PPS after Geoffrey de Freitas was promoted: 'If he wanted to encourage a visitor to leave, which was rarely necessary – they were usually ready to go – he'd take his pipe from his mouth and put it carefully on his blotter, lift himself out of his chair slightly, look across at the clock, and give a little grunt. It never failed.'

Every weekend, Chequers revived his spirits and recharged his batteries. Clem and Vi loved Chequers and the Buckinghamshire countryside in which it was set. As often as possible they travelled there on Friday evening, and returned after an early breakfast on Monday morning. They generally spent their holidays there. They played tennis, croquet and bridge, Vi criticising her husband's bridge without inhibition in front of the private secretaries whom they recruited for a foursome. They played golf at the nearby golf club, and the ever-present detective caddied. Clem read, but not the great poetry of his youth, for which perhaps his heavy workload no longer left the mental energy, but Agatha Christie, Jane Austen, Gibbon or the Brontës. Jane Austen was still the favourite novelist for both Clem and his brother Tom, who re-read her every year. At nights he often read to Vi – at the end of 1949 he was reading her Kipling's *Captains Courageous*.

On one Sunday Herbert Morrison arrived and asked the Prime Minister if he had seen the reports in the newspapers. Clem said he never read the Sunday papers. 'I never know if he's telling the truth or not,' said Morrison afterwards. Morrison, who lived and breathed politics, could not imagine a politician who could take or leave the daily papers.

'It was a pleasure,' says Sir David Hunt, who became Clem's Private Secretary in 1950 and grew exceptionally fond of him, 'to see how he enjoyed himself at Chequers, strolling in the grounds in a bright suit of tweed. He invited me there for lunch the first weekend I was with him. He seemed to like having me there.'

'On one occasion I was required to partner him at tennis,' writes Mayhew. '. . . We must have looked a strange pair – one of us short, static and elderly, and the other tall, mobile and young, both wearing colourful Old Haileyburian sweaters.'

Clem and Vi decided they would retire to that part of Buckinghamshire, and in 1949 they bought Cherry Cottage at Great Missenden, just a few miles away from Chequers. Kenneth Harris depicts Vi as a difficult and neurotic woman, but her daughter Felicity thinks that is unfair. 'They had a terribly happy marriage,' she says simply, and that is certainly true. 'She was a basically happy woman. We used to laugh together a lot. Little things bothered her but big things she took in her stride.' Vi once wrote three pages of closely typed notes about being the Prime Minister's wife, and these show us a rather livelier, more contented and more intelligent woman than Harris describes, with a startling if naive clarity of vision. She was frustrated when she felt that civil servants were putting a barrier of protocol between her and her husband, around whom her life revolved. She resented getting Clem's messages via their respective private secretaries. She insisted on seeing the Prime Minister's engagements and opening all her own letters: 'If I had handed everything over to my secretary I shouldn't have remembered anything about the letters.' Nor was she impressed by the civil servants' first attempt at drafting a speech for her, writing to Clem while he was away: '[The draft] was far too involved for me. It conveyed no meaning to me. We eventually got out quite a good little speech.' Once, so she assured her family, she shared a platform with a lady who rose to her feet and said 'unused as I am to public speaking' three times before falling down in a faint.

Her happiness was very important to Clem. The work was arranged so that he could spend the maximum amount of time with her, going up to the flat for lunch and tea. After breakfast, they took the Welsh terrier Ting for a walk in St James's Park, the policeman a few paces behind. She was happy with the allotted role of Prime Minister's wife, giving interviews in which she complained that 'his habit of shrugging his shoulders when he sits down gives a suit no chance', and broadcasting the nation's gratitude to volunteer women who had looked after Britain's soldiers: 'You darned socks and how you darned them,' says the script, on which someone has helpfully underlined 'how' and the second 'darned' for emphasis.

'It was extraordinary', she wrote in her private account, 'how soon No 10 felt home to me. I was determined to keep the homely atmosphere we had always had . . . There is a wonderful atmosphere at No 10. Everybody there is so kind and helpful.' She took pleasure in being able to use the address to help charities in which she interested herself: the Save the Children Fund, the National Association of Girls' Schools, King George's Fund for Sailors and the one for which she had done hundreds of hours of voluntary work, the Red Cross.

Labour MPs found her puzzling. Tony Benn, newly elected to Parliament in 1950, was one of a group of young Members invited to tea in the flat at Downing Street. He wrote in his diary for that day: 'There had been a row at Questions over the appointment of an American admiral over NATO sea forces . . . We had been warned by Clem's PPS not to talk shop and so we were slightly taken aback when Vi went for Clem and asked why he had knuckled under to the Americans yet again.' He concluded: 'I think [Clem] has an inferiority complex . . . Vi was very la-di-da in her latest creation, with long red fingernails. She might have been a leader of society and her comments were very "upper class".' Vi would have felt she was letting her husband down if she had not been well turned out. The fact that Clem failed to notice does not seem to have bothered her. Felicity says: 'With three daughters, he thought he ought to try, so sometimes he'd say "That's a nice dress, my dear."' On one occasion he returned to work after tea and Vi's private secretary asked her: 'What did the Prime Minister say about the new fox fur?' 'He didn't notice,' said Vi.

When Sir David Hunt arrived in 1950, his predecessor warned him that Vi was impossible, and Sir David recalled for me the painful occasion when he made an appointment for the Prime Minister which clashed with something she wanted her husband to do. 'She stormed into the Cabinet Room, shouted for a bit, said it was very inefficient, a shame we couldn't get someone to do it properly. He was the other side of me, waving to her to calm down.' But Hunt decided that she was 'a good-natured woman at heart' and that 'the reason for her desire to have all arrangements perfect was her fierce devotion to her husband and her determination to save him trouble at the cost of her own.'

Clem gave Hunt what he still thinks is the oddest and yet the most natural job interview for private secretary. He asked nothing about the job, or about politics, but wanted only to talk about Hunt's time at Oxford and in the army. He became very animated when he learned that Hunt had served on Alexander's staff, describing Alexander as the greatest general in the war. Hunt warmed to Clem quickly. They talked military history together. 'He enjoyed that in the way you enjoy something you know you do well. He had a very well-stocked mind. He must have been a very good regimental officer in the war because he was efficient and decisive. That infected his politics. He thought people should stay faithful to what they'd enlisted in. He'd have thought it beneath him to do a crooked deal. He disliked anyone who intrigued against the line. That's why he was fond of old trade union leaders.'

Hunt, who years later in his retirement became television's *Mastermind* champion, is sure Clem could have been a Mastermind champion. He had that sort of mind, and he was still exercising it with his mind games: doing *The Times* crossword, typing out lists from memory. One day in 1950 he sat down and typed out the name of every person who had served in his government. Then he counted them – there were 135 – and wrote carefully beside most of the names either 'TU' or 'Ox' or 'Cambs'. He re-typed them out against the offices they occupied, and wrote beside each name the dates during which they occupied it. Finally, he typed out a list of the public school-educated Ministers, under the name of their school. Eton came first, with seven names including Dalton and John Strachey. Next, unsurprisingly, was Haileybury, with five names, then Winchester with three, including Cripps and Gaitskell. Marlborough, Wellington and St Paul's boasted two each, and Harrow, Cheltenham, Tonbridge, Dulwich, Rugby and Oundle had one each. He wisely showed this to no-one: it would have been regarded as a rather suspicious activity for a Labour Prime Minister. But it was no different from typing lists of all eighty-five boys at prep school with him, or the boys in his class at Haileybury, or the men he had served with in Gallipoli. It kept his mind sharp and provided a little harmless nostalgia at the same time.

There were other pleasures. Seeing plays. Watching tennis: at Wimbledon in 1950 he saw 'the finest men's doubles that I can remember. Particularly satisfying as Australians beat Americans', he wrote to Tom. Visiting the King: if anything Clem's affection for the monarchy increased, and he wrote to Tom that the princesses Elizabeth and Margaret were turning into very bright young women, especially Margaret; and that Prince Charles was 'a fine little boy running about with great vigour. He shook hands with grave courtesy.' And Clem still found time to interest himself in ecclesiastical appointments. 'Thank you very much for your useful letter on the Truro vacancy,' he wrote to Tom in November 1950.

But in the end he had always to return to the increasingly intractable task of enabling Britain to pay her way in dollars. This meant tighter money, restricted imports, giving exports priority over the domestic market. It also meant a wage freeze and no major strikes. London's 1948 dock strike provoked perhaps his most effective broadcast ever. In a firm voice charged with anger, he told listeners of 'an unofficial strike in the Port of London', snapping out the word 'strike' as though it were a deadly insult.

Is there anybody who knows better than the docker what unemployment means? Didn't you have enough of the means test? This strike is not against capitalism or your employers. It is a strike against your mates . . . I lived in Dockland for many years . . . I remember what casual labour meant . . . Do you remember what it was like to go home and your wife

would say 'Any work today?' 'No.' For over forty years the union . . .
argued that if men turned up every day they should be paid. They
should have a guaranteed weekly wage. And during the war your old
leader, Mr Ernest Bevin, then Minister of Labour, introduced it . . .
Who advised you to [strike]? A small nucleus who for political reasons
want to take advantage of every little dispute that takes place . . . Your
clear duty to yourselves and your fellow citizens is to return to work.

The strike ended forty-eight hours later, and Clem's broadcast was
one of the main reasons. The TUC agreed a wage freeze, encouraged
by the fact that Cripps retained a tax system which redistributed
wealth and kept prices under strict control. But TUC leaders could
not prevent another dock strike in 1949. Gold and dollar reserves
continued their decline. There was severe inflation. The rearmament programme and the welfare state were costly. A recession
in the USA, and a decision by other European countries that the
drawing-rights of Marshall Plan debtors should be freely convertible
into dollars, made the position worse.

In July 1949, Hugh Gaitskell led a group of younger Ministers
who convinced the Prime Minister that the right course was to
devalue the pound; the alternative orthodox methods had destroyed
MacDonald's government in 1931. Cripps was still doubtful, but
Clem overruled him, and on 18 September 1949 Cripps announced
that the exchange rate with the dollar would be reduced from 4.03
to 2.80. His radio broadcast was designed to counter Churchill's
propaganda:

I am sure you've read and heard a good deal in the last few months
about the difficulty we, and other European nations, have in earning
enough dollars to buy what we need in the way of food and raw
materials especially from America and Canada. It's referred to as 'the
dollar shortage' or 'the sterling-dollar problem' and it has been with us
more or less since before the first world war – but it has become much
more intense since the last war and, indeed, in the last few months
our dollar difficulty has become very very serious indeed . . . We must
sell more goods and services for dollars. This is especially important
now before the Marshall Plan, with its dollar aid, comes to an end –
as it does in 1952 . . .

Pre-war governments solved the problem by creating unemployment.

The unemployed wouldn't need any imported raw materials, for they
had no work; nor would they have been able to buy much food, for

they had no wages. That would have reduced overseas expenditure. And when enough people were unemployed, fear and misery would have made it possible to cut down the general wage level, and bankruptcy would have forced a cutting down of the industrial costs . . .

But devaluation meant spending cuts. Where were they to come from? Defence? Over Ernest Bevin's dead body. The NHS and social services? Only if Clem wanted to precipitate the resignation of Nye Bevan and a full-scale parliamentary rebellion. In the end most things were cut, but nothing decimated: defence, housing, government departments, though not social services.

It was not the happiest atmosphere in which to call a general election. But there had to be an election by the summer of 1950 at the latest, and Cripps did not think it right to produce a Budget before it. The British government needed to talk to US bankers and politicians with the strength of a new mandate around them, he believed. The election was fixed for February 1950. This time Clem and Vi travelled in comparative style. The Hillman had been traded in for a Humber, in the back of which, Vi tells us in her Downing Street notes, sat the detective and 'Mr Philpott from the *Daily Herald*'. Another car followed containing the *Time Life* reporting team from the USA. 'The chauffeur very kindly put my car away, bringing it round ready for the road in the morning.'

Clem's speeches had not changed. 'Many who listened, and especially some of the active party workers, would have liked to have heard more rousing speeches than those which Clem gave,' says Jack Jones. 'But if you listened closely his message was clear, forthright, honest, dignified and essentially humane. These are the qualities the British people respect and still want to hear.' There were grounds for optimism. Despite its financial worries and an unremittingly hostile press, the government had won all thirty-five by-elections of the Parliament. But there had been what James Margach has described as 'five years of ceaseless press harassment'. The task of making people frightened of the government was made harder by the Prime Minister's immensely reassuring personality. The way round that was to present him, quite falsely, as a weak character unable to stand up to dangerous left-wingers like Nye Bevan. Before the election Charles Wintour, later editor of the *Evening Standard*, introduced Clem the Wimp to *Standard* readers in a review of Roy Jenkins's interim biography of Clem:

Clement Attlee was a young man who couldn't quite. He couldn't quite get his house colours at Haileybury. He couldn't quite get a first at Oxford. He couldn't quite earn a living at the bar. In fact he couldn't quite make a success of his early life ... What brought this staid and uninspiring gentleman to the leadership of a powerful Party? ... Not brains. Not ambition ... It was too much spare time in his twenties that set Clement on the road to fame.

Come the election, the *Standard* sent to one of his election meetings an American woman journalist with sharp claws, Emily Hahn:

> He looks a dear little gentleman, with good chiselled features and small feet ... If you aren't a big tough guy you can be a little loveable guy that everybody in the club respects and handles gently for fear of breaking him ... I wonder whether it has occurred to Mr Attlee that this is a rough and naughty world, and that quite a lot of it is outside England. He talked as though England could decide to be a socialist state all by itself ...

Clem was not at all surprised that the *Daily Worker* took the same line as the capitalist press. Under the headline 'MIDDLE CLASS AND MEDIO-CRE' its acerbic news editor, Allen Hutt, wrote of Clem's early years in Limehouse: 'Boredom drove him to the well recognised English middle-class pastime of slumming it in the East End.' During the election the Conservative newspapers have a surprisingly modern ring to them. 'VOTE FOR FREEDOM AND LOWER TAXES' ran a headline in the *Daily Graphic* on the Monday of election week, 'VOTE FOR A HOME YOU CAN OWN' on the Tuesday, 'VOTE TODAY—VOTE TORY' on Thursday.

The result was a triumph and a disaster. Labour achieved the highest popular vote any party had ever polled, even more than in 1945, and nearly three per cent more than the Conservatives. The swing to the Conservatives was only 3.3 per cent. But Labour's overall majority was down to five, because many of its votes went to build up massive majorities in safe Labour seats. The redistribution of seats which had taken place during the Parliament had transferred huge blocks of Labour votes from marginal seats to safe seats and probably lost Labour about thirty MPs. One consequence of the redistribution was that Clem, for the first time, had a different constituency, Walthamstow East. He was widely respected there but never quite at home in the way that he had been at Stepney. Ellis Kopel was a young reporter on the *Walthamstow Guardian*, who used to take tea each month with the Labour Party and Clem: 'They were rather uncomfortable occasions because he seemed to be a man totally without small talk, and they did not feel they could raise matters of state with the Prime Minister. Tea and sandwiches went round for 20–30 people and the atmosphere was leaden.'

After the election there was, Clem wrote to Tom, 'the distasteful business of reconstructing the government . . . It always means relegating some good friends to the back benches.' Six Ministers were dropped, and Clem managed for the first time to get the average age of his Cabinet below sixty: it was now fifty-nine and a quarter. He and his Ministers now had to do a good deal of their work in the House of Commons, in case there was a snap vote which might bring down the government. How could Labour ensure a better result next time? Morrison ran Labour's NEC sub-committee on publicity. He became the first of a long line of top Labour politicians – his grandson Peter Mandelson is the latest – to use control of the publicity machine to influence policy. Their argument is this. Labour can rely on its core support among the industrial working classes. The people whom it must not offend are the middle classes, where the floating voters are found and who are easily alarmed. Morrison had a phrase for it: he wanted 'all the useful people'. Labour in 1950 kept its support in the industrial north, but lost it in the south.

So the question for policy-makers is: how much of Labour's traditional agenda will middle-class voters stand for? If the answer is 'not very much', or even none at all, then that is how much Labour should advocate. To do anything different is to risk electoral suicide. Morrison, in his post-mortem on the 1950 election, wrote that Labour should 'modernise' – a word which has recently enjoyed a resurgence in Labour circles, its meaning entirely unchanged. The election setback confirmed his view that it should abandon nationalisation and 'consolidate'. It should not promise or plan any more activity on the welfare state or nationalisation fronts.

This strategy brought Morrison into direct conflict with Nye Bevan and a significant group of influential Labour MPs. The election result convinced Hugh Gaitskell that 'the Morrison policy of going slow and retrenchment . . . would have been appropriate.' The big unanswered question was: who would Clem line up with? Bevan? Or Gaitskell and Morrison? Clem's method was to avoid coming down on either side unless it became clear that the wrong side was about to lose. Now he said just enough to make sure that the party did not formally adopt 'consolidation' as a policy.

When Parliament met, he teased Churchill for his efforts to woo

Liberal votes: 'He has been a very ardent lover of this elderly spinster, the Liberal Party . . .' Privately, he wrote a song about it.

> The Winston would a wooing go
> Hey Ho says Eden
> Whether old Smithers would let him or no
> With a roly poly gammon and spinach
> Sing Ho for Anthony Eden.
>
> So off he set in his Churchill hat
> Hey Ho says Eden
> And on the way he fell in with a rat
> With a roly poly gammon and Simon
> Sing Ho for Anthony Eden.
>
> Soon they arrived at the Liberal House
> Hey Ho says Eden
> And knocked on the door for Violet Mouse
> With a roly poly gammon and Simon
> Sing Ho for Anthony Eden.
>
> In return on the wireless you shall have your say
> Hey Ho says Eden
> And turn all the Liberals to ballot our way
> With a roly poly gammon and Simon
> Sing Ho for Anthony Eden.
>
> But just as they were about to begin
> Hey Ho says Eden
> Clem Davies and Megan came tumbling in
> With a roly poly gammon and Simon
> Sing Ho for Anthony Eden . . .

Violet Mouse is a reference to the leading Liberal Violet Bonham Carter. Hearing that the Liberals were not using her in any of their allotted election broadcasts, Churchill offered her one of the Conservative slots, which she turned down on the advice of Liberal leader Clement Davies and of Megan Lloyd George. Clem's poetry seems to have revived in 1950. With it came a late-flowering energy and lightness of touch. Yet the Parliament which lasted from February 1950 to October 1951 was a miserable one for him. It saw the Korean war; the death of his closest colleague, Ernest Bevin; and the political explosion that blew his party apart.

On 25 June 1950, North Korean forces entered South Korea. Two days later President Truman ordered in US forces, and the United Nations Security Council called for the withdrawal of North

Korean forces. British forces were sent to help, but privately Clem was restraining Truman from doing things which might spread the conflict – flying reconnaissance missions over Soviet territory, for example. The British arms budget was increased, and conscription was raised from eighteen months to two years, imposing an enormous extra strain on the economy. Churchill accused the government of sending insufficient troops, too late, but the Labour Party's instincts were against committing money on armies and armaments which could be spent on health and education.

Korea quickened the formation of two camps in the Labour Party, and in October Clem was faced with a decision which could hardly fail to re ignite the conflict between them, whichever way he jumped. Cripps wrote from his Zurich clinic enclosing a gloomy doctor's report: 'Unless I now go off for a prolonged rest I shall probably do irreparable harm to my health. Under these circumstances I see no alternative but to hand you my resignation and to apply for the Chiltern Hundreds.'

Clem's real choice as Cripps's successor was between Hugh Gaitskell and Aneurin Bevan. Dalton or Morrison might have had a strong claim if they had pressed it, but they both advocated Gaitskell. Morrison was no economist: 'I listen to Stafford explaining those figures, and I just know I could not do it,' he said. Dalton's main interest now was in advancing the careers of his young protégés, and he was satisfied with his own position as Minister of Town and Country Planning, having turned down the Colonial Office and explained to Denis Healey afterwards, with the discretion for which he was famous: 'Colonial Office! A lot of syphilitic niggers! All kicks and no halfpence!'

Harold Wilson was a possibility. The youngest Cabinet Minister this century was doing well as President of the Board of Trade. Clem liked him, and preferred him to Gaitskell: he told David Hunt that he thought Gaitskell frivolous. Wilson was the only one of the rising stars who was not among the Dalton coterie – in fact, Dalton considered Wilson 'a weak and conceited minister', but Clem wrote privately that he was 'the outstanding success' among the new boys. Years later Clem liked to recall how Nikita Khrushchev told him he had been right to send Wilson to negotiate a food deal with the Soviet Union: 'It takes a Yorkshireman to beat a Russian in negotiation.'

But Wilson was still only thirty-five. Gaitskell was forty-four and, at Dalton's urging, had become Minister of State at the Exchequer after the 1950 election, handling a great deal of the Chancellor's workload as Cripps's health declined. It would have looked very strange now to appoint Wilson over his head. Gaitskell or Bevan? Either way there was likely to be trouble. The Treasury had always been anxious to make charges for some NHS services. Bevan defended like a tiger the concept of a service entirely free at the point of use. The month before the election, Morrison's Lord President's Committee agreed to make a prescription charge of one shilling. Bevan persuaded the Prime Minister that it would be foolish to do this just before an election, but the problem was only shelved.

After the election, Harold Wilson brokered a compromise. Cripps gave up seeking prescription charges, and Bevan accepted a Cabinet committee to keep a weekly watch on NHS spending. But at this committee, Gaitskell continued to press the case for charges, and the weekly meetings started to turn into regular battlegrounds.

Clem inclined towards Bevan's view on charging for NHS services. He had painful memories of people he had known in the East End, who used useless old wives' remedies for their children's ailments because they could not afford proper treatment. But putting Bevan at the Exchequer would cause trouble with Morrison. It would also be an acceptance that there would never be any charges for NHS services, and Clem liked to keep his options open. Gaitskell got the job. Bevan was furious because he knew that charges could now only be held off by constant trench warfare. He expressed himself freely to the Prime Minister, but to no effect.

In the following month, November, the focus was back on Korea, as the Chinese pushed General MacArthur's army back towards the sea. MacArthur clearly wanted to launch a full-scale war to re-establish Chiang Kai-shek as China's ruler. Truman made a statement which sounded as though he was giving MacArthur permission to use the atom bomb in Korea. The House of Commons heard this news with something like panic, and Clem announced that he would at once seek a meeting with the President in Washington. (Bevin was too ill to fly.) But would the President see him? He tried to contact him, then went into the House of Commons Dining Room and sat with some Ministers, including Harold Wilson. No-one wanted to raise the subject of the US visit, though it was on all of their minds; Clem turned to Wilson abruptly and said: 'Just been reading Philip Guedella. Tell me, which of the popular historians do you prefer? Guedella or Arthur Bryant?' 'Bryant,' replied Wilson, and they talked over supper about the Peninsular War. At 9 pm the President's agreement to the visit came through and steadied everyone's nerves.

It was a curious four days in Washington. There was a lot of superficial banter, with Major Attlee and Captain Truman singing First World War songs together after dinner at the British embassy, including a chorus of 'Tipperary'. They chided their respective military chiefs, the new CIGS, Field Marshal Sir William Slim, and US Secretary of State General Marshall, that generals knew nothing of war and should leave it to those who had been on the ground among the bullets. Clem planned all that, says Sir David Hunt, to create a mood of military camaraderie with the President. How much was achieved, we do not know. Dean Acheson, Marshall's deputy, claimed afterwards to have foiled Clem's clever ploy to manoeuvre the President into promising never to use the atom bomb without British agreement. But Truman had promised, stipulating only that the agreement could not be in the official communiqué. It was the old story.

What we know is that the bomb was not used; the Americans neither withdrew from Korea nor broadened the conflict into a global war with China; and eventually Truman screwed up his courage to fire MacArthur. Those were the three things Clem wanted. He would not have wasted time wondering how much he had contributed to the result.

The price he paid was a huge rearmament programme which would require great sacrifices from the British people, and great strains in the Labour Party. This added to the problems of running a minority government which was constantly harassed by the opposition, in daily danger of losing a vote in the House of Commons and had a new Chancellor who did not yet have his own standing in the party or the country. This was no time for Clem to lose the rock-like figure of Ernest Bevin, but he could see – though Bevin couldn't – that his Foreign Secretary was now far too ill to carry on. Bevin was the man to whom he owed most, whose loyalty had sustained him, who had resolutely turned down his own chance of becoming Prime Minister out of loyalty. But Clem's greatest political friend was no longer up to his job, and he had to go. Bevin was desperately upset, and almost insulted by his consolation prize – becoming Lord Privy Seal. 'I am neither a Lord, nor a Privy, nor a Seal,' he is said to have commented. At a Foreign Office party to celebrate his seventieth birthday he told his officials with tears in his eyes: 'I've been sacked.' He was even more upset when he found out that his replacement was to be Morrison, who was appointed because foreign affairs was thought to need a 'big name', and Morrison's was the biggest available.

He arrived at the Foreign Office just as everything started to go wrong. Two Foreign Office officials, Guy Burgess and Donald Maclean, defected to the Soviet Union in May 1950. Bevin's Middle East policy was beginning to unravel, and Morrison was in charge at the time. Clem vetoed Morrison's wish to use troops to defend British interests in Persia. Of greater importance in the long term, Morrison strengthened Bevin's line against the emerging European Economic Community, and ensured that Germany and France, not Britain, would be at the centre of the new Community.

Morrison was blamed, rather unfairly, and was criticised for not spending enough time on foreign affairs, which was also unfair because he had to deputise for a sick Prime Minister. Clem's duodenal ulcer flared up again, and he had to go into St Mary's Hospital for an operation. While he was there the pent-up tension in the Labour Party and the Cabinet – over Korea, over armaments, over health charges – exploded into open warfare, as he must have known it would. It was the worst possible time to be absent, and Clem, as usual, had an understatement instantly available. 'It is annoying to have to go to hospital,' he wrote to Tom. '. . . One's memory of early days is very vivid. I can always conjure up the sights and smells of Northaw.'

The spark which turned the smouldering embers in the party into a destructive bush fire was Gaitskell's determination to charge NHS patients half the cost of false teeth and spectacles in his first Budget. Nye Bevan was now Labour Minister, and Gaitskell had prepared the ground carefully, lining up his allies for an assault on the heart of Nye Bevan's old territory, producing in March 1951 a joint memorandum with the new Health Minister, Hillary Marquand, and the Scottish Secretary, Hector McNeil. 'In a sentence we propose to reduce the hospital estimates by £10 million and to find the balance of £20 million by what seems to us the only practical method, viz the introduction of charges.'

Teeth and spectacles were a symbol: for the principle of a totally free health service, which Gaitskell believed was not sustainable; for the principle of rearmament, which Bevan believed was wrong in principle and foolish in practice. Cripps had been reluctant to force the issue to the point at which Bevan would resign. The new Chancellor not only failed to share this reluctance; he seemed positively to want Bevan's resignation. Bevan thought of Gaitskell as a jumped-up civil servant with no standing in the Labour Party, telling John Strachey that he was 'nothing, nothing, nothing' and ignoring Strachey's warning that the Chancellor had a 'will like a dividing spear'.

On 9 April 1951, with the new government two months old and Bevan and Gaitskell firmly in their trenches, Morrison chaired a Cabinet meeting in Clem's absence, at which Gaitskell presented the Budget he was to deliver the next day. Morrison reported that the Prime Minister thought it would be 'stark folly' to split and precipitate another general election. It would put the Tories in power for ten years and people would blame Bevan. He added, how accurately we cannot know, that Clem believed they must stand by their Chancellor. The Cabinet backed Gaitskell. The one person who could save the situation was laid up in St Mary's Hospital, Paddington. Throughout the next morning, with the Chancellor due to deliver his Budget at 2.30 pm, the leading actors made separate pilgrimages to the hospital. First to arrive, at 10.30 am, were Bevan and Wilson with a draft compromise: a ceiling on NHS expenditure, a mention of the need for charges, but no actual charges. Next, at 11.30, came Gaitskell, carrying the Budget speech he intended to deliver in the afternoon, and fortified by having already rejected the Bevan/Wilson compromise three times that morning – the last time when it was put to him by the formidable Ernest Bevin. Clem spent a full hour trying to persuade Gaitskell to accept it. Gaitskell said he would either announce the charges or resign. At last Clem, by Gaitskell's account, murmured 'what I took to be "Very well, you will have to go." In a split second I realised he had said, "I am afraid they will have to go."' The die was cast.

Seconds before Gaitskell rose to deliver his Budget, Morrison had a hurried word with him, and he removed from his speech the date on which charges were to be imposed. It seems likely that Morrison was the bearer of an instruction from the Prime Minister, because Morrison himself was keen for the Chancellor to stand firm.

When Bevan and Wilson went to St Mary's again that evening, Clem urged them to do nothing until the Parliamentary Labour Party met the next day, and probably suggested that Gaitskell had left the door open to compromise by omitting the date. After that

Clem was exhausted, and refused to see Morrison. When the PLP met, Bevan made a last throw for compromise, probably inspired by his hospital visit. He would not resign, he said, but 'others' should do their bit for party unity, as he was doing. By 'others' he meant Gaitskell, and by 'doing their bit' he meant refraining from announcing a date for the introduction of charges.

Ernest Bevin died that weekend, five weeks after ceasing to be Foreign Secretary. 'My dear Nye,' wrote Clem from hospital, 'I gather that all went off well at the Party meeting and I am grateful to you for the line you took. The death of Ernie has rather over-shadowed these differences, and I hope that everyone will forget them. I think that it is particularly essential that we should present a united front to the enemy . . .' But Gaitskell pressed home his advantage: at the next Cabinet meeting he and Morrison insisted that health charges be introduced straight away. Gaitskell gave the impression of being determined that Bevan should either be humiliated or forced out of the Cabinet. Bevan said that if a date was set, he would resign. That night a delegation went to St Mary's: Morrison, Gaitskell, Chuter Ede and the chief whip, William Whiteley. They persuaded Clem to send Bevan an ultimatum; Clem's letter to Bevan ended: 'I shall be glad to know today that you are prepared to carry out loyally the decisions of the Government.'

Bevan, Wilson and John Freeman resigned from the Cabinet, stating that their reasons were not only 'teeth and spectacles' but also the rearmament programme, and they led a rejuvenated left on the back benches. With a parliamentary majority of just five, and a general election likely at any moment, Labour looked – and was – split beyond hope of repair. It was Labour's defining moment, the moment when the battle between left and right assumed its post-war form. It is a tribute to its leader that it had taken six years to arrive. He and Harold Wilson were always sure that they could have prevented it from arriving then if Clem had been well. But he was ill, and Cripps and Ernest Bevin were dying. The tactic of deferring the date of the charges was almost certainly Clem's, and he could have prevented Gaitskell from torpedoing it. As for rearmament, Clem knew that they could not spend the arms budget anyway – the raw materials were not there.

The wounds of 1951 are still raw today. Michael Foot cannot forgive Clem for not giving Bevan support against Gaitskell. Denis Healey cannot forgive him for not giving Gaitskell full support against Bevan. Clem had been furious with Morrison, and desperately sad to lose what he considered were three of the best members of his Cabinet. Hugh Gaitskell was an accomplished technician whose skills he valued, not a man who was close to the soul of the party as he and Nye Bevan understood it. Not a poet, as he and Bevan were; not a man whose adult life had been dominated by a rage against poverty and injustice, as his and Nye Bevan's had been.

'Nye should have been given more time, Morrison and Gaitskell should not have dug in,' Clem told Kenneth Harris. He advised Labour MPs: 'Keep this here, at Westminster. Do not take it into the constituencies.' But it was not practical advice. Everywhere they went, Labour activists only wanted to know about one subject: the great split.

'The Bevan business was a nuisance,' Clem wrote to Tom, with his marvellous capacity for alighting upon the inadequate word. '. . . With this and Ernie's death I did not have as restful a time as I should have had.' His letters to Tom now begin to display his physical ailments and his sixty-eight years. The writing is even more cramped and careless and most letters mention the death of one or two old friends. His reading, for a man whose joy was literature, and whose boyhood dream was to become a poet, is also becoming arthritic, and it is sad to find him writing to Tom: 'I got through a lot of reading in hospital, but I don't find some of the moderns, whom they laud to the skies, very much good.'

Altogether, the eighteen months after the 1950 election were not a happy time for the Labour government. Yet Clem, once out of hospital, seemed full of bounce and vigour. He kept up his private letters: the letters to Tom, the lifelong correspondence with his old batman Charlie Griffiths, 'Griff'. Most of the correspondence with Griff has not survived but Sir David Hunt saw some of it at the time: 'It was a correspondence between equals, no deference on the one side nor patronage on the other – which was quite difficult to pull off in the circumstances.' One day in June 1951, when nothing seemed to be going right, Clem found a poem in his basket of work, sent in by fifteen-year-old Ann Glossop, of Penrhos College, Colwyn Bay. One of the private secretaries must have thought it might amuse the Prime Minister, and put it in his box instead of sending the usual acknowledgement – 'The Prime Minister wishes me to say . . .' – or passing it to the Education Minister.

Would you please explain, dear Clement
Just why it has to be
That Certificates of Education
Are barred to such as me? . . .

I've worked through thirteen papers
But my swot is all in vain
Because at this time next year
I must do them all again . . .

Please have pity, Clement,
And tell the others too.
Remove the silly age-limit
It wasn't there for you.

Clem composed his reply. It was sent to Ann Glossop with 'SECRET' typed on top of it, and has lain in Clem's daughter-in-law's filing-cabinet ever since:

I received with real pleasure
Your verses my dear Ann
Although I've not much leisure
I'll reply as best I can.

I've not the least idea why
They have this curious rule
Condemning you to sit and sigh
Another year at school.

You'll understand that my excuse
For lack of detailed knowledge
Is that school certs were not in use
When I attended college.

George Tomlinson is ill, but I
Have asked him to explain
And when I get the reason why
I'll write to you again.

Clem would have imagined the thrill it must have given Ann Glossop to receive a piece of doggerel from the Prime Minister. He enjoyed young people. He loved hosting a children's Christmas party at Chequers each year, and in the winter of 1950–51 he spent a happy evening as guest of honour at the London School of Economics Labour Club dinner, at which two students performed a cabaret satirising the right-wing nature of Clem's Cabinet. Bernard Crick remembers him almost splitting his sides with laughter at the lines: 'We'll make Herbert Morrison scrub the steps of Transport House, When the Red revolution comes . . .'

'I can't thank you enough,' he told them as he left. 'Best evening I've had for ages. People normally treat the PM with such caution and such respect that it is very, very boring for Clement Attlee. Not so here.'

There were occasional diversions. One day he sent for his new Minister of Works, George Brown. Brown, a young man in his first ministerial job, had ensured that he was fully briefed, on every conceivable topic the Prime Minister might ask about, and took himself off to the Cabinet Room. There Clem asked him: 'About that statue of Smuts, Minister. Who's going to do it? I do hope not that fellow X – all holes and triangles.' Brown's bulging briefcase was never opened. Looking at the statue in later years, he thought X might have made a better job of it.

But for Clem, there was a pressing dilemma. When should he call an election? He did not want to soldier on with a majority of five until the Conservatives finally managed to pull sufficient of a surprise to defeat him. But 1951 was not a good year for Labour, and Morrison wanted to hold on in the hope that something would turn up: better economic news, the hoped-for improvement in meat supplies, signs of peace in Korea, peace in the party.

In 1952 the King was due to make a six-month tour of Australia and New Zealand. The Australians had wanted the King in 1951, but this would have clashed with the Festival of Britain, which relied on his presence to maximise its potential as a dollar earner. 'My view is that [the tour] should wait until 1952,' Clem had minuted late in 1949, and it did. Postponing the tour yet again would seem insulting. But both Clem and the King were horrified by the idea of a political crisis occurring in the King's absence. So Clem decided that the election had to be in 1951.

Today it would be inconceivable for a Prime Minister to time an election round a royal tour; but the episode also tells us something about Clem himself. Others did not like the decision, even then. Morrison was shocked, and the General Secretary of the Labour Party, Morgan Phillips, asked Clem for a postponement of the election because the party's national agent had just died. Afterwards Phillips walked gloomily across to Alice Bacon at the funeral and said in a passable imitation of Clem's voice: 'Carry on, Morgan, carry on.'

A few days after Clem gave the Cabinet the election date, the King informed him he had to have a major operation, and might have to cancel the tour after all. Consideration for the King still seems to have been uppermost in Clem's mind. He minuted the following: 'Postponement of election would, I am sure, be contrary to King's wishes. It would appear to contemplate the worst. It is contrary to constitutional practice to allow illness of King to interfere with working of the constitution.' So he announced an October election, for the first time using the radio for the purpose. 'The Prime Minister's capacity for making everything sound sensible and unimportant was seldom heard to better advantage,' commented the *New Statesman*.

During the election he said something which showed how different Clem's world was from the one we inhabit in the 1990s. 'I am convinced that the more we can put our appeal to the people on the basis of what people can give rather than what they could get, the more successful we shall be,' he told an audience in Slaithwaite, adding, incredible though it seems: 'I do not like appealing to cupidity and stupidity.'

The Labour Party conference, which Clem had hoped would provide a boost at the start of the campaign, merely proved how strong the Bevanites were in the party. Bevan came top in elections to the National Executive, with Bevanites also coming second (Barbara Castle), third (Tom Driberg) and sixth (Ian Mikardo), and all improving their votes. Leadership figures – Morrison, Dalton, Griffiths – were elected with reduced votes.

A few days later Clem arrived in Tom Driberg's Chelmsford constituency to address an afternoon meeting. Driberg had taken the precaution of asking Vi if there was any food her husband particularly liked for lunch, and after a few moments' thought she answered: 'Rice with treacle.' This was part of the homely quality about Vi which Clem found comforting, and which helped him to project a reassuring image. Everyone knew that she drove her husband everywhere. They also knew (thanks to the *Daily Mirror*) that she sucked mints as she drove, ironed her husband's trousers each morning with a portable iron, and listened carefully to every one of his dry, sensible, reassuring speeches.

Another constituency he visited was Eastbourne, not because Labour stood the slightest chance of winning there but because Tom's son, Chris Attlee, was the candidate. 'We had some 3,500 in the audience with a large proportion of Tories,' he wrote to

Tom. 'Chris made his points clearly and economically. Vi drove me down from Manchester via Chequers doing just under 400 miles for the day without being fatigued. We have had a remarkable tour, immense crowds and great enthusiasm, but what it will all mean in votes I can't tell. Vi always gets a great ovation and received floral tributes everywhere.'

The result of the election was the most unfair in recent political history, and offers a serious indictment of our electoral system. Labour received more votes than the Conservatives, but fewer seats; it therefore lost the election. Labour once again increased its vote, receiving 48.8 per cent of the popular vote against 48 per cent for the Conservatives. But once again, thousands of working-class votes piled up in already strong traditional Labour seats. The Conservatives had 321 seats, Labour 295, the Liberals six and Irish parties three. The Conservatives had an overall majority of seventeen and a majority over Labour of twenty-six. Clem went on the radio. 'Our defeat is not due to any falling away of Labour support, but to the fact that in most constituencies Liberals voted Tory not Labour.' Through the quiet, calm delivery you can just hear the disappointment in his voice.

For the first time in eleven years, Clem had no responsibility for conducting the nation's affairs. He seems to have felt something like relief. He and his top Ministers were exhausted. Vi was disappointed for her husband, but for herself, she was looking forward to living in Cherry Cottage, into which she now tried to cram Clem's 2,000 books. She said a fond farewell to David Hunt, mentioning that their relationship had been stormy. He made deprecating noises, but she said: 'I know what I'm like. I don't know what would have become of me if I hadn't been married to the best man in the world.' She wrote privately some of those naively honest sentences: 'Though the last thing I had wanted was to be the wife of the Prime Minister, yet I wouldn't have missed those six years. Never before had I been a person of any importance and I suppose I enjoyed being made a fuss of! . . . Many outstanding events took place while my husband was Prime Minister. I met many interesting people. I have dined with seven Prime Ministers.'

Clem's sister Mary, the missionary who was eight years his senior, wrote: 'These 6½ years have been to all your brothers and sisters a time of unsullied pride and gladness in you.' His sister Margaret, five years older than Clem, wrote to their brother Tom: 'Looking back to our old CSU [Christian Social Union] days – did we ever dare to hope that we should get right into the Promised Land in our lifetime? That it should have been done with Clem as Prime Minister makes me give thanks every time I think of it.' The night after the election there was a happy family dinner-party in the Downing Street flat. Perhaps the only member there who was full of unalloyed disappointment was the youngest daughter, Alison. She was about to be married and had hoped for a reception at Chequers, like Janet's. But then, she could hardly complain at the result. Her fiancé was a Conservative and neither of them voted. 'We've agreed to pair,' she told her father.

10

An Earl and a Knight of the Garter

In 1951 Clem was sixty-eight. His unremitting workload since 1939 would have killed many people. Sixteen-hour working days had been the norm for twelve years.

There were more deaths to sadden him. In February 1952, the King and Stafford Cripps both died. Apart from his respect for the monarchy, Clem and George VI had grown fond of each other. Michael Foot writes that the King's death was the only event which he ever knew to affect Clem emotionally, in public. He could speak calmly even of the death of Ernie Bevin 'but when he spoke of George VI's death, tears were in his eyes and voice.'

'I was much attached to the king and knew him very well, seeing him week after week,' Clem wrote to Tom. 'I had very nice messages from Queen Mary on my article in the *Observer* which she said was just what a mother would like to have written about her son.' When he heard the news, he had just begun to write to a new friend who was to play a growing role in his life, and provide a great deal of happiness in his old age. The second sentence of his letter, written ten days after the first, reads: 'I began this letter but then supervened the death of the king and I have been so busy with writing and preparing speeches that I neglected to carry on.' The letter was to a young American journalist called Patricia Beck, who had been part of the *Time-Life* team covering the 1951 election. She was assigned to follow Clem's campaign. Her job, she says was 'to nursemaid the photographer and make sure we knew everyone in the pictures'. Clem always enjoyed her company, and a few years later she was calling him 'Uncle Clem'.

He was awarded the Order of Merit in 1951, and the *Walthamstow Guardian* arranged a celebration party, inviting many members of the Cabinet and other distinguished people. The party was arranged for a Thursday night and the *Walthamstow Guardian*, like most local papers, went to press on Wednesday and appeared on Friday. So the report of the event was already printed, including Clem's speech which he had provided in advance. Clem and Vi set off in the car from Great Missenden at 4.30 pm, and a great smog came down; by the time they telephoned from a Buckinghamshire pub to say they could not get there, the party was almost over. Clem and Vi did not arrive home until six in the morning. The paper gave a detailed description of the reception he was given when he arrived, and report of his speech, and had to run an apology the next week.

Clem was Labour's best electoral asset, but he began to be a little detached. 'I want you to go to this new thing called the Council of Europe,' he told Alf Robens, George Brown and Geoffrey de Freitas. 'I don't know much about it, but in *your* time you'll *have* to.' He seems to have assumed that the split in the party over teeth and spectacles would all blow over, if only people didn't talk about it too much. There was no chance of that. When the party line on defence – to accept the government's proposed levels of expenditure – was announced, fifty-seven Labour MPs refused to vote for it. The rebels' fury was increased by the government's announcement that they were not going to be able to spend all the money Gaitskell had earmarked for defence. If anyone was in any doubt that Gaitskell had deliberately picked a fight with the Bevanites in order to impress trade union leaders whose votes could help him up the slippery pole, here was evidence. They could not, of course, see Gaitskell's diary, to which he confided that he could hardly have strong loyalties with the trade union leaders 'and continually refuse to do any of the dirty work for them and with them'. These union leaders, led by Ernest Bevin's grim successor at the TGWU, Arthur Deakin, demanded that the fifty-seven rebels should recant or be expelled.

Clem believed they would refuse to recant, and that he faced the prospect of expelling a fifth of his MPs, including some of the brightest and best of them. Deakin might view that with equanimity, perhaps even enthusiasm, but Clem did not. Throughout the summer the battle raged among Labour MPs, setting the scene for a bitter Labour Party conference.

In Morecambe in September 1952, the weather was vile, with rain and high winds, but not as vile as the tempers of the delegates. One of the earliest speakers, miners' leader Will Lawther, set the tone for the conference by shouting at a heckler, 'Shut yer gob.' The big test of party opinion was the election of members to the constituency section of the NEC. It had been Clem who, in the Thirties, had persuaded the reluctant union leaders, in particular Ernest Bevin, to allow the constituencies to elect their own NEC representatives, instead of having them chosen in essence by the block votes of the big unions. Now Arthur Deakin could only watch in helpless rage as the constituencies elected Bevan in first place, Barbara Castle second, Tom Driberg third, Harold Wilson fifth, Ian Mikardo sixth and Dick Crossman seventh. The only successful candidate who was not on the Bevanite ticket was Jim Griffiths, who came fourth. Morrison and Dalton lost the NEC seats they had held for a quarter of a century, and Gaitskell's attempt to win a seat failed.

Clem was shocked. Nye Bevan was a nuisance, but a nuisance Clem understood, a man who was in politics for the same reason as Clem himself. The clever young men around him were another thing entirely. Clem had no time for Crossman or Driberg, considering them untruthful dilettantes. Worse, Driberg was in hock to the unspeakable Beaverbrook; and Clem must have known, because everyone did, about Driberg's sensational private life. Privately Clem thought, as Deakin did, that the NEC result was partly due to successful Communist infiltration. Publicly, he infuriated Deakin by accepting, without a word of reproach, the verdict of the constituencies. Not so Hugh Gaitskell, who endeared himself to the powerful union leaders by claiming publicly that 'the Communist Party has now adopted a new tactic of infiltration into the Labour Party' and that many of the party delegates were 'Communist or Communist-influenced' (the source for this was apparently a journalist on the News Chronicle); he talked of 'mob rule by a group of frustrated journalists'. Driberg, Crossman and Foot were journalists by trade, and their articles, especially in Foot's Tribune, were equally unrestrained in their attacks on Gaitskell and his supporters.

Gaitskell was mistaken about the Communists. In the late 1930s the Communist Party had been good at infiltrating the Labour Party, and the result was that in 1945, in addition to two elected Communist MPs, half a dozen Labour MPs were secretly Communists. Some of them were expelled from the Labour Party during the life of the 1945 government. But by 1952 the Communist Party had neither the people, nor the subtlety, nor even the desire to infiltrate the Labour Party. It did not matter. The battle for the soul of the Labour Party was out in the open, and any weapon was fair game. It was being fought, writes Brian Brivati in his biography of Gaitskell, not just between two sets of policies, but between two different sorts of people: 'The Bevanites were a drunken night in Soho, at the Gay Hussar . . . the Gaitskellites . . . were a night dancing at the Café Royal . . .' The Labour Party was feeding greedily off its own flesh, and its leader, who in Brivati's analogy was a small sherry before dinner and a train home to Great Missenden after it, struggled desperately to bring the meal to an end.

When Labour MPs returned to the House, Clem personally moved a resolution which banned unofficial groups within the party. 'What is quite intolerable', he told the PLP, 'is the existence of a party within a party with a separate leadership, separate meetings, supported by its own press . . . Drop it. Stop this sectionalism. Work with the team. Turn your guns on the enemy not on your friends.' He convinced Bevan that the group must be disbanded, and, feeling optimistic, left for a tour of India.

There he celebrated his seventieth birthday in January 1953. 'About half a million locusts arrived to assist in the celebration,' he wrote to Patricia Beck. 'The trouble in the Party has broken out again just as I thought that I had got things running smoothly. An article in the *Tribune* upset the applecart.'

He still hoped that the 'least said soonest mended' approach would work, and at Labour's 1953 conference in September, it looked as though it just might. He had quietly encouraged a move to the left in the policy document proposed by the National Executive Committee, which included further nationalisation measures and the removal of all charges on the NHS. It was passed with little criticism. A trade union-sponsored motion giving the deputy leader an automatic seat on the NEC brought Morrison back without a fight.

Back in London, Clem had time to think of pleasanter things. 'It was only by chance that I learned you were back in England and was given your address,' he wrote to Patricia Beck in November. 'I should so much like to see you and hear your [news?]. I have been wanting to thank you for that fine picture of [?] that you sent us from the USA, but I did not know where to write. Vi and the family join in thanking you. Could you come and lunch or dine at the House some time?' (A calligraphy expert with a microscope might be able to decipher the subject of the picture.) Vi was probably happier than she had been for years, in Cherry Cottage in Buckinghamshire. 'We are very happy in our country home, being blessed with a homely house – all that could be desired in the way of neighbours – and lovely country,' she wrote. Their builders were a little dilatory but, Clem wrote to Tom, 'Vi put the fear of God into them' and they got on with it. Sir David Hunt would have sympathised with the builders. Clem managed some reading, including a biography of his father's hero Gladstone. 'He was a dreadful person,' Clem wrote to Tom. 'His guidance by the almighty was worse than Cromwell. He seems to have had as little idea of managing a Cabinet as he did of dealing with Queen Victoria.'

He wrote his autobiography. This was a mistake. He should have waited until he retired and felt freer to say whatever he liked. *As It Happened* is one of the least interesting political autobiographies ever written. Clem was still leader and had the lifelong habit of watching every word and never making an unnecessary enemy. The only interesting passages therefore were all expunged before the book was published, and languish to this day in an archive at Churchill College, Cambridge.

He found time to be President of the Old Haileyburians in 1953–4. 'It was the quickest AGM we've ever had,' says Bill Tyrwhitt-Drake. 'If you didn't speak before the question was put, that was it.' The AGM normally lasts half a day. Clem's lasted less than forty-five minutes.

Clem's elder statesman image was enhanced, and the division in his party narrowed, by an impressive parliamentary speech calling for a summit meeting to stop hydrogen-bomb testing. But the split was never far beneath the surface, and it opened up again a week after the speech, when Foreign Secretary Anthony Eden announced that Britain and the USA would discuss collective defence of South East Asia and the Western Pacific. To Bevan this looked like an effort to encircle China which would prejudice talks aimed at ending the war in Vietnam, where the French had been forced to the negotiating table after their defeat at Dien Bien Phu. But the Labour leadership supported the government. Bevan, despite being a member of Labour's Shadow Cabinet, in effect disowned his own leader in questions to Anthony Eden in the House of Commons. Clem was heard to mutter: 'Just when we were beginning to win the match our inside left has scored against his own side.' Bevan resigned from the Shadow Cabinet, but this decision split the Bevanites. Harold Wilson had come thirteenth in the Shadow Cabinet elections and was faced with the choice of whether he should fill Bevan's vacated place. He decided, quite quickly and rather pointedly, to take it. Refusal would have made him Bevan's permanent poodle.

The next battleground was German rearmament. Churchill and Eisenhower were in favour, because they wanted a rearmed

Germany to act as a buffer against the Soviet Union in the East. Labour's growingly aggressive right wing, led now by Morrison and Gaitskell, agreed with Churchill and Eisenhower. The Bevanites did not.

The future of Germany was one of the few subjects on which Clem was never quite rational. He believed Germans were an arrogant, imperialistic people, and not to be trusted with weapons. He took a watchful stance while he waited to see which way events were going to fall. He decided to 'live to fight another day', falling in with the views of the NEC and the Shadow Cabinet. At the 1954 conference in Scarborough, he and Morrison narrowly carried the conference on German rearmament; then the left and right lined up for a big set-piece battle over the post of Labour Party Treasurer.

Arthur Greenwood had been the Treasurer since 1943. The post has always carried considerable weight in party policy-making, and its holder could expect his chances of the leadership to be significantly enhanced. The Treasurer was elected by the whole Labour conference and anyone who could get the block votes of most of the six big trade unions could be sure of being elected; Arthur Deakin could normally speak for all six. Hugh Gaitskell had proved to Deakin and his fellow union leaders that he would stand up to the left. Deakin liked men who stood up to the left. Years later Frank Chapple, another powerful right-wing union leader, said of Neil Kinnock: 'He's got balls.' That was what Deakin thought of Gaitskell. Greenwood died in June 1954. Deakin and Gaitskell met for lunch and agreed that Gaitskell should run. Bevan stood against him, and everyone knew that the post was a great deal more significant than the controller of the party's pursestrings over the next twelve months. Deakin lined up the unions for Gaitskell, and he won handsomely.

The next day Bevan told the annual *Tribune* rally that the Labour Party should not be intimidated by powerful trade union leaders. Clem had asked the conference not to be 'swayed by emotionalism' on German rearmament, and Bevan said: 'I know I shall be accused of emotionalism. I know now that the right kind of leader is a desiccated calculating machine who must not allow himself in any way to be swayed by indignation.' Myths gather as memories dim: the desiccated calculating machine was not Hugh Gaitskell, but Clem Attlee. 'We'll have him [Bevan] out in six months,' commented Deakin.

Back in the Commons, the split could not be kept off the floor of the House. Bevan, after attacking his own leader in the chamber, led sixty-two Labour MPs in a refusal to support Labour's position that it was 'necessary as a deterrent to aggression to rely on the threat of using thermo-nuclear weapons.' Deakin and Morrison demanded Bevan's expulsion. Once again Clem demurred. When the Shadow Cabinet met he acted most unusually: he stated his view right at the start. Before anyone else had spoken, he said: 'I'm against expulsion.' He reluctantly accepted the majority view, pressed by Morrison and Gaitskell, that, at the very least, the Parliamentary Labour Party should be asked to withdraw the whip. Clem hated the resultant PLP meeting: 'There was far too much personal scrapping, malice and uncharitableness,' he wrote to his old friend Jack Lawson. Which side was responsible, he did not say; he probably thought both, but he was more angry with Gaitskell than with Bevan. He answered a letter of support from Oliver Baldwin, Stanley Baldwin's socialist son: 'It was a pretty miserable morning but these things do occur from time to time.' Gaitskell, Hugh Dalton and Alf Robens had been worried that he might not take a sufficiently hard line. 'It turns primarily on the little man tomorrow,' Dalton noted in his diary. 'If he's firm, he'll win.' They tactfully handed him some speech notes prepared by Gaitskell. Clem followed the notes faithfully in his speech to the PLP, put them down, looked up, and said: 'Remember the Liberals.' It was the only moment when he expressed publicly the terror that was eating at him from inside.

Bevan lashed out generally. If he was disloyal to Clem, what about George Brown, who in 1947 had tried to get signatures demanding Clem's resignation? If he was making personal attacks, what about Gaitskell? The PLP withdrew the whip, but only the National Executive could expel Bevan from the Labour Party. It looked as though expulsion was certain unless the party leader was determined to prevent it – and even then he might not succeed. But would he try? Dozens of people wrote to him and they all had a courteous reply, never more than two sentences long. John Strachey wrote that he was against expulsion, but Nye was in the wrong; what did Clem think? 'A lot of vague rumours are going about but I don't take a great deal of notice of them,' Clem replied.

Gaitskell and Alf Robens went to see him to try to stiffen him against Bevan, and found their heads being bitten off. 'You made me the spearhead of a policy in which I did not believe,' he barked at them. Three of the most powerful union leaders, Deakin, Tom Williamson and Ernest Jones, went to see Clem to threaten that unless Bevan was expelled, Labour might find itself very hard up at the coming election, which was expected any week. This was serious. Without their money it would not be possible to fight an effective election campaign.

At the NEC, Clem said nothing and doodled on his pad until it became obvious that, left to themselves, the NEC would expel Bevan. Then he made his move. Bevan, he said, should be asked to prepare a statement for the NEC and submit to questioning by a sub-committee. This was carried, by the tight margin of fourteen votes to thirteen. Then, privately, he saw Bevan and they agreed a statement which Clem thought he could sell to the NEC. Bevan was cross-examined, and the statement was accepted by the NEC after another angry debate.

Both sides have carried into their retirement their annoyance at Clem's handling of this episode. For the Gaitskellites, Roy Jenkins says today: 'Where was he in the Gaitskell/Bevan tribal warfare? There was always some ambiguity in that. It was irritating at the time and went with him being a very reserved man and not pronouncing on issues he did not have to pronounce on.' On the Bevanite side, Michael Foot and Barbara Castle find it hard to forgive him for waiting until the last moment. 'He came down on the right side in the end, to his credit, but why did he wait so long?' says Barbara Castle. Clem never bothered in his lifetime to defend or explain the way he had handled the business, but he achieved what he wanted to achieve; he might not have succeeded if he had shown his hand earlier.

On 15 April 1955, Anthony Eden, who had replaced Churchill as Conservative leader, announced an election. The whip was restored to Bevan a week later. Twenty years earlier, in 1935, Clem had led into a general election a party which had been bitterly divided on defence. Now he had to do it again. In 1935 the leader of the TGWU, Ernest Bevin, had brutally removed the leading pacifist, George Lansbury, from the party leadership. In 1955 Bevin's successor Arthur Deakin tried to have the leading disarmer thrown out of the party. In 1955 as in 1935 Clem, whose own convictions on the issues were as strong and as immovable as anyone's, had brought to the situation the skills of a quiet but expert conciliator and had managed to avoid the worst fracture. But in 1955 as in 1935, he was leading a party that did not look like a winner.

The anti-union feeling engendered by recent strikes and vigorously stirred by the newspapers did not help, either. Arthur Deakin had made the unions look like Labour's power-brokers in recent weeks, and had tried to blackmail Clem, but Clem would never have dreamed of trying to distance himself from them. Irritating they might be, blockheaded their leaders sometimes were, but they represented organised labour and had founded the Labour Party. A Labour leader could not, in his view, embrace the unions when they were popular and wealthy and doing what he wanted, and distance himself from them when they were unpopular, poor and being awkward. He could not have known that after 1992, Tony Blair would do precisely that. Without the unions, his party was rootless.

For the last time, Vi drove her husband the length and breadth of the land and listened to him exhort, warn against last-minute stunts, ridicule the idea that Conservatism meant freedom and socialism meant slavery, nail the lies as they appeared – for example, that Labour would bring back rationing. But none of it was effective enough. Clem Attlee was popular and respected, but his party looked a mess. The result was: Conservatives 345, Labour 277, Liberals 6.

For Morrison, Gaitskell and Deakin, this result could be explained in two words: Aneurin Bevan. Clem did not think it was that simple. For him, the key factors were that the Conservatives had much more money and the support of the press.

It was time to retire. Clem wanted to be out of harness as soon as the election was over, but the Shadow Cabinet and Labour MPs urged him to stay. Bevan was the most fervent in his plea for Clem to stay – not just until an agreed date, but indefinitely. Bevan knew that if Clem went now, his successor would probably be Morrison. Clem held on because he wanted to hand the Labour Party on in good order. He did not want to leave it split, nor to leave it under the leadership of Morrison, whose instinct was to use the machine to bludgeon the left into line. Morrison had been in the forefront of the battle to keep Communists out of the Labour Party, becoming known as Labour's witchfinder-general. He had been intolerant of the rebel Poplar councillors in the early Twenties, of the ILP rebels in the late Twenties, of the Socialist League in the Thirties, and now he was squaring up to the Bevanites.

Clem, whose views on most issues were noticeably to the left of Morrison's, thought that losing the left would mean ditching the radical dynamism which alone made the party worth supporting. He wanted to heal the split and select a successor. It is unlikely that he was motivated by a desire to frustrate Morrison, but he was human enough to regard that as an incidental advantage. He did not, after all, owe Morrison much personal loyalty; and some of his laconic remarks about Morrison when he did eventually retire sound uncomfortably like discreet gloating.

Clem and Morrison had come through a lot together. They met as East London local politicians after the First World War, and they knew each other pretty well, not much liking what they knew. But Clem was tired. He left Morrison to do most of the speaking in that session. Morrison tried hard to sound like the next party leader, but he was sixty-seven and the prize was slipping, slowly but irretrievably, from his grasp. It seems likely that by the time Clem left for his holiday, leaving an unfinished parliamentary session and two major debates for Morrison to handle, he had decided on his preferred successor.

Writing to Patricia Beck from the farm where he spent the holiday, he sounded more relaxed than he had been for years, with time to reminisce and enjoy the wonderful Pembrokeshire coastline. '... It hardly seems ten years ago since the events of 1945 and that memorable campaign. Our campaign this year went very well but I felt that the tide was against us. I have nearly completed 20 years leadership of the Party – quite long enough as I told them after the election, but at present they won't let me go.' Patricia, an American living permanently in London, wished to become a British citizen, and there was some delay in the naturalisation process. He offered to help by having a word with a Minister – a real sign of esteem, for he almost never used influence for anyone outside his own family circle.

They were staying on a farm five miles from St David's. 'It's a fine coastline with a lot of jolly bays mostly fairly unfrequented,' he wrote to Tom. They had a new German maid, 'a very nice girl who has done something to mitigate my prejudice against that people.'

After his holiday he had a slight stroke and then an attack of eczema. The major trade union leaders wanted him to go quickly to make way for Morrison. Morrison tried to get up a round-robin petition among MPs for Clem to stand down in his favour, but he could get little support. The left still wanted Clem to stay, on the Belloc principle: 'Always keep ahold of nurse, For fear of finding something worse.' But what did Clem want? Clem, typically, never said, and left nothing to indicate his wishes, but it seems now fairly clear that he wanted to go as soon as possible. He did not want to be succeeded by Morrison. He had reluctantly given up the idea that he could be succeeded by Bevan. He wanted the leadership to skip a generation, and had by now decided, with some reservations, that this had to mean Gaitskell: but a Gaitskell who could demonstrate that he had not only technical competence and an iron will, but some sort of commitment to the ends for which the Labour Party was created, and a Gaitskell who would unite the party, not split it further. Clem went to Labour's conference in Margate in September looking for these qualities.

His nephew, who had been a Labour parliamentary candidate, was a delegate and sat opposite the platform. 'I frequently caught expressions on his face reminiscent of you,' Clem wrote to Tom. What Clem was looking for appeared during a rather dry speech of Gaitskell's on nationalisation, full of facts and figures. Gaitskell unexpectedly looked up from his prepared speech and said:

> I became a socialist quite candidly not so much because I was a passionate advocate of public ownership but because at a very early age I came to hate and loathe social injustice, because I disliked the class structure of our society, because I could not tolerate the indefensible differences for status and income which disfigure our society, because I hated poverty and squalor . . .

Two months later in Parliament Clem watched the two young economists, Hugh Gaitskell and Harold Wilson, increasingly working together to present a credible economic strategy. In late November he told Herbert Bowden, his chief whip, that he was resigning, and they agreed a date for the announcement. 'Shall I tell the contenders?' asked Bowden. 'Tell Gaitskell,' replied Clem. Morrison, who lost all sense of dignity when he thought the leadership might be within his grasp, scuttled round trying to persuade Gaitskell and Bevan to withdraw in his favour. He was humiliated by the leadership election result: Gaitskell 157 votes, Bevan 70 and Morrison 40.

Clem believed Labour should be led from left of centre not right of centre, and in a perfect world he would have liked Bevan to succeed him. He was angry with Bevan for making that impossible, and angry with Gaitskell for coldly provoking Nye, but he recognised that Gaitskell's coolness under fire was necessary to a leader. Coolness under fire had sustained him in the job for twenty years. He was able to pass on to Gaitskell a relatively united party, and while the Bevanite group broke up, Gaitskell and Bevan worked together.

Clem went to Gaitskell's New Year party in Hampstead after the election and, calling for silence, raised his glass in a toast to the new Labour leader: Gaitskell rushed in from the next room, where he had been serving drinks, saying, 'Oh, Clem, thank you, I never expected this.' 'And you'd no right to,' Clem muttered under his breath, just loud enough to be heard by Edna Healey, Denis Healey's wife, who was standing beside him.

Clem gratefully handed over his burdens to a much younger man and went back to Cherry Cottage. For the next nine years, until 1964, he was as happy an elderly retired gentleman as Buckinghamshire could boast. Few politicians retire without regrets, but Clem did. This was in part because he did not let regrets bother him; but also because he did not have the causes for regret that most politicians have. He was, and still is, far and away the most successful leader Labour has had. He led the party for longer than anyone else and he is the only Labour Party leader so far to retire with a reputation intact, or before dying in office. And he had the rare satisfaction of knowing that he had gone a long way towards achieving the aims he adopted as a young man. He had done this largely by keeping his tongue silent. This was what gave him his reputation for having no conversation. He had conversation, but profligate speech was dangerous as leader of the Labour Party. In retirement he let his tongue loose. We hear less of cricket and Haileybury than at any time for twenty years. They had served their purpose as conversational gambits to cling to when it was unwise to talk about topics that really interested him. 'I have arrived', he said happily in 1959, 'at the years of irresponsibility. It doesn't matter a hoot what I say.'

He suddenly became, as Michael Foot put it to me, rather garrulous. Foot feels there was something self-satisfied and unkind about his new-found talkativeness. It led him to sharp repudiations of old opponents like Harold Laski, one of Foot's heroes. In a television interview in 1959 Clem said: 'Rather saw himself too big, did Harold. Funny for a student of political science. He couldn't quite work the thing out.' More noticeable, though it distressed Foot less, was the attitude towards Herbert Morrison. 'Poor little man – didn't know he was eaten away with ambition' was one of the most unkind comments.

'My dear Driberg,' Clem wrote in 1956, 'Thank you for sending me your book on the Beaver. I have delayed replying until I had read it. This I did with much interest. I note that in *The Times* the advertisement is next to one headed "A Bad Man". The heading might have been extended across the page.' When Beaverbrook died Clem refused to write an obituary on the grounds that he could think of nothing good to say about him. Clem's dislike, not often incurred, was not lightly withdrawn.

Arthur Skeffington, an MP who wanted an honour and asked Clem for a letter to support his claim, suffered one of Clem's put-downs. 'Dear Skeff, I hope you get the honour you deserve, Yours Attlee.' Skeffington showed the letter around, but received no honour. 'Just signing Attlee, not Clem, was a giveaway for his friends,' says Lord Longford.

His one worry was that he would leave Vi without enough money to be comfortable. She was thirteen years younger than him, and they wanted a bungalow built near Cherry Cottage for her old age without him. He had £2,000 a year pension, three guineas a day attendance allowance for the House of Lords, and little else. Henry Attlee's money had been spent long since. So he took every decently-paid piece of work he was offered. He broadcast as often as he was asked, wrote endless book reviews and fragments of autobiography, and did the American lecture-tour circuit, on subjects such as 'The Future of Europe', 'World Government or World Chaos' and 'The Future of Democratic Government'. He started to act like a freelance journalist, becoming irritable with people who did not mention how much they would pay, cheerful when he was paid surprisingly well for not very much work and clear about comparative rates. The BBC paid '75 guineas for a pleasant chat with Francis Williams', but with newspapers, he noted to Tom, 'payment is in inverse ratio to the character of the paper'. *Time Life* paid handsomely: £710, i.e. about £200 an hour. When Churchill was ill in 1958, everyone rushed to Clem for obituaries which, when Churchill recovered, were 'kept in cold storage, but paid for' as he told Tom.

'He rather flogged himself and I don't think he much enjoyed those American tours,' Roy Jenkins told me. I am not sure he is right. Clem's letters from the USA suggest that he is having a whale of a time, meeting new people and marvelling at American young people as only an elderly Englishman can do.

In a note, apparently to himself, he puts his money-matters into context: 'When I became Prime Minister my money worries were at an end, for now I had the prospect of a pension at the end of my time, but it made no provision for a widow and one could not save very much with the family growing up ... Nowadays I don't have to worry about every pound while the allowance to members of the House of Lords enables me to lunch well and to hire taxis instead of travelling by the underground. I shall not leave much at death, but I hope that Vi will live reasonably comfortably.'

When his thirty-year-old Corona typewriter 'conked out' he wrote to the company and asked if it could be repaired. 'They came down handsome with a new one,' he wrote triumphantly to Tom, 'but as you can see I am not expert in its use yet.' In fact his typing, always erratic, was slightly better with the new machine, and his letters became more frequent, chattier, and easier to read, except when he wrote them by hand.

His journalism was interesting but not stylish. It was not easy to stop producing work as though from a concrete mixer, but he did have a gift for the succinct phrase. He reviewed the memoirs of old friends and colleagues with a caustic wit. Morrison's memoirs were 'a fine work of fiction', in Dalton's 'we see his cheerful exuberance and his enjoyment of the political fight . . . mingled with a certain insensitiveness to the feelings of other people.'

In broadcasting he could be an interviewer's nightmare. A good interviewer could get him talking, but there were many bad interviewers, and he did not consider it his duty to do their work for them. In 1958, in a voice pregnant with dark meaning, a radio interviewer asked, 'Are people naturally good?' Lord Attlee replied: 'Yes, with exceptions,' and then stopped, presumably because he had answered the question. A long follow-up question, hastily composed, provoked a little elaboration: 'There are some people who are just born bad. Hitler was just a nasty piece of work.' The programme was called *Frankly Speaking* and had three interviewers. It being 1958, one of them asked, with a well-bred sneer, whether he had ever been an angry young man. 'The young men who used to annoy me were after the first world war, they'd had such a bad time in the war, you know. Don't know much about angry young men, never met one.' No, he never lay awake in bed. 'Made up my mind years ago that there was no point in worrying about anything.'

What did he dream of being when a small boy? Being Prime Minister? Lawyer? 'A poet,' he said, promptly and firmly. What poetry did he like? 'Don't like the moderns. John Masefield's the last for me . . .' 'Is that because they don't have the romanticism . . .' 'No, just old age.' Politely embarrassed, the interviewers decried the idea that their seventy-five-year-old guest might not be young, but Clem, in his usual hard-headed way, was just facing the sad truth.

His passion was poetry, he had dreamed of being a poet, yet could not appreciate Betjeman, Auden, or Larkin.

He liked modern detective stories, he said, but not the American ones. 'American detectives don't play the game according to the rules.'

They then tried to tease him about politics. They should have known better. He waited patiently until the end of a long, tortuous question which somehow linked socialism with Machiavelli, and answered: 'No.' After which someone had to lift the interview off the floor again.

His correspondence flowered. 'I am so glad you liked my review of Winston's book,' he wrote to Patricia in April 1956. He had written of Churchill's *History of the English Speaking People*: 'It might indeed be better called "Things in history which have interested me."'

'I was so glad to hear that we are now fellow subjects,' he wrote to her in December 1958 after her naturalisation had come through. He thought she would be amused by a remark he had heard from an Englishman on his last US tour: 'I don't mind you throwing the tea into Boston harbour, but I wish you would not dredge it up and serve it to me.' He was delighted with a letter from one of the boys from his old Haileybury Club days in the East End, now living in Canada – 'a charming letter' he told Tom in 1956. 'He is keeping Christmas with 8 children and 19 grandchildren.' He kept up with the obituaries. 'I noticed the death of C. Reed of our house,' he told Tom in 1958. 'I last saw him at an OH dinner at Rawal Pindi in 1928.'

His poetry now was mostly little snatches of rhyme which went into his letters. If what he was writing inspired a few lines of verse, he wrote them down. The limerick which has become most famous was written to amuse Tom, and probably shown to no-one. It was found years after his death in one of his letters. It was inspired by being enrolled as a Knight of the Garter:

> Few thought he was even a starter
> There were many who thought themselves smarter
> But he ended PM
> CH and OM
> An earl and a knight of the garter.

Each day when the House of Lords was sitting, Vi drove him to Great Missenden station, and he travelled in a third-class compartment to Baker Street, then on the underground to Westminster. He was a very conscientious peer, 'always coming up to me', says his friend Lord Longford, 'and saying, is there going to be a division tonight, I don't want to leave before a division.' 'I am the eighth Univ MP of my time to go to the other place,' he wrote to Tom with that sure touch for the irrelevant detail.

He followed political events with a keen if detached interest, loving the freedom to say, within limits, whatever came into his mind. He was shocked at his old friend Eden's bungled invasion of Suez. At first he approved of Eden's successor Harold Macmillan, because he had made himself unpopular with the Conservatives in the Thirties by his stand for the unemployed. He was not at all impressed with Hugh Gaitskell's crusade to get rid of Clause 4 from the Labour Party's constitution. 'The Labour Party's passion for definition should always be resisted,' he said. 'Hugh excited it. He should have sedated it.'

He became, as he wrote to Patricia, 'a keen supporter of world government. Impractical they say, but not so impractical as trying to run a world of sovereign states equipped with hydrogen bombs . . .' He was active in the Movement for World Government. This developed the idea which had started in a letter to Tom on New Year's Day 1933. In the intervening years he had done what he could, trying to bolster the UN at every opportunity; but now, in retirement, he had a chance to realise his dream.

One of the most attractive things about Clem was that he had no sense whatsoever of his own importance. The LSE's Social Administration department, where he had once taught, sent round a standard invitation to all of its former staff to celebrate its fiftieth anniversary. The organisers thought that the early staff members had died, but just as the platform was settling down in the Shaw Library, someone noticed a small, elderly man arriving inconspicuously and taking a seat at the back. Bernard Crick remembers: 'One of the platform party ran to the back in embarrassment to apologise and try to persuade him to come up to the front. He refused, or rather demurred. The audience as he was recognised, rose to its feet and applauded. Only then would he join the platform. Afterwards they asked when his car was coming. "No car, came from Kings Cross on the 68 bus. A very reliable route." They had great difficulty persuading him to take a lift back.'

Lord Longford recalls inviting Clem and Vi to a restaurant for dinner after a House of Lords debate. Clem insisted that it was his turn to buy the meal, but he knew no restaurants: when he was in office, he only ate out at the Oxford and Cambridge Club. So Longford suggested one, being careful to choose a moderately-priced restaurant because he knew Clem was careful with money. At the end of the meal Clem asked if Longford would pay, and Clem would repay him. 'They don't know me here, they might not take my cheque,' he said.

In the summer of 1959 Clem's old prostate trouble returned and he had to go into Westminster Hospital for a few days. Driving out of Amersham to visit him, Vi had a serious accident. A car drove out of a side road and hit her car. The driver's brother-in-law was killed, and Vi had a broken arm and was badly bruised. The accident caused a good deal of speculation, most of it hurtful and unjustified. For years there had been stories of Vi's poor driving, the standard 'woman driver' jokes of the Fifties, and the family suspected, with some justification, that on the few occasions she did have a crash, the police tipped off the press. She had passed her advanced driving test, and Clem always insisted his wife was a wonderful driver. But not everyone agreed. When Clem was Prime Minister, Sir David Hunt and the detective sometimes sat in the back of the car. Hunt was horrified at the speed with which she took blind corners in the narrow roads around Chequers. The detective used to keep his eyes closed.

To Clem she was always in the right, especially now. In defence of Vi he could be heartless about others. He wrote to Arthur Moyle (now Lord Moyle): 'The fellow killed his brother-in-law. I hope he gets a sentence. Vi has been overwhelmed with sympathy.'

Vi's driving duties were lighter in the October 1959 general election. Although Clem took on a heavy round of speaking engagements in the home counties, Kenneth Harris did some of the driving. Clem had by now decided that Harris should write his authorised biography, and was ensuring that he had access, not only to papers, but to Clem and Vi as well. As they drove home one night to Great Missenden, Harris remembers snatches of a monologue: 'Was the school librarian once . . . Never be lonely if I've got my books, and if I haven't I know quite a bit by heart. Would be all right in gaol.' Labour lost the election.

The following year, Tom died. Though he was nearly eighty, it still came as a shock to Clem. He had seemed well, and was looking forward to the dinner which Clem had proposed at the House of Lords to celebrate his birthday. A stay in hospital – he too had the family trouble with his 'hydraulics' – did not seem serious, but his heart failed suddenly while he was there. Tom had recently helped John Betjeman to produce his *Guide to English Parish Churches* by providing copious notes on Cornish churches. 'I feel that some of the other counties are not done with the love and thought you and I gave to Cornwall,' Betjeman wrote to him. But like most of the things Tom did, it did not pay well: ten guineas, plus £2.10s for a reprint.

Tom lived by his beliefs. Clem lived in the world and lived by its rules, and when he disliked the rules, he worked to change them. They had one serious disagreement, in 1914. Since then, the only signs of any disagreement in their letters is over codes of dress. For Alison's wedding, Clem had once written, almost apologetically, 'Vi would like you to come in top hat and tails.' Tom's attitude to top hat and tails would have been similar to Aneurin Bevan's. Tom and Kathleen had consciously hidden themselves in deepest Cornwall and lived a life that suited them. Vi was shocked by the way they lived, the more so when Kathleen turned up at Chequers one day wearing hessian.

Clem's last letter to Tom, written a few weeks before Tom died, revived another sharp disagreement between them. Tom's grandson Jeremy, whose mother was a Catholic, had been sent to a top Jesuit public school, Beaumont. Jeremy decided in 1960 not to go to an Oxford college, but to the Jesuit training college in Oxford, Campion Hall. 'He will miss so much of Oxford,' lamented Clem. 'I should think that the Jesuit training is pretty narrowing and Campion Hall is a poor substitute. However, I suppose being a Catholic priest even a Jesuit is better than becoming a Communist.'

Religion had divided the brothers as much as pacifism. Even in his old age, Clem's tough-minded honesty refused to allow him this indulgence. Tom could not claim him for the church. Once Clem died, Christians like Lord Longford, who seem offended by the idea that an atheist can live a good life, made efforts to claim him for Christianity, but there is no evidence at all that his rejection as a young man of the God of his fathers was not utterly final.

There were to be none of the rituals of death which help the grieving process. Tom had decreed no funeral because his body was to go to medical research, and no memorial service, simply a pause in his local parish church on the first Sunday after his death, during which the congregation were to be asked to think kindly of him. Nye Bevan died the same year, and Hugh Gaitskell died three years later. The deaths of two much younger men, one whom he liked and admired, the other whom he only admired, brought sadness, but it also brought Harold Wilson to the leadership of the Labour Party, and Clem had always thought Wilson the best of his generation. Labour would, as he wanted, be led from left of centre not right of centre. He left Gaitskell's funeral with Denis Healey, telling Healey: 'I thought Hugh would go to *my* funeral.' He was now eighty, and Arthur Moyle asked how that felt. 'Better than the alternative,' said Clem.

By the time Gaitskell died, Clem and Vi had moved out of Cherry Cottage into the bungalow, where there was not enough room for all his books. With some sadness, he gave a part of his library to the new university at York. They held a house-warming party. 'I am so glad you can come,' he wrote to Patricia. 'It will be a bit of a squash but there are a lot of people to whom Vi wishes to show our little bungalow or semi-bungalow.'

He had also had two bouts of serious illness – the duodenal ulcer again – while Vi was suffering with lumbago. For a time they were both in King Edward VII Hospital for Officers in Marylebone. Clementine Churchill wrote to Vi: 'My dear Vi, I'm so anxious about Clem and keep thinking of you both the whole time. This just brings you both my love. Clemmie.'

Still keenly interested in political events, Clem vigorously opposed British entry into the Common Market on the grounds that it would damage the Commonwealth. This made him, as he told Patricia, 'a strange bedfellow with the old Beaver. I never expected to be asked to write for his publications.'

He told her the Americans were being stupid about Fidel Castro: 'I think they have unnecessarily driven him into Khrushchev's arms.' He took against Enoch Powell: 'He is a singularly arid person. One would never take him for a Professor of Greek and a former GSO in the war.' He admired Macmillan's 'wind of change' speech and his colonial policy, but was shocked at his 1962 'night of the long knives' when he got rid of half his Cabinet. His views on that event, set out in a letter to Patricia, give some idea of how he had himself, as Prime Minister, tried to ease the pain for sacked Ministers: 'It is not decent to distinguish those alleged to have retired and those sacked. According to Harold's talk to the 22 committee the whole object of the exercise was to get efficiency, a pleasant thought for his former colleagues to take with them into retirement, yet he gets rid of Kilmuir, much his best man, and retains ridiculous people like Mr Brooke, the Hampstead wonder.'

For Arthur Moyle he wrote a poem about the carnage:

> Hail to our splendid Mac
> Long live our glorious Mac
> What though we've got the sack
> Enoch and Pete got back
> Why should not we?
>
> Hail to our fine new look
> Though Selwyn Lloyd's forsook
> Still we've got Henry Brooke
> Surely he'll find a nook
> Somewhere for me . . .

In June 1964 came a death that, for a while, knocked the bounce out of him. Vi collapsed with a cerebral haemorrhage in the kitchen of the bungalow while cooking Sunday lunch, at the age of sixty-eight. She was taken to hospital but died during the night. It was a shattering blow. They had been in love with each other, without a pause, from the day they met. He seemed oblivious to her occasionally difficult temperament, and she appeared not to have resented his preoccupation with work. She suffered from lumbago all her adult life, and her illness after their visit to India left her permanently unsteady in the dark. Yet he had not for a moment imagined that she might die before him. All their plans for the future had been based on the assumption that he would die first.

Felicity, Martin and Alison rushed to the bungalow and found their father, on the surface, calm. He had burnt the huge pile of letters he had written to his wife over the years. He never explained why, but we may suppose that they were for her, and that if he left them behind, in future years strangers would trawl over them.

He remembered he was due to go that evening to the Indian High Commission. He went to the telephone, dialled the number, and his horrified children heard him say: 'I'm sorry, I can't come to the reception tonight. My wife's just died and there's no one to drive me.' They realised at that moment the deep shock he was in. He was being held together only by years of practice at ferocious self-discipline. It was sad for his friends to see his shrunken, grief-stricken figure at her funeral.

He moved out of the bungalow for a while, into the Tudor Court Hotel in Cromwell Road, Kensington, where Martin stayed with him. 'I should have written before but I have had such a huge mail of very kind letters,' he wrote to Patricia. 'So many of them like yours showed real affection and appreciation of Vi. The children have been so good to me.' He could not stay in the bungalow. 'The house is so much a projection of Vi's personality and most of my friends are in town.' So he started thinking seriously about where and how to spend the rest of his days. With his characteristic swift, decisive despatch of business, he soon had it sorted. The house was to be sold. He would seek a flat in the Temple, right in the heart of the city, and he would engage a young ex-soldier to look after him, just as his old batman Griff used to do.

That settled, he got on with it. He found a four-room flat at 1 Kings Bench Walk in the Temple, one of the very few blocks in the Temple which had been bombed during the war and rebuilt, and therefore had a lift. He engaged, he wrote to Janet in the USA, 'a very nice fellow', Alf Laker, to look after him, 'formerly in the RAMC and the catering corps which gives him the right background . . . As a bencher I shall have a delightful club just across the road and a good many old friends in the Temple.'

For years, Vi had handled their moves. This time he had to do it himself, and he did it methodically, like a military operation. Laker had to measure all the furniture and pictures he intended to take with him. He then cut pieces of card to scale and arranged them on a floor plan of the new flat.

In the midst of the move came the 1964 general election. He was delighted with Harold Wilson's performance. 'I had a good talk with HW yesterday and found him in great form,' he wrote to Janet. 'He says that the reports from the constituencies are most encouraging, a '45 feeling.' He took to the road himself, offering his simple, sharply-focused message, the distilled wisdom of his political life, at dozens of meetings. The difference between the two parties, he told his audiences, was that the Conservatives were only interested in profit, while Labour wanted to serve the community.

Labour won with a majority of four, and among Wilson's first guests for a weekend at Chequers were Clem Attlee and Laker. Wilson took great care to make sure that his old boss had a good weekend. Clem found Wilson 'in fine form' he told Patricia Beck. On Patricia's behalf he once again wielded a little influence. She was starting her own public relations business. Clem sent her an introduction, to the President of the Board of Trade, Douglas Jay. His old friend Jay, if he saw the letter, must have known at once that it was genuine, for it was in his usual execrable typing: 'This is to introduce to you a great friend of mine Miss Patricia Beck who is engaged in important wor [sic] for our exprt [sic] market. If you can be of any assistance I shall be greatly obliged.'

She, increasingly, was making him happy when few others could. 'I always enjoy seeing you so much and it is good of you to give so much pleasure to an old man,' he wrote in March 1965, and again in April: 'You do not know how much your visits cheer me up.' Just occasionally she made a few notes on the back of an envelope of their conversations. These show that he was still keeping his mind sharp, for she writes: 'Showed me his list of all places slept in since 1899!!! (600+ & 202 journeys.)' They also show her affection for him: '22nd – dinner at The Angel – beautiful clear evening for Our Clem – a nightcap at the flat.' '19th – rang to see if he was at home. Yes, cheerful.' He did not, presumably, also show her his lists of those who had served in his government, under the two headings: fifty-three 'dead' and fifty-seven 'alive'.

He was still going regularly to the House of Lords and Arthur Moyle, Sir Frank Soskice and Frank Longford were frequent visitors to his home, as were Felicity and Alison, Martin, and Martin's wife Anne.

He grew to love the flat. It was just like being back at Oxford, he said. He provided a television for Laker but never watched it himself. He had always hated television – it was a part of the modern world he never learned to accept, and the family had not owned one until the late 1950s when someone gave them a very unreliable second-hand set. He accepted an invitation from Sir Frank and Lady Soskice to watch the boat race on television at their house, but when it was over and wrestling came on he turned to Laker and muttered, 'Time we went home.'

Laker turned out to be an excellent cook and an entertaining companion, and they got on well. 'Laker returned some time after 12 when I was in my bath and confessed that he had one over the eight,' he wrote to Patricia Beck. 'Clearly a good time was had by all.'

Churchill died in 1965, along with other old friends and colleagues, and Clem could feel himself getting weaker. On the way to a memorial service for Chuter Ede, who had been his Home Secretary, he said to Alice Bacon, now a Home Office Minister in Wilson's Cabinet: 'Alice, I've been to a number of funerals lately of my old colleagues – do you think I will be the next?' They travelled in her official car. He was dressed, she says, 'in a superb old-fashioned morning-suit with silk hat and rolled umbrella' which, he told her, was very old. 'People say I'm a Victorian,' he told one of his visitors, serenely.

There was to be a rehearsal the day before Churchill's state funeral. Clem was told that at his age and state of health (he had been suffering from sickness and shaking, and was quite weak), he need not go, but he insisted: he was not going to make a mistake at Winston's funeral through missing the rehearsal. It was a bitterly cold day, there was a good deal of standing around, and by the time he got back to the flat he was in a state of near collapse. Laker put warm slippers on him, wrapped a blanket round him, and offered him brandy. He refused that, so Laker put brandy in his tea. 'He must have known, but he drank it, probably to please me.' He slept badly, and was not in a fit state for the funeral, but he was determined to go. He got through it, though he stumbled and some newspapers had pictures of him, a small figure, sitting alone on the steps of St Paul's, recovering himself.

'I was taken ill on Tuesday,' he wrote to Janet in October, 'with violent shivering followed by vomiting. My doctor told me that I should be all right next day.' He was not up to campaigning in the 1966 election but was delighted with Wilson's victory. His new typewriter was getting a little too much for him – perhaps it would have been kinder of Corona to repair the old one – and a letter to Janet ends: 'Foreign affairs remain very sticky without eeeeeeeeeeeeee I don't know what has happened to my typewriter so I must close love to all.' After that more of his letters were handwritten.

He was still able to visit the Lords sometimes, and to review books, which gave him much pleasure and sometimes other emotions. 'I am reading Gallipoli', he wrote to Patricia, 'but it makes me so damned angry that I can't stand more of it than half an hour at a time. I recall meeting one of the most boneheaded generals when I entered the House in 1922. I marvel now at my restraint in not saying to him "you bloody old butcher, it was due to your crass stupidity that most of my good lads were killed ..."' Sadly, he was more judicious when he came to write the review for the *Spectator*.

He was also well enough to correspond with new young friends. 'my dear geoffrey', he wrote in January 1966 to a teenager who had written to ask for an autograph; 'thank you for your charming letter. what a contrast to the american autograph hunters who constantly plague and seldom enclose even a stamp for return postage.

'why should I spend frequent tanners
on these folk who have no manners.'

Clem cannot make the shift key of his typewriter work, and the
entirely lower-case typing has a feel of 'archy and mehitabel'. Clem's
next letter to him begins: 'my dear Geoffrey, To address me as my
lord is quite all right.' He told Geoffrey that the South African
government was the most reactionary since Hitler.

'I don't suppose I shall last much longer,' he wrote to Patricia
Beck. It was not self-pity, just an unsentimental statement of fact.
He wrote the same to his daughter Janet in the USA, adding that
he hoped she could come and see him – he did not add 'before
I die' but she knew and came. To Patricia he defined how he
felt about death, with a burst of feeling and exhilaration and his
usual grand disregard for punctuation: 'By the time I die people
will say that old man only just dead I thought he died ages ago.
I shan't mind. I recall what one of my good comrades in the war
said "Anyway I have lived in the greatest country in the world for
22 years." I have had 60 more than that, 60 more years of memories,
of friendships and kindness.

'Je serai sous la terre
et phantome sans os
Par les ombreux myrteux
Je prendrai mon repos.

'I shall die with lots of poetry in my heart and perhaps on my
lips. However for you my dear remember the last line of the sonnet
Cueillez dès aujourd-hui les roses de la vie.' The phrase 'lived in
the greatest country in the world' must have been at the top of his
mind all his life, for he had closed his autobiography with it more
than a decade earlier.

As 1966 drew to a close he could not type any more; the handwriting was poor even by his standards, and he was puzzled to find
that it always went diagonally across the page. He was having a great
deal of 'tummy trouble', colds and sickness, he had a constant flow
of saliva to his mouth, and his sight and hearing were beginning to
fail. He saw, with the clarity which had always been his strength, how
his body was slowly, bit by bit, 'conking out', as he might once have
put it, just as his trusty old Corona typewriter had done.

He hated most of all the loneliness of old age and illness. 'I had
a very dull weekend seeing nobody and having only two telephone

calls to break my loneliness,' he wrote to Patricia. On Christmas Day, staying with Felicity and her children, a slight stroke temporarily deprived him of the power of speech. 'I got along with nods and shakes and in fact won all games such as Scrabble and card games,' he wrote to Patricia. In January both Laker and Patricia had to spend short periods in hospital. He stayed with Felicity again, writing to Patricia: 'I am glad you are not allowed to overwork. Even a very tough old bird like me could not do more than about 16 hours a day. Stafford Cripps killed himself by overwork.' The following year, 1967, saw him mostly travelling by wheelchair, generally pushed by the faithful Laker, who was now effectively a nurse as well as a batman.

He was re-reading old favourites – Jane Austen and John Buchan – and finding the Wilson government disappointing. He still believed, as he had always done, that you should set out your stall honestly and then try to achieve it. Trimming never did any good. 'When I remember Harold Wilson and Nye Bevan I am amazed by time's revenges . . . They seem to adopt Tory policy in everything . . . I have not bought any new clothes for years. With any luck my present supply should last me out.'

At the end of June he went for a stay in Osborn House on the Isle of Wight, once Queen Victoria's home and now a convalescent home for officers. 'This is a lovely spot,' he wrote to Patricia, 'and they look after me very well, but I am rather bored to tears. I have not really contacted the other residents and I tend to get left by myself.' It took him a while to realise what the problem was, and then he took swift action. 'Things have improved,' he wrote two days later. 'My good Laker without instructions had told people I wanted to be left alone. I have disabused them so I am no longer treated as a leper'; but 'I seem to get feebler every day.' And a week later: 'I shall be glad to get away from here next week although everyone is very kind and it is really a lovely spot, but I get very tired of being left about the place.' One imagines, on a cliff overlooking the sea, a wheelchair, and inside it a small, frail old man with a bristling grey moustache, wrapped in a blanket, being left in peace with nature, and wanting nothing so much as a good talk with somebody. He was home by 30 July. He wrote his last letter to Patricia on 3 September. 'I don't think much of Wilson's reshuffle. Douglas Jay is sacked. I don't know why. The Government seems to me to be very weak with no one much coming up. I think they will get an almighty smash at the next election though the Tories are not much good.'

Five days later he was admitted to Westminster Hospital, where he developed pneumonia. He read *Pride and Prejudice*, his favourite novel in all the world, yet again. He kept up his mind games, 'I've been remembering the name of every boy in my form at Haileybury,' he told Felicity, and she thought he would recover. But on her next visit he said, 'I can't remember the seven wonders of the world.' Then she knew the end was near.

His children, Patricia and Griff visited continually, and Laker was there most of the time, shaving him and helping him to eat. It was Laker who was holding his hand when his grip slowly slackened.

A Note on Sources

As far as possible, I have given the sources, where they are needed, within the text of the book. This note is intended as a guide to further research.

Clement Attlee did not feel the need to unburden himself, even to a private diary. This may have been good for his blood pressure but bad for that of his biographers, because he probably left fewer clues to his mental processes than any other Prime Minister. Of the papers he did leave most are in three collections.

The biggest, by quite a long way, is in the Bodleian Library, Oxford, which contains all the letters to Tom and a host of government papers. More recently, the Bodleian acquired the letters to Patricia Beck, which have never been used before.

Churchill College, Cambridge, has a small but interesting collection of private papers. They include several fragments of autobiography which are far more illuminating than what Clem chose to publish, and some wartime correspondence with Churchill. Churchill College also houses the papers of key figures such as Ernest Bevin, Philip Noel-Baker and A. V. Alexander. It was among Bevin's papers, for example, that I found the letter to Bevin from Stafford Cripps about Clem's finances, quoted in Chapter Four.

The third collection is held by Clem's daughter-in-law, Anne, Countess Attlee, at her North London home. She has a good deal of private correspondence; all of Clem's poems; a few letters between Vi and Clem and notes by Vi (most of their correspondence did not survive); the very early letters by Clem, his brothers and sisters and his father, which are quoted in Chapter One; and the World War One reminiscences quoted in Chapter Two.

The British Library of Political and Economic Science – the LSE library – holds the records of the Independent Labour Party and has some useful material relating to Clem's time in the ILP. It also houses the Dalton diaries and some early Attlee pamphlets.

In addition to these collections, the National Sound Archive can play the keen researcher Clem's broadcasts; and there is, of course, a wealth of material about Clem in government between 1940 and 1951 at the Public Record Office in Kew, most (though not all) of it in the classes PREM 5 (for the war), PREM 8 and CAB 21. Clem's own wartime collection of papers is in the class CAB 118.

More material is released to the PRO every year; but there are some important documents which, despite fine-sounding talk about open government, we are still not allowed to see, half a century after the events: for example, correspondence during the war between Clem and the Home Secretary, Herbert Morrison, presumably on security matters.

I am grateful to the knowledgeable people in all these places who guided me through their treasures: Helen Langley at the Bodleian, Angela Raspin at the BLPES, Tamsin Pert at Churchill College, Chris Mobbs at the National Sound Archive, Simon Fowler at the PRO, and of course Countess Attlee herself, who guards her treasures carefully and has been tireless and generous in helping me find my way through them. Many people kindly talked to me, or corresponded with me, about their memories of Clem. Every one of them provided a new insight of some sort.

The most important interviews for this book were with Clem's second daughter, Lady Felicity Harwood, and I am most grateful for her kindness, patience and hospitality. Mrs Peggy Attlee, Tom Attlee's daughter-in-law, has also been most helpful, and I had an interesting talk with the third Earl Attlee.

Some distinguished politicians, trade unionists and diplomats kindly gave me their memoirs and impressions of Clem: Lord Boyd-Carpenter; Lord Bruce; Baroness Castle; Michael Foot; Sir David Hunt; Lord Jenkins; Jack Jones; Lord Healey; Lord Longford; and John Platts-Mills. Denis Healey recalled for me the song on p. 108, and Cyril Cooper the song on p. 105.

Commentators, journalists and academics have shared their memories and insights: Bernard Crick; Kenneth Harris; Professor Peter Hennessy; and Baroness Hollis.

At Haileybury, my thanks are due to David Jewell, the Master, Dan Hearn, head of politics, and Bill Tyrwhitt-Drake for the Old Haileyburians. At the Law Society, John Randall and Lynn Quinney helped me to find out about past Law Society President, Henry Attlee. Billy Dove at the Attlee Foundation pointed me towards some useful sources.

A Note on Sources

Some old friends of mine turned out to have met Clem or heard him speak, like Ellis Kopel, a young reporter on the *Walthamstow Guardian* when Clem was MP for Walthamstow. John Beckett's unpublished autobiography, lodged in Sheffield University Library, provided additional information for Chapters Three and Four. For Chapter Seven I drew heavily on research by Raymond Smith and John Zametica, published in 1985 as *The Cold Warrior: Clement Attlee Reconsidered.*

There were many useful interviews with Clem in his retirement on which I also drew. The interview with Francis Williams is well known, but I also had a verbatim note of an interview with Mark Arnold-Forster, which Jake Arnold-Forster found among his late father's papers and showed to me. Peter Hennessy's lectures are splendid sources of insight about a man whom Hennessy admires as much as I do, especially 'The Statecraft of Clement Attlee' (Queen Mary and Westfield College, 1985) and the Gresham College lecture 'A Sense of Architectonics' (November 1995).

The author and publishers wish to thank the following for permission to reproduce illustrations:

TEXT PAGES
Vicky, © Solo Syndication/Cartoon Collection, University of Kent.
   Title page
E. H. Shepard, *Punch*: pages 131, 245
A. W. Lloyd, *Punch*: page 168
Low, *Evening Standard*/Cartoon Collection, University of Kent: page 209
Illingworth, *Punch*: page 253

All other illustrations are courtesy of members of the Attlee family: Countess Anne Attlee, Lady Felicity Harwood and Mrs Peggy Attlee.

Select Bibliography

Attlee, Clement, *As It Happened*, Heinemann, 1954
———, *The Labour Party in Perspective*, Gollancz, 1937
———, *The Social Worker*, George Bell and Sons, 1920
Attlee, Peggy, *With a Quiet Conscience* (a privately published life of Thomas Attlee)
Barnett, Correlli, *The Lost Victory*, Macmillan, 1995
Benn, Tony, *Years of Hope*, Diaries 1940–62, ed. Ruth Winstone, Hutchinson, 1994
Brivati, Brian and Jones, Harriet, *What Difference Did the War Make?*, Leicester University Press, 1993
Brivati, Brian, *Hugh Gaitskell*, Richard Cohen Books, 1996
Brockway, Fenner, *Towards Tomorrow*, Hart-Davis MacGibbon, 1977
Brome, Vincent, *Clement Attlee*, Lincolns-Prauger, 1949
Brown, George, *In My Way*, Gollancz, 1971
Brown, Gordon, *Maxton*, Mainstream, 1986
Bullock, Alan, *Ernest Bevin*, Heinemann, 1960
Burridge, Trevor, *Clement Attlee*, Cape, 1985
Castle, Barbara, *Fighting All the Way*, Macmillan, 1993
Churchill, Winston, *The Second World War*, Cassell, 1948
Clemens, Cyril, *The Man from Limehouse*, International Mark Twain Society, 1946
Cross, Colin, *The Liberals in Power*, 1905–14
Dalton, Hugh, *Memoirs*, Frederick Muller, 1953
Dove, Billy (ed.), *Attlee As I Knew Him*, Borough of Tower Hamlets, 1983
Fielding, Stephen, Thompson, Peter and Tiratsoo, Nick, *England Arise*, Manchester University Press, 1995
Foot, Michael, *Aneurin Bevan*, McGibbon and Kee, 1962
Glennerster, Howard, *British Social Policy Since 1945*, Blackwell, 1995
Harris, Kenneth, *Attlee*, Weidenfeld and Nicolson, 1982
Hattersley, Roy, *Who Goes Home?*, Little, Brown, 1995

Healey, Denis, *The Time of My Life*, Michael Joseph, 1989

Hennessy, Peter, *Never Again*, Vintage, 1993

———, *The Hidden Wiring*, Gollancz, 1995

Hunt, David, *On the Spot*, Frank Davies, 1975

Jenkins, Roy, *Mr Attlee*, Heinemann, 1948

———, *Nine Men of Power, Truman*, Collins, 1986

Kramnick, Isaac and Sheerman, Barry, *Harold Laski, A Life on the Left*, Hamish Hamilton, 1993

Laffin, John, *Damn the Dardanelles*, Osprey, 1980

Margach, James, *The Abuse of Power*, W. H. Allen, 1978

———, *The Anatomy of Power*, W. H. Allen, 1979

Mayhew, Christopher, *Time to Explain*, Hutchinson, 1987

McSmith, Andy, *John Smith*, Verso, 1993

Morgan, Kenneth O., *Labour People*, OUP, 1987

Nicholas, H. G., *The British General Election of 1950*, Macmillan, 1951

Pimlott, Ben, *Hugh Dalton*, Cape, 1985

Rolph, C. H., *Kingsley*, Gollancz, 1973

Seaman, L. C. B., *Life in Britain Between the Wars*, B. T. Batsford, 1970

Seymour-Jones, Carole, *Beatrice Webb*, Allison and Busby, 1992

Skidelsky, Robert, *Politicians and the Slump*, Macmillan, 1967

Thompson, Paul, *The Edwardians*, Weidenfeld and Nicolson, 1975

Tiratsoo, Nick (ed.), *The Attlee Years*, Pinter, 1991

Vaughan, Paul, *Doctors Commons: A History of the BMA*, Heinemann, 1959

Vernon, Betty, *Ellen Wilkinson*, Croom Helm, 1982

Wheen, Francis, *Tom Driberg*, Chatto and Windus, 1990

Wyatt, Woodrow, *Confessions of an Optimist*, Collins, 1985

Index

Index

Index

Index